The State, the Financial System and Economic Modernization

The role of the state is of paramount importance in the historical development of modern financial systems, and governments have long had need of large-scale finance related thereto. Unlike private parties, however, the state possesses powers of taxation, lending it a greater ability to borrow and repay debts than private economic entities. In addition, the state has had the power to create financial institutions and markets, and to shape their development through legislation and state regulation.

With chapters focusing on a number of European countries, as well as North and South America, and covering approximately 150 years of development, this book demonstrates the key role that finance has played in economic change. Thanks to the variety of countries studied, it is shown that financial systems did not develop uniformly; on the contrary, divergent systems came into being and persisted. Insights into the primacy of the state's role in the financial development of the pre-industrial era have not carried over into the historiography of the industrial era itself, so never before have the insights developed here been brought together in a systematic manner. The aim is to demonstrate through comparative historical analysis the richness of the history of modern financial systems, and to restore the state to its primary role in the shaping of those systems. The book makes a unique contribution to financial historiography, and thus will be of interest to economists and to financial, economic and world historians.

RICHARD SYLLA is Professor of Economics in the Leonard N. Stern School of Business, New York University.

RICHARD TILLY is Professor of Economic and Social History at the University of Münster.

GABRIEL TORTELLA is Professor of Economic History at the University of Alcala.

The State, the Financial System and Economic Modernization

edited by

Richard Sylla, Richard Tilly and Gabriel Tortella

CAMBRIDGE
UNIVERSITY PRESS

PUBLISHED BY THE PRESS SYNDICATE OF THE UNIVERSITY OF CAMBRIDGE
The Pitt Building, Trumpington Street, Cambridge CB2 1RP, United Kingdom

CAMBRIDGE UNIVERSITY PRESS
The Edinburgh Building, Cambridge CB2 2RU, United Kingdom
http://www.cup.cam.ac.uk
40 West 20th Street, New York, NY 10011–4211, USA
http://www.cup.org
10 Stamford Road, Oakleigh, Melbourne 3166, Australia

First published 1999

Printed in the United Kingdom at the University Press, Cambridge

Typeset in Plantin 10/12 pt   [SE]

A catalogue record for this book is available from the British Library

Library of Congress Cataloguing in Publication data

The state, the financial system, and economic modernization / edited
  by Richard Sylla, Richard Tilly, and Gabriel Tortella.
     p.   cm.
   ISBN 0 521 59123 6
   1. Banks and banking – Government policy – History.   2. Finance,
public – History.   3. Capital markets – History.   I. Sylla, Richard
Eugene.   II. Tilly, Richard H.   III. Tortella Casares, Gabriel.
HG1725.S72   1998
332.1–dc21   98-14397 CIP

ISBN 0 521 59123 6 hardback

In honour of Rondo Cameron

Contents

List of figures   *page* ix
List of tables   x
List of contributors   xi
Preface   xiii

1 Introduction: comparative historical perspectives   1
   RICHARD SYLLA, RICHARD TILLY AND
   GABRIEL TORTELLA

2 Politics and banking in revolutionary and Napoleonic France   20
   FRANÇOIS CROUZET

3 Belgian banking in the nineteenth and twentieth centuries: the
   Société Générale and the Générale de Banque (1822–1997)   53
   HERMAN VAN DER WEE AND MONIQUE VAN DER
   WEE-VERBREYT

4 Banking liberalization in England and Wales, 1826–1844   75
   P. L. COTTRELL AND LUCY NEWTON

5 Banking in Europe in the nineteenth century: the role of the
   central bank   118
   FORREST CAPIE

6 Public policy, capital markets and the supply of industrial
   finance in nineteenth-century Germany   134
   RICHARD TILLY

7 The role of banks and government in Spanish economic
   development, 1850–1935   158
   GABRIEL TORTELLA

8 Central banking and German-style mixed banking in Italy,
   1893/5–1914: from coexistence to cooperation   182
   PETER HERTNER

9   State power and finance in Russia, 1802–1917: the Credit
     Office of the Finance Ministry and governmental control over
     credit institutions   210
     BORIS ANAN´ICH

10   The origins of banking in Argentina   224
     ROBERTO CORTÉS CONDE

11   Shaping the US financial system, 1690–1913: the dominant
     role of public finance   249
     RICHARD SYLLA

12   Cosmopolitan finance in the 1920s: New York's emergence
     as an international financial centre   271
     MIRA WILKINS

     Index   292

Figures

3.1 Summary of liabilities of the Générale de Banque,
1823–1913   *page* 62

3.2 Summary of assets of the Générale de Banque, 1823–1913   64

3.3 Origin of revenue of the Générale de Banque, 1823–1919   70

6.1 Industrial investment and new issues in Great Britain and
Germany, 1883–1913   144–5

6.2 Realized inflation-adjusted returns on securities portfolios
in the UK and Germany, 1871–1913   147

6.3 Standard deviation among sixteen German security classes,
1871–1913   148

7.1 Bank-note creation and budget deficit, 1874–1935   164

7.2 Peseta–pound sterling exchange rate, 1890–1913   168

7.3 Bank of Spain: collateral credits, total line and actually
drawn, 1904–35   170

7.4 Securities portfolios in Spanish banks and Bank of Spain's
collateral credits, total line and actually drawn, 1904–35   172

10.1 Banco de Buenos Aires, 1823–6   228

10.2 Banco Nacional issue, deficit and gold premium, 1826–9   229

10.3 Casa de la Moneda issues, 1837–61   229

10.4 Money supply and gold premium, 1823–52   229

10.5 Banco de la Provincia de Buenos Aires, metallic and paper
deposits, 1855–8   231

10.6 Banco de la Provincia de Buenos Aires, issues, deposits and
reserves, 1864–80   232

10.7 Banco de la Provincia de Buenos Aires, issues, deposits and
reserves, 1880–91   233

10.8 Banco Nacional, issues, deposits and reserves, 1873–9   234

10.9 Banco Nacional, issues, deposits and reserves, 1880–91   235

10.10 Interest rates, 1829–47   238

10.11 Interest rates, 1864–90   239

10.12 Reserves and gold premium, 1863–1891   242

Tables

4.1 Joint-stock bank creations in England and Wales,
    1826–43   *page* 84
4.2 Geographical sources of initial subscriptions to the
    shares of the Wilts & Dorset Banking Company, 1835   101
6.1 Numbers of business incorporations and initial equity capital
    raised, 1826–1907   136
6.2 Rate of return on equity investment, 1871–83   139
6.3 Average annual industrial investment and industrial new issue
    activity in Germany and the United Kingdom, 1882–1913   142
6.4 Sectoral rates of growth and distribution of new issues   143
6.5 Two measures of investment banking spread on the issue of
    German industrial securities, 1885–1913   150
6.6 Structure of new industrial security issues in London and
    Berlin, 1883–1913   151
9.1 Numbers of different types of credit institutions in Russia in
    September 1910 compared with May 1913   217
9.2 The growth in business operations of the joint-stock
    commercial banks   219
10.1 Deposits of the Banco de la Nación, 1892–1909   244
10.2 Deposits in private banks, 1897–1909   245

Contributors

BORIS ANAN'ICH is Professor in the Institute of Russian History, St Petersburg.

FORREST CAPIE is Professor in the Department of Banking and Finance at City University Business School.

PHILIP COTTRELL is Professor in the Department of Economic and Social History at the University of Leicester.

FRANÇOIS CROUZET is Professor in the Centre Roland Mousnier at the Université Paris IV–Sorbonne.

ROBERTO CORTÉS CONDE is Professor in the Department of Economics at the Universidad de San Andres.

PETER HERTNER is Professor in the Institut für Geschichte at Martin-Luther Universität Halle-Wittenberg.

LUCY NEWTON is Lecturer in Economic and Social History, School of History, University of East Anglia.

RICHARD SYLLA is Professor of Economics in the Leonard N. Stern School of Business, New York University.

RICHARD TILLY is Professor of Economic and Social History in the University of Münster.

GABRIEL TORTELLA is Professor of Economic History in the University of Alcala.

HERMAN VAN DER WEE is Professor in the Centrum voor Economische Studien at the Katholieke Universiteit Leuven.

MONIQUE VAN DER WEE-VERBREYT, wife of Herman Van der Wee, is co-author of their chapter in this volume.

MIRA WILKINS is Professor in the Department of Economics at Florida International University.

Preface

Around five years ago (in 1993) the three of us realized that we shared an interest in a theme of comparative financial history which deserved book-length treatment. That theme was the role of the state in the financial development of nations and the links between public and private finance. In order to ensure a broadly international comparative perspective, we set about recruiting knowledgeable scholars in various different countries. As planning progressed, we began to see that the book would combine three fields of interest – financial history, economic development and international comparison. These interests, we realized, were also striking features of the work of an influential economic historian, Rondo Cameron. Since we and our collaborators continue to draw on Rondo Cameron's work, we thought it fitting to say a few words about his influence here.

Three aspects of Rondo Cameron's work are of particular interest today. First came his demonstration, supported by rich archival evidence and published in *France and the Economic Development of Europe* (1961), that the dynamic development role played by private business institutions could be fruitfully treated in an explicitly international comparative framework of analysis. Second, subsequent works, *Banking in the Early Stages of Industrialization* (1967) and *Banking and Economic Development* (1972), both of them team efforts headed by Rondo Cameron, put banks in the centre of the stage and upgraded their importance and, implicitly, the importance of financial institutions generally in the process of economic development. After they appeared, there was less chance that historians and economists would continue to slight those institutions, as they had in the past. Third by drawing attention to the positive roles played by private economic agents, the 'Cameron' studies fostered a more critical attitude towards government policies and state intervention in economic history than had been typical among economists and historians in the decades after the Great Depression and World War II. This was controversial at the time; some of it still is.

And that is the point: Rondo Cameron's work has shaped our

perceptions of the problems in financial history that need to be addressed and of possible approaches to their solution. Our book does not follow Cameronian suggestions at every turn. Our occasionally differing interpretations of the role of the state are cases in point. But even when our conclusions differ from those he reached in his work, we share and build on his judgement that 'finance matters' and that comparative history is indispensable in showing why that is so. That is why we dedicate this volume to Rondo Cameron.

RS, RT and GT

1 Introduction: comparative historical perspectives

Richard Sylla, Richard Tilly and Gabriel Tortella

The more one studies the historical origins and development of modern financial systems, the more it becomes apparent that at most of the critical points when financial systems changed, sometimes for better and sometimes for worse, the role of the state was of paramount importance. That is hardly surprising. Long before private economic entities – trading, transportation and manufacturing enterprises may be cited – came to require financing on a scale beyond the capabilities of individual proprietors and partners, governments had needs for large-scale finance. The most durable reasons for these needs involved the political ambitions of governments: solidifying and extending their authority, unifying the disparate components of their states under a central administration, promoting state-led and state-financed economic development projects as a means of increasing state power, and, perhaps most important of all, waging wars against other competing states. But the state not only had a need for large-scale finance. It also had the coercive power of taxation that, among other things, gave it a stronger credit, that is, a greater ability to borrow and pay debts, than was possessed by any private parties. Moreover, the state had the power to create financial institutions and markets, and to shape their development through legislation and state regulation. States used all of these powers from the European middle ages up to and including the eighteenth century, when the modern industrial era commenced.

Curiously, the insights into financial development coming from the pre-industrial era, insights that point to the primacy of the state's role, have not carried over into the historiography of the industrial era itself. Here the fascination with industrialization reigns supreme, with commercial, agricultural and financial developments relegated to secondary, ancillary, facilitating roles, and with the role of the state itself pushed well into the background, where, many have argued, it not only was, but also ought to have been. The *laissez-faire*, anti-mercantilist traditions of classical and neoclassical economics were in major ways responsible for this shift of historical emphasis. So has been the division of labour among modern economists, which has made public finance and private finance into separate sub-disciplines, each with its own practitioners, courses of study, students, textbooks and journals, and with few interactions between the two groups.

Those of us specializing in financial history have not been unaffected by these strong currents of thought. For one thing, they relegated us to the study of something that was inherently less important than the one big thing that was important, namely industrialization. For another, they fragmented finance itself into two fields, private and public, each with its own sub-fields, and each having seemingly little to do with each other. Most of us studied private finance – the economics of money and banking, other financial intermediaries, money and capital markets, the rate of interest and the returns of equity shareholders. Public finance divided itself into two sub-fields, the economics of taxation and of governmental expenditures, neither of which had much to do with any of the private-finance fields.

As financial historians buffeted by these currents, our strategy to be relevant was a simple one. Private banks were the one type of financial institution present throughout the era of industrialization in one form or another, and so we would gain attention for our work by studying what banks did, how their nature and functions changed over time, and how banks did or did not contribute to industrialization. This we did, in numerous dissertations, articles and books.

Since the 1960s, consequently, the literature on the role of banking in economic development has grown enormously. This represented at the time an overdue correction of the older view that 'money and banking' had much to do with short-run cyclical phenomena, but little to do with long-run economic change. In the meantime, however, the fields of finance, monetary economics and even financial history have moved on. It has become clearer that finance involves and involved much more than banking. Developments in economic theory (the theory of expectations, the economics of information and especially the economics of institutions) have helped here by making the interactions between financial markets, institutions such as banks and shifts in public policy more amenable to systematic generalization. We have begun to see new significance in the breadth and variety of institutions incorporated within financial systems – non-bank intermediaries, money, debt and equity markets, and stock exchanges.

In tracing these variegated institutions and markets back to their origins, we are no longer distracted by finding that the financial needs and intents of the state were of primary importance; that public or state banks to serve state financial interests arose almost simultaneously with private banks; or that these public banks set patterns that private banks sometimes followed; and that they also evolved into central banks that regulated and controlled the activities of the private banks. New significance can be attached to the discovery that private banks themselves, though they may have begun in many instances as proprietorships and partnerships without governmental sanction or interference, evolved towards business corporations chartered and regulated by the state, in the state's financial interest. And it is no surprise that the money, debt and equity markets that eventually became mainstays of industrial and business finance, invariably began as issuing and trading markets for government debt obligations before there were many private obligations.

In our historical work we learned further that financial systems did not develop according to some uniform pattern dictated by the logic of industrial finance. Instead, there were divergences of systems. In Continental Europe, financial systems came to be dominated by large banks; open debt and equity markets were of relatively minor significance. In the 'Anglo-Saxon' countries, however, banks played a lesser role, and relatively more financing of enterprises, especially long-term financing, took place through the open bond and equity markets. What accounts for the differences that emerged among financial systems? Very often they resulted from the ways in which the state formulated financial legislation and regulated financial institutions and markets.

And yet these various insights, these rediscoveries being made for different sets of national historical experience, have not yet been brought together in a coherent, systematic manner. That is the purpose of this book. Its intent is to demonstrate, through comparative historical analysis, the richness of the history of modern financial systems, and to restore the state to its primary role in the shaping of those systems. The financial history of the era of industrialization, to repeat, is much more than the history of banks. And in this era the role of the state in determining its own notions of proper financial legislation and regulation, is far greater than one would gather from earlier accounts.

Economic historiography has of course long recognized that the state has exerted ongoing influence on the financial system through rules and regulations, e.g. through controls over the money supply, interest rates and so on. What has not always been appreciated, however, is that the non-intended consequences of state operations, especially the handling of public finances, could have had long-lasting effects upon the development of private financial arrangements. Take the emergence of the modern national state in the early modern period (since *c.* 1500). That development involved war-making and hence public borrowing from private sources on an unprecedentedly large scale. In some cases this generated financial distress among private wealthholders, and produced long-lasting results; in others, initially pernicious effects could be rapidly overcome. A brief survey of the historiography can illustrate the connection.

A key historical concept here is that of 'financial revolution'. Originally developed to describe the history of English public finance between the 'Glorious Revolution' of 1688 and around the middle of the eighteenth century (Dickson 1967), its basic idea can be generalized: the rising importance of bourgeois, capitalist wealthowners coupled to the above-mentioned increase in governmental financial needs led European states to adapt their financial practices to capitalist standards, e.g. by making their financial accounts more transparent, by improving their revenue bases or – in the extreme case – by making the power to spend and tax contingent upon the approval of a political body dominated by property-holders. The end result was emphasis on an appeal to the self-interest of capitalists in the form of an offer of assets that had an attractive combination of return, liquidity and risk of default. All of this represented a radical departure from such time-honoured practices as debasement of the coinage and confiscation of wealth through forced loans or default.

In one sense, the story of financial revolution should begin with the Netherlands. For in the seventeenth century, the Netherlands, or rather Holland, emerged as the first nation with public finances based on the honouring of capitalist principles, above all a power to spend and tax subject to the scrutiny and approval by legitimate representatives of the bourgeoisie – which dominated political affairs to an extent matched nowhere else in the world. The financial demands of the Dutch state consequently reached an entire class of investors, not just a privileged circle of wealthy capitalists, as was the case in all other countries at this time (De Vries 1976: 211–13, 218, 220). The combination of private wealth and the consent of the citizenry made for a strong state and provided the basis of the Netherlands' amazing great-power status (Kennedy 1988: 101–2). Since the emergence of an identifiable Dutch state was coterminous with capitalist-oriented institutions of public finance, there was no 'financial revolution', only evolution. For reasons which need not detain us here, the Netherlands were unable to exploit their head start in financial institutions as the basis for a head start in industrializing (Riley 1980). Instead, the country's main, lasting contribution to European economic modernization was in serving as an example for England and, indeed, in supplying the latter with a monarch, William of Orange, whose presence eased the implementation of the modern, Dutch principles of public finance.

At the heart of England's 'financial revolution' was the emergence, at the end of the seventeenth century, of a balance of power there between the executive branch of government (the king and his ministers), on the one hand, and the legislative branch (parliament), on the other. The executive initiated policy, but its executing depended upon parliamentary approval. As North and Weingast (1989) have pointed out, this represented a division of labour which was favourable from a transaction costs point of view and one which – applied to the government finances – had enormous implications. The fact that the state's finances depended upon parliamentary approval did not merely enhance capitalist confidence in the former; it also encouraged the state to adopt financial measures likely to impress private capitalists: e.g. the chartering of the Bank of England, the creation of more liquid (and more tradable) forms of government debt, the publication of annual government budgets, and the development of a more efficient and centralized system of tax collection (Dickson 1967; Neal 1990; O'Brien 1988; Brewer 1989). These arrangements can be viewed as institutions which offered, in North's phrase, 'credible commitments' by the British state to a policy of monetary and fiscal soundness – which coincided with the interests of British capitalists.

There are good reasons to see this set of changes as an important basis for Britain's subsequent economic development. As a recent survey of Britain's 'industrial revolution' (Deane 1996: 23) commented:

The upshot of this transformation in the English (and after the 1707 Union with Scotland, the British) system of public finance was twofold. In the first place it strengthened the economic power of the central government by giving it virtual immunity from the financial crisis that plagued most of its European rivals. In the second place, and as a by-product of the massive increase in the National Debt, it contributed directly to the modernization of the nation's credit institutions, to the integration of its capital market and to the development of a prosperous and efficient financial sector.

And as Larry Neal has recently argued, the declining risk and increasing liquidity of government debt made its yield an increasingly convenient indicator of the opportunity cost of capital to private investors throughout the country, enhancing the integration of its capital markets (Neal 1994: esp. 153–5, 171–81; also Pressnell 1960). Indeed, it has been argued that falling yields through much of the eighteenth century may have induced ('crowded in') more investment in the private sector, while the increased demand of government war finance from the 1790s temporarily led to a 'crowding out' of that investment (Ashton 1948; Williamson 1984; Heims and Mirowski 1987; also Mokyr 1987).[1]

Whatever one may think of the 'crowding out' argument, there can be no doubt of the relative superiority of Britain's financial position at the end of the eighteenth century. Its strength can be illuminated by comparison with another great-power contender of the times, France. Britain's financial revolution, according to Charles Kindleberger (1984), put it, financially speaking, one hundred years ahead of France. Kindleberger emphasized the collapse of John Law's bank project, the Mississippi Bubble and the ensuing state bankruptcy of 1720, for this left France with a legacy of popular mistrust of banks and government debt which could only be overcome in the nineteenth century, roughly one hundred years later (Cameron 1967). It should be added, however, that French financial backwardness followed not from the collapse of 1720 alone, but from the continuing unreformed character of eighteenth-century French political institutions and the resultant weakness of public finance. The crisis of state finances, we recall, led directly to the Revolution, and in the Revolutionary and Napoleonic eras which followed public finances remained precarious (Marion 1914–33; White 1989; Weir 1989; Velde and Weir 1992). The role of the *assignats* illustrates that precariousness. In François Crouzet's chapter in this book we see that role, as well as the emergence of Napoleon's cautious if ill-fated financial policies, as a reaction to this legacy. The reaction may have included ultimately constructive measures, e.g. the founding of the Bank of France, but in any case it was one with powerful and long-lasting consequences for the French monetary and banking system. The proverbial propensity of the nineteenth-century French financial system to accumulate gold and silver – which braked, even if it did not prevent, French industrialization – thus derived from a series of short-term responses to the state's immediate financial needs at the century's beginning.

Anglo-French comparison would seem to support strongly the notion of 'financial revolution' as a major historical force in the shaping of modern financial systems. A broader comparative perspective, however, leads to a less unitary view and offers, in particular, two important qualifications. First, in a number of successful industrializers modernization of the system of public finance came in bits and stages, and not in the form of a one-shot, unidirectional shift in fiscal mechanisms; and in such cases it hardly seems to deserve the name 'financial revolution'. Second, the state did not respond to its financial problems and influence private systems of finance through fiscal and borrowing mechanisms alone; it frequently relied on administrative measures and regulation (and deregulation) as well. These qualifications are documented throughout the book. The first point can be well illustrated by a brief survey of German experience.

We begin with Prussia, the most important German state. Its 'financial revolution' could be said to have entered an initial phase during the Napoleonic Wars. This phase followed a long period covering virtually the entire eighteenth century in which Hohenzollern Prussia, in contrast to Western countries, adhered to an older, paternalist view of finance based on the parsimonious principle of 'living within one's means', i.e. holding expenditures to the minimum essential to the state's survival, mainly in order to keep the monarchy independent of the provincial estates and to avoid surrendering some power over the state in exchange for additional powers to tax.[2] The decisive defeat of Prussia at Jena in 1806 shattered the Hohenzollern state and the internal balance of power between monarchy, landed aristocracy (Junker) and the largely agrarian population of peasant producers (the small urban bourgeoisie was not yet a significant factor). The response was to free the economy from corporatist, quasi-feudal restraints, e.g. by abolishing serfdom, and to centralize government administration, i.e. to strengthen the central government bureaucracy at the expense of the Junker (and to some extent at the expense of the absolutist monarchy). However, the financial measures adopted – new taxes and borrowing from private merchants and bankers – did not have much effect until after the war had been won (in 1815), and they produced, in any case, only promises of parliamentary controls over government finances and no concrete concessions. Moreover, the major loans of 1810, 1818 and 1820 were actually mobilized along traditional lines, contracted through foreign bankers (the Rothschilds), and were not part of a new strategy to tap the financial resources of an indigenous class of capitalist investors.[3] Indeed, secrecy remained a hallmark of Prussian finances in these years. For neither the king nor bureaucracy welcomed the guarantee of public credit which a parliament of property owners could have granted. Thus, in the subsequent period the Prussian government's policy stance was highly restrictive, marked by monetary and fiscal restraint, a return to the older Prussian 'Hausvater' tradition of parsimony, even down to considerable reliance on non-tax revenues which had a low political profile.[4]

This changed in the 1840s, when railway building attained high priority in government policy; but the unresolved question of the power to tax and borrow became a major issue. It was one of the problems which led to the Revolution of 1848–9; and one of the most significant results of the Revolution was the second phase of Prussia's financial revolution. For with the adoption of a constitution came the creation of a parliament of property owners with the right to review the government's budget and to control its power to tax and spend. And it is interesting to note the strong increase in government borrowing and related state spending on infrastructure which was registered at this time.[5]

Prussia was important, but Germany's financial modernization transcended Prussian history. Two developments are relevant here. First, the south German states of Bavaria, Baden and Württemberg modernized their systems of public finance earlier and more thoroughly than Prussia.

By the late 1820s they had established accountable systems of government debt administration with taxing and spending powers limited – and legitimated – by parliamentary controls; and these seem to have had financial pay-off in the better borrowing terms which these states enjoyed *vis-à-vis* Prussia from around 1820 to the 1840s (Homer and Sylla 1996; Borchard 1968: 25–9; Ullmann 1986). These states, however, did not go as far as Prussia with respect to deregulation of their economies, e.g. the liberalization of trade, occupational entry or reform of land tenure, so their relative advantage in public finance was offset by Prussia's lead in other policy areas.

Second, for political reasons, Prussia pursued the goal of a German-wide customs union in these years, the realization of which had important financial implications. It turned out that the net revenues generated by the Zollverein were the latter's most attractive argument for many of the states, at least initially; and the distribution of those revenues led to an agreement on fixed exchange rates between the south German Gulden and north German Thaler areas, and eventually even to restraints on the issue of state paper money by the individual member governments (Dumke 1984; Holtfrerich 1989). Customs revenues outweighed seignorage potential, and thus unification of monetary standards and a built-in commitment to price stability and strict controls over the money supply developed out of the Zollverein as an instrument of public finance.[6] These institutional changes, then, born of the need to respond to short-term problems of public finance, powerfully shaped the subsequent development of the German banking system.

British financial history, though it represents the classic case of 'financial revolution', nevertheless supplies a good illustration of our second point, which stresses the ongoing and general importance of the state as regulator of the private financial system. As noted above, one of the legacies of the English 'financial revolution' of the eighteenth century was the privileged position of the Bank of England and related limitations placed on the development of private, joint-stock banks (through the Bubble Act of 1720). The chapter by Cottrell and Newton in this volume demonstrates the importance of this legal arrangement by showing how rapidly joint-stock banks grew in the 1830s after the law was modified by Acts passed in 1826 and 1833. Their argument is reinforced, moreover, by reference to the slowdown in bank growth which followed another important piece of legislation – Peel's Act of 1844 – which regulated not just the Bank of England but entry into banking generally. Public concern for the status of the Bank of England, an early element of the country's 'financial revolution', thus continued to be an important determinant of its financial development.

That chapter, however, also helps identify a more subtle point about British financial development. For Cottrell and Newton note that the loosening of the Bank of England's monopoly only led to an increase in the number of new joint-stock banks after restrictions on their participation in the London market for small and liquid bills of exchange had been lifted in 1833. This improved their competitive position *vis-à-vis* private bankers but it did so by permitting them to operate in the well-organized London money market. Legislation, that is, encouraged them to do, on a somewhat larger scale, what their predecessors, the country banks, had already been doing, and therefore strengthened the 'market-orientated' elements of the British financial system.

This is worth stressing since, by a species of dialectic, these strong market elements also shaped the further development of British financial institutions.[7] In Forrest Capie's chapter on central banking, it becomes clear than when the Bank of England began to try to assume lender-of-last-resort responsibilities (e.g. in the 1870s) it defined these in terms of anonymous relationships (sometimes termed 'arms-length' relationships), and was concerned with 'keeping in touch with the market', infusing liquidity, but not with monitoring the individual institutions involved and keeping watch for bad risks. Thus Britain's central bank – whose behaviour pattern proved not to be a model for Continental Europe – had to respond to a market development which was, in turn, at least in part a response to the Bank of England's own history.

The case of the United States offers yet another relevant chapter of historical experience, for in that country decentralization of political power was even more pronounced than in the German case. The institutions which determined public finance reflected that decentralization. Yet it is worth remembering that centralization of power is, and always has been, a part of the American experience. Conflicts between decentralizing and centralizing forces were always present, but for the most part they were accommodated into a framework of stable politics by the country's ingenious federal system that, under the Constitution of 1787, divided up sovereignty between federal and state governments. Sylla's chapter explores, within the federal-system framework, how the fiscal needs of governments at several key times in US history gave lasting shape to the country's financial system. Thus, however 'exceptional' the United States may have been in some respects, in terms of the thesis of this volume it was not at all exceptional.

Sylla's first example antedates US independence. Fiat paper money appeared for the first time anywhere in the Western world in colonial Massachusetts as a solution to a pressing short-term problem of public finance. But it quickly became a solution to the problem of providing the means of exchange to accommodate long-term economic expansion throughout the American colonies, and in time throughout the world.

The historical concept of 'financial revolution' has already been raised here in connection with England and the Netherlands. It applies as well, Sylla argues, to the United States, where the Federalists of the 1790s, led by an able finance minister, Treasury Secretary Alexander Hamilton, engineered a sharp break with America's previous financial history by introducing, in just a few years, a modern financial system with specie-based currency and public debt, corporate banks issuing convertible notes, a central bank and active securities markets. This financial system became a key underpinning of the country's early start on the road to economic modernization.

Public finance considerations also figured prominently in the proliferation of American banks under the auspices of state charters. The states saw that their bank charters had value and learned to appropriate some of that value for public purposes. The lessons learned early by the states were instrumental in the development of the federal government's national banking system, which came in during the Civil War of 1861–5 to aid in the government's wartime bond sales. The occasion was also used to introduce for the first time a uniform national paper currency backed by the credit of the federal government.

Mira Wilkins' chapter in a sense provides a sequel to Sylla's. The United States, in no small measure because it possessed a dynamic, modern financial system from its first years as a nation, grew over the course of the nineteenth century into the world's largest economy. Until the First World War, however, the country remained an importer of capital as well as the world's largest debtor nation. The war changed all that. When it ended the United States had become the largest creditor nation. By the 1920s, New York City had become the hub of international finance. This came about, Wilkins says, 'not because of any action or lack of actions of the US government, but because the United States was where the capital and the capital markets were'. The suddenness of the change in America's international position, coupled with the lack of governmental financial involvement and leadership in the 1920s, led to some of the abuses that became painfully evident at the decade's end. Wilkins notes that the ensuing crisis of the 1930s brought new governmental regulatory structures in finance that once again reshaped the US financial system. These changes, however, lie beyond the purview of this volume.[8]

The history of the other industrializing countries offers many variations on the same general theme. In the case of Belgium, as explained in the chapter by Herman Van der Wee, fiscal problems in the aftermath of the Napoleonic Wars were behind the unwillingness of the Dutch parliament to sanction the state-owned development bank proposed by King William for the southern Netherlands (later Belgium). That refusal led in 1822 to the chartering of a *private* institution which did not require parliamentary approval. Thus was born an institution which was to play a dynamic role in Belgian industrialization and which was eventually to become one of the world's most successful universal banks, the Société Générale de Belgique. What it became, however, went far beyond the initial mission, which was to alleviate the state's financial situation. Ironically, perhaps, it was the king himself who initially weakened the Société Générale's role as government fiscal agent. He did so by pushing that institution into its universal banking activities, on the one hand by enlisting its support for a number of infrastructure projects and on the other hand by encouraging it to build up a national network facilitating the use of bills of exchange as credit and payments instruments. Even before the Revolution of 1830 led to the creation of the kingdom of Belgium, the Société Générale had begun to assume its leading role as a universal bank which combined its support of heavy industry and transportation investments with successful commercial banking operations. The correlation between the business activity of this single institution and Belgian industrial growth is truly remarkable.

Germany's economic history supplies yet another case in which repeated, though infrequent, shifts in the policy stance of the state continued to shape the contours of private financial development. In chapter 6, Tilly documents two short-run responses to financial crises with long-run effects. First, in the 1840s, the Prussian state's answer to crisis was to establish a government-controlled bank of issue which soon acquired a dominant position in the country's system of payments and short-term credit, thus encouraging private institutions to concentrate their resources in riskier, longer-term activities. Second, the boom and bust of the 1870s reflected short-run political changes, but it eventually led to a reform of the German system of corporate finance which encouraged concentration among both banks and industrial enterprises. The long-run implications were thus of major importance.

The cases discussed up to now represent, so to speak, scenarios not only in which significant shifts in the conditions of public finance took place which had readily identifiable, if long-run, effects on the development of private financial institutions, but in which rapid industrialization and economic growth also came about, presumably in part as a result of the operations of such institutions. For there can be no question but that the histories of nineteenth-century Britain, Belgium, France, Germany and the United States are success stories from the perspective of long-run economic growth. That is, the theme of 'economic modernization' is not an undeserved component of our book's title. That warrants emphasis in this introduction, since neither economic growth nor the mechanisms which link it to financial development are explicitly investigated here.[9]

Of course, an historical generalization based on the early industrializers alone cries for extension – in time and place. The book supplies that extension by including within its purview some industrial 'latecomers'. The Spanish case provides a different angle on the interrelationship between the state and the financial system, a case which also illustrates the ability of institutions to stimulate or arrest economic development, and provides an example of what one may call 'Cameron-Gerschenkron' modernization, when banks and the state largely replace the market in mobilizing funds for industrialization. In the early modern period, the profligacy of the Spanish state and its disregard of economic logic played havoc with the country's financial institutions (Tortella 1997: esp. 230–2). It was the state's financial predicament which favoured the foundation of Spain's first modern bank (Banco de San Carlos, 1782) and its demise. A state-sponsored plan to stimulate growth of the banking system as a means of financing the railway network in the mid-nineteenth century also ended in partial fiasco. It was not until the twentieth century that the birth of a strong private banking system, the state's decision to put its financial house in order after the 1898 débâcle, and the development of a special triangular relationship between the central bank (the Bank of Spain), the large private banks and the Ministry of Finance permitted the establishment of a surprisingly robust set of mixed banks, able to finance the development of heavy industry (metallurgy, chemicals, electricity) and public works without suffering – at least not with the same acuteness – the recurrent crises which affected other European 'mixed' systems. Undoubtedly, the fact that Spain was on a silver standard (which was *de facto* fiduciary) contributed to lend flexibility to this rather unique setup. In the Continental tradition, the capital market played a secondary role in Spain, and it was the large banks, with strong support from the central bank and the state, that took the lead in industrial finance.

Peter Hertner's chapter considers the experience of yet another industrial latecomer – Italy. As its title suggests, the main theme concerns the links between central banking and private, commercial banks. The initial weakness of those links documented here is striking and raises two sets of questions pertinent to the general concerns of our book. First, to what extent did the underdeveloped character of central banking itself, as reflected in the plurality of banks of issue and the failure to maintain convertibility and exchange rate stability, derive from the political and financial weakness of the Italian state? Second, given that underdevelopment and given the rapid growth of the activities of the two large mixed banks in the period, should we not conclude that successful 'industrial banking' owed little to effective central banking institutions?[10] Hertner does not deal with the first issue directly, but his account suggests that the initial weakness of central banking was gradually overcome, partly because the Bank of Italy's position strengthened, partly because its chief, Stringher, began to redefine the bank's role in the country's financial system. There are thus some grounds for believing that the Italian mixed banks – and the Italian economy – would have done less well had central banking not strengthened over these years.

Our list of important 'industrial latecomers' includes Czarist Russia. Here, too, state financial priorities had consequences for the development of private financial institutions. Throughout the nineteenth century, the state faced the problem of reconciling its imperial, expansionist ambitions with a Russian economy that developed so slowly that it became more and more backward relative to the industrializing economies to its west in Europe. Russia's solution was autocratic: the state itself, meaning the Czar and his ministers, would exercise vastly greater control over the Russian economy and financial system than was the case elsewhere in Europe. In his chapter on Russia, Anan´ich gives a detailed account of how, during the century before 1917, the Russian state exercised nearly absolute control over the country's public and private financial arrangements through the Credit Office of the Ministry of Finance. During that period, the Credit Office centralized in one bureaucracy financial functions that were widely diffused in other countries. These included public debt negotiation (including foreign loans and state-guaranteed loans for railway building), debt management, the chartering and supervision of public (state-operated savings, mortgage and central) banks and most types of non-public (e.g. joint-stock land and commercial) banks, tax administration, coinage at the mint, foreign exchange dealings and stock exchange supervision.

In Czarist Russia, therefore, very few fiscal, monetary and credit institutions were beyond the ken and regulation of the Credit Office. Anan´ich's account provides a concrete example of what autocratic centralization of financial authority meant in practice. Autocratic rule in finance in Russia's case proved to be not inconsistent with industrial modernization, for by the 1890s the country embarked on an industrial upsurge. Russia's financial system, under the eye of the Credit Office, grew apace with this move towards modernization.

All of this happened, interestingly, without a 'financial revolution' in the Western European sense described earlier. In one respect, to be sure, Czarist Russia did adapt to Western bourgeois rules: in order to finance its ambitious programme of economic modernization, it adapted to the demands of private financial institutions abroad, from the 1850s by reliably honouring its foreign debt commitments, then dramatically in the 1890s by adopting the gold standard. The related success story of capital inflow and economic growth is well known (e.g. Gregory 1994). This did not reduce the Czarist state's wish to control the financial system, however; and nor could it prevent the end of the *ancien régime* in 1918. A poignant element of Anan´ich's narrative is his account of how the finance minister during the last months of the Czarist regime was confronted by a seeming need to increase the regime's autocratic control over finance to cope with crises, and an opposed need to reduce such control – to deregulate a highly regulated system – in the interest of a stronger Russian economy. The Czar's regime was not given time to resolve this conflict.

Our comparative perspective necessarily widens as we move from our European centre to the periphery. That could be seen in the case of Czarist Russia. It is even more apparent if we consider the case of Argentina. With this example we take up a developing economy in which real economic development and its concomitant financial development were extremely dependent on foreign political and economic influences – on exports, on capital imports and also on immigration. Nevertheless, internal political conditions had great influence – more than is often thought (see Marichal 1989 on this). Cortés Conde shows how domestic political fragmentation encouraged the development of a weak banking system, in which governments founded banks to favour special interests but also to ease their own financial problems (by imposing, in effect, a seignorage tax). When fragmentation increased, for whatever reason, weak financial institutions proliferated, their growth potential magnified by European investors who were 'bullish' on Argentina. The episode known in European economic history as the 'Baring Crisis' of 1890 had its origins in an almost anarchic expansion of provincial state banks and their corresponding note circulation in the second half of the 1880s. This was facilitated by an attempt at 'free banking' regulation (law of 1887) reminiscent of the US. Only when the crisis had broken the banks and foreign creditors as well did thorough-going reform of the banking system come. And even at that it took nearly a decade, for the decisive legislation first came in 1899, in association, significantly, with Argentina's adoption of the gold standard.

It is time to draw together the strands of the foregoing comparative observations. Three, or possibly four, general themes stand out. They correspond to questions deserving further research attention and represent issues raised, directly and indirectly, in the chapters which follow.

The first theme is the great inter-country differences in the mix of public and private finance and in the way states influenced private financial development. The differences range from the increasingly market-orientated development of Great Britain to the continuing strong controls exercised by the state in Czarist Russia. They call for further attention since they bear on the general question of what and how well financial institutions contributed to economic modernization in the countries considered. If it is true, for example, as Sylla has argued for the US case, that major financial innovations came about largely in response to changes in the arrangements governing public finances, then great interest necessarily attaches to those changes. An important caveat calls for acknowledgement here, to be sure: the differences noted may result from fundamental differences in the nature of the polities of the countries, e.g. in the degree of political fragmentation (or decentralization), or as a result of a country's position in the international system of power politics. They certainly do *not* simply reflect different development strategies.[11] Still, the national differences in this respect do offer an intriguing possibility for understanding how and how well financial systems have developed.

Second, the way in which the state affected private financial development had much to do with its influence on the flow of information relevant to private financial decision-making. This is obvious in the case of public finance: the institution of such rules as parliamentary controls over state budgeting, for example, could serve as useful information about the future expected real rate of return on government debt instruments. Another obvious and quite general example can be seen in the adoption of gold standard rules by nineteenth-century governments: this represented a signal to investors at home and abroad. Less obvious, but important, were the regulation of business incorporation and the conditions under which private corporate debt and equity could be traded in organized markets. At one extreme, stringent government controls could prevent competitive financial markets from developing; and at the other, lax disclosure requirements could allow such nascent markets as might have emerged to atrophy.

A third issue, related to that just mentioned, concerns the relative effectiveness of 'market-orientated' as opposed to 'bank-orientated' financial systems of private finance as development mechanisms. The chapters which follow include historical success stories associated with both types of system and offer illustrations of both costs and benefits of the underlying institutional arrangements. Comparative assessment of these two 'ideal types' (Weber) is related to the relative merits of hierarchies in overcoming problems of information asymmetry between providers and users of financial capital as weighed against the presumed disadvantages (or costs) of having less competition than under the alternative, market-orientated arrangements. Readers will have to judge for themselves how clearly our book resolves this issue. Nevertheless, it is worth noting here that financial problems currently faced by countries in the process of economic transformation and development have analogies in the historical experience discussed here.

Finally, short-run state policy responses to immediate problems, economic and non-economic in nature, could have long-run effects on a country's financial development and on its overall pattern of economic modernization as well. Put somewhat differently, a country's long-run financial development can be said to reflect the historical sequence of events experienced, i.e. it is path-dependent. The histories of all of the countries considered in this volume illustrate the point. War and revolution seem to have powerfully influenced the private financial structures which emerged for example in France, in Belgium, in the US, in Germany. What remains to be seen, to be sure, is not only whether the paths of development observed varied significantly across the countries studied, but whether – and the extent to which – their doing so reflected uniquely different sequences as opposed to uniquely different sets of purely economic forces, such as relative prices and quantities of factors of production.

NOTES

1 It should be noted here that not all of the changes associated with 'financial revolution' necessarily contributed to improvement of the private financial system. The Bubble Act of 1720, for instance, may well have served to keep English banking smaller scale and more fragmented for a longer period of time than the needs of industry would have dictated. See Cameron 1967.
2 On this point see the insightful comments by Braun (1975).
3 Although this class developed strongly over the period, as the considerable growth of financial activity (including the sale of foreign securities in Berlin's capital market) between 1815 and 1840 indicates. On this see Brockhage 1910 and Borchardt 1961. See also the essay by H. Schissler and the documents edited by her and H.-U. Wehler in *Preussische Finanzpolitik 1806–1810* (Kehr 1984).
4 This policy stance even included restraints on military spending. Prussian money stock growth in the 1820s and 1830s was low by comparison with France or England; and its borrowing per capita, the highest among the fifteen most important German states in 1815, was by 1815 the lowest of that same group. See Cameron 1967; Borchard 1968. Borchard shows how Prussia's investment was restrained by its self-imposed fiscal conservatism.
5 On this see, in addition to Borchard 1968, Tilly 1966.
6 Of course, the individual German states were able to charter and *did* charter

the private banks of issue, but since users of their notes were able to discriminate between the different issuers a general overissue did not take place, and the largest state bank of issue, the Bank of Prussia (with around two-thirds of total circulation), set the pace for the rest. See on this Thorwart 1883.

7 That implies that the older studies which stressed the importance of the London money market were on 'the right track' (see King 1936; Pressnell, 1956). From around the 1860s the inland bill declined in importance, but the growth of foreign bills more than offset the decline; and the London money market became, if anything, more important for British banks. See Nishimura 1971.

8 For a perspective on twentieth-century changes in US financial development and regulation, see Bordo and Sylla 1995.

9 This question has been at the heart of many publications, including some written by the editors and also by Rondo Cameron. Two further points may be worth making here, however. First, the histories discussed in this volume include evidence of a positive connection between financial and economic modernization. One might even go so far as to claim that swings of more rapid economic development were favoured by changes in financial institutions, for example by a contraction of government demands for savings after a prior expansion of such demands had whetted investors' appetites, so to speak, by demonstrating the advantages of supplying them. Second, economic modernization, associated with capital-intensive technologies on the one hand, and with rising incomes on the other, will also have had powerful effects on financial institutions. An obvious point, no doubt, but worth remembering.

10 One could even go a step further and suggest – thanks to available evidence on rapid industrial growth in the period – that banks were less crucial for Italian industrialization than has been often argued. On this see Federico and Toniolo 1991: esp. 202–6.

11 We also acknowledge the fact that financial innovations deriving from changes in state policies need not have been primarily benign in their effects on economic modernization potential. Many scholars have noted the dialectical relationship linking state regulations with innovations which did not more than offset some of the negative effects of the former.

BIBLIOGRPAHY

Ashton, T. S. 1948. *The Industrial Revolution*. Oxford.
Borchard, Karl 1968 'Staatsverbrauch und öffentliche Investitionem in Deutschland 1780–1850', dissertation, University of Göttingen.
Borchardt, Knut 1961. 'Zur Frage des Kapitalmangels in der ersten Hälfte des 19. Jahrhunderts in Deutschland', *Jahrbücher für Nationalökonomie und Statistik* 173: 401–21.
Bordo, Michael D. and Sylla, Richard (eds.) 1995. *Anglo-American Financial Systems: Institutions and Markets in the Twentieth Century*. Burr Ridge, Ill.
Braun, R. 1975. 'Taxation, Sociopolitical Structure, and State-Building: Great Britain and Brandenburg-Prussia', in C. Tilly (ed.), *The Formation of National States in Western Europe*, pp. 243–327. Princeton, NJ.

Brewer, John 1989. *The Sinews of Power: War, Money and the English State, 1688–1783*. London.

Brockhage, B. 1910. *Zur Entwicklung des preussisch-deutschen Kapitalexports*. Leipzig.

Cameron, Rondo 1967. *Banking in the Early Stages of Industrialization: A Study in Comparative History*. Oxford.

Deane, Phyllis 1996. 'The British Industrial Revolution', in M. Teich and R. Porter (eds.), *The Industrial Revolution in National Context*, pp. 13–35. Cambridge.

De Vries, Jan 1976. *The Economy of Europe in an Age of Crisis, 1600–1750*. Cambridge.

Dickson, P. G. M. 1967. *The Financial Revolution in England*. Oxford.

Dumke, R. H. 1984. 'Der Deutsche Zollverein als Modell ökonomischer Integration', in H. Berding (ed.), *Wirtschaftliche und politische Integration in Europa im 19. und 20. Jahrhundert*, pp. 71–101. Göttingen.

Federico, G. and Toniolo, G. 1991. 'Italy', in R. Sylla and G. Toniolo (eds.), *Patterns of European Industrialization: The Nineteenth Century*, pp. 197–217. London.

Gregory, Paul 1994. *Before Command: An Economic History of Russia from Emancipation to the First Five-Year Plan*. Princeton, NJ.

Heim, Carol and Mirowski, Philip 1987. 'Interest Rates and Crowding-Out during Britain's Industrial Revolution', *Journal of Economic History* 47: 117–39.

Holtfrerich, Carl-Ludwig 1989. 'The Monetary Unification Process in Nineteenth-Century Germany. Relevance and Lessons for Europe Today', in M. De Cecco and A. Giovanni (eds.), *Monetary Regimes and Monetary Institutions: Issues and Perspectives in Europe*, pp. 216–43. Cambridge.

Homer, Sidney and Sylla, Richard 1996. *A History of Interest Rates*. New Brunswick, NJ.

Kehr, E. 1984. *Preussische Finanzpolitik 1806–1810. Quellen zur Verwaltung des Ministeriums Stein und Altenstein*, ed. H. Schissler and H.-U. Wehler. Göttingen.

Kennedy, Paul 1988. *The Rise and Fall of the Great Powers*. London.

Kindleberger, Charles 1984. 'Financial Institutions and Economic Development: A Comparison of Great Britain and France in the Eighteenth and Nineteenth Centuries', *Explorations in Economic History* 21: 103–24.

King, W. T. C. 1936. *History of the London Discount Market*. London.

Marichal, Carlos 1989. *A Century of Debt Crises in Latin America*. Princeton, NJ.

Marion, Marcel 1914–33. *Histoire financière de la France depuis 1715* vols. II–IV. Paris.

Mokyr, Joel 1987. 'The Industrial Revolution and the New Economic History', in J. Mokyr (ed.), *The Economics of the Industrial Revolution*, pp. 293–325. Totowa.

  1987. 'Has the Industrial Revolution Been Crowded Out? Some Reflections on Crafts and Williamson', in *Explorations in Economic History* 24: 293–325.

Neal, Larry 1990. *The Rise of Financial Capitalism: International Capital Markets in the Age of Reason*. Cambridge.

  1994. 'The finance of business during the industrial revolution', in R. Floud and D. McCloskey (eds.), *The Economic History of Britain since 1700*, I, pp. 15–181. Cambridge.

Nishimura, S. 1971. *The Decline of the Inland Bills of Exchange in the London Money Market 1855–1913*. Cambridge.

North, Douglass and Weingast, Barry 1989. 'Constitutions and Commitment', *Journal of Economic History* 49: 803–32.

O'Brien, Patrick 1988. 'The Political Economy of British Taxation, 1688–1815', *Economic History Review*, 2nd ser., 41: 205–41.

Pressnell, Leslie 1956. *Country Banking in the Industrial Revolution*. Oxford.

1960. 'The Rate of Interest in the Eighteenth Century', in L. S. Pressnell (ed.), *Studies in the Industrial Revolutions*, pp. 178–84. London.

Riley, James 1980. *International Government Finance and the Amsterdam Capital Market, 1740–1815*. Cambridge.

Thorwart, F. 1883. 'Die Entwicklung des Banknotenumlaufs in Deutschland von 1851–1880', *Jahrbücher für Nationalökonomie und Statistik* N.F. 7: 193–250.

Tilly, Richard 1966. 'The Political Economy of Public Finance and the Industrialization of Prussia', *Journal of Economic History* 26: 484–97.

Tortella, Gabriel 1997. 'Banking and Economic Development in Spain', in Alice Teichova, Ginette Kurgan-van Hentenryk and Dieter Ziegler (eds.), *Banking, Trade and Industry: Europe, America and Asia from the Thirteenth to the Twentieth Century*, pp. 229–44. Cambridge.

Ullmann, Hans-Peter 1986. *Staatsschulden und Reformpolitik: Die Entstehung moderner öffentlicher Schulden in Bayern und Baden, 1780–1820*. Göttingen.

Velde, François and Weir, David 1992. 'The Financial Market and Government Debt Policy in France, 1746–1793', *Journal of Economic History* 52: 1–39.

Weir, David 1989. 'Tontines, Public Finance and Revolution in France and England, 1688–1789', *Journal of Economic History* 49: 95–124.

White, Eugene 1989. 'Was There a Solution to the Ancien Régime's Financial Dilemma?', *Journal of Economic History* 49: 545–68.

Williamson, Jeffrey G. 1984. 'Why Was British Growth So Slow during the Industrial Revolution?', *Journal of Economic History* 44: 687–712.

2 Politics and banking in revolutionary and Napoleonic France

François Crouzet

During the early 1790s, France went through a period of government intervention in the economy, the scale and scope of which had no equivalent in Western countries until World War I.[1] However, the intervention was purely a reaction to immediate pressures and not a matter of doctrine. Almost to a man, members of the revolutionary assemblies and their leaders, including the *Montagnards* who ruled in 1793–4 when *dirigisme* prevailed, were in favour of a market economy and of *laissez-faire*. They broke with their principles under the pressure of circumstances: to make up the budgetary deficit which they had inherited from the Old Regime (and made worse), to finance war against most of Europe, and last but not least to appease the *sans-culottes* – the lower-middle-class and working-class militants who, from August 1792 to July 1794, were both the main plank of support of the revolutionary governments and a threat to their existence. Stimulated by extreme leftists (*les enragés*), the Parisian *sans-culottes* were not ready to accept cuts in their living standards, even for the defence of the Republic; they held archaic, unrealistic, antimarket, moral-economy views, to which the Jacobins had to make concessions in order to enlist and retain their support. In addition, revolutionary leaders believed in the priority of politics over economics; the general will of the nation, which they embodied, was superior to the laws of political economy.

In December 1795, the *émigré* and royalist journalist Mallet du Pan wrote that the forced loan, which the French government had just imposed, was 'an operation of Tartars–Kalmuks, who treat France as a conquered country and plunder it utterly in order to retain their power for a little longer'; and the following month he added: 'The French government eats up every year a morsel of the Republic's capital; it devours France as a spendthrift eats up his patrimony.' In less picturesque terms, the nineteenth-century historian René Stourm stated: 'The financial views of the Jacobins were exclusively to exhaust present resources to the utmost, and to sacrifice the future.' Indeed, revolutionary rulers, whatever their faction, regularly gave priority to immediate needs, to the pressures of the moment. The fashionable expression 'short-termism' might have been coined at their intention! This chapter intends to explore the long-run consequences that policies which had been improvised to answer immediate problems may have had upon the French economy, and especially upon its financial system.

First, two aspects of government intervention will be briefly considered:[2] on the one hand, the massive creation of paper money by the revolutionary regimes, from 1790 to 1796, which led to an outburst of inflation and finally of hyperinflation; on the other hand, the *dirigiste* or 'command' system, which was imposed upon the French economy for just over a year, in 1793–4, and which may be called the 'economic terror' as it roughly coincided with *la Terreur*. This second aspect will be mentioned first, as its long-term consequences were rather limited, while paper money and inflation had more far-reaching effects. They are connected with the problem of the Revolution's policy in banking affairs – or rather the lack of policy in this field – so that it devolved upon Bonaparte to lay the French banking system's cornerstone.

The economic policies which the *Montagnards* followed from May 1793 to July 1794 were the product of circumstances – the dangerous position of the French Republic, the apparent necessity of drastic measures of 'public safety' and the pressure from the *sans-culottes*. This *dirigisme* included prices and wages controls (the 'laws of the maximum'), commandeering of supplies with the help of the military, rationing of basic foodstuffs in large cities, forced loans to be subscribed to by rich citizens, a kind of nationalization (or state monopoly) of foreign trade, foreign exchange control, state factories for producing armaments, soldiers' uniforms, etc.

This system has been praised by some historians, but actually it did not work well, though its main objective – to supply bread to the army and to Paris, plus arms to the former – was roughly achieved; but all other commodities disappeared and could only be obtained on the black market.

As far as this system worked, it was through coercion and repression, through terror and the apparatus of a police-state. Therefore it disintegrated fast and collapsed after the fall of Robespierre (28 July 1794) and the end of Terror. The abolition of the *maximum* by the National Convention, on 24 December 1794, only ratified a *fait accompli*, as for several months price control had become a dead letter.

Nonetheless, the command economy of the Year II had serious though not long-lived consequences. Farmers were furious when the product of their toil was requisitioned and paid for, at *maximum* prices which they thought far too low, in a depreciated paper currency with which they could hardly buy anything. So they reduced the cultivated acreage; they killed and ate their cattle. Moreover, as weather conditions were poor, the harvest of 1794 was bad, and that of 1795 not much better (ploughing and sowing had taken place in 1794 before the *maximum* had been abolished). Consequently, a severe food shortage developed in most parts of France and it was made worse by the exceptionally cold winter of 1794/5. Quite a few people died of starvation and/or disease. This last famine in French history was the perverse backlash of the 'economic terror', which had generated a supply crisis.

But this crisis did not last. Once the *maximum* had gone, farmers eagerly went back to work and there was a bumper harvest in 1796; those of 1797 and 1798 were also very good, so that the late 1790s were characterized by the abundance and cheapness of foodstuffs.

In non-agricultural sectors, the combination of *maximum*, requisitions and inflation was harmful to many traders and manufacturers. They could not hoard their goods as easily as peasants did; they often gave long credit to their customers; the state, which had become a major customer, was notorious for only paying after long delays, and in a currency which was fast depreciating. So many businessmen were obliged to sell at a loss and much circulating capital was destroyed; some firms were thrown out of business, and those which survived had a difficult recovery, when more normal conditions had been restored. This was one of the reasons for the sluggishness of industrial recovery during the late 1790s.

Nonetheless, these harmful after-effects of Jacobin *dirigisme* pale beside those of inflation – which were serious in the short, medium and even long term. To be fair, however, it must be pointed out that, thanks to massive issues of *assignats*, which were the main factor of inflation, the revolutionary governments extracted from the French people very large resources, which they used for defending the Republic against its enemies.[3] On the other hand, it can be maintained that equivalent resources could have been mobilized, with a lower rate of inflation (and no hyperinflation), if government had resisted the obsolete and selfish demands of the *sans-culottes* and preserved the market economy.

On 2 November 1789, the Constituent Assembly 'nationalized' all Church property, with the idea that its sale to the public would give the means of reducing the national debt and its servicing. As the sale would take time, it was decided on 19–21 December to issue a limited amount of a paper currency, called *assignats*, which creditors of the state would receive and with which they would be able to buy 'national properties'. As the budgetary deficit was large and increasing, fresh issues of *assignats* had to be regularly ordered, specially after France had become involved in war

(April 1792). The first *assignats* were issued in August 1790, and the value of those in circulation in January of each year is given here (in millions of livres):

1791	1792	1793	1794	1795	1796
560	1,420	2,350	4,800	7,000	30,000

So the increase in the circulation of paper was rather regular and only in 1795 was there a sharp acceleration. As in 1790 and 1791, the rise in *assignats* circulation was accompanied by a gradual withdrawal of specie from circulation, total money supply did not increase and there was no inflation. A general rise of prices only started in 1792, when some supply shocks also occurred. On the other hand, *assignats* had depreciated, in relation to precious metals and to foreign currencies, from the end of 1790, i.e. shortly after the first issues. Their depreciation, however, was neither very fast, nor uninterrupted, except in 1795; as measured by the value of gold which could be bought with 100 livres in *assignats*, it is given here for January of every year (in livres):

1791	1792	1793	1794	1795	1796
91	72	51	40	18	0.5

In 1795, *assignats* circulation increased at a monthly average rate of 11%, while the price of gold rose at 34% and most other commodities at 30% or more. This bout of hyperinflation did not result from the abolition of the *dirigiste* system, as many historians have maintained, but from the disruption of production and distribution which that system (and especially the *maximum*) had caused.

By late 1795, payment in *assignats* was increasingly refused and only specie accepted; the movement spread gradually from the countryside to the towns. For once, this was a case of good money driving away bad. Moreover, the economy was in chaos, business at a standstill, tax revenue close to zero in real terms, and the inflation tax itself becoming useless to the government. So the latter decided to get rid of *assignats* and, on 19 February 1796, all the apparatus and machinery for printing them was solemnly destroyed and burnt. A new kind of paper money, the *mandats territoriaux*, was to replace the *assignats*, but the change was badly managed[4] and within two months the new currency had depreciated as much as the *assignats* in six years. Eventually both *assignats* and *mandats* were demonetized,[5] but during the summer of 1796 France had *de facto* returned to a metallic currency. Unlike many other cases, this ending of inflation involved neither devaluation of the former currency nor the creation of a new one – only a change of name![6] As for the economic consequences of inflation, it is striking that French industrial production and trade reached a nadir during hyperinflation and started to recover in 1796 (though the quasi-famine of 1795 was also a factor). On the other hand, a serious after-effect of inflation – and also of revolution – was the inadequacy of the money supply.

During the early years of the Revolution, specie had been gradually withdrawn from circulation, either through the hoarding or through the exporting of precious metals. Many people, worried by the Revolution's radicalization and distrusting the *assignats*, hoarded the specie they had in hand, while a flight of capital from France and deficits in the balance of trade created a drain to foreign countries. By April 1793, when trading *assignats* for specie – or vice versa – was forbidden except at par, the circulation of specie had come practically to an end. The French metallic stock had been hoarded or exported. However, during the last stage of hyperinflation and after its end, a good deal of the specie which had been hoarded emerged from hiding and went into circulation. Moreover, there was an inflow of precious metals into France, from two sources: conquest and speculation. From September 1795 to January 1796, the *assignats* depreciated more in relation to gold than to foreign currencies, so that it was profitable to send gold to France, either to remit money or as a speculation, especially from England as the rate of exchange of sterling had fallen below the gold points; a good deal of gold was therefore exported from London to Paris. Moreover, from 1794 onwards, the French armies occupied several neighbouring countries, from which heavy war contributions and indemnities were demanded; a rough guess is that this policy of 'supranational requisition' resulted in the import into France, from 1795 to 1799, of about 200 million livres in specie and bullion.

However, these imports were not enough, and the French metallic stock in the late 1790s, and even after 1800, was markedly below its pre-Revolution level. Gaudin, Bonaparte's Minister of Finance, estimated that 'we are left with only 1500 to 1800 millions', against 2 billions or more before 1789. He also thought that people kept on hoarding, so that the whole of the specie was not really in circulation. Possibly, moreover, trade needed more specie than before the Revolution, because the use of trade credit and bills of exchange had decreased and cash or short-credit transactions now prevailed.

On the other hand, there is a consensus that the French economy was rather depressed during the period of the Directory (1796–9), while documents from that period are full of complaints about the 'shortage of specie', which was made responsible for the difficulties which prevailed. A serious problem was the fall in farm prices, of grain, cattle, wine, etc., which went on for three years from the autumn of 1796 to the summer of 1799. This fall was not a collapse and a lot of people in towns, and also in the countryside, benefited from the cheapness of food, but many farmers undoubtedly suffered: in January 1799, it was reported that around Paris 'the low price of grain plus the rise in labour costs make cultivators hopeless and ruin them'. A succession of good harvests was certainly a major factor in the fall of prices, but in November 1798 a report from Angers (western France) mentioned a complete cessation in the sales of wine – at a period when usually they were the most active – and added: 'What is the cause of this baleful stagnation? The shortage of specie . . .' In February 1799, another report, this time from southwestern France, gave the same explanation for 'the absolute distress' of cultivators, who were 'overstocked with foodstuffs and cannot sell them even at the lowest prices'.

In industry, there was a clear recovery for some branches and in some areas under the Directory, and striking progress for the cotton industry. On the other hand, many documents confirm the relationship between stagnation and the monetary factor. In an inquiry which was carried out at the end of 1797 and early in 1798, the *maximum*, the requisitions, the depreciation of *assignats* and the recent shortage of specie (which hindered the buying of raw materials) are described as major causes of the fall in output and of the losses which have reduced manufacturers' capital in the important textile district of Nord (Lille, Roubaix, etc.). Some years later, reports from many *départements* by Bonaparte's prefects gave the same explanation for industrial depression. As late as 1802, it was said that the hosiery manufacturers of Troyes were unable, 'for lack of specie, to answer all the orders which they received'. Several recent works confirm these views. In Dauphiné, under the Directory, manufactures were 'hit by a monetary famine and a fall in prices: markets narrowed, profit margins were reduced' (Léon 1954: I, 359). At Elbeuf, the woollen industry remained depressed as late as 1800, because 'specie had disappeared from circulation'.[7] According to Woronoff (1984), ironmaking firms greatly suffered in the late 1790s from the shortage of specie and from high interest rates. That the latter were much higher than before the Revolution cannot be doubted; according to an expert, J.-B. Le Coulteux, the common rate of interest in France on deposits was 2% per month; the discount rates of private banks fluctuated, according to circumstances, between 1.5 and 3% (even at some periods 4%) per month (Crouzet 1993: 502).[8] The shortage of specie and more generally of capital[9] was certainly – with the lack of confidence – a major cause of such 'usurious' rates.

However, monetary factors were not solely responsible for the sluggishness of industry's recovery under the Directory, and several other causes can be detected, mainly the continuance of war (which, *inter alia*, hindered French exports) and the political instability of the Directorial regime. In 1797 and 1799, political and military disturbances generated crises which broke any spurt of growth. Nonetheless, France's financial and economic difficulties in the late 1790s resulted, partly at least, from a supply of money in circulation which was inadequate for the country's needs. The culprit was inflation, which, during the early years of the Revolution, had forced specie to emigrate or to hide, so that politicians had resorted to inflationary issues of fiat money. Under a specie standard, which prevailed again after the demise of paper money, banks were able to introduce some flexibility, by changing the money supply according to business conditions and needs; so there was, under the Directory, an interest in banks and in banking innovations. This brings us to the central theme of this chapter: the role of politics in the shaping of the French financial system. To this end we shall have to go back a few years.

During the eighteenth century – except for three short and separate episodes adding up to twenty-five years – France had no bank of issue. One major reason was the disastrous experience of John Law's Banque Royale (1716–20) and the final collapse of the *Système de Law*. Although a number of plans to establish a bank of issue – generally on the lines of the Bank of England – were drawn up during the decades which followed, none of them came to fruition before 1776. On the other hand, this does not mean that France was as backward in banking as has often been maintained. If she lacked a large public bank, she had many private bankers, even if the word is used according to the practice at the time to exclude 'financiers' who were involved in government finances. *Sensu stricto*, bankers financed private, especially international trade. Actually, the separation between the two groups was not fully watertight and became less so in the Old Regime's last years. In any case, public opinion generally amalgamated the two categories and bankers suffered from the bad name which financiers had, as blood-suckers of the people. It is generally accepted that this kind of 'banking system' was roughly adequate to the needs of the French economy: merchants did not want a circulation of banknotes, which was, in their eyes, the expedient of governments in dire financial straits; and they did not need them, as they were perfectly happy with bills of exchange, which enjoyed their confidence and of which there was an enormous and growing circulation.

Another important trait of the banking scene was that banking was an unregulated profession, outside the corporate structure of the Old Regime's society, with freedom of entry; there was thus no obligation for bankers to be catholics, and indeed many of them were protestants – in numbers disproportionate to the number of protestants among the eighteenth-century French population. More precisely, many of them belonged to Huguenot families who had emigrated – especially to Geneva – during the persecutions of protestants under Louis XIV (or earlier); a number of their descendants came back to France, especially to Paris and Lyons, during the eighteenth century, to set up as bankers. One of their reasons was that citizens of Geneva had subscribed for huge sums (especially in proportion to the city's population) to French government stocks and that agents in Paris were needed to manage their affairs. This group of protestant, Genevese and Swiss bankers was no part of the Old Regime system and therefore was not involved in its collapse – unlike the 'financiers', who were clearly linked with the monarchy and were swept along with it. They survived, to take advantage of post-revolutionary opportunities and to become the core of the *haute banque protestante* (top protestant bankers), which was a crucial component of the French nineteenth-century banking system. Obviously, the latter owed a great deal to circumstances, such as the emigration and return of Huguenots and the inflow of capital from Geneva and Switzerland to support tottering royal finances.

Protestant bankers played a leading part in the establishment in 1776 of the Caisse d'Escompte, which was the first French bank of issue – but for Law's ill-fated Banque Royale; in this respect, it is significant that the word 'bank' was carefully avoided, in order not to revive unpleasant memories. Though enjoying an official authorization from the government, it started as a purely private enterprise, organized as a limited joint-stock company; its main function was to discount bills of exchange (at a maximum annual rate of 4%); it also soon started to issue bank-notes (of large denominations), which were redeemable upon demand in coin, and it had a de facto monopoly of such issues. It was basically a bankers' bank and, unlike other early central banks, the Caisse provided assistance to bankers and not credit to the state.

However, this exception did not last, and the Caisse's independence was threatened by the increase in the government's budgetary deficit. During the War of American Independence, it did not lend to government, but it was very helpful to the latter by providing credit to the bankers who handled the distribution of new government securities. Then, in August 1783, the Caisse had to make to government a loan of 24 million livres; this caused a rush to change notes into specie, and cash payments had to be temporarily suspended. Still the bank recovered from that crisis and prospered during the next few years, while the need to redeem its notes on demand for coin prevented for a time excessive pressures from the government.

But as the financial situation worsened, ministers became more demanding. In February 1787, Calonne, the chief minister, decided that the Caisse's capital would be raised from 15 to 100 million livres (through the issue of 20,000 new shares), of which 70 million would be advanced to the Treasury (at an interest of 5%). In August 1788, his successor, Brienne, raided the Caisse's liquidities and decreed the suspension of its cash payments, thus making its notes legal tender; this decision was to be several times renewed up to December 1789, though the Caisse went on making some payments in specie. Shortly afterwards, Brienne was dismissed and replaced by Jacques Necker, himself a banker, who obtained from the Caisse a succession of advances, thanks to which government muddled through up to the meeting of the States General in May 1789 and during the months which followed (up to the creation of the *assignats*). As a result, the state's debts to the Caisse rose to 130 million by 5 May 1789 and to 166 million by 23 November 1789. The note issue also increased, of course, though up to July 1789 the cash/circulation ratio remained above its statutory level of 25%; but by 31 December 1789, note circulation had reached 129 million (against 80 in May), while cash reserves had fallen to 5 million. As E. N. White stresses, the Caisse's notes had become fiat money.

This unhappy story of the Caisse's growing subjection to government, which transformed it from a bank intended to sustain foreign trade and give cheap credit to merchants, into a virtual state bank, had some influence in the long term, as it was remembered by many people, especially some of its directors and managers who, a decade later, were to hold office in the newly founded Bank of France. Indeed, the short-lived Caisse d'Escompte was a training-ground for bank staff; it also made Parisian businessmen (its notes only circulated in the capital) familiar with banking operations and especially with bank-notes.

Still, by late 1789, it was on the verge of bankruptcy. Necker wanted to rescue it. Moreover, the Constituent Assembly had just 'nationalized' the Catholic Church's property and some means had to be found to 'mobilize' this huge capital fast enough to fill up the budget deficit. Necker was convinced that issues of inconvertible notes were necessary, but he wanted to control them and restrict their dangers. Therefore, he revived a project which had been put forward by Calonne in 1787, and he proposed to the Constituent Assembly that the Caisse d'Escompte be transformed into a 'national bank'. The latter would have a privilege (of at least ten years) to issue bank-notes, which would be inconvertible for the time being, but would be guaranteed by the government, up to a sum of 240 million; 170 million (i.e. the expected budget deficit for 1789 and 1790) would be lent to the state at 3%, and the rest would be used to discount commercial paper. Those advances would be gradually repaid from the proceeds of 'national properties'.

There was thus an opportunity to establish a large bank of issue, and some writers consider that Necker's plan might have created public credit in France, but it was not accepted by the Constituent Assembly and the opportunity was missed, for reasons which were ideological and political.

Many deputies distrusted the Caisse d'Escompte, which had been a prop of the Old Regime in its last days, and many were also suspicious of any kind of bank, which to them meant speculation. The Caisse also had a set of resolute foes (who were also Necker's enemies): the friends of Isaac Panchaud, who had inspired its foundation but had been expelled from its board in 1778. They reproached the Caisse with having become subservient to government, instead of supplying cheap credit to the economy; they included bankers, like Clavière, and at least two influential politicians who aspired to replace Necker as chief minister, Talleyrand and Mirabeau.[10] Moreover, some deputies feared that a national bank would be either too independent from the state – and thus a danger to it – or too subservient to government and then a powerful weapon in its hands. The precedent of the Bank of England was invoked both in favour of and against the project. The duke of La Rochefoucauld maintained that British trade had prospered despite the Bank and not thanks to it, that any state bank, any monopoly of issue, was harmful to business, and that the Bank of England had contributed to corrupt English politics. An extreme royalist, the baron de Batz, proclaimed: 'We have nothing to gain from making ourselves English, bankers and financiers, against nature and reason.' In his view, banks were useful only in industrial and commercial nations, and France was not one of them. Mirabeau flattered the voluntarist prejudices of his fellow-deputies by claiming that the French nation needed no 'useless intermediaries' to manage its finances; indeed, many deputies did not want public finances, which had just been freed from the yoke of private financiers, to fall now under the hold of bankers. Some even thought that the state might create money according to its needs and for the first time loud praise for paper money was heard. On the other hand, the projects for an independent central bank or for free banking had few supporters, though Du Pont de Nemours, in a very modern and radical speech, demanded the extension to banking of the principles of free enterprise and abolition of privileges. Talleyrand answered that competition between many banks would be dangerous; he condemned both a state-sponsored central bank and the issue of banknotes.

The debates were interesting but inconclusive, though mainly hostile to Necker's plan. J.-B. Le Coulteux de Canteleu, a well-known banker, summarized the majority's opinion, as spokesman for the Assembly's Finance Committee, by stating, on 17 December 1789, that one ought 'to find the nation's true resources in the nation itself . . . [and] not to make public safety solely dependent upon the stability of a Bank'. So Necker's plan was shelved and the Constituent Assembly preferred to create the *assignats*, by decrees of 19–21 December 1789, with consequences which are well known. They were issued by a special state agency, the Caisse de l'Extraordinaire, and from January 1793 directly by the Treasury, and not by a bank.

Since the seventeenth century, the incompatibility between absolutism and a national bank had often been stressed, but France, which was becoming a constitutional, limited monarchy, also refused to experiment with a central bank of issue.

The decrees which created the *assignats* also stipulated that the Caisse d'Escompte would receive 170 million livres in *assignats*, as repayment of the advances it had made to the Treasury in 1789 and of 80 million more it would advance during the first semester of 1790. The Caisse was authorized to raise its capital to 200 million, but it would remain a private establishment; its connection with government and its help to the latter would come to an end. Actually, the break was gradual, particularly because of delays in the fabrication of *assignats*, the issue of which only started on 10 August 1790. From January to August 1790, the Caisse had therefore to make renewed and large advances to government, in bank-notes, which, when intended to be sent to the provinces (where they were unknown), were stamped with the formula: 'Promise to supply *assignats*.' On 17 April 1790, the Assembly had decreed that *assignats* would be first allocated to be exchanged against the Caisse's notes (including the 'promises'), up to the state's debt towards the bank being entirely paid off; the bank-notes thus exchanged would be destroyed. The exchange actually started on 15 August 1790, when over 300 million livres in bank-notes were in circulation; it was almost over in September 1791, and alto-gether 400 million in bank-notes were exchanged for *assignats*, which is roughly the amount of the state's indebtedness to an institution, without the help of which bankruptcy – which the Constituent Assembly had solemnly renounced – could hardly have been avoided. The Assembly's members were indeed ungrateful! Still, on 8 October 1790, they author-ized the Caisse to make fresh issues of notes, but they would not be legal tender any more. These issues were much inferior to the earlier ones (the notes circulation was about 30 million in 1791), and they were made illegal by a decree of 8 November 1792 which prohibited all bearer bills or notes. The Caisse had lost its main source of profits, and eventually on 24 August 1793 it was suppressed, like all joint-stock companies, by the Convention, which the left-wing *Montagnards* dominated. This was the end of France's first bank of issue.

The problem of a national bank, which had been discussed in November–December 1789, was not to be revived for six years, but in 1790–2 there was an experience of free banking, under the pressure of circumstances, which was brief but not without consequences for the future.

An early effect of the creation of *assignats* had been a withdrawal of specie from circulation – to be hoarded or exported. The shortage of coins created serious difficulties for small, daily transactions, although to the early *assignats*, which had large denominations (200 livres and more), were gradually added much smaller ones;[11] an effort was also made to increase the minting of small coins. Nonetheless, local authorities and private entrepreneurs made many attempts to supply additional means of payment. The most significant was the establishment of *caisses patriotiques* (this was the most common name for these institutions). At first, they just exchanged *assignats* against *billets de confiance* (bills of confidence), i.e. notes of lower (and often very low) denomination than *assignats*, which were redeemable into *assignats* but never into specie. However, from mere *bureaux de change*, many of them soon became fractional reserve banks of issue. From the spring of 1791 onwards, these banks sprang up everywhere in France, even in very small towns. White (1990) has identified 1,666 patriotic banks, which were active in the summer of 1792.

It is significant that this proliferation of unregulated banks was soon brought to an end by the revolutionaries, and that all historians have considered it as a shocking case of 'monetary anarchy'; they have trusted contemporaries who accused the banks of frauds and swindles, and believed that their *billets* were counterfeited on a large scale. One had to wait for articles by White (1990; 1991) to have a radically different but convincing interpretation. White sees in the *caisses patriotiques* episode an experience of free banking which government unwittingly allowed to develop very fast, and which, though short-lived, was successful. The caisses' management was generally sound; cases of fraud and forgery were rare. The *billets de confiance* were widely accepted by the public, and their contribution to inflation was quite small, as their total value even at its peak was under one tenth of the circulation of *assignats*.

However, this free banking was disliked by many politicians, as an infringement upon the sovereignty of the state, which alone has the right to issue money. As for the *sans-culottes*, they accused the caisses of encouraging the hoarding of foodstuffs and the rise of prices. From early 1792, a campaign against the new banks developed; it was helped by the failure of one leading Parisian caisse. The Legislative Assembly and then the Convention adopted a succession of decrees which increasingly restricted the activities of the caisses (and undermined confidence in their notes).

Eventually, on 8 November 1792, any further issue of *billets* to the bearer was forbidden, and all of them had to be withdrawn from circulation by 1 January 1793. Banks of issue were thus made illegal.

Historians have generally stated that the Convention closed the caisses in order to protect the public against their malpractices. Actually, its decision must be related to changed political circumstances, to the 'first Terror', which succeeded the fall of the monarchy on 10 August 1792. There was a reaction against *laissez-faire* and a return to centralization, and it was normal that they prevailed in a field as sensitive as the currency. Moreover, the abolition of a currency – the *billets de confiance* – which was a substitute for the official currency was liable to increase the income which government obtained from seignorage and the inflation tax, which had become its major resource.

This was a minor, though fascinating, episode but it left many revolutionary politicians with a distrust of a plurality of banks of issue. This dislike had been voiced by Talleyrand in 1789, as mentioned earlier; it was to emerge again during the early days of the Bank of France. This episode also reveals that the French revolutionaries could be more imbued with the idea of a centralized and unitary state than the tenants of absolutism had been. After all, one of their favourite slogans was: '*La République une et indivisible*'; this principle also applied to banking.

During the Terror, banks and bankers were suspected of treason by the Jacobins and *sans-culottes*, especially for helping the flight of capital from France to England. A number of bankers were imprisoned, a few were executed, while others fled the country; the rest kept a low profile. After the fall of Robespierre, private banking revived and the list of Parisian bankers of 1797 was not very different from that of 1792, though a number of well-known names had disappeared. On the other hand, in 1795 the financial and monetary situation sharply deteriorated; inflation turned into hyperinflation. When the Convention separated and the new regime of the Directory was installed (2 November 1795), the circulation of *assignats* exceeded 20 billion (against 6.6 billion a year earlier), and they had fallen to 0.8% of their face value. It was under those circumstances that new projects for establishing a central or national bank emerged and were discussed at the end of 1795 and early in 1796.

It was generally agreed that drastic steps were needed to stop hyperinflation, but politicians were divided between those who wanted to get rid of the *assignat* altogether, and others who preferred to revalue it. Among the first group was the Finance Minister, Faipoult, who had recommended, in a pamphlet published before his appointment, the establishment of a central bank, independent of government; it would issue bank-notes convertible into specie, which would gradually replace the *assignats*. On 13 November 1795, Echassériaux, a member of the Legislative Council, 'the Five Hundreds', recommended encouraging 'the establishment of free banks' which 'would help government stimulate the progress of the economy', and would be, 'like in England and Holland, the source of national prosperity'. On 26 November 1795, the Five Hundreds voted a resolution which ordered that the circulation of *assignats* be raised to 30 billion and that afterwards the apparatus to print them would be destroyed (this destruction eventually took place on 19 February 1796); and, following Echassériaux's advice, they also invited the Directory to encourage proposals by banking companies (on 21 November, 'financial companies', which the Convention had banned, had been again authorized), which would be able to make advances to the Treasury; as a guarantee of their advances, they would receive certificates of mortgage (*cédules hypothécaires*) on national properties. On 3 December, André Laffon-Ladébat (who had been a director and then the liquidator of the defunct Caisse d'Escompte) announced that a bank was in the process of being founded. It would receive from government national properties worth 1,200 million livres, on the guarantee of which it would exchange *assignats* against new bank-notes and make monthly advances to the Treasury.

However, this project was rejected on 5 December by the Upper House (Conseil des Anciens); the latter included many former members of the Convention, and in their eyes there was a strong link between the Republic and the *assignats*; the former had survived thanks to the latter. To give up *assignats* was equivalent to disavowing the Republic. Moreover, the most leftist members of the Council remained, like the *Montagnards* of 1793, suspicious of banks and bankers. Other parliamentarians considered that a bank which was not yet established and the credit of which was unknown could not be of much use to the Treasury in the dramatic circumstances of hyperinflation which prevailed. They were probably right, as the magnitude of the bank's programme was disproportionate with the means which a new institution was likely to obtain at the time.

Therefore the Directory and the Councils opted for a different solution: a forced loan (which was voted 10 December 1795) for an amount of 600 million livres, *metallic* (i.e. gold) *value*, equivalent to 60 billion in *assignats* at their market price, i.e. double their circulation at that moment. Actually, government only obtained 200 million, and after long delays.

The monetary problem remained unsolved and new debates about a central bank took place in February 1796 (the month when equipment for printing *assignats* was destroyed). Many politicians were, by then, ready for a return to a metallic currency, but it was represented that the stock of specie that France had retained was much below its pre-Revolution level and would not be adequate to the country's needs, so that a bank would be necessary.

On 6 February 1796, there was a meeting of financiers and bankers, which included both survivors of the Old Regime or of the Caisse d'Escompte and newly rich profiteers of the Revolution. They drew up a plan (akin to that of Necker in 1789) for a large bank, which would be private, but chartered by the state. It would discount bills of exchange on a large scale and issue its own notes. This would be a remedy to the depreciation of *assignats* and to the scarcity of specie. The government would hand over to the bank most of the national properties; in return, it would receive each month 25 million in notes payable at sight in specie or of fixed maturity; but the circulation of those notes could never exceed the value of securities held by the bank, which could be cashed when the notes came to maturity.

On the same day, Minister Faipoult wrote to Laffon-Ladébat, who was soon to be elected as Director General of the 'National Bank of Issue' (on its board were many stars of Parisian banking). He stated that the Directory was interested in his plans and was ready to assign to the new bank national properties for 883 million (metallic value), against a monthly service of 25 million, in specie or its equivalent; he added the promise that the bank would enjoy 'the most complete independence in its operations'.

However, as had happened two months earlier, this project came up against strong opposition, in the Councils and in the press; significantly, Robert Lindet, a former member of the Committee of Public Safety during the Terror, was a leading opponent. The very word 'bank' stirred up an invincible hostility among men whom the slogans of 1793 had deeply marked. They feared that the bank, far from helping the government, would actually dominate it; its promoters were accused of having deliberately discredited the *assignats*, the Republican currency, in order to replace them with their own paper. If a new currency was necessary, it behoved the state, not private interests, to create and control it. As for the right-wing members of the Councils, they were hostile to the project because it was supported by a government they disliked.

Eventually the Legislative Councils did not reject the plan, but on 23 February 1796 they refused to approve explicitly the foundation of a bank; the Directory considered that they were hostile and the project was given up. Government was in a serious quandary, as the printing of *assignats* had come to an end, while money was badly needed for a new campaign in the spring against Austria. So they resorted to the creation of a new paper money, the *mandats territoriaux*, which would, within two months, depreciate as much as the *assignats* had within six years. On 17 July 1796, they ceased to be legal tender at their face value.

Once more, the legislature had refused to establish a national bank. Nonetheless, the idea was not dead and discussions went on. Indeed, government wanted the support of a powerful bank, the notes of which would enjoy public confidence; bankers were, of course, interested, and also merchants, who wanted better and cheaper discount facilities; and, as earlier on, the example of the Bank of England was often invoked by people who were in favour of a central bank.

In November 1796, Ramel, who had succeeded Faipoult as Finance Minister, invited the bankers and merchants of the main French cities to send delegates to Paris, in order to discuss the foundation of a bank. The delegates were favourable to a 'super-bank', more powerful than the private caisses which had been or were to be established.[12] But they wanted such a bank to be independent of government, while its notes would be guaranteed by the latter. They gave these views to Ramel, and the conference failed. Ramel tried again a year later, without greater success.

At the same time, the legislature received a number of petitions and projects about banks which would be linked to the state and receive from it part of their capital. In 1799, the Lower House set up a special committee to examine these various plans. Two reports were prepared in April and August 1799: they favoured a larger number of banks, but on condition that they would be private undertakings; their notes ought not to enjoy any official recognition, and particularly would not be acceptable for the payment of taxes. Anyhow, it was unlikely that a projected state-supported national bank would be adopted in 1799, when public finances were in a disastrous condition and when there was a revival of Jacobinism, which was hostile to banks. Nonetheless, it is significant that the idea of a powerful bank with links to the state had been discussed again during the last months of the Directory.

Moreover, some innovations in banking had been achieved during that period, despite the failure of the grand plans which have just been described. In the late 1790s, a number of people were conscious that banks of issue would be useful to make good the loss by France of part of her metallic stock. On the other hand, the resources of private bankers were certainly inferior to those which had been available before the French Revolution, so that initiatives were taken to establish 'public', i.e. joint-stock, banks, which could raise relatively large capitals, and discount bills of exchange at reasonable rates. Thanks to the decree of 21 November 1795, which had been taken in preparation for establishing a national bank, a second period of 'free banking' opened in 1796. It was different from the first (1790–2), as the new banks were far fewer in number than the pullulating *caisses patriotiques*, but of much larger size; their notes (which were of larger denomination) were exchanged upon demand into specie, and not into government-supplied fiat money.

Only three months after the 'national bank' project had failed, the Caisse de Comptes Courants (Counting House for Current Accounts; henceforth CCC) was founded, on 26 June 1796, with a capital of 5 million livres. The number of its shareholders was not large, but they included some well-known Parisian businessmen and some former directors of Caisse d'Escompte. 'This was in essence a revived Caisse d'Escompte' (White 1990). Indeed, its main function was to discount; it only accepted short-dated bills (up to ninety days), with three signatures (including one by a banker), but its rate was much lower than at private banks. Soon it started to issue bank-notes, which were convertible into specie at sight. Their circulation rose gradually to 14 million in the autumn of 1798 (while its discounts had peaked earlier at 24 million per month). The CCC survived a serious crisis and panic caused by the flight of its Director General in the autumn of 1798, and it was reasonably prosperous up to its merger with the Bank of France in February 1800.

However, many businessmen complained that the policy of the CCC was too restrictive, that it was a bankers' bank, that only an oligarchy benefited from its discounts. So a dozen merchants established in November 1797 the Caisse d'Escompte du Commerce (CEC); it was to supply credit to medium-sized firms, which would be freed from the 'tyranny' of the third signature, as bills with only two signatures would be discounted, provided that their maturity came within sixty days. Still, the new institution was also a kind of close club, as it granted credit only to its shareholders (but they were more numerous than at the CCC, rising to 253 in 1799). Its bank-note circulation reached 20 million in April 1802.

Later, in July 1799, the Banque Territoriale (Land Bank) was founded; it would lend on the security of houses and buildings, by issuing notes or accepting drafts. The idea was to mobilize real estate (many businessmen had bought 'national properties'), in order to grant credit to traders. However, this bank was not successful and went into liquidation in 1803.

These were the three main establishments which emerged in Paris, but there were some others, far less important, which also discounted and issued bank-notes, plus some which received deposits and made advances on securities but did not issue. In the provinces, a number (unknown) of small banks were founded. They were not bankers' banks and gave credit to merchants.[13] The best known is the Société Générale de Commerce, established in 1798 in Rouen, which was both a seaport and a manufacturing town. Its discounts appear to have been quite useful to local trade and industry; but they were made mainly in specie, and the value of its notes circulation was only 253,000 francs in February 1799.

Indeed, the importance of the 'public banks' which emerged under the Directory must not be overestimated. Admittedly they were 'psychologically useful' (Ramon 1929): their management was sound (but for the crisis at the CCC in 1798), so that the distrust of banks and bank-notes was reduced; they reintroduced some techniques which had disappeared since 1793, especially the use of bank-notes. But from an economic point of view, the new banks' role was modest, though not negligible. In three years, the CCC discounted on average 120 million in bills per year; the defunct Caisse d'Escompte's discounts had averaged 300 million per year and those of the Bank of France, during its first decade, were about 400 million per year. So the CCC's activity was lower than that of the two great banks which preceded and followed it, but by no means ridiculous; it helped to revive credit during a period when much instability – economic and political – endured.

Nonetheless, one can wonder why businessmen and capitalists did not take more advantage of the 'free banking' which prevailed under the Directory and of the opportunities it might have offered. One reason, mentioned above, was the uncertainty and instability that held sway under the Directory, a feeble regime which was threatened by royalists on its right and neo-Jacobins on its left, which only survived thanks to some kind of *coup d'état* every year, and which was unable to impose or to accept a general and durable peace. Such an environment certainly acted to discourage ambitious enterprises such as joint-stock banks. In 1797, an official reported that, in Paris, 'trade languishes owing to scarcity of specie and excessive rates of interest; no large undertakings, no useful speculations are started . . . Commerce can prosper only with peace; it is impatiently waiting for it' (Crouzet 1993: 510).

There was also a shortage of capital relative to the country's needs, as is revealed by extremely high rates of interest.[14] Since 1789, a lot of liquid capital had been destroyed, especially when maximum prices had been enforced and when hyperinflation had raged. Moreover, during the Directory , some capital was diverted towards dealings with government, especially towards supplying the armed forces. As war contractors were paid only after long delays and in instruments which were not easily monetized, this was tantamount to a systematic policy of short-term borrowing, and therefore to a crowding out of the private sector. Another diversion of capital was investment in real estate, in buying 'national properties'; many of them were still unsold in the late 1790s and their prices were low, so that the return on investment in land and/or buildings might be high, and less risky than in commercial, financial or industrial ventures. Lastly, banks – admittedly private ones – were already thick on the ground in Paris.

Under such circumstances, it is quite possible that moneyed men did not want to launch ambitious plans for public banks of issue without the *non obstat* from government, or rather without its support. In one of the petitions which were presented to the legislature in 1799, a group of capitalists stated that they would be able to raise a capital of 10 million, but this would not be enough for their bank to have a strong impact upon the country's prosperity.

During the revolutionary decade, the plans for establishing in France a powerful national bank, which were put forward first in late 1789 and later in late 1795–early 1796, had come to nothing, and the embryonic central bank, which the Caisse d'Escompte had been before 1789, had been destroyed. Admittedly, these plans had all been conceived as means to solve the state's acute financial problems; they had also aimed at associating the state and great private bankers, with government supplying part of the capital and receiving advances in return, though some experts, like Du Pont de Nemours in 1789 and Saint-Aubin in 1795, had argued that governments would always try to obtain loans that would cause banks to issue too many notes, so that banks ought to be completely independent of the government. This association of the state with private banks had been a major reason why the plans of 1789 and 1795–6 had been rejected by the Constituent Assembly and by the Directory's Councils, because left-wingers did not want private interests to get a hold upon the country's finances. In both cases, political circumstances of the time had also been influential: the hostility to Necker of some politico-financial clans, the ambitions of men like Mirabeau and Talleyrand, the relationship between Republic and *assignats*, the Jacobin background of many politicians under the Directory, etc. And there was also, of course, the sheer magnitude of the state's financial problems, which looked insuperable, even for a 'national bank'. On the other hand, since 1796, free banking had prevailed and France had, in 1799, a number of private banks of issue, but they existed on sufferance, as no law, no statute about banking had been adopted. The supporters of *laissez-faire*, who had been dominant during both the early and the last years of the French Revolution, had thus failed to build up the framework of a modern banking system. It was therefore upon the authoritarian regime of Bonaparte that this task devolved; it approached this task with its usual alacrity but, unsurprisingly, it gave to the institution it created its own imprint.

The establishment of a 'national bank' took place almost as soon as Bonaparte had come to power and had started to reorganize France on authoritarian lines. Actually, it was one component of this reorganization and it is thus no wonder that the new bank – the Banque de France (BKF) – was to be closely subordinated to government. However, this dependence was not imposed at once and some years elapsed before it took definite shape.

The regime which the coup of 18 brumaire (10 November 1799) established enjoyed the support of a group of bankers (it is likely that they had promised it before the coup). They included men like J.-B. Le Coulteux and J.-F. Perregaux, who had been among the promoters of the aborted projects of 1796 and 1799, and soon after the coup, they proposed the creation of a new bank to Bonaparte and to Gaudin, his Finance Minister, who welcomed the idea, as they needed the bankers' goodwill, at a time when the Treasury's coffers were as good as empty.

On 6 January 1800, Le Coulteux, Perregaux and four other bankers wrote to Gaudin that the statutes of a new bank had been settled and that they had been elected as regents. The BKF's capital would be 30 million francs, but the regents doubted that such a sum could be raised fast enough for their enterprise to succeed. So they asked that the Sinking Fund (for the National Debt, which had just been created) deposit at the BKF the 10 million in security deposits which general receivers of taxes had to pay; one half of this sum would be converted into BKF shares. In return, the BKF would pay on demand the general receivers' mandates up to 5 million, plus the sums deposited on current account by the Sinking Fund.

These propositions were accepted by two decrees of 18 January 1800; *Le Moniteur*, the government's newspaper, published an article which stressed that the new bank, unlike the Bank of England at its foundation, would not hand over to government its capital; rumours were unofficially spread that Bonaparte would subscribe thirty shares of the BKF and that his family and friends would imitate him.[15]

The first shareholders' general meeting was held on 16 February 1800. The deed of partnership was signed, the statutes approved. The capital would be 30 million francs, with 30,000 shares of 1,000 francs each. The BKF would receive deposits, make discounts, issue notes payable at sight in specie to the bearer. It would be managed by fifteen regents and supervised by three *censeurs* (auditors), whom the shareholders' general meeting would elect; each of them had to own at least thirty of BKF's shares. A 'central committee' of three regents, elected by their colleagues, would manage the BKF's affairs; its chairman would also preside over the regents' council and the shareholders' meetings.

A striking aspect is that the Bank of France started with the financial support of the government, which, behind the façade of the Sinking Fund, acquired shares for 5 million francs and deposited as much on current account. This contribution was to make up for some time most of the BKF's effective capital, as the public was slow to subscribe.[16] This was a major difference from the Bank of England, which, 106 years earlier, had raised from private subscribers its capital of £1.2 million, and then had lent it to the English government. On the other hand, the BKF requested from the start that the French government become its shareholder. But it has been mentioned earlier that a capital endowment by the state had been a constant in the various projects for a national bank which had been put forward since 1795; the difference was that, under the Directory, the endowment would have been in national properties and for a huge sum, while the Consulate granted it in cash, but for a relatively small amount.

One can thus wonder about the motives of a government as impecunious as the Consulate at its beginnings, and why it introduced into the network of public finances a new player, which, according to Michel Bruguière (1986: 147), made this network unnecessarily complex. Of course, there was an idea at large that a 'national bank' was useful, nay necessary, and a regime which wanted to make a new start had to establish one, though it could not hope for large advances from the BKF in the near future. There was a kind of gamble by Bonaparte and Gaudin, who calculated that, in the long run, a great bank would benefit both the French economy and the state's finances. There was also, as Michel Bruguière suggested (1986: 151), a recognition that government could not dispense with the collaboration of rich people, and a wish to please the business community, especially bankers.

Actually, the initiative came from the latter. They faced substantial risks when dealing in bills of exchange, because of sharp fluctuations on markets of commodities such as colonial produce.[17] They wanted a kind of mutual insurance and assistance fund, to which they would resort in times of strain. Indeed, the BKF started as a rather exclusive bankers' club, which was concerned with rediscount rather than discount. By subscribing to its shares, private bankers obtained access to rediscount facilities, with credit available in proportion to the number of shares they owned. According to Bruguière (1986: 147, 149–50), though the BKF did not get any 'exclusive privilege', it was a privilege for its promoters to get new discount facilities without having sunk much capital. They were also hoping to revive the large circulation of bills of exchange, which had prevailed before 1789 and which had contracted during the Revolution, because of lack of confidence and decline in production and trade.

The next important step in the new bank's progress was the take-over of the Caisse de Comptes Courants. Several great bankers were both directors of the CCC and promoters of the BKF; negotiations had started as early as January 1800, but they lasted some time; the CCC's representatives tried to take advantage of its anteriority and of its being a going concern, but they realized that the BKF, with its large capital, could eventually put the CCC out of business. When, thanks to Perregaux, some generous conditions were offered to CCC's shareholders, an agreement was reached on 20 February 1800, and on the same day the BKF started business, in the building where the CCC had operated.

This absorption created, through the CCC, a strong link between the defunct Caisse d'Escompte and the new BKF, and this continuity has been stressed by Alain Plessis (1985). It was obvious as far as some men were concerned: some directors and shareholders of the Caisse became regents and shareholders of the BKF, which employed in its offices many former clerks of the Caisse and of the CCC. On the other hand, during its first twenty years, the BKF was not basically different from the Caisse in the nature and volume of its operations, and Plessis considers that it was not a radical innovation, that it started where its predecessors had stopped. And the BKF resumed the punctilious care with which bills presented for discount had been examined and selected at the Caisse. However, there were also some significant differences between the two institutions. The BKF did not fix a ratio between its specie reserve and its notes circulation – as the Caisse had decided in 1784; it did not take up the constraint of a fixed discount rate of 4%, and it only discounted bills with three signatures (the Caisse had no such rule).

At its beginnings, the BKF wanted to be independent; on 17 September 1800, Perregaux, chairman of the central committee, stated: the Bank 'is free, free by its creation which was the work of individuals, independent by its statutes, freed from any conditions which a contract with government or an act of the legislature could have imposed; it exists under the protection of the country's laws and only through the collective will of its shareholders. When it deals with government, its transactions have the features which are the rule in a free country' (Crouzet 1993: 539). However, the BKF was under an obligation towards the government: Bonaparte, his family and friends had set the example in subscribing to its stock; the Sinking Fund (i.e. the state) had subscribed for 5 million francs and was depositing funds at the BKF, as did the National Lottery. Since August 1800, the BKF was entrusted with paying interest on the National Debt and pensions.

On the other hand, it did not enjoy a monopoly of notes issue. It had taken over almost at once the CCC, but Paris still had two separate issuing establishments: the Caisse d'Escompte du Commerce (CEC), which was prosperous, and the Comptoir Commercial, which had been founded in December 1800. Early in 1802, the government suggested that the CEC should unite with the BKF, but the CEC's shareholders were hostile; they were mostly merchants and had grievances against bankers; they complained that the BKF had adopted the CCC's restrictive policies; in their eyes, the BKF and the CEC had different aims and had to remain separate. However, they could not prevail against the will of Bonaparte, whose centralizing dispositions did not accept the coexistence in Paris of three banks, 'which fabricated . . . paper money'. On the other hand, he also had some grievances against the BKF, which made too easy the discounting of its shareholders' bills and which had not achieved the sharp cut in interest rates which he wanted.

Barbé-Marbois, head of the Treasury, invited the banks to consult together, but with no results. Then the position of the CEC was weakened by the flight, in December 1802, of one senior employee – with a pot of money. The BKF was confirmed in its hostility to any circulation that it would not exclusively control. Moreover, the danger of a new war with Britain was increasing and the government was conscious of the mischief which the fall of one of the three banks of issue would produce.

In January 1803, Bonaparte made up his mind that there ought to be a single bank of issue, and after complicated negotiations the decision was taken at a meeting on 16 March 1803 between the First Consul, three ministers, three members of the Conseil d'Etat,[18] plus Le Coulteux and Perregaux for the BKF.[19] But the latter did not like the degree of control and the limitation of the Bank's dividend, which were demanded by the government. This conflict became known in the business world, which worried; the funds and Bank stock fell. On 29 March, the regents wrote to Bonaparte that the bill which was contemplated did not enjoy a general consensus, as some clauses 'went against the general principles by which banks are ruled, from the point of view of the independence they must enjoy'. Bonaparte made some concessions and a law of 14 April 1803 gave to the Bank of France its charter (it had had none during its first three years).

The BKF was granted for fifteen years the monopoly to issue in Paris notes payable at sight and to the bearer. Outside Paris, no bank of issue could be established without the government's permission; its notes would not be under 250 francs[20] and would have to be printed in Paris. On the other hand, BKF's shareholders would lose their discounting privileges, so that the monopoly could be justified by the interest of the public and not of the shareholders. To finance the take-over of its two rivals, the BKF's capital would be raised to 45 million francs, through the issue of 15,000 new shares.[21] On the other hand, the yearly dividend could not exceed 6% – to prevent BKF stock from competing with government funds which bore 5% interest. The management of the BKF was, as pre-

viously, entrusted to fifteen regents, but seven of them and the three auditors would have to be elected from the shareholders who were merchants
or manufacturers, so that the interests of the 'merchant body' would be
represented; conversely, the influence within the Bank of private bankers
would be reduced.[22]

The fate of the two other banks of issue was thus settled: they would not
be allowed to make fresh issues and their outstanding notes would be
withdrawn from circulation before 23 September 1803. The conditions
of the take-over were not the same, however: the CEC was just absorbed
by the BKF, like the CCC in 1800, and most of its shareholders were
compensated by receiving BKF shares. As for the Comptoir Commercial,
it was allowed to survive as a kind of branch office of the BKF for discount
operations (but it did not issue its own notes).

The law of 14 April 1803 brought to an end the period of 'free banking'
which had opened in 1796. It also gave to the BKF its basic charter,
which, however, was only one stage in the definition of its relationship
with the state. Some tension persisted: Bonaparte continued to criticize
the BKF's discount policy; though the latter had become more flexible, he
persisted in the view that it was too restrictive and he wanted more facilities for war contractors (this would have been equivalent to indirect
advances to government). In 1805, however, he accused the BKF of
accepting too easily what were actually accommodation bills. In two
words, he thought that the BKF was too independent. The director of the
Sinking Fund, Mollien, who was hostile to the BKF, wrote to Bonaparte
in 1804 that it was 'well below the duties which the new law [of 1803]
imposes . . . instead of becoming a great public institution [it] remains the
almost exclusive preserve of a few bankers', and he proposed to have it
administered by *one* governor.

This attitude was typical of members of the Old Regime personnel who
had returned to power: these bureaucrats had accepted having to entrust
private 'entrepreneurs' with the task of creating a 'suppletory currency',
because the state had been disqualified from such a function by the *assignats* disaster; however, they wanted to supervise closely the issue of bank-
notes, to restrict their use, to ensure that they enjoyed better guarantee,
and also to neutralize the regents as privileged intermediaries.

Actually a serious crisis, which broke out in the autumn of 1805, put
the BKF into a position of weakness and gave government the opportunity to impose its *diktat*. At the roots of this crisis lay the dealings of a
consortium of large war contractors, *les négociants réunis*. Their leader
was Ouvrard, who had launched in 1804 a gigantic plan for the payment
of a 'subsidy' which Spain had promised to France, through the transfer
from America to Europe of large quantities of Spanish dollars which had

accumulated in Mexico. As war broke out between Britain and Spain in December 1804, things became more complicated, because the permission of the British government was necessary for the transport of the specie on board American ships or even British naval vessels.[23] The operation therefore ran into delays and difficulties; members of the consortium drew bills upon each other. And they succeeded in having them – and other doubtful drafts – discounted by the BKF, thanks to the complicity of Desprez, who was both one of them and a BKF regent, and to the carelessness of Barbé-Marbois, the Treasury Minister.

As a consequence, the circulation of BKF notes sharply increased, its portfolio was filled with accommodation bills, its cash reserves fell (on 22 September 1805, they were only 1,200,000 francs). A panic broke out. People who held bank-notes rushed to have them paid in specie. A rumour spread that a new paper currency would be introduced, so that the rate of exchange of the franc fell and bank-notes depreciated by 10%. However, the BKF managed to avoid a suspension of cash payments, by 'rationing' them.[24]

This crisis had come at an awkward time for Napoleon, who was then fighting the Austrian and Russian armies in central Europe. He was absolutely furious, specially with the BKF's regents, who, in his view, had betrayed their duties; and when he returned to Paris, after his triumph at the battle of Austerlitz and the victorious peace of Presbourg (Bratislava), he exacted severe punishment. Ouvrard and his associates, who had failed, were obliged to give up all their assets. Barbé-Marbois was dismissed from the Treasury department and replaced by Mollien. As for the BKF, a law of 22 April 1806 imposed a reform which was to govern it, in most matters, up to 1937. Admittedly, its privilege was lengthened to twenty-five years and its capital was to be doubled, so that it could discount on a greater scale. However, it would henceforth be directed by one governor, appointed by imperial decree; he would be helped by two sub-governors, also appointed by the emperor. Still, the governor ought to own at least a hundred BKF shares and the sub-governors fifty, so that outsiders were de facto excluded. The governor had a right of veto upon the decisions of the regents' council; the Central Committee, which hitherto had been the supreme authority, was abolished. Moreover, three of the regents would have to be general receivers (of taxes), i.e. civil servants, who would represent the government. Cretet, a *conseiller d'état*, who had been a merchant before the Revolution and a politician during the Directory, was the first governor; he had spoken against the dominance of bankers in the BKF and drawn up the law of April 1806.

This was a 'monarchical reform' (Marion 1925, IV), which was imposed without consulting the BKF's shareholders, and which put it under the close supervision of government. Moreover, a decree of 1808 was to regulate in every detail its activities. Vainly, in a pamphlet, *Sur la Banque de France*, had Du Pont de Nemours extolled free banking, and argued that granting advances to governments endangered banks and that they could only be completely free if they were wholly independent. The acquiescence in the BKF's new regime can be explained partly by the background of many large shareholders and of many regents; twenty of the thirty-eight men who were regents under Napoleon were bankers and many of them had started their careers before 1789. They were thus steeped in an Old Regime tradition of a 'special relationship' between the state on the one hand and top financiers and bankers on the other.

The narrative of the BKF's beginnings can stop here. When the law of 1806 was being prepared, Napoleon stated: 'The Bank does not solely belong to its shareholders; it also belongs to the state which granted it the privilege of creating money . . . I want the Bank to be just enough, and not too much in the hands of the government.'[25] He thus expressed his wish for a kind of balance, which, strangely enough, was to be achieved. The state enjoyed henceforth some control over the BKF's affairs, but neither Napoleon nor his successors up to 1914 misused this control. They did not make the BKF an annex to the Treasury; they did not oblige it to print money in order to satisfy the latter's needs – a policy which would have destroyed the confidence which a fiduciary currency needs and which BKF notes actually enjoyed during the nineteenth century. The BKF's independence was partial, limited, but the duty of its leaders not to grant to government financial support which could endanger the national currency was respected.

This attitude was normal for the men who led both the state and the bank during the period which followed the revolutionary typhoon; they had known the pressures by Louis XVI's ministers upon the Caisse d'Escompte, and then the irreversible tidal-wave of the *assignats*. After such experiences, they were frightened by any prospect of a new runaway inflation, with its disastrous economic consequences and its threat to the social order; they closely subordinated the notes' issues to the discount of genuine commercial paper; they opposed an excessive exploitation by the state of the BKF's credit. This compromise held good for over a century.

The Bank of France was to be one of Napoleon's lasting creations, but it bore his imprint and that of the bureaucrats who worked for him, and this was an authoritarian imprint. The BKF was part of the 'national business machine' (Bosher 1970) of the financial bureaucracy, which Napoleon built up, and which may have been the equivalent, in matters of government, of the modern industrialization that Britain pioneered. It was to make the Ministry of Finance the true master of the French state.

According to Rondo Cameron (1967: 102), the new regime, which emerged from the 18 brumaire coup, 'had a free choice of financial institutions', but made the wrong choice. Actually, taking into account the personality and background of Bonaparte and his associates, and the circumstances of the time, especially the consensus, after years of chaos, in favour of strong, centralized government and institutions, the freedom of choice was theoretical.

The *assignats* disaster left French people deeply and lastingly allergic to 'paper' – not only to fiat money but also to convertible bank-notes. Moreover, the arbitrariness, the bad faith, the sheer dishonesty which their rulers had displayed could not but strengthen the traditional distrust of Frenchmen towards *l'état de finances*, which, in the words of Bordo and White (1990), had dilapidated 'its modest reserve of credibility'; its ability to borrow was restored only slowly. In some respects, this was positive. Napoleon did not want to borrow, in order not to be dependent upon capitalists, but he could not have obtained loans even if he had wanted to. He financed his wars through increasing taxation at home,[26] war indemnities and plunder abroad. The Old Regime had been crushed under the burden of the national debt. During the inflation of the early 1790s, the load had been gradually reduced by the *assignats*' depreciation. When paper money had been demonetized, the debt ought to have been serviced in specie, but the Directory was unable to do so and, in 1797, it decided 'the bankruptcy of the two thirds', which de facto cancelled the capital of two thirds of the national debt.[27] The Napoleonic wars did not increase the debt, except for paying the heavy indemnity of 700 million francs, which was imposed upon France after the Hundred Days and Waterloo. So post-1815 France had a public debt which was much lower than Britain's, and, of course, much lower than in 1789. On the other hand, though banks and joint-stock companies had been among the victims of the 'economic terror' of 1793–4, they remained under a cloud of suspicion, as under the Old Regime.[28]

Those archaic prejudices were widespread, and not only among the common people. Guy Thuillier (1983) has pointed out how significant is the *Traité d'économie politique*, which was written in 1808–10 by the ideologue Destutt de Tracy. It expresses the almost instinctive reactions of many members of the upper class under Napoleon and the Bourbon restoration – a class which was landed, enlightened and hostile to government. Destutt had condemned the *assignats* as early as 1790 and he stigmatized them as a kind of 'universal robbery'. This unhappy experience led him into an extreme monetary realism; he rejected any notes issue by the state and even distrusted government's borrowing. Many rich and influential people had similar views, up to the 1830s and 1840s. For instance, they believed in a causal relationship between a policy of lavish money issues and easy credit on one hand, and irregularity in business cycles on the other. They also wanted to protect people with savings from risky investments.[29] According to Thuillier, one finds in those attitudes 'the roots of a kind of French economic malthusianism' (1983: 247–8), and a major factor for the slow development of the French banking system, with consequences for the economy's other sectors.

The policy followed by the Bank of France is a clear and important example. Undoubtedly, the experience of its leaders during the French Revolution led them, quite naturally, to extreme caution, to a search for security. The main aspects were the strictness of rules in the matter of dis-counts, which hindered their growth,[30] a high cash reserves/notes in circulation ratio (which was higher than at the Bank of England), and recurrent efforts to limit the number of banks of issue.[31] So Cameron considers that the BKF imposed artificial and useless restrictions upon the global volume of credit, which caused a scarcity of short-term credit for working capital (Cameron 1967: 115, 127).

On the other hand, the BKF's policy was in harmony with the French people's compulsive appetite for precious metals. During the first half of the nineteenth century, France acquired silver from America on a massive scale; in the 1840s Léon Faucher estimated that she possessed one third of all the precious metals in Europe. After the gold discoveries in California and Australia, France was to absorb 40% of the total increase in the world's stock of gold.

As, on the other hand, the growth of non-metallic money was severely compressed (at least up to 1848), the French monetary situation was characterized by an unusual predominance of specie. In 1850, 93% of all transactions in France were settled in specie, against 35% in England and only 10% in Scotland.[32]

So, in the 1830s and 1840s, France

supported the charge of a stock of sterile metals almost five times as large as that of contemporary Britain. Had France managed with the same proportion of gold and silver in its money supply as England and invested the surplus (by means of imports) in real resources yielding a return of only 5 per cent per annum, the annual addition to real income would have been of the order of 1 to 1 1/2 per cent – an increase in the annual growth rate of between 50 and 100 per cent. This is a measure of the cost to France of its financial system.[33]

For a later period, J. Foreman-Peck and R. Michie (1986, II: 403–4) have calculated that, by 1889, France's gold reserves – 3.6 times those of England – were equivalent to 11% of national income. If this ratio had been reduced to 5% – to the benefit of investment, of course – the yearly growth of national income would have been 1.5% higher.

Cameron (1967) considers that 'the restricted vision and inflexible

attitudes of the men who controlled its destinies' (the BKF) were responsible for the banking system's deficiencies and for the 'inelastic and
unnecessarily expensive stock of money' which France carried. However,
as was mentioned earlier, those attitudes were shared by a large body of
opinion, and possibly by a majority of the nation's elites. Repeatedly,
during the nineteenth century, economists stressed the political importance of France's large gold and silver stock, which was an insurance
policy against crises, both internal and international, both economic and
political. Those writers had a point: it was not useless to have large
reserves of precious metals, for a country like France, which was subject
to revolutions and, on the other hand, surrounded by hostile great powers
– Britain, Prussia, Austria. The crushing war indemnity of 5 billion gold-
francs which France had to pay after the Franco-Prussian war can be used
– with hindsight – to support this view.[34]

Another qualification is suggested by the recent book of Marc
Flandreau, who criticizes the estimates of the French metallic stock by
Cameron (1967) and Lévy-Leboyer (1976: 405–11, 416–20), and who
has built up a new series from 1840 onwards (Flandreau 1995: 126–8,
148–50, 159–60, 249, 337). He finds that *c.* 1840, France owned 2.3
billion francs of gold and silver coins, while previous estimates were
over 3 billion (and the Bank of France's reserves were only a small
share of the total). He has also calculated that the specie stock per
capita in 1844 was in France only 18% higher than in Britain (but after
1850 the gap between the two countries, in that respect, widened).
Nonetheless, he concedes that the French had a strong propensity to
retain specie; in 1848, they held about 23% of the world stock of precious metals.[35]

Altogether, it is difficult not to side with the economists who
denounced the incoherence of the massive hoarding of precious metals
and its perverse effects upon the real economy.[36] Likewise, Rondo
Cameron has rightly added the deficiencies of the banking system to the
list of factors which contributed to the 'slowness' of French industrialization and modernization during the nineteenth century.

Therefore, the shadow of the *assignats'* mega-inflation has had for a
long time afterwards a baneful influence upon the wealth and welfare of
the French people.

NOTES

1 This paper covers such a wide range of problems that it has been impossible to
  give full references.
2 The first part of this chapter is much abbreviated, but is necessary – especially
  the section on inflation – to the main content of the chapter; it also gives more
  examples of the dialectics of short and long term.

3 S. E. Harris (1930) calculated that, within six years, the *assignats* brought in the equivalent of 7 billion gold-livres, i.e. fourteen times the tax revenue of the Old Regime's last years, and the GNP for 1788.

4 Particularly, the rate of exchange of *mandats* against *assignats* was fixed at too high a level.

5 Officially, and definitively on 4 and 10 February 1797.

6 From *livre* to *franc*. However, on 15 August 1795, the Convention had defined the franc as worth 5 grams of silver, only a small fraction different from the Old Regime's *livre-tournois*.

7 At the fair of Beaucaire, where much of the output of the Languedoc woollen industry was marketed, shortage of specie was also a problem, as lack of confidence reduced sales on credit and cash payments were often demanded.

8 Only some 'public banks' (see below) discounted more cheaply: at 0.5% per month for bills at thirty days, at the Caisse de Comptes Courants, but the quantity of bills discounted at such 'low' rates was relatively small.

9 On capital, see p. 37.

10 In 1785, Mirabeau had published a venomous pamphlet, *De la Caisse d'escompte*.

11 Eventually, on 23 December 1791, the fabrication of *assignats* of 50, 25, 15 and 10 sols (1 sol = $\frac{1}{20}$ livre) was ordered; but they only came into circulation late in 1792.

12 See pp. 36–7.

13 Some issued low denomination notes, which were redeemable in copper coins.

14 See p. 25.

15 The shares were of 1,000 francs; Bonaparte's step-daughter, Hortense de Beauharnais (later Queen of Holland), took ten shares.

16 By 22 September 1800, only 1,853 shares had been acquired by private persons; subscriptions greatly increased in the spring of 1801, after peace had been restored on the Continent. By January 1802, the 30,000 shares had been subscribed; soon the Sinking Fund sold its 5,000 shares to a group of bankers.

17 For example, a crash of colonial produce in Hamburg in July 1799 had been badly felt in the French ports and in Paris.

18 An Old Regime institution, which Bonaparte had revived. One of its functions was to scrutinize projects of decrees and laws.

19 Only in Napoleonic France would a decision of this kind be taken by such a *soviet*!

20 500 francs was the minimum denomination of Bank of France notes. This deliberately excluded all but businessmen and the well-to-do from using them.

21 The subscription was slow, partly because war with Britain started again in May 1803.

22 However, the general assembly of the 200 largest shareholders was to represent all shareholders and to elect regents and *censeurs*, so that power would be concentrated in the hands of the very rich.

23 In return, the British government would receive some specie, which they badly needed.

24 On 12 February 1806 it was to lay down the rule that its metallic reserves would always be at least one third of its outstanding notes.

25 This idea was indeed expressed in the law's preamble: 'The ownership of the Bank belongs to the state and to the government as much as to its shareholders.'

26 He again set up indirect taxes, which the Constituent Assembly had abolished.

27 Earlier, in 1793, the registration and consolidation of all claims upon the state, in the *Grand livre de la dette publique*, had given an opportunity to cancel some of them. In 1801, under the Consulate, the 'bankruptcy' of 1797 was confirmed, but henceforth interest on the debt's last third was paid in specie.

28 The traditional assimilation of bankers and financiers, and the idea that most of the former were crooks persisted; they are obvious in the novels of Balzac and Stendhal. Much later, Clemenceau liked to say that bankers are always 'free on bail'.

29 This inspired the policy of the Conseil d'Etat, which had to approve the creation of joint-stock limited companies and actually did in rare cases give its authorization. (There was also the idea of reserving the financial market to the Treasury's securities.) In 1827, it rejected Jacques Laffitte's application for a large joint-stock bank which would finance industry.

30 The BKF could only discount bills bearing three signatures (for persons who had an account at the Bank, two signatures would do); the signatories had to be resident in Paris; bills' maturity was limited to ninety days. After 1817, the discount rate remained at 4%; the majority of the regents refused any kind of manipulation, which, in their view, might aggravate business cycles; the BKF's mission was to help the economy in times of stress, and not to encourage speculation by lowering its rate at other moments. As a result, the BKF had too much specie most of the time and only filled its portfolio of commercial paper in times of crisis.

31 After 1815, the BKF tried to limit the development of banks of issue which had been set up in several *départements*, and to prevent the creation of new ones. Eventually, thanks to the crisis resulting from the Revolution of 1848, it obtained the monopoly of notes issue for the whole of France.

32 Cameron 1967: 116 (table IV, 3), 117. In 1845, 82% of the French stock of money was specie; in 1870, 81%; in 1900, 44%.

33 Cameron 1967: 128. Moreover, there was a drift of savings towards government securities.

34 This war, like earlier the Revolution of 1848, had made necessary a suspension of cash payments by the BKF.

35 On the other hand, according to Flandreau, France played, thanks to her large metallic stock and to her bimetallism, a pivotal role in the system of international settlements; she acted as shock absorber during the disturbances which resulted from the enormous increase in gold production from 1849 onwards. Her metallic stock was the necessary complement of the credit edifice which Britain operated.

36 In 1838, H. d'Esterno wrote: 'The unemployment of specie is a loss as real as that caused by the unemployment of land' (p. 11).

SELECT BIBLIOGRAPHY

Aftalion, Florin 1990. *The French Revolution: An Economic Interpretation*. Paris and Cambridge.
Asselain, Jean-Charles (ed.) 1989. *Révolution de 1789, guerre et croissance économique*, special issue of *Revue Economique* 40(6).
Aubin, Christian 1991. 'Les assignats sous la Révolution française: un exemple d'hyperinflation', *Revue Economique* 42(4): 745–62.
Bergeron, Louis 1968. *Banquiers, négociants et manufacturiers parisiens du Directoire à l'Empire*. Paris.
Bigo, Robert 1927. *La Caisse d'escompte (1776–1793) et les origines de la Banque de France*. Paris.
Bordo, Michael N. and White, Eugene N. 1990. *British and French Finance during the Napoleonic Wars*, Working Paper 3157, National Bureau of Economic Research, Cambridge, Mass.
Bosher, J. F. 1970. *French Finances 1770–1795: From Business to Bureaucracy*. Cambridge.
Bruguière, Michel 1986. *Gestionnaires et profiteurs de la Révolution*. Paris.
    1992. *Pour une renaissance de l'histoire financière: XVIIIe–XXe siècles*. Paris.
Cameron, Rondo (ed.) 1967. *Banking in the Early Stages of Industrialization: A Study in Comparative History*. Oxford.
Capie, Forrest H. (ed.) 1991. *Major Inflations in History*. Aldershot.
Caron, Pierre 1909. *Tableaux de dépréciation du papier-monnaie réédités avec une introduction*. Paris.
Comité pour l'histoire économique et financière de la France 1991. *Etat, finances et économie pendant la Révolution française. Colloque tenu à Bercy les 12, 13, 14 octobre 1989 à l'occasion du Bicentenaire de la Révolution française*. Paris.
Crouzet, François 1993. *La grande inflation: la monnaie en France de Louis XVI à Napoléon*. Paris.
d'Esterno, H. 1838. *Des banques départementales en France*. Paris.
Flandreau, Marc 1995. *L'or du monde: la France et la stabilité du système monétaire international 1848–1873*. Paris.
Fohlen, Claude 1968. 'Une expérience de crédit foncier. La Banque territoriale (an VII–an XI)', in *Mélanges offerts à G. Jacquemyns*, pp. 275–85. Brussels.
Foreman-Peck, J. and Michie, R. 1986. 'The Performance of the Nineteenth Century International Gold Standard', in W. Fischer, R. M. McInnis and J. Schneider (eds.), *The Emergence of a World Economy*, 2 vols. Stuttgart.
Furet, François and Ozouf, Mona (eds.) 1988. *Dictionnaire critique de la Révolution française*. Paris.
Furet, François and Richet, Denis 1965–6. *La Révolution française* 2 vols. Paris.
Gaudin, M.-C. 1826, 1834. *Mémoires, souvenirs, opinions et écrits du Duc de Gaëte*, 3 vols. Paris.
Hampson, Norman 1988. *Prelude to Terror: The Constituent Assembly and the Failure of Consensus 1789–1791*. Oxford.
Harris, R. D. 1986. *Necker and the Revolution of 1789*. Lanham.
Harris, S. E. 1930. *The Assignats*. Cambridge, Mass.
Harsin, Paul 1933. *Crédit public et banque d'état en France, du XVIe au XVIIIe siècle*. Paris.

Jacoud, Gilles 1991. 'La monnaie fiduciaire: d'une émission libérée au privilège de la Banque de France (27 octobre 1795–14 avril 1803)', in Comité pour l'histoire économique et financière de la France, *Etudes et documents*, III, pp. 87–135. Paris.

Kindleberger, Charles P. 1984a. *A Financial History of Western Europe*. London.

1984b. 'Financial Institutions and Economic Development: A Comparison of Great Britain and France in the Eighteenth and Nineteenth Centuries', *Explorations in Economic History* 21(2): 103–24.

Lefebvre, Georges 1951. *La Révolution française*. Paris.

Léon, Pierre 1954. *La naissance de la grande industrie en Dauphiné (fin du XVIIe siècle – 1869)*, 2 vols. Paris.

Lévy-Leboyer, Maurice 1964. *Les banques européennes et l'industrialisation internationale dans la première moitié du XIXe siècle*. Paris.

1976. Three chapters in F. Braudel and E. Labrousse (eds.), *Histoire économique et sociale de la France*, III/1, pp. 347–471. Paris.

Marion, Marcel 1914–31. *Histoire financière de la France depuis 1715*, 6 vols. Paris. (Vols. II–IV deal with the Revolution.)

Mémoires de G.-J. Ouvrard sur sa vie et ses diverses opérations financières, 1826, 3 vols. Paris.

Merino, J.-P. 1989. 'L'affaire des piastres et la crise de 1805', in Comité pour l'histoire économique et financière de la France, *Etudes et documents*, I, pp. 121–6. Paris.

Meyer, Jean, Corvisier, André and Poussou, Jean-Pierre 1991. *La Révolution française*, 2 vols. Paris.

La pensée économique pendant la Révolution française 1990. Actes du Colloque international de Vizille, 6–8 septembre 1989, *Economies et Sociétés* 24 (7–10).

Plessis, Alain 1985. 'Les rapports entre l'Etat et la Banque de France jusqu'en 1914: tutelle ou indépendance?', in *Administration et contrôle de l'économie, 1800–1914*. Paris and Geneva.

Ramon, Gabriel 1929. *Histoire de la Banque de France d'après les sources originales*. Paris.

Schnerb, Robert 1984. 'La dépression économique sous le Directoire après la disparition du papier monnaie (an V–an VIII)', *Annales historiques de la Révolution française*, pp. 27–49.

Stourm, René 1885. *Les finances de l'Ancien Régime et de la Révolution*, 2 vols. Paris.

Szramkiewicz, Romuald 1974. *Les régents et censeurs de la Banque de France nommés sous le Consulat et l'Empire*. Geneva.

Thuillier, Guy 1983. *La monnaie en France au début du XIXe siècle*. Geneva and Paris.

White, Eugene N. 1990. 'Free Banking during the French Revolution', *Explorations in Economic History* 27(3): 251–76.

1991a. 'Experiments with Free Banking during the French Revolution', in F. Capie and G. E. Wood (eds.), *Unregulated Banking: Chaos or Order?*, pp. 131–57. London.

1991b. 'Measuring the French Revolution's inflation: the Tableaux de dépréciation', *Histoire et Mesure* 6(3–4): 245–74.

Woronoff, Denis 1984. *L'industrie sidérurgique en France pendant la Révolution et l'Empire*. Paris.

3 Belgian banking in the nineteenth and twentieth centuries: the Société Générale and the Générale de Banque (1822–1997)

Herman Van der Wee and Monique Van der Wee-Verbreyt

Introduction

From its founding in 1822 the Société Générale de Belgique occupied an essential place in the economy of Belgium. Its contribution to the definitive breakthrough of the Belgian Industrial Revolution – the first to be realized on the European Continent – was indeed so decisive and so comprehensive that any attempt at historical analysis of the phenomenon without integrating that contribution into the explanatory picture would distort reality. The Société Générale was from its beginning, albeit with ups and downs, a real 'mixed bank' (also called 'Universalbank'): in fact it was the first effectively working mixed bank on the Continent. On the basis of this specific structure the Société Générale was able to maintain a predominance in the country's economy throughout the whole of the nineteenth and the beginning of the twentieth century, remaining by far the most important and most powerful financial institution in Belgium. In 1934, under the pressure of the Great Depression and because of specific Belgian political circumstances, the Société Générale was forced to split into a holding company (keeping the name of Société Générale de Belgique) and a commercial bank (given a new name: the Banque de la Société Générale de Belgique, later the Générale de Banque). The holding company and the commercial bank remained – and remain up to the present day – in their respective spheres of business the two largest and most influential financial institutions of the country.

The purpose of this chapter is to present a general overview of the two institutions during the last two centuries, focusing in particular on the banking aspects of the activity of the Société Générale. As far as the period 1822–1934 is concerned, the chapter will pay special attention to the acquisition of resources by the Société Générale and to its global investment strategies. From 1934 onwards the Société Générale, having lost its functions as a commercial bank, will be studied only in its role of main shareholder of the Générale de Banque, the new commercial bank under its control. Thus an examination of the global investment policies of the

53

Société Générale from 1934 onwards will be left out: its influence upon the decisions made by the Générale de Banque, on the contrary, will still be included in the overview. But the overview as such will be very brief and will be presented as a conclusion, being beyond the scope of this chapter.

The chapter is based on research in the archives of the Société Générale and the Générale de Banque, and on the analysis of documents pertaining to William I, King of the United Kingdom of the Netherlands after the defeat of Napoleon in 1814–15 (the southern Netherlands, having been under Austrian rule in the eighteenth century, were annexed by France in 1795; they became in 1814–15 part of the United Kingdom of the Netherlands and during the revolution of 1830 proclaimed themselves an independent state under the name of Belgium).

The origins of mixed banking in Belgium, 1822–30

The new bank, created by William I of the Netherlands, was conceived in statutory terms as a type of development bank, the purpose of which was to encourage the country's trade and industry by means of its activity as a commercial and investment bank, accepting deposits, extending short-term commercial credit, issuing bank-notes, extending long-term loans to industry and even participating in industrial enterprises.

In fact, the activities of the Société Générale during the first years of its existence do not wholly correspond to this description, because William I wanted the bank to perform other functions as well, mainly functions of cashier and banker of the state, and moreover managing the public debt. These last functions would predominate in the bank's activities during the 1820s, although the activities as a private commercial and investment bank, it should be emphasized, were not negligible. To explain the contrast between the aims of the bank as specified in the statutes and the business of the bank in reality, the difficulties faced by the king in governing his country should be taken into consideration. These difficulties will be summarized briefly in what follows.

William, as a young man, had been educated in the spirit of Prussian Enlightened Despotism. Later, during the French Revolution, living in exile overseas, he had been impressed very much by the ongoing English Industrial Revolution. The combination of his education and his English experience led the king to believe that he could play a crucial role in developing his kingdom economically: his dynamic action would make it industrially the most advanced region of the Continent, the north being already advanced commercially and financially, the south having the full potential to become a modern industrial area. To realize his programme William, of course, needed extra financial means. The very traditional

Amsterdam money and capital market, however, was not interested in industrial investments in the south, the central bank of Amsterdam (the 'Nederlansche Bank') was unwilling to be flexible as far as credit to the king was concerned, and Parliament (the 'Staten-Generaal') simply refused to accept any deficit spending by the king's government, rejecting also any proposal to increase taxes in the northern provinces, taxation being already at a high level there to alleviate urban unemployment and poverty since the economic decline of the eighteenth century. Public debt being at a peak at the end of the French Revolution (double the value of GDP), Parliament's main priority was now to get rid of the debt as soon as possible, or at least to decrease it quickly. An increase, in any case, was to be avoided. The king, therefore, was looking for extra income from other sources: new fiscal income or new channels of credit to be found in the southern provinces and extra income and credit from public land in both north and south.

William's government increased taxes in the south substantially: these taxes were producing 90% of the increase in total fiscal revenue of the kingdom between 1814 and 1830. The government also transferred substantial amounts of fiscal revenue from the south to the north: between 1814 and 1830 the south generated 46% of total fiscal revenue of the central administration of the kingdom, but only 19% of total expenditure of the central administration returned to the south. Finally, William wanted to make public land more useful in solving the kingdom's financial difficulties. Public land was abundant, particularly in the south, but it did not contribute much to the improvement of the health of the public finances, although in principle land could make such a contribution. Land, for example, could be used as a mortgage for obtaining long-term loans; it could be made more productive by privatizing its exploitation; it could even be helpful in liquidating public debt by selling off land in redemption of bonds and annuities. Early in 1822 William proposed therefore to create a public bank in Brussels, which would manage all public property of the kingdom. The new bank would use income from public property to finance the service and eventually the redemption of the public debt. It would also be allowed eventually to sell parts of the land in view of the redemption of the debt. Parliament, however, refused to vote in favour of the government's proposal, fearing that the king would take advantage of the new institution to engage in large borrowing, based on mortgaging public land.

The king, after the negative vote of the Parliament, changed his tactics. He took up a recent request of a group of private bankers in Brussels to be allowed to create a private commercial bank with a statute of a joint-stock company and integrated the idea into his own original proposal. The new bank which he intended to create would be a private institution and for that reason did not need parliamentary approval, only the approval of the government, i.e. an approval by royal decree. It would have a capital of 50 million guilders (some 106 million francs). Forty percent of the capital, representing 20 million guilders, would consist of the contribution by the king of personal crown land, i.e. some farmland and tithes in the northern part of the kingdom, mostly forests and woods in the southern part of the kingdom. From the revenue from these lands, the new bank should pay to the king an annual sum of 500,000 guilders. From 1824 onwards, additionally, the bank should pay a sum of 50,000 guilders to the 'Amortisatie-syndicaat', a new public institution to be created especially to redeem the public debt with the help of sales of public land and of revenue from public land and from crown land, donated to the new bank. This sum of 50,000 guilders should be increased annually by 50,000 guilders until a ceiling of 500,000 guilders was reached in 1835. It was clear that by privatizing the exploitation of his crown land, the king expected a considerable increase in its return.

The remaining 60% of the capital, representing 30 million guilders, would consist of 60,000 nominal shares of 500 guilders each. The issue of the shares, however, was a great failure, even after the king had personally guaranteed a minimum annual dividend payment of 5%. Only 5,426.5 shares were subscribed by the public, the king himself subscribing 25,800 shares. Moreover, most of the subscriptions were paid up with public securities. Nevertheless, the bank, having more than half of its share capital subscribed, was founded in December 1822 as a private commercial bank, with a statute of a joint-stock company, its headquarters being located in Brussels. The main objective of the bank was to develop trade and industry in the kingdom by extending commercial short-term credit to the private sector, by issuing convertible money, *inter alia* for that purpose, by extending long-term loans to the private sector and by participating in industrial enterprises. Notwithstanding the private character of the bank's charter the governor had to be appointed by the king, the appointment implying a political decision. No wonder therefore that Minister of State Ocker Repelaer van Driel, a Dutch nobleman and close collaborator of the king, was to become the first governor.

The government, moreover, would confer some public functions upon the new institution. In 1823 the Société Générale was made the official cashier of the kingdom and with a view to organizing this function efficiently the bank created sixty-three branch offices throughout the kingdom. The Société Générale, its subscriptions having been paid up with public securities mainly, lacked liquid funds. The bank felt obliged, therefore, to devote itself in the first place to the exploitation of the land it had received from the king, to its role of state cashier, to selling the state securities it had received in paying up the share capital, and to the placement of new public loans. As a matter of fact, the Société Générale was in the first place a financial instrument in the hands of William I, managing the public debt and helping him in finding new resources and in particular new credit facilities to alleviate the pressure of servicing the debt and the pressure of the government's growing budget deficit.

But soon the Société Générale was also prompted to provide other help to the government. Within the framework of the king's 'enlightened' policy of economic progress, grand projects were periodically launched, aimed at improving the infrastructure. The bank was asked to provide financial support for these projects, *inter alia* some of the financial means for digging the Pommeroeul–Antoing canal (1823–6), aimed at creating a direct waterway link between the coal basin of the Borinage (in the Mons region) and the whole of Flanders/northern France, including the metropolitan area of Paris. The Société Générale also provided financial support for facilitating exports. For example, the 'Nederlandsche Handel-maatschappij', created by William I in 1824 to organize the kingdom's external trade – in particular the exports of cottons produced by the Flemish mechanized industry to the Dutch colonies in Asia – each year received substantial advances from the bank against the security of merchandise, shares or government bonds. Finally, under heavy royal pressure, the Société Générale also granted long-term credits to modern industry, for example in 1829 a long-term loan to John Cockerill, the industrialist from Liège, who in the same year brought his first blast furnace into service (see Figure 3.2).

From its foundation the Société Générale, as was mentioned earlier, was also active as a commercial bank, providing short-term credit to the private trade and modern industry sectors and using for that purpose its own bank-notes as well as liquid assets derived from its function as a state cashier. The king encouraged the bank to extend this activity, in particular through multiplying the discounting of bills of exchange and the issuing of bank-notes for that purpose. The managers of the Société Générale did not react very enthusiastically, because the extension included discounting bills of exchange from all over the country, which would enhance the risks. In the end the Société Générale had to give in to the king, creating an independent branch office at Antwerp under the name of Banque d'Anvers which controlled its own discount-house ('comptoir'), and setting up, with the help of local businessmen of good reputation, several discount-houses at the main office in Brussels and at the dependent branch offices in Mons, Tournai, Liège, Ghent and Verviers.

The new network of local discount-houses proved to be very efficient. The discounting activity of the Société Générale was to expand quickly from 1825 onwards. As a matter of fact, discounting paradoxically formed a solid basis for achieving greater independence *vis-à-vis* the king and the impact of public finances. In the beginning most of the bills discounted originated from the Brussels discount-house, but soon the share of the other discount-houses would increase remarkably. In 1829 the share of the houses outside Brussels had risen to 74% of the total amount of discounted bills (the large Antwerp discounting activity once again not included). The share of the discount-house of Mons was 50% of that total. Thus a fundamental shift was already taking place in the commercial investment policy of the Société Générale during the period of the United Kingdom of the Netherlands: a shift away from royal tutelage and away from the links with public finances, and a rapidly increasing interest in supporting the expansion of the modern industrial sectors (coal mining and heavy metal industry) in the Borinage (Mons) and in the region of Charleroi, both in the western province of Hainault at the border with France.

The completion of the Pommeroeul–Antoing canal was responsible for the sudden upsurge of exports of coal and cast iron by waterway to Flanders and France. The merchants paid the colliery owners and the metallurgists by means of bills of exchange that were presented regularly for discounting at the local private bankers in Mons, who in their turn presented them for rediscounting at the local discount-house of the Société Générale in Mons. The colliery owners and metallurgists themselves, in order to finance some of their long-term investments, were also drawing bills on their local bankers, who once again presented them for rediscounting at the Société Générale: a dangerous situation if a crisis should occur.

The Belgian revolution and the definitive breakthrough of the Société Générale's mixed banking activities, 1830–50

The Belgian revolution in 1830 disturbed the economy of the southern provinces seriously and had a deleterious eVect on the coal and metal industries in the region of Mons and Charleroi and on their export trade to France. The Société Générale was giving support to the local bankers, who had been the major promoters of industrial activity in the region but who were now experiencing great diYculties in maintaining a healthy liquidity position. In the process of repaying their debts, the local bankers transferred to the Société Générale shares in industrial Wrms of the region and some participations in canal and other companies which they had had in their portfolio for some time or which they themselves had received recently in repayment of debts. Chance thus played an incontestable part in the abrupt reorientation of the investment policy of the Société Générale, though a much more determining factor was to be the conscious attempt on the part of its management, at the start of Belgium's independence in 1830, to initiate a new, original and autonomous investment strategy, based on a profound belief in the modern industrial future of the Mons and Charleroi region.

The Belgian revolution was more than a period of economic crisis, difficult to overcome even for as large a bank as the Société Générale. It was also a period of political crisis, particularly critical for the Société Générale, which was accused of being a bank of William I, the great enemy of the new regime. Fortunately, the Société Générale received financial support from the Rothschilds of Paris. The revolutionaries, for their part, were in urgent need of money to finance their revolt and the creation of an independent state, and therefore were eager to receive help from the Société Générale, the only big financial institution in the south. The appointment by the revolutionaries of a new governor of the bank, Ferdinand Meeûs, a strong, independent personality and politically acceptable to the leaders of the new regime, was a second factor in placating the Belgicist critics against the 'Orangist' (i.e. considered as a pro-William) institution.

Meeûs was an excellent banker. He realized immediately that the Société Générale's traditional investment policy and the main banking activities had to be changed drastically, investment in Dutch public debt and placement of Dutch state bonds and annuities among the public in the north and in the south being now entirely out of the question. What were the alternative profitable investment opportunities for the bank? A policy of organizing, in collaboration with the Rothschilds of Paris, the issuing of Belgian state loans would be an obvious choice. Meeûs would indeed become very active in the field, but he realized that as long as there was no peace between Belgium and Holland (the treaty would be first signed in 1839, King William I not being willing to recognize Belgian independence before that year), the Belgian government would not inspire much confidence and therefore would not be able to borrow on a large scale, in any case not sufficiently to satisfy the expansionary ambitions of governor Meeûs.

More promising to Meeûs was the interest in 1830 of Belgian business and of Belgian municipalities in building an 'Iron Rhine' between Germany and Antwerp, which would not cross Dutch territory and would be able to attract a large part of German transit-trade. The government in 1832 integrated the idea into a more global scheme of providing the whole country with a full network of public railways. The Belgian Parliament discussed the proposal in depth, all members agreeing with the idea of building a network of railways, but disagreeing bitterly on how to organize the realization of the idea. Many members supported the government's proposal to build a system of public railways, but many other members wanted a system of private railway companies, receiving concessions from the state. Meeûs, himself a Member of Parliament, was of course advocating a private system, which would open an entirely new perspective for investment by the Société Générale. He was already in touch with the Rothschilds and other bankers with a view to organizing bankers' syndicates for the construction of railways which would make French and German transit-trade via Belgium especially attractive.

Meeûs was disappointed by the decision of the Belgian Parliament in early 1834 that the government itself should create the basic network of public railways, leaving the construction of the secondary lines to private initiatives after the completion of the public system. But Meeûs, though disappointed, did not withdraw from the scene. He understood immediately the long-term implications of the construction of railways in Belgium, even if it was realized in a first stage by the government itself. Railways would be large consumers of coal, iron and machinery. Because the principal objective was to attract the transit-trade of France and Germany, the construction of the Belgian railways would imply also the construction of railways in the two neighbouring countries and the construction of links between the different national systems: the Belgian coal and metal industries, being at that moment technically and technologically much ahead of their French and German counterparts, would greatly benefit from these fundamental structural changes in overland transport. Meeûs therefore reorientated the investment strategy of the Société Générale resolutely in the direction of the sectors of coal mining, of heavy industry, of engineering and of the transport sector. This shift was made easy by the circumstances of crisis in 1830, the Société Générale having already acquired at that moment some participation in the sectors of heavy industry and of transport, as mentioned above.

How did governor Meeûs organize *in concreto* his new investment strategy? In fact, he did it in a very innovative way. Meeûs realized that the demand for coal, iron, and steam engines would increase so dramatically that only a large-scale industrialization policy would be able to satisfy that demand. Such a dramatic increase in scale could be achieved only by a significant increase of capital input and by a modernization of industrial management. In Meeûs' view the traditional small-size family firms of the Hainault region were structurally not fitted for this fundamental change. Meeûs therefore started to advocate the transformation of the family firms into joint-stock companies. The Société Générale in his view was best suited to help with this transformation: it could offer its juridical know-how, it could also offer financial help by participating in the capital of the firms, and it could attract external capital by organizing the issue of new shares on the capital market of Brussels and Antwerp. Finally, the transformation of the family firms into joint-stock companies, with a controlling participation of the Société Générale, would allow the latter to modernize management and to adapt it to the increase in scale of production and to the mechanization of that production.

The Société Générale was very successful in its new investment strategy. Between 1832 and 1839 the bank acquired many controlling participations in coal mining and in the sector of metallurgy in the region of Charleroi and Mons in the province of Hainault, and also in the region of Liège. The bank, furthermore, acquired participations in companies engaged in river, canal and maritime transport, in French railway companies, in companies for the construction of steam engines, in companies of the glass and crystal sector and of the flax spinning and linen weaving sector, in sugar refining and in real estate companies. The success of the new investment strategy of the Société Générale is illustrated by the evolution of its industrial portfolio: it rose from 3.8 million francs in 1835 to 38.7 million in 1840 and to 54.8 million in 1850 (see also Figure 3.1).

In 1835 the Société Générale introduced an even more sophisticated form of industrial banking by founding three subsidiary companies whose specific task it was to look after industrial investment. In addition to the management of the parent company's participations in industry and transport, the subsidiary companies were entrusted with the creation and management of their own industrial portfolios. Moreover, they had to stimulate, coordinate and control the modernization of all the patronized companies and reduce their number. In this way the management of their portfolios contributed to the development of more centralized company techniques (horizontal and vertical integration). Above all, the subsidiary companies were already holdings *avant la lettre*, also taking capital from outside the parent company.

The Société Générale was not the only bank to develop at that moment as a mixed bank. The Belgian liberals, who had organized the Belgian revolution, remained distrustful of the Société Générale, suspecting that its sympathy still lay with the Dutch House of Orange. For that reason they founded the Banque de Belgique in 1835, aiming at an imitation of the successful investment policy of the Société Générale. In tandem the Société Générale and the Banque de Belgique indeed formed a dynamic financial power and a motive force of Belgian and European industrial development. The total amount of capital invested in the 150 newly created joint-stock companies in Belgium between 1833 and 1838 reached about 288.5 million francs, of which the Société Générale

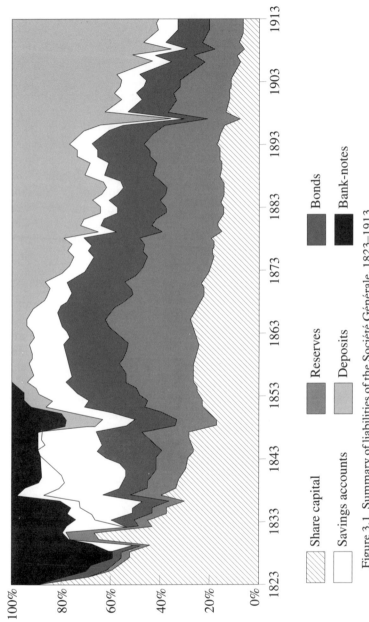

Share capital

Savings accounts

Reserves

Deposits

Bonds

Bank-notes

Figure 3.1 Summary of liabilities of the Société Générale, 1823–1913

accounted for 102 million, or 35%, and the Banque de Belgique 54 million, or 18%. The banks' industrial participation went along two lines: directly by taking up shares and indirectly by granting long-term loans. Moreover, the banks were granting short-term commercial credit to the companies they controlled, by means of discounting bills of exchange and allowing overdrafts in current account.

One can wonder why the system of mixed banking was so successful in the early stages of Belgian industrialization. We are inclined to follow the Gerschenkron hypothesis, suggesting that the link of the mixed banks with the heavy industries fuelled the Belgian industrialization process. The need for long-term fixed capital being quite high in the sectors of heavy industry and the Belgian financial sector being still very primitive at that moment, the mixed banks could supply the necessary capital where self-finance could not suffice. It is indeed significant that the Société Générale and the Banque de Belgique concentrated their investment in particular on the expanding coal and metal industries of Wallonia. The increasing collaboration between the Walloon heavy industries and the Brussels system of industrial banking, even the osmosis of both interests, or still better the absorption of the interests of industry by the banks – the so-called 'Bruxellisation de la Wallonie' – meant an organizational progress, that in setting the pace for growth became the real core of the Belgian industrialization pattern. The organizational progress was especially important when it came to making decisions on long-term investments. Owing to the system of mixed banking, the decision-making process was transferred from a decentralized, segmented market to a strong centre of power, creating a sort of mini-capital market, which clearly had better information and better instruments of coordination and control at its disposal.

How was the Société Générale able to increase its resources for bringing to a good end the reorientation of its investment policy? The bank was given, in 1836, the authorization of offering for sale the 28,773.5 shares that had not been subscribed in 1822. The subscription was successful but in the end it did not increase the bank's liquid assets, as the bank had to buy back at a high price the shares still in the hands of William I and his heirs after the signing of the peace treaty in 1839. It decided to keep these shares in portfolio in order not to depress further the value of the shares at the Exchange.

It was principally the realization of the crown lands during the early 1830s that gave the Société Générale the necessary additional funds to carry out its new investment policy. Being afraid that the liberal Belgicists in the government would decide to confiscate the crown lands, because they were considered as having some connotation with William I, now the

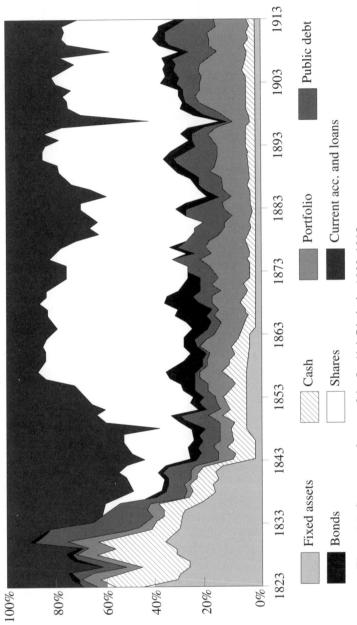

Figure 3.2 Summary of assets of the Société Générale, 1823–1913

Fixed assets   Cash   Portfolio   Public debt

Bonds   Shares   Current acc. and loans

main enemy of the country, Meeûs and his board of directors wanted to get rid of that asset as soon as possible. From 1831 onwards a substantial portion of the crown lands was sold off. The sale resulted in a gross profit of 60 million francs. Equally crucial, but much less stable in character, was the role played by the Caisse d'Epargne, the saving fund of the Société Générale which was set up officially in 1832 after the bank had taken over several municipal saving banks in distress during the revolution period. The Caisse d'Epargne became a great success. Saving deposits increased rapidly from 0.88 million francs in December 1832 to nearly 61 million in 1842. The management attempted to persuade savers to subscribe to longer-term bonds, but the attempt failed to a large extent.

The issuing of bank-notes was a third source of means for financing investment by the bank. But the government, by imposing a strict maximum upon the amount of bank-notes to be issued, excluded any spectacular expansion of short-term credit activities by the bank through discounting. As bank deposits and current account transactions were not yet very developed in Belgium, the government measures, limiting the issuing of convertible paper money, were therefore also a causal factor in the decision of the Société Générale to focus in the first place on investment banking by taking participations in modern industrial enterprises and by extending long-term loans, mainly to the patronized enterprises.

Notwithstanding the success of the Société Générale as a mixed bank, the formula as it evolved was not without danger. Because of the long-term immobilization of a large part of their assets the Société Générale worked with low liquidity ratios (see Figure 3.2). Such ratios increasingly threatened the smooth functioning of deposit and, especially, of saving and issue banking. Indeed, the low liquidity ratio caused acute problems when the bank faced sudden panic withdrawals. The financial crisis of 1838–9 already underscored the shortcomings of the system. The Société Générale resisted that crisis better than the Banque de Belgique, because it was able to sell its French assets on the French capital market. But in 1848 international events and a panic withdrawal in Belgium itself badly affected the Société Générale too.

The crisis of 1848 and its consequences for the Société Générale, 1848–1934

During the crisis of 1848 the formula of mixed banking was questioned for the two main financial institutions of the country, i.e. the Société Générale and the Banque de Belgique. Walthère Frère-Orban, the leader of the liberal party who would dominate political life in Belgium for the next thirty years, was convinced that no mixed bank would ever be able to combine the functions of bank of issue, deposit bank and industrial bank in a satisfactory way, the constraints of liquidity in deposit and issue banking being fundamentally irreconcilable with the long-term requirement of investment and industrial banking. Frère-Orban accused the Société Générale of having invested all the deposits of its saving division into participations in industry and in loans to its patronized companies, the latter, because of the crisis, being all frozen. He also accused the Société Générale of not having expanded its discounting and issuing activity, which would have put short-term credit at the disposal of the economy as a whole and would have served the common good. The Société Générale, he said, had concentrated instead all its credit facilities, short-term as well as long-term, on helping its own patronized companies.

The Belgian liberal party, and its leader Frère-Orban in particular, had well-defined ideas of how the government should run a modern state. The liberals were very distrustful of the big mixed banks, which under the cover of the free market economy would monopolize financial power and by doing so would become a state within the state. The liberals, of course, advocated the idea of a free market economy, but wanted it to operate within the framework of a fragmented industrial and financial structure, which would guarantee the full impact of free competition. The liberals also championed a second principle: the government had to intervene directly and actively in organizing economic life, not only when the working of the free market economy was falling short of pursuing the common good, but also whenever the common good was at stake, even if the private sector was taking good care of it.

The liberals, being in power since 1848, would turn their principles into practice. When the Société Générale and the Banque de Belgique got into trouble during the financial crisis of that year, Frère-Orban was prepared to help on condition that both institutions accepted a fundamental restructuring of the Belgian banking system, the state being given a large and active role in the new system. Frère-Orban, moreover, wanted to get rid of the formula of the mixed bank and wanted to introduce the Anglo-Saxon formula of a more specialized banking system. A specific public institution should be given the monopoly of issuing bank-notes in view of extending short-term commercial credit by discounting bills of exchange of good quality. A specific public institution should be created to organize the short- and long-term borrowing by municipalities, provinces and other local administrations. A specific public institution should be created for receiving the savings of the great masses, to manage these savings properly and turn them into optimal pension schemes.

Frère-Orban was able to realize most of his ideas. The three institutions mentioned above were founded between 1850 and 1865 and were all three very successful. What happened meanwhile to the mixed banks? Frère-Orban wanted them to become pure investment banks (*banques d'affaires*). Indeed, when founding the National Bank of Belgium in 1850 he withdrew the right of issue from the mixed banks and forced the Société Générale to transfer to the National Bank all its local branches and discount-houses. With the founding of the public saving and pension bank the Société Générale would also lose most of its previous function of a saving bank. Of course, the Société Générale could still receive deposits, but in fact these deposits and the current account activities connected with them had to relate mainly to short-term transactions with the patronized industrial companies and with the bankers' correspondents from foreign countries. Short-term credit activities, by means of discounting and issuing bank-notes in general, were now to be dominated entirely by the central bank.

As a result of the restructuring of the financial system in Belgium the Société Générale between 1850 and 1870 withdrew heavily into investment banking, concentrating increasingly on acquiring participations in Belgian heavy industry and related sectors (see Figure 3.2). Within these limits, however, the bank again became very successful. It now took few risks in its long-term investments. An extensive investigation always determined the credibility and profitability of the companies that were the objects of its participation policies. It also always kept an eye on its own financial structure: discounting was maintained within the group; if liquidity problems in the field of the Société Générale's deposit banking division eventually arose, they could be solved by appealing to the central bank of issue through the technique of rediscounting.

The Société Générale maintained its former investment strategy and even accentuated it still more in the direction of coal mining, heavy industry and railways. The involvement in railway promotion is especially striking. Within one decade, from 1850 to 1860, the share of participation in railway companies in the total portfolio rose from 4.2 to 25.9%. At least three reasons may explain that special interest. First, the need for fixed capital was very high in railways and the return very slow, one reason why entrepreneurs turned to credit institutions such as the Société Générale when they decided to create railway companies. Second, since railway construction induced an enormous demand for the products of the patronized iron companies and linked with them for products of the patronized coalmines, the interest of the Société Générale in the modern transport sector is obvious. Third, in 1865 the Société Générale created a subsidiary company, the Société Belge des Chemins de Fer, that concentrated exclusively on creating companies for the construction and exploitation of railways. The Société Générale and its subsidiary not only participated directly in new railway companies but also often acted as issuers of shares and bonds to the Belgian public. The proceeds of the issues were then used to pay the Belgian patronized companies, supplying the rails, the rolling stock and any other equipment connected with railway transport. As soon as the construction of the railway was finished – that is as soon as the demand for Belgian materials ceased – the Société Générale or its subsidiary often started to sell their own shares on the Exchange.

The Société Générale was also the first Belgian investment bank to extend its international activities in a systematic way. The national railway market being quickly saturated, the Société Générale had to widen the geographical range of its investment policy to guarantee sufficient outlets for the patronized firms. The Société Générale participated directly in the creation of new foreign companies, but more often it acted via its subsidiary, the Société Belge des Chemins de Fer, which obtained between 1877 and 1883 many concessions for the construction of railways in France, Germany, Austria, Italy, Spain, the Netherlands, Russia, China, and Central and South America. The construction and exploitation of these lines were entrusted to branch and filial companies of the Société Belge, in which the latter kept a major share. The Société Belge developed therefore into one of the first specialized holding companies, in the modern sense of the word.

The international railway market in turn becoming saturated, the Société Générale gradually broadened its investment strategy to new sectors, *inter alia* the real estate sector and the gas sector in Belgium, later also the electricity and tramway sector in Belgium and still more in other European countries and in many countries overseas, in particular when electrification became an integral part of the urban transport system. At the end of the century the Société Générale started also to integrate mining and heavy industry into its international investment strategy. In earlier decades such investment had already taken place in nearby Luxembourg and French Lorraine, but from 1896 onwards Russia became the country *par excellence* for investment in mining and heavy industry. The Société Métallurgique Russo-Belge, a subsidiary of the Société Générale, was the organizing medium. Finally, from 1906 the Société Générale started to invest heavily in the Belgian Congo: investments in copper, cobalt, gold, diamond and later uranium mining, in transport, in agriculture and so on. In the interwar period the colonial participations would become predominant in the portfolio, an important factor of increasing sclerosis of its composition and the main reason for the decline of the holding company after World War II.

The Société Générale, as a matter of fact, had never been happy with the idea of Frère-Orban that it should limit its activities to those of a *banque d'affaires*. From the beginning of the restructuring of the Belgian banking system, the Société Générale had been looking for a way out of this, in its view, too narrow straitjacket. In the late 1860s and early 1870s a way out was found effectively in imitation of what was going on in England. Deposit banking for the general public, using current accounts and cheques, was becoming very successful indeed in England, as well as the system of provincial joint-stock banks. The Société Générale decided to integrate both systems in its own banking practice. In 1866 the formula of interest-bearing current accounts for the general public was introduced. From 1870 onwards a network of patronized but autonomous provincial joint-stock banks was created in collaboration with local bankers, in order to attract deposits from the general public and to promote medium- and small-sized enterprises in and outside the main industrial areas. The idea proved to be very successful. In 1900 the Société Générale already patronized twelve regional joint-stock banks. In 1913 the number had risen to eighteen, which together controlled a network of sixty-one branches throughout Belgium. From the 1890s the Société Générale focused its efforts also on creating outside Belgium a powerful international financial network under its control. Participations were taken in banks active in France, South America, Russia and China. The real start, however, is usually attributed to 1902, when the Banque Sino-Belge was created under the full control of the Société Générale. In 1913 this bank was transformed into the Banque Belge pour l'Etranger, a bank with a much broader outlook.

The combined strategy of expanding the Société Générale's control over international and domestic banking resulted in an impressive increase in the share of financial participations in its total portfolio: it rose from 16.4% in 1880 to 39.7% in 1913 (see Figure 3.3). The increase also reflects a structural renewal of the banking activities of the Société Générale since the beginning of the 1850s. The Société Générale had taken its revenge *vis-à-vis* Frère-Orban's policy. It had again become a mixed bank in the fullest sense of the word, albeit via the intermediate route of introduction of its deposit banking to the general public and via the expansion of its provincial and foreign patronized banks, which also introduced deposit banking for the general public on a large scale. A powerful factor in the expansion of deposit banking for the general public was the remarkable growth of intangible wealth during that period and the simultaneous spectacular expansion of the trade in industrial shares and bonds and in government securities. The Société Générale offered a service of managing personal fortunes, which expanded quickly. All these

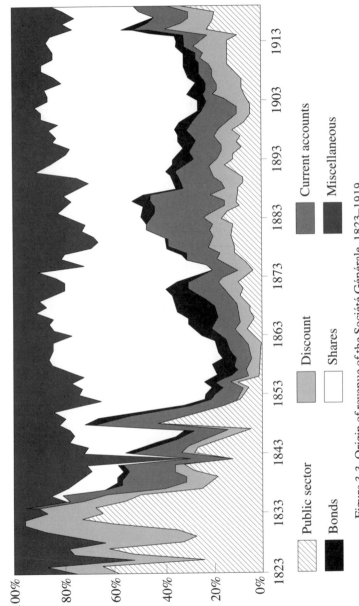

Figure 3.3 Origin of revenue of the Société Générale, 1823–1919

Public sector

Bonds

Discount

Shares

Current accounts

Miscellaneous

customers opened personal current accounts, which stimulated transfer payments via these accounts.

The network of provincial and foreign banks also stimulated discount banking within the group. Firms would present bills of exchange to their banks, being now patronized companies of the Société Générale. The latter would present these bills eventually for rediscounting to the Société Générale, which if needed could always present them for rediscounting to the National Bank of Belgium. Thus personal and commercial short-term credit and payment by transfer from one account to another were gradually gaining in importance and, on the eve of the First World War, they were already overshadowing the commercial activity of the National Bank and even its function of creating means of payment. Private bank money became gradually more important in aggregate than the bank-notes of the National Bank.

The revival of the mixed bank activity of the Société Générale gave it again such power over the Belgian economy that it took advantage of it to subdue the National Bank in the 1920s to the interests of the private banking system. With the reform of 1926 the management by the Board of Directors of the National Bank was to be controlled entirely by a Council of Regents, all members of the private banking sector and domi-nated by the Société Générale. This control, however, would not last; the Great Depression would once again change the situation.

A last but important remark: the structure of the Société Générale with its group of patronized industrial companies and its other group of patronized banks was, in its initial stage, a factor of great organizational progress, in the Chandlerian sense of the word, creating a subtle but very efficient balance between a centralized control, as far as the making of strategical decisions was concerned, and an autonomous management for the daily operations.

Conclusion: the end of mixed banking in Belgium

The Great Depression of the 1930s weakened the Société Générale and the other private mixed banks so much that they were all in urgent need of financial support by the government. However, since the end of the First World War socialists and Christian democrats had gained much political influence. Being now important partners in the government coalitions, they imposed their views and conditions upon political decision-making. In 1934, by government decree, the mixed banks had to be split into pure holding companies and commercial banks, the latter having to limit their activities exclusively to short-term commercial banking operations. The Société Générale de Belgique became a holding company and its previous commercial banking division was transferred to a new company, the

Banque de la Société Générale de Belgique, later to be called the Générale de Banque, and to be referred to here as the Banque. The holding company, however, remained the main shareholder of the commercial bank.

In 1935 the government issued a decree putting the commercial banks under the strict control of a new public institution, the Banking Commission, with the aim of safeguarding the interests of savers and the public interest in general. After the Second World War the control was tightened not only by imposing liquidity and minimum capital requirements upon the commercial banks, but by introducing in addition an investment ratio: the large banks, in particular the Banque, had to invest a minimum 65% of its deposits into short-term government paper. This ratio was to help the government in financing its social security and welfare policy after the war. But as the financial needs of private business grew quickly in parallel with reconstruction and postwar economic growth, the government policy of imposing a strict investment ratio on the commercial banks in favour of the state had to be abandoned gradually. Nevertheless banking would never become the same again as it had been before the First World War. A new era of banking came into being, the banking sector being integrated into the creation and further development of the modern mixed economy in Belgium.

SOURCES

The main sources for this article are unpublished documents in the archives of the Société Générale de Belgique, the Générale de Banque, and the National Bank of Belgium (a section of the documents concerning the early history of the Société Générale has been transferred to the General Archives of the Kingdom). Some papers of governors, preserved in private archives, were also studied, as were the reports, published yearly by the three institutions mentioned above.

The study presented here refers to research the authors undertook for a book on the history of the Société Générale and the Générale de Banque (1997). For more detailed information on sources and literature used during the research we refer the reader to that book. For more information on the graphs we refer to a similar but more extended study on the same subject, written by several Belgian historians under the editorship of Herman Van der Wee (1997).

BIBLIOGRAPHY

Baudhuin, F. 1944. *Histoire économique de la Belgique (1914–1939)*, 2 vols. Brussels.

Cameron, R. 1971. *La France et le développement économique de l'Europe, 1800–1914*. Paris.

Cameron, R. (ed.) 1967. *Banking in the Early Stages of Industrialization*. Oxford.

Cameron, R. and Bovikyn, V. (eds.) 1991. *International Banking, 1870–1914*. Oxford.

Le centenaire de la Société Générale de Belgique, 1822–1922, 1922. Brussels.

Chandler, A. D., Jr, 1962. *Strategy and Structure: Chapters in the History of the Industrial Enterprise*. Cambridge, Mass.

1990. *Scale and Scope: The Dynamics of Industrial Capitalism*. Cambridge, Mass.

Chlepner, B. S. 1926. *La banque en Belgique: étude historique et économique*, I, *Le marché financier belge avant 1850*. Brussels.

1930. *Le marché financier belge depuis cent ans*. Brussels.

Crombois, J. F. 1994–5. 'Les activités bancaires de la Société Générale de Belgique, 1870–1914. Facteurs de développement d'une grande banque mixte', *Revue Belge d'Histoire Contemporaine* 25: 1–29.

Daems, H. 1977. *The Holding Company and Corporate Control*. Boston.

Da Rin, M. 1996. 'Understanding the Development of the German Kreditbanken, 1850–1914: An Approach from the Economics of Information', *Financial History Review* 3: 29–47.

Demoulin, R. 1938. *Guillaume Ier et la transformation économique des Provinces belges*. Liège and Paris.

De Trannoy, J. 1905. *Jules Malou de 1810 à 1870*. Brussels.

Durviaux, R. 1947. *La banque mixte: origine et soutien du développment économique de la Belgique*. Brussels.

Gille, B. 1965. *Histoire de la maison Rothschild*, I, *Des origines à 1848*. Geneva.

Horlings, E. 1995. *The Economic Development of the Dutch Service Sector, 1800–1850: Trade and Transport in a Premodern Economy*. Amsterdam.

Kauch, P. 1950. *La Banque Nationale de Belgique, 1850–1918*. Brussels.

Kindleberger, Charles P. 1993. *A Financial History of Western Europe*. Oxford.

Kurgan-Van Hentenryk, G. 1992. 'Finance and Financiers in Belgium, 1880–1940', in Y. Cassis (ed.), *Finance and Financiers in European History*, pp. 317–35. Cambridge and Paris.

1996. *Gouverner la Générale de Belgique: essai de biographie collective*. Brussels.

Laureyssens, J. 1975. 'The Société Générale and the Origins of Industrial Investment Banking', *Revue Belge d'Histoire Contemporaine* 6: 93–115.

1989, 1992. 'Financial Innovation and Regulation. The Société Générale and the Belgian State after Independence', *Revue Belge d'Histoire Contemporaine* 20: 223–50; 23: 61–89.

Lebrun, P., Bruwier, M., Dhondt, J. and Hansotte, G. 1979. *Essai sur la révolution industrielle en Belgique, 1770–1847*. Brussels.

Lévy-Leboyer, M. 1964. *Les banques européennes et l'industrialisation internationale dans la première moitié du XIXe siècle*. Paris.

Luyten, D. 1986. 'Pressiegroepen in de eerste helft van de negentiende eeuw. Een concreet geval: de Société Générale tijdens de financiële crisis van 1848', *Belgisch Tijdschrift voor Nieuwste Geschiedenis* 17: 127–62.

Malou, J. 1863. *Notice historique sur la Société Générale pour favoriser l'industrie nationale, établie à Bruxelles, 1823–1862*. Brussels.

Maziers, M. 1972. *La Société Générale de Belgique, 1822–1972*. Brussels.

1994. *Histoire d'une forêt péri-urbaine: Soignes, 1822–1843. Sous la coupe de la Société Générale*. Brussels.

Thonissen, J. J. 1863. *La vie du comte de Meeûs*. Leuven.

Tilly, R. 1989. 'Banking Institutions in Historical Perspective: Germany, Great Britain, and the United States in the 19th–20th Century', *Journal of Institutional and Theoretical Economics* 145: 188–209.

Van der Wee, H. 1982. 'La politique d'investissement de la Société Générale de Belgique, 1822–1913', *Histoire, Economie et Société* 4: 603–19.

Van der Wee, H. (ed.) 1993. *A Financial History of Europe*. Antwerp.

1997. *The Generale Bank, 1882–1997*. Tielt

Van der Wee, H. and Verbreyt, M. 1997. *The Generale Bank, 1822–1997: A Continuing Challenge*. Tielt.

Van Elewijck, E. 1913. 'La Société Générale avant 1850', *Revue Economique Internationale* 10: 96–129.

4 Banking liberalization in England and Wales, 1826–1844

P. L. Cottrell and Lucy Newton[1]

The predominance of corporate commercial banks possessing nation-wide branch networks in the industrial economies of Europe during the late twentieth century has been seen as a consequence of a process akin to Darwinian evolution. It has been attributed to the joint-stock bank's innate superiority and the onset of concentration within banking, with the latter being considered by some to have been inevitable. Drawing from an almost world-wide review of banking structures, Wilson (1986: 1–14) put forward a general rule that there has been a 'gradual reduction in the number of banking units', 'a growth in their average size' and 'a more widespread resort to branch banking'. However, surveys undertaken during the 1950s pointed to regional, but especially local, banking within the French system, the still flourishing condition of private banking in the German Federal Republic and the sustained independence of local banks in the southern German Federal Länder. Furthermore, there was a persistence of unit banking in Norway, and 'diversity' and the 'absence of strong connecting links' within Danish banking. (Clayton 1962: 260; Opie 1962: 55, 58; Sayers 1962a: 300; Wilson 1962: 6–7.)

The continuing vitality of these 'hybrid' banking systems, namely the coexistence of major institutions possessing significant branch networks alongside regional or local banks, after a century or more of industrialization has required some explanation from practitioners of comparative banking. Yet, it is only in the case of France that this has been provided in terms of the countervailing effects arising from certain social, almost psychological, attitudes. These consist of deeply rooted individualism; loyalties persisting over generations within some social groups to certain banks; a demand for personal service; and particularism as in local patriotisms or ties (Wilson 1986: 134–7, 217). This stress upon social factors accords in part with the emphasis of Rondo Cameron when he considered the 'efficacy' of banking systems in performing the roles of intermediaries, financial entrepreneurs and providers of the means of payment to facilitate the division of labour (Cameron 1970: 9–10).

There is also scholarly agreement over the importance of differing economic circumstances leading to significant variations in banking structures and the financial functions they discharge (Cameron 1970: 11). In somewhat of a Cameronian vein, Wilson (1986: 12–15) argued that economic growth and arising structural change have played a central part in the unfolding of the process of concentration. However, what Wilson largely ignored, along with many others interested in comparative banking, is the role of the state. This contrasts markedly with Cameron's comparative *historical* perspective in which he maintained that: 'Legislation has been one of the most important factors in shaping the structure of banking systems and thus influencing their performance' (Cameron 1970: 10).

The development of joint-stock banking in England and Wales was not an evolutionary, secular process but rather, in its initial phases, took place through two bursts of bank promotions. The first occurred over the late 1820s and the first half of the 1830s, resulting in 117 joint-stock banks being in business by 1843 (see Table 4.1). The second wave came during the mid-1860s and early 1870s (Shannon 1930–3; 1932–3) and led to the number of such institutions rising from 98 in 1857 to 128 in 1880 which was to prove to be their historic maximum. Each of these spurts in promotions was related to short-term economic circumstances – the cyclical upswings of the mid-1830s, the mid-1860s and the early 1870s – and to social factors as expressed, for instance, in the persistence of unit banking with the average number of offices per bank in 1880 still being only 6.5 (Nishimura 1971: table 1, 80). Yet, the underlying, secular rate of this development was dictated by liberalizing legislation – by Acts passed in 1826, 1857 and 1862 (Cottrell 1988: 45–9). The 1826 statute permitted the establishment of banks with more than six partners and freely transferable shares, albeit beyond a 65-mile radius of London. However, responding to the speculative excesses of the mid-1830s, Peel introduced further legislation in 1844 which so strictly regulated the creation of new joint-stock banks that only twelve were established while his Act remained in force (Toft 1970). Partial reform from 1857 allowed bank promoters once more to have their sway and this was exerted in full measure after banks became fully assimilated within the generally liberalized company law from November 1862.

This contribution focuses upon the 1826 Act's impact – the growth of provincial joint-stock banking in England and Wales until the early 1840s. As such, little direct attention will be paid either to the post-1826 development of the Bank of England's provincial branch network (Ziegler 1990; also Collins 1972a; Moss 1981, 1992; Jones 1985), or to the rise of joint-stock deposit banks in London from 1834.[2] Whereas the parliamentary inquiries of the late 1830s and early 1840s have frequently been employed as a source by banking historians, here internal evidence is drawn upon – from the surviving papers of those banks that became part of the 'Big Five' and thus were of considerable longevity. Hitherto, such material has not been substantially exploited. This is supplemented by a reading of the *Circular to Bankers*. It is largely a hostile contemporary source since it was the private-country-banking interest's newsletter, although by the mid-1830s it was more reconciled to the new joint-stock banks. Once again, this contemporary commentary has been largely neglected. When employing such industry-related material and evidence, considerable care has to be exercised to overcome their inevitable and various biases but, nonetheless, they allow a fresh view to be taken of the first wave of quasi-corporate bank creations.

In section I the state's attitude towards money and banking is reviewed with particular attention paid to the origins of the 1826 Act. The consequent expansion of joint-stock banking is outlined in section II, where it is also maintained that this development should be considered in terms of two phases: from 1826 until mid-1833, and from mid-1833 until the early 1840s. This temporal division arises from the phases of the trade cycle and equally, if not more importantly, from the likelihood until February 1834 of further legislation affecting the formation of joint-stock banks. Both factors influenced contemporaries' behaviour. However, apart from the declaratory clause inserted in the Bank of England's renewed charter of 1833, the government was not to introduce major banking legislation. Other aspects affecting the creation of joint-stock banks promoted before spring 1833 – local, regional and national – are considered in section III, whereas the mid-1830s promotional boom is reviewed and analysed in section IV. This considers contemporary anxieties aroused by the banking boom of the mid-1830s, especially designs to establish 'district' banks. An attempt at an overall assessment of the impact of banking liberalization after 1826 in England and Wales is made in section V. The conclusions consist of the findings presented here melded with those arising from the work of other scholars.

I

As Cameron pointed out some thirty years ago, 'the sovereign authorities [within Continental Europe] remained extremely suspicious of independent money powers, with the result that they restricted the growth of banking even more severely than in England' (Cameron 1970: 11). If anything, this assessment underplays the extent of the contrast. For instance, the British state played no direct part in sterling's shift from silver to gold, with the government's decision to 'dethrone' silver in 1816 being largely on the grounds that gold had been *in practice* the nation's standard for nearly a century.[3] Likewise, the state undertook no shaping role between 1711 and 1821 in the significant development of commercial banking. Although, in relation to other aspects of institutional change required by the onset of modern economic growth, the English state has been regarded as a passive facilitator, with respect to money and banking, the state stood back for nearly a century after 1711 until it was forced by events to address the problem of stability during the post-1815 reconstruction period.[4] This section considers how the state was drawn into allowing the creation of quasi-corporate banks as a response to the outbreaks of banking crises, beginning in Ireland in 1820/1. Vested interests, such as the private banking community, the Bank of Ireland and the Bank of England, were able to delay but ultimately not block legislation. At the same time, the state, in Lord Liverpool and Robert Peel, had legislators who were more than prepared to act.

The business organization of private banking both in London (Joslin 1954; Melton 1986a, b)[5] and, from the mid-eighteenth century, in the provinces, was solely determined by the Bank of England having a monopoly of joint-stock banking in England and Wales from 1707. This arose from the Bank having provided the state with £1.5m the previous year to finance war with France. The further provision of £2.9m to the government in 1711 went with a more closely framed definition of the Bank's exclusive privilege. Henceforth, 'no [other] corporation or partnership of more than six persons should "borrow owe or take up any Sum or Sums of Money on their bills or Notes payable at demand or at any less Time than Six Months"'.[6] The Bank had been established in 1694 to finance the state's expenditures on war. What was to be an enduring, direct connection with national finances developed from 1706 so that by 1717 'the credit of the country was bound up with' the Bank of England (Andréadès 1924: 121).[7] However, even with the arising exclusive privileges that it thereby acquired for undertaking joint-stock banking throughout England and Wales, the Bank remained until the mid-1820s primarily and particularly a banker to the state and to the elite of metropolitan society. Consequently, the rising circulation of banknotes beyond London after 1750 was predominantly due to the activities of the increasing number of largely small, private banks. These were unfettered by state-imposed restrictions except with regard to the number of individuals that constituted banking partnerships.[8]

Just as war finance had given rise to the Bank of England during the late seventeenth century, so prolonged warfare, inflation and financial instability directed the state's attention to monetary and banking matters over the opening decades of the nineteenth century. A growing public debate from 1802 led to the Bullion Committee of 1810 and its associated pamphlets and parliamentary discussions (Clapham 1944b [1970]: 22–3; Fetter 1965: 37–40; O'Grada 1991). However, in 1811 the House of Commons rejected the Committee's recommendation that the foreign exchanges should be stabilized by the Bank of England through the conduct of its lending and its reserve policies. Thereafter, the onset of deflation from 1814 made the resumption of specie payments politically awkward so that the necessary government decision was postponed in February 1815, in April 1816 and again in April 1818 (Clapham 1944b [1970]: 51, 62–3, 64; Hilton 1977: 30). Ultimately, the administration's hand was forced by the opposition during the 1819 parliamentary session but it was able to bring about the passage of a compromise measure. This, on the one hand, further postponed cash payments to 1823 while, on the other, following Ricardo's proposals of 1816 (Fetter 1965: 91–2), required the Bank of England to meet its notes in gold bars on a downward sliding scale, reaching Mint price on 1 May 1821 (Fetter 1965: 93–5; Horsefield 1949). Even so, cash payments, suspended since February 1797, were finally introduced in spring 1821 owing to a decision of the Bank of England's directors. With bullion holdings of £11.9m, the Bank side-stepped Ricardo's Ingot Plan through announcing its readiness to resume full cash payments, two years in advance of the legislative timetable (Morgan 1943[1965]: 75–6; Clapham 1944b[1970]: 72–3, 75–6; Fetter 1965: 96–9; Hilton 1977: 87–91).

Although country bankers were to point during the late 1820s to an ascendancy within Parliament and the administration from 1819 of 'Economists', resumption's timing had been dictated by the government's postwar reliance on the Bank of England for funds coupled with Bank directors' continuing anxieties over the 'Old Lady's' bullion holdings in relationship to the exchanges.[9] Postwar banking reform in England and Wales – the 1826 legislation – has often been portrayed more positively by historians, although with some stress that the government was forced to act as a result of the calamities of the 1825/6 crisis. Nevertheless, the government had an interest in banking reform from the early 1820s, aroused initially by Irish difficulties.

During 1820 the small and weak private banks of southern and western Ireland were gravely affected by a financial crisis. The situation led the government to introduce an Irish Banking Act in 1821 that allowed banks with more than six partners to be established beyond a 50-mile radius of Dublin. This foreshadowed the 1826 Act for England and Wales, particularly in terms of the restriction of the Bank of Ireland's privileges to a specified 'metropolitan area'. Indeed, the government quickly attempted to place the Bank of England on the same footing. In April 1822, Lord Liverpool suggested that the Bank's charter, although having a life until 1833, should be renewed to run until 1843. However, this was to be on the basis that its monopoly of joint-stock banking applied solely to the area within a 50-mile radius of London. The necessary agreement was sealed on 2 May 1822, although with a modified provision extending the Bank's protected metropolitan radius to 65 miles. Yet, owing to opposition from country bankers, the government's new compact with the Bank of England was not put into effect (Clapham 1944b: 87–8).

Although establishing a template, the 1821 Irish Act had imperfections as its drafters appear to have been primarily concerned with the need to fund £0.5m of short-term debt. In particular, it failed to repeal legislation of 1756 and, consequently, banks still remained required to act legally in the names of all their shareholders, who therefore had to be listed, for example, on notes and receipts. This cumbersome, impractical situation was only addressed in 1824 owing to political pressure exerted by promoters of a Belfast joint-stock bank (the conversion of the Northern Bank, first established in June 1809). Other precedents for subsequent English developments came with the creation of the Hibernian Bank by a private Act, promoted by a group of Roman Catholics excluded from the Bank of Ireland's direction and who sought to conduct corporate deposit banking in Dublin (Barrow 1975: 61–81; Simpson 1975: 16–26; see also Munn 1983; Ollerenshaw 1987).

The 1824 Irish Banking Act also arose from the efforts of an English group, led by Matthias Attwood, a partner in the London bank of Spooner, Attwood & Co. and a Member of Parliament. He thought that a London-based Irish bank, supported by English capital, would be a profitable venture but this was stymied by other clauses of the 1821 Act. These required all shares in Irish joint-stock banks to be held by residents in their areas of operation, thus disbarring the participation of not only English investors but also Dubliners.

Attwood's scheme for the Provincial Bank of Ireland was developed in conjunction with Thomas Joplin, a Newcastle private banker, who in 1822 had proposed the formation of a joint-stock bank on Tyneside. The Provincial's 1824 prospectus attracted the necessary capital but, before the bank could commence business, three outstanding problems required resolution. Joplin attempted to persuade directors of the Bank of Ireland to allow the Provincial both to be incorporated, so gaining limited liability, and to issue notes within the Dublin protected area. He was unsuccessful in these endeavours, not a surprising outcome since the 1821 Act's passage had involved three months of prior negotiation between the government and Arthur Guinness, the Governor of the Bank of Ireland. Thirdly, the full involvement of English shareholders in the bank could only come about after further legislation. The Provincial's promoters moved the bill for the necessary private Act in March 1825 but this was quickly superseded by a government measure permitting the introduction of British capital into Irish joint-stock banks and which received royal assent on 10 June 1825 (Cottrell 1985: 36–7).[10]

The foundation of the Provincial Bank brought to the fore Thomas Joplin, who proved to be a doughty campaigner for the introduction of joint-stock banking into England and Wales over the ensuing decade. He was convinced of the superiority of corporate banks through his familiarity with Scottish banking, gained from the circulation of Scottish banknotes in north-east England. In one of the many versions for his plan for an English joint-stock bank, Joplin argued that the difference in banking stability north and south of Hadrian's Wall was not the result of 'anything different in the nature of . . . money transactions . . . but the nature of their respective banking establishments; the Scotch banks being Joint Stock Companies, while the English banks are private partnerships'. This was a point that members of the government were to take up again in their reactions to the 1825/6 crisis. However, the Provincial Bank proved to be not just a model for future emulation in terms of its constitution. Its directors also spread Scottish banking practice in Ireland by establishing branches (fourteen by 1828), through paying interest on deposits and by making advances in the form of cash credits. Its Kilkenny and Waterford offices during the late 1820s were overseen by J. W. Gilbart. His consequent immersion in Scottish banking methods was to be transferred to London in 1834, when he became manager of the newly established London & Westminster Bank. This institution, like the earlier Hibernian in Dublin, was a joint-stock deposit bank formed on Scottish lines.

The growing debate in the mid-1820s concerned with the constitution of banks was brought to a head by the 1825/6 crisis in England. Although the country banks had been considered to comprise 'a flexible capital market for turning facilities into facts', this was challenged from summer 1825 by a series of incidents, of which the most notorious took place at Bristol. The overture to the crisis began in October with the failure of Sir William Elford's bank at Plymouth. This was followed by that of others in Lancashire and Yorkshire and eventually came to involve the collapse of sixty-three country banks throughout England and Wales (Hilton 1977: 204–10). The climax was reached during mid-December with the demise of two major London banks, that of Pole, Thornton & Co. bringing down in its train forty-three country banks for which it had acted as their metropolitan correspondent (Hilton 1977: 215). Contemporaries not only blamed these events upon the Bank of England, country bankers and

London bankers alike, but also argued that banking required to be over-hauled in order to meet the greater, growing financial needs of commerce and industry (Mushet 1826). Most country banks had equity capitals of at most £10,000, with merely twenty-six having the legal maximum of six partners. Indeed, more than two thirds of the 552 licensed note-issuing banks in England and Wales had three or fewer partners (Ziegler 1990: 5).[11] Lord Liverpool and Robert Peel saw a solution to the banks' lack of equity resources in the introduction of joint-stock banking in England and Wales on the Scottish model.

Peel in particular followed the lines of Joplin's arguments through contrasting the extent of bank failures in England since 1793 with the one and only apparent case that had taken place in Scotland, despite comparable expansions of credit north and south of the border. This went along with criticism of the Bank of England, especially its reluctance to open provincial branches (Thomas 1934: 64–7). However, although then not appreciated, Joplin's and Peel's Anglo-Scottish banking contrast was misconceived. During the mid-1820s, apart from the three so-called public banks with royal charters – the Bank of Scotland, the Royal Bank of Scotland and the British Linen Company – there was only one Scottish joint-stock bank conducting business. This was the Commercial Bank of Scotland formed in 1810, whereas a further two – the National and the Aberdeen & Country – were only in the process of being established as Peel spoke and Joplin reissued his pamphlet. Other Scottish banks – the provincial banking companies – were constituted as either private partnerships or small proprietory companies, and only nineteen of the latter had more than thirteen members. Furthermore, these institutions were almost as failure-prone as private country banks in England and Wales, with a fifth of their number collapsing during the period before 1830 as opposed to a third of the country banks south of the border (Checkland 1975; Munn 1981; Saville 1996). Moreover, in 1830, Henry Burgess, on behalf of country bankers but with some justification, was able to point out that 160, out of the 165 English private banks forced to suspend payments during the 1825/6 crisis, had subsequently paid 20s. in the pound.[12]

Lord Liverpool had long favoured the Bank of England having branches, especially at Manchester where there was no local issue of notes, but his designs had been resisted by the directors at Threadneedle Street (Hilton 1977: 223). He also opposed the continuance of the 'small' £1 note, whose life at Huskisson's behest Parliament had extended in 1822 for a further eleven years in reaction to deflation. Lord Liverpool's views were well known, as was the wider, growing support for the introduction of joint-stock banks into England and Wales. The Bank of

England reacted by establishing a committee to investigate the establishment of branches on 12 January 1826, the day before it officially received a memorandum from Lord Liverpool and the Chancellor, Robinson.[13] The government's communication was pithy and to the point. Without branches the Bank was to lose its monopoly, while 'small' notes were to be abolished and the introduction of joint-stock banks, but without limited liability, was contemplated. The necessary legislation was passed during spring 1826. The cessation of the circulation of notes under £5 took effect from 5 April 1829, although only within England and Wales owing to the successful counter-pressure exerted by Scottish bankers in conjunction with Sir Walter Scott.[14] The Banking Act[15] contained a threat that the government might charter a rival to the Bank of England but otherwise followed the 1825 Irish Act through permitting the establishment of banking co-partnerships outside a 65-mile radius of London. Lastly, to clarify the law, Bank of England 'agents' were specifically empowered 'to carry on banking business in any place in England' (Clapham 1944b[1970]: 76, 91, 103–7).

II

The outcome of the 1826 banking legislation is portrayed in outline in Table 4.1. By 1833, twenty-eight joint-stock banks with unlimited liability (more strictly, banking co-partneries) had been successfully established in England and Wales. Over the mid-1830s boom, their numbers further increased and subsequently reached a peak of 120 in 1840.[16] Failures began in 1834 with that of the Nottingham & Nottinghamshire Banking Co., although subsequently it was able to resume business.[17] The underlying problems of the new banking only became prominent in 1836, with the disappearance of the Bury & Heywood Banking Co., a mayfly of the year's speculative boom in banking promotions, and, more seriously, the collapses of the Gloucester County & City Bank and the Northern & Central Bank (Thomas 1934: 668). Much was to be made of the circumstances that led to the demise of some of the new joint-stock banks from summer 1836. However, the Gloucester County & City became a branch of the County of Gloucester Bank,[18] while the debts of the Northern & Central, amounting to £3.3m, were to be discharged in full although in this process its shareholders lost about £0.6m. Overall, of the 141 joint-stock banks successfully established during the 1826 Act's lifetime, only nineteen either collapsed or closed before the introduction of Peel's new banking code in 1844. Certainly, this was evidence of continuing instability and of the 1826 Act having not put banking on a sounder basis. Yet, the failure rate of joint-stock banks to 1843 – 13.5% of

Table 4.1 *Joint-stock bank creations in England and Wales, 1826–43.*

Year	Number of joint-stock banks promoted	Number of disappearances due to failure or amalgamation	Number of joint-stock banks in existence
1826	3	–	3
1827	3	–	6
1828	–	–	6
1829	7	–	13
1830	1	–	14
1831	7	–	21
1832	7	–	28
1833	10	–	38
1834	11	1	48
1835	9	–	57
1836	59	3	113
1837	5	5	113
1838	1	3	111
1839	6	2	115
1840	6	1	120
1841	2	5	117
1842	2	3	116
1843	2	1	117

Source: Drawn from Thomas 1934: 656–62.

those formed – was considerably less than that of either the private country banks in England and Wales or the Scottish provincial banking companies.

There are grounds for considering joint-stock-bank formations under the 1826 Act in two periods – before and after mid-1833 – arising from cyclical fluctuations and, equally, the continuing question of whether the state would introduce further banking legislation that was to remain open until February 1834.

First, the period from the 1825/6 crisis until spring 1833, as far as contemporaries were concerned, was marked by a long business recession that prompted, albeit belatedly, a government inquiry into economic conditions.[19] Rising prices, and other indications of what observers regarded as a positive change in the state of trade and commerce, were only noticed from July 1833.[20] An improving business climate certainly affected the likely success of bank promotions, especially those involving appeals to the 'blind' investor. However, the mid-1830s cyclical upswing had other implications, possibly more negative, for the further creation of joint-stock banks. By December 1835, the *Circular to Bankers* was arguing, and with some reason, that joint-stock banks formed before spring 1833 probably had a greater solidity since they had commenced business when prices were low and therefore during their early years had faced 'no risk of declining markets'.[21] Indeed, only one bank established before 1833 – the Leith Banking Co., Carlisle – failed outright during the slump that followed the 1836 crisis. This had been a branch of a Scottish bank, although independently registered as an English banking company, and ultimately was unable to compete with the Carlisle City & District Bank (Thomas 1934: 669). The only other fatality amongst this cohort of banks was the Bank of Manchester, formed in 1829 and which closed its doors in 1842. Its creditors were paid 20s. in the pound (as were those of the Leith Banking Co.) and, despite its shareholders experiencing consequent losses totalling over £1m, it was re-established in 1852 (Thomas 1934: 669; Grindon 1877: 242, 245, 246; Gregory 1936, II: 52). The twenty-one further joint-stock-bank failures between 1836 and 1843 were of institutions created during the mid-1830s boom, of which eleven had been promoted during the 'banking mania' of 1836. Three of these twenty-one foundered banks were taken over by other institutions to survive beyond 1843 in different guises.

Economic conditions, especially changes in expectations, played a part in both the timing of bank creations under the 1826 legislation and their subsequent chances of longevity. However, the establishment of joint-stock banks was also affected by intimations of further, harsher legislation. They were first aired by the Duke of Wellington in early 1830, when pressure upon the government was being exerted from both Huskisson's coterie and the landed interest to allow the formation of joint-stock banks having limited liability.[22] Henry Burgess, editor of the *Circular to Bankers*, thought he detected that this had support amongst 'landed proprietors'. Their particular backing arose from a belief that such institutions would be 'more ready to grant accommodation to farmers and graziers . . . because of unlimited confidence in them and [their] managers' who would be under 'no apprehension for sudden demands in consequence of convulsions of general credit'.[23]

These early markers for further banking legislation were not lost in the mounting furore over the franchise and parliamentary reform (Brock 1973; Moss 1990), the excitement caused by the French revolution of 1830 and the activities of 'Captain Swing' in the countryside (Hobsbawm and Rudé 1969). The continuing possibility of new measures was given a focus in the establishment of a Secret Committee to inquire into the renewal of the Bank of England's charter, moved for in the Commons by Huskisson, a known supporter of joint-stock banks. As it was being convened, country bankers were concerned that likely members would be either joint-stock-bank directors or those who favoured further liberalizing legislation.[24] However, some joint-stock bankers, such as directors of the Bank of Liverpool and the Bank of Manchester, already looked to greater state regulation of both the promotion and the business of joint-stock banks. They approached Lord Althorp, the new Whig Chancellor, on 9 April 1832 with a set of 'Propositions'. These included stipulations that joint-stock banks should have minimum nominal capitals of £0.5m, of which 20% should be paid up, contributed by at least a hundred shareholders of whom no fewer than twenty had personal stakes of £1,000. Furthermore, they recommended that branches be established only within a 20-mile radius of banks' head offices, while the business should be conducted by boards comprising at least seven directors, who were elected annually. Moreover, they put forward that banks' annual reports be made publicly available. These 'Propositions' went to the Secret Committee, to which directors of the Bank of Manchester gave evidence (Thomas 1934: 134–7).

The 'banking question' was considered by the Committee, albeit partially and briefly, but no consensus was reached owing to the conflicting interests of the Bank of England, the private country bankers and the new joint-stock banks. Consequently, its arising report made no definite recommendations, leaving Althorp, in whom the private country bankers had confidence, to discuss the matter with the Bank of England. Joplin had already argued that the Bank's monopoly with respect to its protected post-1826 'metropolitan area' only applied to note-issuing joint-stock banks and therefore did not embrace the creation of London joint-stock banks that dealt solely in deposits. Althorp was also subject to parliamentary pressure, with the House being twice petitioned by a group headed by W. R. Douglas, a Scottish merchant resident in London, which sought to establish a metropolitan joint-stock bank 'on the Scottish system'.[25]

Ultimately, Althorp decided simply to renew the Bank of England's charter but with the insertion of a declaratory clause. This followed Joplin's argument that joint-stock deposit banks could be established within the Bank's 'metropolitan' area. Furthermore, the renewed charter remedied one of the defects in the 1826 legislation which prevented joint-stock banks from drawing bills on London that were either under £50 or for less than six months' sight – precisely the paper most wanted in the provinces.[26] The necessary bill was passed in August 1833.

Despite renewal of the Bank of England's charter, further joint-stock-bank legislation continued to be expected, with private country bankers fearing that it might allow the creation of chartered banking companies.

Indeed, the Whig government favoured the establishment of a precise legal code, such as that suggested by the managements of the Bank of Liverpool and the Bank of Manchester. This would permit banks to be formed as corporations (as opposed to quasi-corporations under the 1826 Act), with those that did not issue notes enjoying limited liability. While obtaining the necessary charters would be expensive processes, it was also equally apparent that these instruments of incorporation would contain restrictions affecting the nature of the banking that could be pursued. The possibility of this new code was sufficient to halt the promotion of the Hull, East Riding & North Lincolnshire Banking Co., which in April 1833 had reached the stage of its shares being allotted. The management of another new joint-stock bank, the York City & County, went as far as attempting to organize opposition to the passage of the indicated legislation and, when unsuccessful, submitted a strongly worded memorial to the government (Crick and Wadsworth 1936[1958]: 209). However, no bill could be introduced in June 1833 because of the imminent ending of the parliamentary session. Nonetheless, this did not quell country private bankers' anxieties over the government's intention to suppress their note issues, following the Bank of England's circular issued by Horsley Palmer on 29 May 1827.[27] In all this, private country bankers pointed to the lobby that the new joint-stock banks had at Westminster, with the Bank of Manchester having 'control of parliamentary representation of that giant borough', 'Sir James Scarlett and Lord Stormont consider[ing] Mr Bignold of the Norwich Joint Stock Bank their political patron' and 'Mr Richard look[ing] to his tutelary banking genius of Knaresborough'.[28] Ultimately, this alarm proved to be unnecessary as Althorp announced at the end of February 1834 that no new joint-stock-bank bill would be introduced, a decision which he confirmed a week later.[29]

Althorp's 1833 declaratory clause proved to be more unsatisfactory than the 1826 liberalizing Act as the provisions of the latter did not apply to the four London joint-stock deposit banks that came to be established before 1843, beginning with the London & Westminster in 1834. In particular, these banks could not accept bills at less than six months and nor were they able to sue, and be sued, in the name of an officer. The latter restriction forced the board of the London & Westminster to obtain a private Act to acquire these powers. This was opposed by directors of the Bank of England, who also refused it a drawing account and, moreover, stated in 1836 that they would not discount bills payable at the London & Westminster. Hostility to their development also came from the London private-banking community who refused entry to the all-important Clearing House, an embargo that continued until the 1850s.

III

Having established that the pattern of bank promotions between 1826 and 1843 was affected by both cyclical factors and, before February 1834, the possibility of further legislation, this section reviews aspects of the foundation of the first joint-stock banks during the period until spring 1833. It begins by considering the basic problems of management structures, the competitive edge of the 'new' banks and its first effects, and the flotation of the 'new' banks' shares. These questions are examined with regard to the small local joint-stock banks that were to characterize the 'new' banking, but the section concludes by reviewing the promotion of larger institutions in the north-west, and Joplin's creation of the National Provincial Bank of England, the only nation-wide joint-stock commercial bank to be created before 1843.

Not surprisingly, the new provincial joint-stock banks were opposed by the private-country-banking interest. Their publicist, Henry Burgess, maintained in spring 1830 that: 'Joint-stock-banks are, unequivocally, good institutions in feeble or infantile communities or in States where capital bears an inadequate relation to the demands of industry.'[30] This assessment, which foreshadowed in some respects Gerschenkron's thinking by about 120 years, did not apply in Burgess' view to England and Wales, while he considered 'Scotch banks' to be the product of a particular, organic evolution.

The private-country-banking interest had formed a defensive pressure group on 2 May 1828 under the chairmanship of W. Rickford, a Member of Parliament and a private banker at Aylesbury, Buckinghamshire. It soon became clear that its anxieties focused in particular upon the effects of the cessation of the 'small' note issue from 1829, above all in rural areas, and the competition that might come from the new branches of the Bank of England.[31] Consequently, this interest group was hostile to 'those advocates of bullionism who would, in order to establish their theory, suppress the circulation of all Country Bankers' notes, and of all individual credit to substitute in their stead the notes of the Bank of England and the King's coin'.[32] The private country bankers justified their role by maintaining that: 'In the intercourse which subsists between a Banker and one of his customers, a degree of confidential honour is necessary, which is entirely inconsistent with the principle of a bank established on the joint stock basis'; while 'The great characteristic of a wise and prudent Private Banker is, that being by his business separated and set apart from the general trading affairs of his vicinity, in which he rarely intermixes as a competitor, he becomes the only fit person to be consulted by the active borrowing classes, as a confidential friend in need.'[33]

The new joint-stock bankers were well aware of the problems of conflicting interests that might arise from their relationships with customers and, for instance, when Thomas Wilson joined the board of the newly established Cumberland Union Bank in July 1829, he had to declare that: 'I will not reveal or make known either to the prejudice of the said company or to the prejudice of any of their customers any matters, affairs or concerns which may come to my knowledge as a director to any person or in any manner whatsoever except when officially requested by a board of directors or by any general or special meeting of the proprietors or by any committee of inspection to be appointed pursuant to the provision of the deed of copartnership constituting the said company.'[34] The founders of the Bradford Banking Co. went further by laying down in the deed of settlement establishing the bank on 1 June 1827 that: 'No director shall be authorised to vote in the matter of any . . . advance or credit or on the rolling in, or withdrawing of the same, or as to the discounting any note or bill wherein he solely or in partnership with any other person or persons may be interested.'[35]

Much of the business of the new joint-stock banks would be conducted by managers in the same manner that the private country bankers employed senior clerks. Once more this raised questions of confidentiality but in conjunction with the extent of decision-making that the banks' administrative officials could undertake. Again, the directors of the Cumberland Union were soon conscious of this particular issue, quickly deciding that: 'nothing in future out of the routine of business shall be transacted by the manager without first submitting it to a board of directors and that every matter discussed by the board be entered in the minute book'.[36] Indeed, that minute book had already been opened – to record a meeting in Workington on 12 March 1829 at which Richard Watts became the bank's chairman and Charles Brown its manager, and the directors decided that they would meet weekly to conduct its affairs.[37] Directors of the Bradford Banking Co., formed in May 1827, took other measures by requiring their manager, Samuel Laycock, to provide security of £10,000.[38] These 'insurances' adopted by the senior managements of the Cumberland Union and the Bradford Bank were not to be exceptional as they were replicated in nearly every instance by promoters and directors of subsequent joint-stock banks.

The strength of the private country bankers' case against their new quasi-corporate competitors was undermined to some extent in early 1829 by the failures of a further two London private banks. Nonetheless, Burgess attempted to challenge what ever additional support this gave to the proponents of joint-stock banking by pointing to the concurrent problems of the Provincial Bank of Ireland.[39] However, the private-country-banking interest had been in some difficulty almost from the passage of the 1826 Act since one of the first joint-stock banks to be established was that of Vincent Stuckey. He quickly took advantage of the legislation to consolidate his investments in five West Country banks into one institution. Initially, it had a nominal capital of £65,000, contributed by thirty-nine shareholders and operated through fourteen branches in Gloucestershire and Somerset. Yet, it was a private joint-stock bank since no public appeal of any kind was made for capital, which enabled Burgess to describe it as 'merely a respectable and old-established County-bank extended on the joint-stock principle'.[40] Although the private-country-banking interest continually attempted to regard Stuckey as 'one of them', within a decade he was a leading spokesman for joint-stock bankers.[41] Some other private bankers followed his initiative, but only to the extent of increasing the number of partners constituting their banking houses, a procedure adopted, for instance, by the Bristol banks of Elton, Bailey & Co. and Miles, Harford & Co.[42]

Defections from the 'fold' went along with a grudging acknowledgement that joint-stock banks could undertake business beyond the reach of an average country banker; like, for instance, making advances of £10,000 which Burgess considered to be double the sum that a private bank could provide as accommodation.[43] Inevitably this had its effects, and the development of the Norfolk & Norwich Banking Co., following its establishment in 1826, led one Norwich private banker in 1830 to relinquish his business.[44] Others became fully fledged joint-stock banks, with, for instance, in 1832, Horden & Co. being converted into the Wolverhampton & Staffordshire Banking Co.[45] However, it was not necessarily the case that customers of the new joint-stock banks received more generous treatment than those of private country banks. The Bradford Banking Co., formed to fill the financial vacuum created in the town by the failure of Wentworth, Chaloner & Rishworth (Crick and Wadsworth 1936[1958]: 201, 203, 204–5), took the business of William and Thomas Marshall on 'the same terms which Messrs Briggs & Co. of Halifax now afford them, viz. an advance of £2,500 without security'.[46] Furthermore, its directors declined the custom of James Varley, who had an interest in the Stanningley Mill Co., had previously banked with Brown & Co., Leeds, and, in February 1828, had his account with Beckett & Co.[47] This was despite the likelihood that £15,000–£30,000 would annually pass through his account, thus generating substantial commissions, which were the bank's principal revenue-earning charges as with the private country banks.

The new joint-stock banks were there to stay and, in certain circumstances, came to be tolerated by their private counterparts. Whereas Burgess had taken obvious pleasure in reporting that the Lancaster

Banking Co. had been established in 1826 only 'with some difficulty', subsequently he acknowledged that it was 'well-managed'. This acceptance was due to the bank being located outside of the southern rural shires, the geographical centre of the private-country-banking interest group, and implicitly acknowledged that the 'north' lacked banks, as was indisputably the case at Lancaster which, prior to 1826, had lacked a banking office.[48]

In mid-1830, Burgess pointed out with some satisfaction that, as far as he was aware, merely six joint-stock banks had been established in England and Wales over the past four years, of which one was Stuckey's and another 'the small bank' at Lancaster but which now had a branch at Chorley.[49] But this reckoning overlooked Burgess' own reports of a promotion of a joint-stock bank in Leicester[50] – the Leicestershire Banking Co. – and that the price of the shares of the Bradford Banking Co. had gone to a premium.[51] Indeed, all in all, by 1830, fourteen joint-stock banks were conducting business. Burgess was not alone in being unable to make an exact reckoning of the 1826 legislation's initial impact. Two years later, representatives of the Bank of Manchester thought that there were only nineteen other joint-stock banks, of which they could give precise details for only eleven (Gregory 1936, I: 22). In January 1833, the shares of but seven English and Welsh joint-stock banks were quoted on the London Stock Exchange, of which only three had subscribed capitals of any significant size: the Bank of Liverpool (£25,000), the Bank of Manchester (£20,000) and the Manchester & Liverpool District Bank (£30,000). The four others had individual capitals at best equivalent to that of an average private country bank (£10,000).[52]

As with canal companies and the first railway companies, most of the joint-stock banks established prior to mid-1833 were set up locally, as their very titles indicate. Generally their shares were held by individuals resident within the area of a bank's operations. However, bank promotion was an entirely new venture for which little detailed guidance was at hand. Consequently, institutions were established from the particular conceptions of their founders. For instance, the Halifax Joint Stock Banking Co., formed during November 1829, began with a nominal capital of £0.5m consisting of 5,000 shares of £100 each, a very large denomination, but on which subscribers were initially required to pay a deposit of only £5. Furthermore, its directors decided that individual holdings should consist of no more than 100 shares.[53] The promoters of the Barnsley Joint Stock Banking Co. took a similar approach two years later through restricting shareholdings to a maximum of 100. However, this bank's directors were required to have at least forty shares, whereas voting powers were tiered, with the minimum holding of five shares carrying one vote, those of fifteen shares having two votes and, thereafter, rising by one vote for every additional ten shares held.[54]

Similarly, there was no clear model for either bank promoters or bank directors regarding capitalization and some of the arising problems are indicated in the early development of the Huddersfield Banking Co., formed in 1827. It was established with a paid-up capital of £0.1m, an unusually large sum for an early, pioneering joint-stock institution. This was amassed by a series of calls rapidly made upon its shareholders – 10% on 1 June 1827, 5% on 2 August 1827 and a further 5% on 6 February 1828. With the improvement in business conditions, the bank issued further, new shares in August 1833. But then, within a year, its directors decided that the bank had too much capital and so returned £3 per share on 26 August 1834 and £7 per share on 21 August 1835.[55] This problem persisted even after the promotion of joint-stock banks became a more regular process. For instance, following the formation of the Hull Banking Co. in autumn 1833, its directors resolved to return capital during 1836 to the extent of £5 per share. Yet, this bank's subscription books remained open, and existing shareholders bought further shares during autumn 1833 and entirely new shareholders were gained between 1834 and 1836.[56]

Unallotted shares provided a useful means for attracting custom to a new joint-stock bank. In the case of 500 unissued shares of the Barnsley Bank, it was decided three months following the bank's establishment that they 'be disposed of at a premium of 30s per share to such persons only as shall undertake to keep accounts with the bank and that disposal of and selection of subscribers . . . be left to the discretion of the managing directors'.[57] The use of shares to attract customers was frequently employed to expand the businesses of newly established banks, but the promoters of the Bradford Banking Co. agreed that such accommodation was to be restricted to 'not £1,000 beyond the value of their stock'.[58] Nonetheless, not every potential subscriber was alloted shares[59] whereas, generally, advances from the Bradford Bank during its early years on the security of its shares were restricted to the amount subscribed. If the sum requested by a prospective borrowing shareholder was greater then either 'caution must be exercised in the conducting of this amount', or further security was required.[60]

The Bank of Manchester was of a very different order from many of the English and Welsh joint-stock banks created before mid-1833. After being promoted during 1828 by Joseph Macardy, an Irish journalist and sometime sharebroker, its nominal capital of £2m was held by 600 shareholders, drawn especially from the elite of the town's cotton merchants. The bank began business on 25 March 1829 and initially was well managed – by a former clerk of a private bank. It was not a note-issuing bank because the 1826 Act prevented its notes being payable in London while, furthermore, there was local hostility in south Lancashire to banks of issue arising from the experience of failed private houses. However, the management of the Bank of Manchester encountered difficulties in obtaining Bank of England notes from the Bank's Manchester agent. Subsequently, in 1832, its directors complained of the attitude of the Bank's agent towards it applications for discounts. This eventually had forced them to obtain Bank of England notes from a London broker but which had thereby given rise to the further costs of a fluctuating rate of discount and the payment of commission. However, during 1833 the bank had 'returns' of £25m on which it charged a commission of a ¼% and it also earnt commissions on a further £16m that had passed through accounts placed with it. Unlike some of its peers, the Bank of Manchester did not require its shareholders to keep their banking accounts with it and, furthermore, shareholders were not given any special preference when they applied for accommodation.

The Bank of Manchester not only was a major institution, through which for the first time the Lancashire cotton interest entered banking, but also was the first of a series of Lancashire banks promoted by Macardy. Although some of the first joint-stock banks had either local or regional branch networks, probably the most extensive apart from Stuckey's being that of the Norfolk & Norwich, Macardy appears to have had a considerable interest in creating a joint-stock bank with a substantial number of branches. In this, there is no indication that he was influenced by either Scottish or Irish banking developments. However, his plans for branching were opposed by the directors of the Bank of Manchester with the result that their ways soon parted.[61] Nevertheless, Macardy continued with his own personal conception of the new joint-stock banking and in 1829 formed the Manchester & Liverpool District Bank, possibly spurred by rising expectations engendered by an increase in cotton exports.

The District Bank was established in part by the acquisition of Christy, Lloyd, Winterbottom & Wesley, a Stockport private bank founded during the mid-1820s. However, the improvement in local business conditions proved to be temporary, while negotiations to merge with a further local private bank, Scholes, Titlow & Co., were abortive. As a result, the District's early years were difficult, made worse by the bank being backed by middling local business interests. It soon became apparent that its promotion had been speculative, whereas the commitment it embodied to branch banking came in practice to be associated with local boards in south Lancashire towns where efforts were being made to attract subscribers to its shares. The bank only gained greater foundations after, first, it was taken over by Manchester directors of more solidity in 1832 and, second, the production of cotton textiles increased cyclically from mid-1833. By mid-1834, District Bank shares at £10 paid were being quoted at premium of £18, with its new management having taken a firm grip on its affairs, generated by seventeen branches in south Lancashire, Cheshire and Staffordshire. Although overdrawn accounts were closed, during 1834 the bank had annual 'returns' of £16m arising from deposits and credit running accounts which collectively totalled over £1.2m. However, once more, Macardy quarrelled with the bank's management, but the consequent separation from the second of his banking companies was not to stop his endeavours as a bank promoter. Macardy went on during the mid-1830s boom to create, first, the Northern & Central Bank of England and, second, the Commercial Bank of England, his aspirations becoming increasingly grandiose in the process.[62]

During the period until 1833, Macardy's banking promotion ventures attracted little comment beyond Manchester. Instead, Henry Burgess, on behalf of his private-country-banking subscribers, kept a closer eye upon Joplin's plans to establish a national bank with a head office in London. Joplin's views had played a part in the drafting of the 1826 Act and he had influence at Westminster, whereas the various editions of his pamphlet were frequently cited in joint-stock-bank prospectuses. Initially, Joplin's own venture was called the Royal Bank, for which he began to circulate a prospectus in London during late 1828, renewing his efforts over the opening months of 1829.[63]

Despite having detected 'the flaw' in the Bank of England's charter, Joplin, with the support of Sir Thomas Lethbridge, in August 1829 modified his concept to a solely provincial institution so that it could benefit from the profits of a note-issue. He gained the backing of the Tory *Courier*, which pointed to the 'want of banking'.[64] By March 1830, this reshaped proposal had reached the stage of private meetings involving Althorp and four members of the Commons: Sir Edward Knatchbull (a Tory 'Ultra'), the Hon. H. T. Liddell, Sir Henry Parnell and Thomas Spring Rice who was connected with the Provincial Bank of Ireland. Also associated was Dickinson Hanning, a Somerset landowner.[65] All that Burgess could suggest to oppose this growing scheme was that country bankers themselves should set up a 'National Bank' upon a 'federal principle', from which joint-stock bankers would be disbarred as shareholders.

Although the title of Joplin's projected joint-stock bank continually changed, from the County Bank of England in April 1830 and on whose behalf Wellington was approached[66] to the Metropolitan County Bank of England in June 1830, its backers continued to grow in number. By mid-1830, the support of the Marquis of Bute, Lord Darnley and Sir Rowland Hill had been enlisted.[67] Despite the progress of this gathering venture being interrupted by the dissolution of Parliament and the franchise reform agitation, Joplin remained relentless. With the project renamed the Provincial Bank, it began to make headway once more from February 1831 to the extent that, within a month, its prospectus was being advertised through the offices of thirty-four country solicitors, all located outside of the 'Home Counties' which constituted the Bank of England protected 'metropolitan' area.[68] Re-entitled the National Provincial Bank of England, it was finally got underway by Joplin, his cousin George Fife Angas[69] and Sir Henry Parnell during May 1833. The bank's shares were all subscribed by mid-August and, at the close of 1833, its directors were establishing its branch network. They purchased private country banks, such as Turner & Co. at Gloucester, and were negotiating for the acquisitions of Rotton, Scholefield & Co., Birmingham, and C. Forster & Sons, Walsall.[70]

However, somewhat like the tensions that developed between Macardy and the directors of the two banks that he had promoted in Manchester during the late 1820s, Joplin was soon at odds with the board of the National Provincial. They were led by Sir Henry Parnell and included nine Members of Parliament and Edward Blount, a future force in Anglo-French finance. Joplin wanted the new bank to be a federation of separate companies, each having its own local shareholders coupled with a local board of directors, but this concept ultimately found no favour. It was finally abandoned by the National Provincial directors in spring 1835, which led Joplin to give up his 150 shares in the bank. Instead, the bank was shaped by Daniel Robertson, its general manager from 1835, who had previously been with the Commercial Bank of Scotland and the Glasgow Union Bank. By 1836, the National Provincial had forty branches and twenty-three sub-agencies in England and Wales, forming a unique nation-wide network outside of the Bank of England's protected metropolitan area. Some branches were managed by local boards but, in the case of others, there had been difficulties in finding suitable 'gentlemen of local influence, unconnected with business' and so their affairs were conducted solely on a day-to-day basis by a manager and an accountant. All these branches were inspected annually, while overall the bank was managed by a London board to whom branch managers had to refer all applications for 'cash credits', but retaining their own discretion over the amount of discounting undertaken for customers.[71]

One of the few criteria available by which to establish the early impact of the joint-stock banks is their share of the private bank-note circulation. During the closing months of 1833, it amounted to £1.3m, 13% of the total. Burgess, in the *Circular to Bankers*, saw this as evidence of only a limited incursion into the business of private bankers and also abstracted

£0.2m from the note issues of joint-stock banks on the grounds that this was accounted for by Stuckey's Bank in the West Country.[72] If this line of reasoning is followed, then the share of joint-stock banks 'proper' was only 11% during late 1833. However, note issues of commercial joint-stock banks had been restricted in practice by the 1826 Act. Directors of the Bank of Manchester had decided not to circulate notes since, under the legislation, they could not be payable in London. Furthermore, although the District Bank commenced business with issuing notes, its directors soon retired them because of the 'London problem'. In turn, the National Provincial was a joint-stock note-issuing bank but, in taking that approach, its directors were unable to open a London branch. However, one of the main planks of Joplin's arguments from 1822 for a joint-stock bank had been that it would mobilize the wealth of London for the business affairs of the provinces.

IV

The promotion of joint-stock banks gathered apace from spring 1833 and the rising speculation in their shares quickly led to concerns being expressed over the constitution and organization of the 'new' banking. This section considers such contemporary anxieties. It also reviews what proved to be the attempts to establish 'district' banks which proved to be largely abortive. This was most spectacularly shown by the mushroom rise and fall of the Northern & Central Bank over two years. Its failure in 1836, coupled with the subsequent collapses of the Commercial Bank of England and the Yorkshire District Bank, may have retarded the general development of widescale branch banking over the second quarter of the nineteenth century. Indeed, speculation in bank shares and the creation of 'district' banks went almost hand-in-hand and these features of the mid-1830s are explored in some detail through a case study of the foundation of the Wilts & Dorset bank.

Over the course of the mid-1830s boom, the rate of joint-stock-bank promotions quickened to ten a year, as opposed to four a year between 1826 and 1832, but only reached 'manic' proportions during 1836, when at least fifty-nine new banks were projected. It has been put forward that bank promoters' activities over 1836 were propelled by the prevailing low rates of interest and the excellent dividend records being established by existing banks (Thomas 1973: 13). Certainly, potential subscribers were lured by prospectuses which pointed to premiums on the prices of shares of banks in business, coupled with arising claims that those who supplied capital could expect to see it returned as dividends within three to four years. The continuing creation of joint-stock banks was considered to have a real foundation in the 'prosperity' of the textile manufacturing districts of Yorkshire and Lancashire, and of the Staffordshire and Worcestershire iron trade.[73] Nonetheless, by August 1835, some were sounding alarm bells. 'We find from advertisements in the country papers that the proprietary system of Joint-Stock Banks is being extended in a manner that appears to us exceedingly dangerous to their contributors and proprietors.'[74] The tocsin was finally rung in March 1836: 'that the prevalent speculation in new Banks and in Bank shares must lead to some catastrophe among those enterprizes appear to us inevitable'.[75] During that month, four new banks were proposed in Liverpool, two in Manchester and, over its closing week, the prospectuses of a further five were presented to the public. By then, all the characteristics of a bubble had developed, with issues being 'stagged'. Some bank shares, on which merely 1s. deposit had been paid, were being sold for 25s., while in other cases even the chances of allotment of shares were being traded. In this, bank shares had been caught up in the first 'mania' for railway shares (Reed 1975: esp. ch. 3).

Concerns over the ever-growing number of bank promotions, and their increasingly speculative character, were first expressed in November 1834. Directors of the Bank of Liverpool and the Bank of Manchester once again began, through a public meeting, to mount pressure upon the government to regulate more strictly new bank creations. They reformulated their 'Propositions' of 1832 through putting forward that banks should have minimum capitals of £50,000, while branches located further than 12 miles from head office ought to be constituted as separate companies and so also have minimum capitals of £50,000. In their view, banks required a minimum amount of capital before they commenced business, to be ensured partly through having share denominations of no less than £50.[76] However, the fever of the bank formation boom only began to abate from May 1836, once William Clay had successfully moved a motion in the House of Commons for a Select Committee to investigate the affairs and conduct of the new joint-stock banks. Clay was in favour of banks having limited liability and fully subscribed capitals, and being subject to full publicity of their affairs. Consequently, he wanted greater regulation than the 'Propositions'.[77]

Some of the new joint-stock banks had attempted to trim their sails from late 1835 through their directors taking a variety of measures. These involved calling up further capital,[78] or closing branches or merging. However, the sudden and spectacular collapse in mid-1836 of the Northern & Central, which with its rapid opening of thirty-six branches had been regarded as the 'boom bank', gave all the necessary grounds for Clay's parliamentary inquiry.[79]

Clay's Select Committee, established in 1836, sat until 1838 and soon found fault, largely arising from poor, inexperienced management and lack of equity capital but, on occasion, owing to fraudulent intent and other criminal behaviour. Its adverse criticisms were reiterated by a further Select Committee, which collected evidence between 1840 and 1841. The hearings and conclusions of these two Select Committees paved the way for Peel's Joint Stock Banking Act of 1844, and their minutes of evidence and arising reports have been mined by historians as a source for banking developments over the 1830s. Although the value of this material is not disputed, it has to be reiterated that only nineteen of the 141 joint-stock banks successfully formed under the 1826 Act had ceased business before the introduction of Peel's new banking code in 1844. That is a failure rate considerably less than that of either the private country banks in England and Wales or the Scottish provincial banking companies. More important than the joint-stock-bank crashes of the late 1830s were the 117 English and Welsh joint-stock banks still open for business in 1843. Their longevity can be accounted for by two factors which had been in operation from the passage of the 1826 Act.

One factor was the local nature of most of these successful banks, such as the Liverpool Commercial Bank and the Stourbridge & Kidderminster Banking Co., both formed in 1834, and which was displayed in their titles.[80] Unit banking had its dangers, especially 'insider lending' and through the institutions being closely tied to the vagaries of local business conditions. However, it could also capitalize upon bank directors' particular knowledge and understanding of local and regional economies and the customers that comprised them (Newton 1997; and, for the mid-century, 1996).

Locally based joint-stock banking was reinforced by the second factor – that a significant number of the new banks were conversions of former private country banks. Reports in the *Circular to Bankers* indicate that at least twenty-two joint-stock banks established during the mid-1830s continued in one way or another the previous businesses of private country bankers.[81] However, although much was made of a 'want of banking' during the mid-1830s as grounds for new bank creations, there is also contrary evidence. This was pointed up in April 1836, when the partners in J. W. & C. Rawson, Halifax, decided to convert their banking house into a joint-stock institution. There were within 8 miles of their office three other private banks and six joint-stock banks with branches, giving a total of fifteen competing banking outlets.[82] This is possibly an extreme case, coming as it does from the height of the banking 'mania', which had its epicentre in Lancashire and Yorkshire.[83]

Within the undoubted establishment of joint-stock banking during the

1830s, there was possibly one false, or precocious, start: branch banking over a considerable business catchment area. Contemporaries referred to this as 'district banking', and did not regard either the 'Scottish banks' or the National Provincial as the exemplars, but rather Macardy's creations – the Manchester & Liverpool District Bank of 1829 and the Northern & Central Bank of 1834. By the end of April 1836, there were at least seven other 'district' banks either in business or being promoted: the Commercial Bank of England (formed in 1834) with thirty branches, which had also been founded by Macardy; the Devon & Cornwall (1831); the East of England (1836, which developed out of the Norfolk & Norwich); the Northamptonshire Banking Co. (1836); the West of England & South Wales District Bank (1834); the Wilts & Dorset Banking Co. (1835); and the Yorkshire District Bank (1834) with twenty-five branches.[84] However, the Commercial Bank of England failed in 1840 and the Yorkshire District Bank collapsed in 1843. When coupled with the previous disastrous closure of the Northern & Central in 1836, these experiences gave branch banking, albeit primarily at a 'district' level, something of a bad name. Consequently, the National Provincial was left to be the major exponent of branch banking within England and Wales, and in its case nation-wide beyond London, until the mid-1860s.[85] Then, the directors of the National Provincial decided to forgo the profits that arose from a private note issue in order to open a fully operational London branch. In addition, the London & County Banking Co., a deposit bank established in 1836 under the declaratory clause in the renewed charter of the Bank of England, had pursued a policy of opening branches. These totalled thirty-six offices by 1844 and aided in supplying the bank's deposits which amounted to £1.23m. The policy of branching was reinvigorated by the board of the London & County during the mid-1860s, when the bank's deposits averaged £10.9m, but again, for the most part, this involved an expansion of its network within the Bank of England's protected metropolitan area. As a result, in 1874, the London & County and the National Provincial were the only two English banks that each had more than 100 offices – 149 and 138 respectively – which assisted the gathering of deposits, their principal liability, totalling £19.9m and £22.9 respectively.[86]

The Northern & Central's ultimately abortive attempt to become a nation-wide branch bank during the mid-1830s had initially been met with some acclaim. It was pointed out by disinterested commentators that its thirty-six branches in late 1834 enabled the bank not only to have a greater note issue but also to exploit other advantages which have come to be associated with branch banking. These were the ability to arrange money transfers without resorting to bills, and to balance internally transactions arising from taking deposits on the one hand and discounting on the other.[87] Instead, amongst those seeking to create 'district' banks during the mid-1830s, the promoters of the more humble, yet ultimately longer-lived, Wilts & Dorset Banking Co. received the greatest contemporary criticism.

The *Circular to Bankers* by August 1835 only saw justification for further joint-stock bank creations, of whatever 'kind', if at least one of three conditions was met. These were: rising economic activity within a district; that the existing banks there were either insecure or could 'not afford [their customers] proper accommodation'; and, lastly, that there had been locally a reduction in number of banking offices due to retirement, death or insolvency. In Burgess' view, none of these necessary factors was present within the rural counties of Wiltshire and Dorset. This region lacked mines, its traditional manufacturing trades were in decline and the total trade of its three seaports – Bridport, Poole and Weymouth – did not match collectively that of other minor harbours, such as either Boston in Lincolnshire or Whitby in the North Riding of Yorkshire. Furthermore, the only recent bank failures in south central England were those of Culburne & Co. at Sturminster and of 'a little bank' at Westbury and these financial voids had been made good through both Williams, Cox & Co. of Dorchester and Fry, Andrews of Wimborne opening branches in Sturminster. Burgess therefore concluded that there was no growth in 'safe or lucrative business' that justified the opening of a new bank and, consequently, he saw the Wilts & Dorset as a speculative vehicle of Manchester bank promoters.[88] He provided further evidence for this seven months later, at the boom's peak, in Wilts & Dorset shares being sold at 50*s*. premium in Lancashire, whereas they were trading within Wiltshire at only 30*s*. premium.[89]

The Wilts & Dorset was established in the market town of Salisbury in 1835 and certainly was a 'district' bank, having twenty-four branches within a year of its creation. In some respects, it was part of the 'series' of 'district' bank promotions that took place during the mid-1830s since the organizer of its provisional committee was W. Campbell Gillan, who during 1834 had been the Secretary of the West of England & South Wales District Bank. He was supported by J. W. Gilbart, manager of London & Westminster, who thereby obtained the London agency of the Wilts & Dorset for his own institution. Although Gillan took no shares in the Wilts & Dorset, Gilbart subscribed for fifty. Furthermore, there are indications that Gilbart's connections with the embryonic Wilts & Dorset not only stemmed from his seeking to expand his own metropolitan bank's list of country correspondents but also arose from family connections within Wiltshire.[90]

Although there is no evidence supporting this bank being a Manchester

Table 4.2 *Geographical sources of initial subscriptions to the shares of the Wilts & Dorset Banking Company, 1835.*

Location of shareholders by county, city or country	Total share subscriptions by location (£)	Percentage of aggregate subscriptions (%)
Wiltshire	18,704	27.76
Lancashire	13,000	19.29
Dorset	8,336	12.37
Cumberland	5,432	8.06
Yorkshire	5,272	7.82
Somerset	4,208	6.25
Westmorland	2,960	4.39
Devon	1,672	2.48
London	1,480	2.20
Hampshire	1,432	2.13
Gloucestershire	1,120	1.66
Staffordshire	1,040	1.54
Unknown	880	1.31
Rutland	600	0.89
Ireland	520	0.77
Derbyshire	320	0.47
Scotland	160	0.24
Warwickshire	160	0.24
Cornwall	80	0.12

Source: Lloyds Bank Archive, London: Book Number 3174, Wilts & Dorset Banking Co., deed of settlement, 1835; and Book Number 3177, Shareholders Register (1835).

promotion, Burgess may have had a point in the extent of extra-regional involvement in its creation. Initially, the Wilts & Dorset had about 400 shareholders (Sayers 1957: 18–19, 91–2, 113, 339) and, as Table 4.2 shows, nearly 20% of the bank's initial capital was supplied by Lancashire subscribers. Indeed, Lancashire was the second most important county after Wiltshire in terms of the location of the residencies given by the bank's first shareholders. However, this has to be set against 53% of the paid-up capital that came from Dorset and Wiltshire and adjacent rural counties (Devon, Gloucestershire, Hampshire and Somerset). Although few stockbrokers and comparable financial professionals either signed the bank's deed of settlement or featured in its first share register – only some six, collectively holding sixty shares – what is striking is the twenty-nine bankers (including Gilbart) who held in total 1,215 shares and were resident throughout England and Ireland. Furthermore, prominent among these banker shareholders were directors and employees of the Bank of Lancaster, the Liverpool Union Bank, the Manchester & Liverpool

District Bank, the Northern & Central Bank and the Tidsley Bank (Bolton), indicating either founding support or a speculative interest from Lancashire and in particular its 'district' banks.[91] Burgess' strictures are given even greater force by the almost total absence of a significant Lancashire interest in the Wilts & Dorset nearly two decades after its successful establishment. In 1853, Lancashire residents accounted for only 1% of the bank's capital, whereas shareholders in Dorset and Wiltshire held 74%, rising to 95% when those living in the adjacent counties of Devon, Gloucestershire, Hampshire and Somerset are included.[92] Over the intervening decades, the Lancashire interest had totally receded and the bank had come to be almost entirely locally owned.

The collapse of *the* 'district' bank – the Northern & Central – in mid-1836 was one of the first domestic indications of an imminent financial and monetary crisis. Nevertheless, a domestic drain of gold, from London to the provinces, only developed from July when it joined an external outflow that had been mounting over the first half of the year. Bank rate was increased on 21 July and again on 1 September and the arising pressure in the London money market brought those seeking discounts to the Bank of England. Primarily, the difficulties centred upon the Anglo-American cotton trade and this became plain during the early months of 1837, shown especially by the failure of three Anglo-American houses – the 'three "Ws"' (Clapham 1944b[1970]: 156–9; Lévy-Leboyer 1982; Chapman 1996). However, the undue expansion of credit in the trans-Atlantic trades had also been contributed to by the new joint-stock banks, particularly those established in Liverpool (Collins 1972b: 97–8, 104, 134) and Manchester. Yet, apart from the Northern & Central, which had attempted to become a national institution, only three north-western banks failed between 1836 and 1843: the misnamed Liverpool Phoenix in 1838 within a year of its establishment, the Central Bank of Liverpool in 1839 and the mighty Bank of Manchester in 1842. Furthermore, the collapse of the Bank of Manchester was not directly attributable to the 1836/7 'cotton crisis' but, rather, arose from its directors' abject failure after 1836 to manage their institution. This resulted in their subsequently finding that their 'confidence had been abused – that unwatched servants had gone astray – that capital was lost – reserves spent – and an amount of liability incurred vastly beyond the power of the assets to extinguish' (Thomas 1934: 669–70).

V

What was the initial impact of the liberalization of banking in 1826? This concluding section considers this question in terms of: the secondary securities market; the spread of the 'banking habit'; inter-regional flows of credit; the Bank of England's attempt to police the 'new' banks; and the quality of bank management.

The passage of the 1826 Act led over the following two decades to the successful establishment of 117 joint-stock banks, of which probably at least a fifth arose from the conversion of existing private banks. As was to be the case in Continental Europe from the 1850s, the relaxation of English legislation affecting the creation of banks brought about in part the institutionalization of private banking. However, the late 1820s and early 1830s in England and Wales were marked by something of a conflict between the 'old' and the 'new' bank, especially in the rural, southern shires and above all within London. Nevertheless, it soon proved to be an unequal struggle and, whereas there had probably been something approaching 600 private country banks in England and Wales during the late 1820s, by 1844 their numbers had fallen to 273. Yet in London, although the five joint-stock banks established after 1833 were individually substantial institutions so that by 1844, collectively, they held deposits totalling £7.9m, during that year there were still sixty-three private banks in the 'City' and the 'West End' with, in aggregate, deposits of about £27m (Crick and Wadsworth 1936[1958]: 22).

The creation of joint-stock banks also played a part in the evolution of a secondary market in corporate securities. By 1836, for instance, the shares of fifteen banks were quoted on the developing Liverpool stock exchange, of which two were extra-regional, 'district' institutions: the Wilts & Dorset and the East of England. Other Liverpool and Manchester stockbrokers, apart from Macardy, acted as agents for the new banks by receiving applications for their shares. Moreover, most of the new banks had nominal capitals of £0.2m divided into £10 or £5 shares, unlike the first railway companies which initially used £100 shares, and then £50 or £20 shares. Consequently, bank shares were more accessible to 'smaller' savers, particularly as the deposits required upon them were frequently very low. This practice widened the market and dealings in bank shares were further assisted through the ease given by their denominations in making up marketable lots (Thomas 1973: 13–17).

However, the wider attractions of bank shares diminished after the 1836 crisis, so that the number quoted on the Liverpool market fell to eight in 1847 and to nine in 1860 (Anderson and Cottrell 1975: 599), just prior to the next major wave of joint-stock-bank promotions. Bank shares during the 1840s were replaced by a mania for railway shares which led to a contraction in the geographical dispersion of bank holdings. As was pointed out above, the Lancashire interest in the Wilts & Dorset Bank had almost disappeared by the mid-1850s. In the case of the Liverpool Commercial Bank, formed in 1833, by 1861 61.7% of its shares were in the hands of residents of Lancashire and Cheshire and the only significant extra-regional interest in its equity, amounting to 15.3%, came from London and the Home Counties (Anderson and Cottrell 1975: 612). In this, there was a return after the mania of 1836 to the local and regional bases of these banks. Consequently, the bank promotions of the mid-1830s, and above all of 1836, constitute a further episode in a continuing series of 'manias' which, through boom and bust, led slowly to the development of a national corporate securities market. These speculative splurges had begun, since the onset of marked industrialization, with the canal 'mania' of the 1790s and continued with the railway 'mania' of the 1840s. Bank shares of both home and overseas institutions, together with those of other financial ventures, were to feature again as *the* boom securities during the mid-1860s.

The London joint-stock deposit banks, established from 1833, deliberately tried to attract the custom of the growing middle classes, through, for instance, paying interest on deposits. Yet, given the number of private country banks in existence during the 1830s, it is difficult to see how the provincial joint-stock banks might have further spread the 'banking habit'. However, Henry Burgess claimed that, in 1810, there had been no banks in Blackburn, Bolton, Bury, Oldham, Rochdale or Stockport. As a result, residents of these Cheshire and Lancashire towns had been forced either to discount bills with local shopkeepers or to take their banking business some very considerable distance, to Manchester, or Kendal in the Lake District, or Nottingham in the East Midlands. In this, he saw justification at least for the formation of the Bank of Manchester, but he was more caustic about the subsequent promotion of the Manchester & Liverpool District Bank.[93]

This was a theme to which Burgess returned on a number of occasions and, when his remarks are brought together, it becomes clear that his prime concern was with the changes that had come about in regional cash and credit transfers. As he put in August 1835:

Men, we believe, are still living who carried on business in parts of the country lying north of the mail-road from Liverpool to Hull, who kept their banking accounts in Nottingham; they resorted to a distance of more than seventy miles for supplies of cash and also, probably because they found it more convenient to pass their pecuniary transactions relating to their foreign trade through a bank at that place. Perhaps no bank at Liverpool and Manchester could so promptly and effectually manage such business – not having any resident partner in London.[94]

In this way Smiths Bank at Nottingham, together with Gurneys of Norwich in East Anglia, had risen in importance from the 1780s as private provincial bankers with London connections. By 1750, Smiths at Nottingham held the accounts of customers beyond the town and county in Cheshire, Derbyshire, Leicestershire, Lincolnshire and Warwickshire, but only three resident in Yorkshire and only one possibly north of the 'mail-road'. This would have been a beginning of the type of business to which Burgess was referring, but to go further – to examine in detail the highlighted decades after 1780 – is not feasible with currently available material (Leighton-Boyce 1958: 40–2). However, in 1760, Thomas & John Tipping, a major Manchester cotton merchanting firm, was forced to discount with Smiths at Nottingham, leading to return flows of £2,000 in bullion at a time, brought by a carrier's cart. Moreover, seventy years later, many Manchester manufacturers still banked at Kendal, 70 miles to the north of the centre of the Lancashire cotton industry (Chapman 1979: 51, 57).

This situation Burgess contrasted with developments during the 1830s: 'Whatever else may be said of the new system of Joint Stock Banking, it has accomplished this good purpose, viz. that of drawing capital from the centre where it was too abundant and cheap, and distributing it in distant parts of the country where it was urgently wanted for beneficial purposes.'[95] What was at the forefront of his mind was the extensive use that the new joint-stock banks, located in industrial districts and regions, made of rediscounting bills on the London money market in order to sustain their liquidity. It was what Joplin had envisaged but without the costly intermediation of London corresponding banks, bill brokers and discount houses. Nonetheless, the evolving pattern of money and credit transfers through the balancing mechanism of Lombard Street was far from linear, or clear to discern.[96]

During the late 1820s, Lancashire was a known 'bill', as opposed to a 'bank-note', area with, consequently, bankers there converting large bills – over £2,000 – into smaller ones because of the lack of cash. However, it was put forward that Lancashire was sending up during the closing years of the 1820s 'more cash . . . to London than any other county . . . except Norfolk'.[97] With regard to rediscounting, Burgess maintained that this had been prevalent during the French and Napoleonic wars because the government had been 'the great cormorant customer for all accumulating money'. Consequently, London bankers had had to resort to the Bank of England whilst country bankers had turned to either bill brokers or their London correspondents. Burgess considered that rediscounting in London had a lesser volume at the peak of the 1830s boom than during the French wars, with the practice having fallen away for some time over the 1820s. Consequently, like many others, he came eventually to consider the business of the joint-stock banks, through being avid London rediscounters of bills during the mid-1830s, both 'new and dangerous circumstances', while it was also put forward that their activities were more akin to bill broking than banking. Again, in common with fellow critics, he maintained that joint-stock banks were being enabled, through rediscounting in the London money market, to 'force' credit, for which the remedy was that they should have greater equity capitals. This stricture applied particularly to the joint-stock banks in manufacturing districts, where even a doubling of their subscribed capitals was thought to be insufficient. On the other hand, joint-stock banks in agricultural counties, which had unmobilized deposits – 'an excess of money' – probably were over-capitalized.[98]

This situation could have been remedied to a degree if the 1826 and 1833 legislation had allowed the full development of note-issuing branch banks with operational offices in London. Even Burgess had seen the advantages that might have come about for money and credit transfers with the growth of the Northern & Central's extensive branch network, but that was abruptly halted by this bank's collapse caused by rank mismanagement of its affairs. Instead, the provincial joint-stock banks took the London correspondent system, initially developed by the private country banks, on to a further stage. This was further facilitated by the legislation of 1833, as the partial repeal of the Usury Laws brought about the development of the discount-houses as principals in the London money market – Lombard Street. Discounting in London doubled between 1832 and 1836, an expansion largely accounted for by the activities of the joint-stock banks. By adding their names to bills, these banks enabled this paper to be rediscounted on the London money market whereas, previously, City bill brokers would not have considered a proportion of these bills to be endorsable (King 1936 [1972]: 42–7).

Discounting was one means by which the joint-stock banks were able to get their notes into circulation and, over the first quarter of 1837, they accounted for 34% of the private note issue that totalled £11m. Some control of this situation had been attempted by the Bank of England, at the government's behest, through what came to be called the '3% discount accounts'. The first was offered to the Birmingham Banking Co. in November 1833, involving a minimum facility of £150,000 and a maximum of £200,000. They had developed from an initiative begun in 1829, allowing banks discount facilities with the Bank's branches at 1% below the public rate provided they circulated Bank of England notes in place of their own. From 1833, the Bank's provincial agents were required to gain information from such banks that would allow an assessment of the quality of the bills tendered for discount under these special arrangements.

With this approach, the Bank's agents at its various branches canvassed every new joint-stock bank as it was promoted. It soon proved the case that the Bank's provision of loans at the times of the quarterly tax collections was the most attractive feature of these accounts to prospective joint-stock-bank customers, as opposed to either circulating the Bank's notes or the assurance the accounts offered against the potential dangers of a run. Moreover, the government's decision to widen the Bank's role as the collector of the land and assessed taxes played a part in their take-up. Provincial joint-stock banks that continued to issue their own notes had to arrange pro contra balances, comprising 'good' bills or gold or the Bank's notes, in order to have tax payments made in their own notes accepted.

In practice, the Bank's control aspect of these accounts played second fiddle to its directors seeking new sources of profits, especially when the Bank had unmobilized resources. During the mid-1830s, these arose from the balances of the East India Company and the proceeds of the West Indian Slave Emancipation loan. Pressures arising from the Bank's own business position worked in conjunction with the difficulties that its provincial agents found when trying to establish the soundness of the institutions that they approached. Moreover bankers, both private and joint-stock, reckoned that their note issues contributed 2.5 to 3% to profits and, accordingly, attempted to reduce the Bank's 'special' discount rate to $2^1/_2$% for bills which they had discounted at 5%.

Over the mid-1830s boom, the Bank's discounting at its provincial branches nearly quadrupled, rising from £7.2m to £24.7m, and, of the latter figure, 85% was accounted for by bills presented by bankers during 1836. Yet, ultimately, this had not led to either the Bank's control of discounting in the provinces or a measurable tempering of the provincial private note issue. When monetary pressure developed during the autumn of 1836, the Bank's provincial agents, despite earlier warnings from Threadneedle Street, were forced to discount freely. They had no other choice since their banker clients with the 'special' facilities invoked the maximum provisions in their discount arrangements with the Bank's branches, while to have refused assistance would have led to a crisis on the scale of that of the previous decade.[99]

Discounting and rediscounting, either with the Bank's provincial branches or on the London money market, were to prove to be a continuing threat to stability until the early 1870s. Yet, over the 1820s and 1830s, this activity constituted one mechanism by which the amount of capital invested, at least in the north-western cotton industry, was expanded. During the 1820s, before the advent of the joint-stock banks, a significant number of mills in Manchester were financed either by bills 'in dead advance', or, and more rarely, by 'a dead loan upon the mortgage of a building' (Farnie 1953: 436). Poorly secured credits supplied by the new joint-stock banks proliferated in south Lancashire during the easy-money years of the mid-1830s as they competed against the seven established private banks in Manchester and amongst themselves. Consequently, during the late 1830s, the District Bank had bad debts of over £0.5m owed by nine firms, while the so-called assets of the Bank of Manchester and the Northern & Central were of comparable quality or worse. This was evidence of the borrower's advantage during very particular years – the mid-1830s boom – when, over the half-century from 1790, the Lancashire cotton industry exceptionally experienced an ease in credit conditions (Chapman 1979: 56–8, 59–60, 66–7).

The bad debt evidence points to the poor management of some of the joint-stock banks, together with the rising expectations generated by the upswing of the 1830s boom. There were constraints of the availability, and the quality, of human capital for the growth of joint-stock banking over the decade and a half after 1826. This was partially ameliorated by many of the 'new' banks being conversions of existing private banks, or employing clerks of private banks as managers, or, as in the cases of the London & Westminster and the National Provincial, the new banks taking as managers those who had prior Irish or Scottish experience – Gilbart and Robertson. The problem of the quality of bank staff was not to be addressed until the creation of the Institute of Bankers in 1879 aided the professionalization of banking, despite a recognition of this need from the early 1840s (Green 1979).

The quality of bank managements constituted a significant difficulty which, by and large, legislation, within a mid-nineteenth-century mindset, could not address. Instead, Peel, in 1844, conscious of the need to attempt once more to resolve the problems of banking instability, turned to a line of argument that had begun with the 'Propositions' of the Bank of Liverpool and the Bank of Manchester, first put forward in 1832. Consequently, his banking regulation code dealt with the registration of *new* banking companies and laid down minimum subscribed equity capitals, minimum share values, etc. Because it was concerned only with new joint-stock banks, the 117 already in existence were unaffected; twenty-five of these failed before the formation of joint-stock banks began to be liberalized yet again from 1857. However, Peel's 1844 code was regarded as so draconian by bank promoters that only twelve new joint-stock banks were established during the thirteen years it was on the statute book, three of which were concerned with international banking. This effectively gave existing domestic joint-stock banks quasi-monopoly positions, especially as the number of private banks declined from 273 to 157 over these years, and this was reflected in their dividend levels during the mid-century.

NOTES

1 This chapter draws upon some of the findings of a Leverhulme Trust-funded project, 'The Constituencies of English and Welsh Joint Stock Banks, 1825 to c. 1885'. We are grateful for the support so generously provided, and also for the valuable assistance of all the archivists who have so willingly given of their time and informed guidance: John Booker (Lloyds Bank); Edwin Green and Sara Kinsey (Midland Bank); Fiona McColl and Susan Snell (National Westminster Bank); and Alison Turton and Philip Winterbottom (Royal Bank of Scotland). We are equally in the debt of Edwin Green for reading an early draft, of Fiona McColl for assisting in resolving some queries, and of the editors for their patience and critiques.

2 There is still only one major institutional history of long-standing: Gregory 1936.

3 Clapham 1944b [1970]: 51–2; Fetter 1965: 57, 65–83. This decision was forced by what had become a perennial silver supply problem, which had led to the increasing importation of French coin over previous years. For background, see Ashton 1955 [1964]: 167, 168–9, 170–2. The decision of 1816 was in accordance with the recommendations of the Privy Council Committee on Coin of 1798, and in particular of Charles Jackson, first earl of Liverpool, who had put forward that the gold standard should be adopted, coupled with a fiduciary issue of silver coin.

4 See, in general, Checkland 1983; and esp. pp. 20–3 with respect to money and banking.

5 For the growth of banking before the 'Financial Revolution', see Kerridge 1988.

6 7 Anne c.30, Sect. 66. See Clapham 1944a [1970]: 58–65.

7 For the origins of the Bank, see Horsefield 1960; and, with regard to the 'fiscal-military state', Dickson 1967; Brewer 1983 and Bowen 1995.

8 For authoritative overviews and analyses of this development, see Pressnell 1956 and Cameron 1967. The most recent, and informed, synthesis is Collins 1988.

9 Continued borrowing from the Bank (and other sources of funds) arose from the government's defeat in 1816 over a two-year extension of the property tax. In spring 1818 the Bank sought repayment of previous advances before being prepared to renew Exchequer bills and, a year later, would not consider resumption unless £10m was repaid. For its part, the Bank had been preparing for resumption in May 1816, which the Governor stated to the House. Certainly there is evidence of this in December 1816 when the Bank's measures were assisted by favourable exchanges and sovereigns were once more being minted. Nonetheless, by early 1819, the Bank was maintaining that considerably more time was required, an attitude possibly shaped by the experience from August 1817 of continually falling bullion holdings. Furthermore, when the postponing legislation of 1818 expired, the Bank anticipated that the exchanges would be unfavourable in March 1820 and so urged the government to mount an inquiry into resumption in order to inform the public. Before the arising parliamentary committees of 1819 were convened, the Chancellor of the Exchequer argued in April 1819 for continued

restriction because of the monetary impact of proposed foreign loans. See Clapham 1944b: 62, 64; Fetter 1965: 82–5; Hilton 1977: 31–6.

10 Attwood and Joplin were also involved in the creation of the Imperial Continental Gas Association; see Hill 1950: 1–6.

11 There were about a further 250 country banks that did not issue their own notes, located especially in Liverpool and Manchester; see Clapham 1944b: 90–1.

12 *Circular to Bankers*, 90 (9 Apr. 1830).

13 On Robinson's minor role, see Jones 1967: 113–17.

14 7 Geo. IV c. 26. See Hilton 1977:221–2.

15 7 Geo. IV c. 46.

16 For a further assessment, see Munn 1988.

17 On its development, see Gregory 1936, I: 238–300; II: 118–19, 128–35.

18 For the history of the County of Gloucester Bank, see Sayers 1957: 18, 65, 75, 77, 149, 162, 172, 187, 188, 208, 210–12, 221, 229, 235, 243, 265, 280.

19 B.P.P. (1830), Select Committee on Manufactures, Commerce and Shipping. For the change in contemporaries' perception of economic conditions see various issues of the *Circular to Bankers*, a weekly, during March and April 1833. For a historian's analysis, see Matthews 1954.

20 *Circular to Bankers*, 262 (26 Jul. 1833).

21 *Circular to Bankers*, 386 (11 Dec. 1835).

22 *Circular to Bankers*, 92 (23 Apr. 1830).

23 *Circular to Bankers*, 86 (12 Mar. 1830).

24 *Circular to Bankers*, 197 (27 Apr. 1832); 260 (12 Jul. 1833); for the publication of Horsley Palmer's circular see *The Courtier* (29 May 1827).

25 On parliamentary pressure see *Circular to Bankers*, 262 (26 Jul. 1833); 263 (2 Aug. 1833).

26 3 & 4 Will. IV c. 98, Ss. 2, 3. On the bills question, see Gilbart 1828:61.

27 *Circular to Bankers*, 255 (7 Jun. 1833).

28 *Circular to Bankers*, 269 (13 Sep. 1833).

29 *Circular to Bankers*, 293 (28 Feb. 1834); 294 (6 Mar. 1834).

30 *Circular to Bankers*, 88 (26 Mar. 1830).

31 *Circular to Bankers*, 3 (8 Aug. 1828).

32 *Circular to Bankers*, 1 (25 Jul. 1828).

33 *Circular to Bankers*, 10 (21 Nov. 1828).

34 Midland Bank, Archive, London [henceforth MBA]: G5, Cumberland Union Bank, Minutes of the Board of Directors, 9 Jul. 1829.

35 MBA: B1, Bradford Banking Company, Deed of Settlement, 1 Jun. 1827.

36 MBA: G5, 21 Jan. 1830.

37 MBA: G5, 12 Mar. 1829.

38 MBA: Bradford Banking Co., Minutes of the Board of Directors, Order Book No. 1, 21 Jun. 1827.

39 *Circular to Bankers*, 25 (9 Jan. 1829).

40 *Circular to Bankers*, 55 (7 Aug. 1829). On the development of Stuckey's Bank, see Saunders 1928; and, for a biographical sketch of Vincent Stuckey, see Gregory 1936, II: 144–57.

41 *Circular to Bankers*, 413 (17 Jun. 1836).

42 *Circular to Bankers*, 299 (11 Apr. 1834). For the growth of banking in Bristol, see Ollerenshaw 1988.

43 *Circular to Bankers*, 7 (5 Sep. 1828).

44 *Circular to Bankers*, 88 (26 Mar. 1830).

45 *Circular to Bankers*, 196 (20 Apr. 1832).

46 MBA: Bradford Banking Company, Minutes of Board of Directors, Order Book No. 1, 6 Sep. 1827. See also 13 Sep. 1827.

47 *Ibid.*, 14 Feb. 1828; see also 6 Mar. 1828 with respect to Brancker, Brown & Co. of Leeds.

48 *Circular to Bankers*, 17 (14 Nov. 1828). See also National Westminster Bank, London, Archives: 12084, The Lancaster Bank, Deed of Partnership, 1 Feb. 1826.

49 *Circular to Bankers*, 102 (2 Jul. 1830).

50 *Circular to Bankers*, 32 (27 Feb. 1829); and Crick and Wadsworth 1936[1958]: 249.

51 *Circular to Bankers*, 17 (14 Nov. 1828). See also Gregory 1936:22.

52 *Circular to Bankers*, 233 (4 Jan. 1833).

53 Lloyds Bank, Archive, London [hereafter LBA]: Book No. 5354, Halifax Joint Stock Banking Co. [subsequently West Yorkshire Bank], Deed of Settlement, 25 Nov. 1829.

54 MBA: Barnsley Joint Stock Banking Co., Reports of Annual Meetings, 28 Nov. 1831.

55 MBA: H 24, Huddersfield Banking Company, Share Register and Transfer Book. On the Huddersfield Banking Co., see Crick and Wadsworth 1936[1958]: 203, 204; Collins and Hudson 1979; Hudson 1981; 1986.

56 MBA: Hull Banking Co., Proprietor's Ledger, No. 1. On the Hull Banking Co., see Crick and Wadsworth 1936[1958]: 209–11.

57 MBA: A12, Barnsley Banking Co., Proceedings and order of the directors, 28 Feb. 1832, f.11. See also Newton 1997.

58 MBA: B1, Bradford Banking Co., Deed of Settlement, 1 Jun. 1827.

59 MBA: Bradford Banking Co., Minutes of the Board of Directors, Order Book No. 1, 12 Jul. 1827, with reference to William Davison and Mr Kirk, who had each applied for five shares.

60 *Ibid.*, for example, 26 Jul. 1827 with respect to Jonathan Anderton, Swithin Anderton and Thomas Milthorp; and 6 Sep. 1827, Joseph Hobson, who was refused a further ten shares.

61 *Circular to Bankers*, 10 (21 Nov. 1828); 319 (29 Aug. 1834); 333 (5 Dec. 1834). See also Thomas 1934: 88, 126, 133–4; Stuart-Jones 1975; 1978.

62 *Circular to Bankers*, 294 (6 Mar. 1834); 333 (5 Dec. 1834); Jones 1971; 1978; Reed 1983:5–6.

63 *Circular to Bankers*, 17 (14 Nov. 1828); 30 (13 Feb. 1829); 31 (20 Feb. 1829).

64 *Circular to Bankers*, 55 (7 Aug. 1829).

65 *Circular to Bankers*, 86 (12 Mar. 1830). Knatchbull was MP for Kent in 1830, and from 1832 until 1845 sat for East Kent. He opposed corn-law repeal and Irish emancipation, and declined a post in Grey's administration. Like Knatchbull, Liddell opposed reform but Joplin's connection with him may have stemmed more from him being the Member for Northumberland and,

subsequently (1837–47), for North Durham. Spring Rice was the MP for Limerick and thereafter for Cambridge until 1839, when he was ennobled. He was a somewhat different politician from others in Joplin's backing group, having been Under-Secretary for the Home Department from 1827, and as such had initiated the reform of the Irish administration. Spring Rice did join Grey's administration as Secretary to the Treasury and subsequently (1835–9) was Chancellor of the Exchequer. He introduced the 'penny post'.

66 *Circular to Bankers*, 91 (16 Apr. 1830) reprinting from the *Salisbury and Winchester Journal* (12 Apr. 1830).

67 *Circular to Bankers*, 98 (4 Jun. 1830).

68 *Circular to Bankers*, 136 (25 Feb. 1831); 137 (4 Mar. 1831).

69 Angas was also associated with the Bank of South Australia and the Union Bank of Australia. See Hodder 1891.

70 *Circular to Bankers*, 250 (3 May 1833); 265 (16 Aug. 1833); 283 (20 Dec. 1833). On private banking in Birmingham, see Moss 1982.

71 See the evidence of D. Robertson to the Select Committee on Joint Stock Banks (1836). Withers 1933: 17, 35, 44, 49–50, 56; and Reed 1983: 10–11.

72 *Circular to Bankers*, 299 (11 Apr. 1834).

73 *Circular to Bankers*, 386 (11 Nov. 1835).

74 *Circular to Bankers*, 370 (21 Aug. 1835).

75 *Circular to Bankers*, 399 (11 Mar. 1836).

76 *Circular to Bankers*, 333 (5 Dec. 1834).

77 *Circular to Bankers*, 407 (6 May 1836). Clay was the liberal Member for Tower Hamlets from 1832 and held the seat until 1857. The son of an eminent London merchant, he became the Chairman of the Grand Junction Railway, and of the Southwark and Vauxhall water companies.

78 *Circular to Bankers*, 386, (11 Dec. 1835); 415 (1 Jul. 1836).

79 *Circular to Bankers*, 289 (31 Jan. 1834); 291 (14 Feb. 1834); 319 (29 Aug. 1834); and Jones 1971.

80 *Circular to Bankers*, 291 (14 Feb. 1834). On the Liverpool Commercial, see Chandler 1968: 230, 232, 237, 238, 493; and Anderson and Cottrell 1975. For the Stourbridge & Kidderminster, see Crick and Wadsworth 1936[1958]: 59 *et seq.*

81 E.g. *Circular to Bankers*, 334 (12 Dec. 1834); 406 (29 Apr. 1836); and 416 (8 Jul. 1836).

82 *Circular to Bankers*, 406 (29 Apr. 1836).

83 *Circular to Bankers*, 407 (6 May 1836).

84 *Circular to Bankers*, 406 (29 Apr. 1836); 407 (6 May 1836). The Devon & Cornwall was based upon the past business of Higston & Prideaux, Plymouth, whereas the Norfolk & Norwich had been the conversion of Bignold's Bank at Norwich. The Yorkshire District arose in part from the conversion of Perfects & Co., Leeds (12 Dec. 1834). For the Devon & Cornwall, see Sayers 1957: 17, 66, 68, 73, 76, 114, 123, 129, 136, 147, 153, 181, 223, 228–30, 235, 243, 265, 282, 342, 352; for the Northamptonshire Bank, see Sayers 1957: 21, 55, 174, 285, 351; for the Wilts & Dorset, see pp. 100–2.

85 The other major exceptions were joint-stock banks in Wales, such as the Glamorganshire Banking Co., the Monmouthshire & Glamorganshire Banking Co. and, above all, the North & South Wales Bank. On the general

reluctance of English joint-stock banks to develop extensive branch banking before the 1880s, see Munn 1997.

86 Crick and Wadsworth 1936[1958]: 36–7: Nishimura 1971: Table 2, p. 84. National Westminster Bank, Archive, London: 10043, London & County Bank, annual reports and balance-sheets, 30 Jun. 1865, 31 Dec. 1874; 12240, National Provincial Bank of England, annual report and balance-sheet, 31 Dec. 1874.

87 *Circular to Bankers*, 334 (12 Dec. 1834).

88 *Circular to Bankers*, 370 (21 Aug. 1835).

89 *Circular to Bankers*, 399 (11 Mar. 1836).

90 LBA: Book Number 3177, Wilts & Dorset Banking Co., Shareholders Register (1835) contains the following entries: Anne Gilbart, spinster, 10 shares; Jane Gilbart, spinster, 10 shares; Joseph Gilbart, jnr., gentleman, 10 shares; all of whom were resident in Puckshipton nr. Devizes, Wilts.; together with Thomas Gilbart, Marden nr. Devizes, farmer, 10 shares and William Gilbart, Milton Pewsey, Wilts., farmer, 30 shares.

91 LBA: 3174, Wilts & Dorset Banking Co., deed of settlement, 1835; and Book Number 3177, Shareholders Register (1835).

92 Calculated from LBA: Book Number 3177, Shareholders Register (1853).

93 *Circular to Bankers*, 333 (5 Dec. 1834).

94 *Circular to Bankers*, 370 (21 Aug. 1835).

95 *Circular to Bankers*, 355 (8 May 1835).

96 For recent attempts to establish flows, see Black 1989; 1995.

97 *Circular to Bankers*, 8 (12 Sep. 1828). See also Ashton 1953; Checkland 1954; Collins 1972a.

98 *Circular to Bankers*, 415 (1 Jul. 1836).

99 The previous four paragraphs have been drawn from Moss 1995.

BIBLIOGRAPHY

Anderson, B. L., and Cottrell, P. L. 1975. 'Another Victorian Capital Market: A Study of Banking and Bank Investors on Merseyside', *Economic History Review*, 2nd ser., 28: 598–615.

Andréadès, A. 1924. *History of the Bank of England*. London.

Ashton, T. S. 1953. 'The Bill of Exchange and Private Banks in Lancashire, 1790–1830', in T. S. Ashton and R. S. Sayers (eds.), *Papers in Monetary History*, pp. 37–49. Oxford.

   1955. *An Economic History of England: The 18th Century*. London (rep. 1964).

Barrow, G. L. 1975. *The Emergence of the Irish Banking System. 1820–1845*. Dublin.

Black, I. S. 1989. 'Geography, Political Economy and the Circulation of Capital in Early Industrial England', *Journal of Historical Geography* 15:366–84.

   1995. 'Money, Information and Space: Banking in Early-Nineteenth-Century England and Wales', *Journal of Historical Geography* 21: 398–412.

Bowen, H. V. 1995. 'The Bank of England during the Long Eighteenth Century', in R. Roberts and D. Kynaston (eds.), *The Bank of England: Money, Power and Influence 1694–1994*, pp. 1–18. Oxford.

Brewer, J. 1983. *Sinews of Power: Money and the English State 1688–1783*. London.

B[ritish] P[arliamentary] P[apers] 1830. Select Committee on Manufactures, Commerce and Shipping.

Brock, M. 1973. *The Great Reform Act*. London.

Cameron, R. 1967. 'England 1750–1844', in R. Cameron (ed.), *Banking in the Early Stages of Industrialization*, pp. 15–59. Oxford and New York.

1970. 'Banking and Credit as Factors in Economic Growth'. Moscow (mimeo, Vth International Congress of Economic History, Leningrad). 23pp.

Chandler, G. 1968. *Four Centuries of Banking*, vol. II, *The Northern Constituent Banks*. London.

Chapman, S. D. 1979. 'Financial Restraints on the Growth of Firms in the Cotton Industry 1790–1850', *Economic History Review*, 2nd ser., 32: 50–69.

1996. 'The Fielden Fortune. The Finances of Lancashire's Most Successful Ante-Bellum Manufacturing Family', *Financial History Review* 3:7–28.

Checkland, S. 1954. 'The Lancashire Bill System and Its Liverpool Protagonists, 1810–27', *Economica*, n.s. 21: 129–42.

1975. *Scottish Banking: A History*. Glasgow.

1983. *British Public Policy 1776–1939*. Cambridge.

Clapham, Sir John. 1944a. *The Bank of England. A History*, vol. I, *1694–1797*. Cambridge (rep. 1970).

1994b. *The Bank of England. A History*, vol. II, *1797–1914*. Cambridge (rep. 1970).

Clayton, G. L. 1962. 'Denmark', in Sayers 1962b: 53–123.

Collins, M. 1972a. 'The Bank of England at Liverpool, 1827–1844', *Business History* 14: 144–59.

1972b. 'The Bank of England and the Liverpool Money Market 1825–1850', unpublished Ph.D. thesis, University of London.

1988. *Money and Banking in the UK: A History*. London and New York.

Collins, M. and Hudson, P. 1979. 'Provincial Bank Lending: Yorkshire and Lancashire, 1826–1860', *Bulletin of Economic Research* 31: 69–79.

Cottrell, P. L. 1985. 'The Business Man and Financier', in S. and V. D. Lipman (eds.), *The Century of Moses Montefiore*, pp. 23–44. Oxford.

1988. 'Credit, Morals and Sunspots: The Financial Boom of the 1860s and Trade Cycle Theory', in P. L. Cottrell and D. E. Moggridge (eds.), *Money and Power: Essays in Honour of L. S. Pressnell*, pp. 41–71. Houndsmills and London.

Crick, W. F. and Wadsworth, J. E. 1936. *A Hundred Years of Joint Stock Banking*. London (3rd edn, 1958).

Dickson, P. J. M. 1967. *The Financial Revolution in England: A Study in the Development of Public Credit 1688–1756*. Oxford.

Farnie, D. A. 1953. 'The English Cotton Industry 1850–1896', unpublished MA thesis, University of Manchester.

Fetter, F. W. 1965. *Development of British Monetary Orthodoxy*. Cambridge, Mass.

Gilbart, J. W. 1828. *A Practical Treatise on Banking*. London.

Green, E. 1979. *Debtors to Their Profession: A History of the Institute of Bankers 1878–1979*. London.

Gregory, T. E. 1936. *The Westminster Bank through a Century*, 2 vols. London.

Grindon, L. H. 1877. *Manchester Banks and Banking*. Manchester.

Hill, N. K. 1950. 'The History of the Imperial Continental Gas Association 1824–1900', unpublished Ph.D. thesis, University of London.

Hilton, B. 1977. *Corn, Cash Commerce. The Economic Policies of the Tory Governments 1815–1830*. Oxford.

Hobsbawm, E. J. and Rudé, G. 1969. *Captain Swing*. London.

Hodder, E. 1891. *George Fife Angas, Father and Founder of South Australia*. London.

Horsefield, J. K. 1949. 'The Bankers and the Bullionists in 1819', *Journal of Political Economy* 57: 442–8.

1960. *British Monetary Experiments: 1650–1710*. London.

Hudson, P. 1981. 'The Role of Banks in the Finance of the West Riding Wool Textile Industry, c. 1780–1815', *Business History Review* 60: 379–402.

1986. *The Genesis of Industrial Capital: A Study of the West Riding Wool Textile Industry c. 1750–1850*. Cambridge.

Jones, F. S. 1971. 'Instant Banking in the 1830's: The Founding of the Northern and Central Bank of England', *Bankers' Magazine* 211: 130–5.

1978. 'The Manchester Cotton Magnates' Move into Banking, 1826–50', *Textile History* 9: 91–111.

1985. 'The Bank of England in Manchester, 1826–1850', *Bankhistorisches Archiv* 11: 28–47.

Jones, W. D. 1967. *Prosperity Robinson: The Life of Viscount Goderich 1782–1859*. London.

Joslin, D. M. 1954. 'London Private Bankers, 1720–1785', *Economic History Review*, 2nd ser., 7: 167–86.

Kerridge, E. 1988. *Trade and Banking in Early Modern England*. Manchester.

King, W. T. C. 1936. *History of the London Discount Market*. London (rep. 1972).

Leighton-Boyce, J. A. S. L. 1958. *Smiths the Bankers 1658–1958*. London.

Lévy-Leboyer, M. 1982. 'Central Banking and Foreign Trade: The Anglo-American Cycle in the 1830's', in C. P. Kindleberger and J.-P. Laffargue (eds.), *Financial Crises: Theory, History and Policy*, pp. 66–116. Cambridge.

Matthews, R. C. O. 1954. *A Study in Trade Cycle History: Economic Fluctuations in Great Britain*. Cambridge.

Melton, F. T. 1986a. 'Deposit Banking in London 1700–90', *Business History* 28: 40–50.

1986b. *Sir Robert Clayton and the Origins of English Deposit Banking, 1658–85*. Cambridge.

Morgan, E. Victor. 1943. *The Theory and Practice of Central Banking 1797–1913*. Cambridge (rep. London, 1965).

Moss, D. J. 1981. 'The Bank of England and the Country Banks: Birmingham 1827–1833', *Economic History Review*, 2nd ser., 34: 540–53.

1982. 'The Private Banks of Birmingham, 1800–27', *Business History* 24: 79–84.

1990. *Thomas Attwood: The Biography of a Radical*. Montreal and Kingston.

1992. 'The Bank of England and the Establishment of a Branch System, 1826–9', *Canadian Journal of History* 27: 47–66.

1995. 'Central Banking and the Provincial System: The Bank of England and the 3 Per Cent Discount Account 1832–1837', *Financial History Review* 2: 5–24.

Munn, C. W. 1981. *The Scottish Provincial Banking Companies 1747–1864*. Edinburgh.

1983. 'The Coming of Joint-Stock Banking in Scotland and Ireland', in T. M. Devine and D. Dickson (eds.), *Scotland and Ireland: Parallels and Contrasts in Economic and Social Development*, pp. 204–18. Edinburgh.

1988. 'The Emergence of Joint Stock Banking in the British Isles: A Comparative Approach', *Business History* 30: 69–83.

1997. 'Banking on Branches: The Origins and Development of Branch Banking in the United Kingdom', in P. L. Cottrell, A. Teichova and T. Yuzawa (eds.), *Finance in the Age of the Corporate Economy*, pp. 37–51. Aldershot.

Mushet, R. 1826. *An Attempt to Explain from Facts the Effects of the Issues of the Bank of England upon Its Own Interests, Public Credit, and Country Banks.* London.

Newton, L. A. 1996. 'Regional Bank-Industry Relations during the Mid-Nineteenth Century: Links between Bankers and Manufacturing in Sheffield c. 1850 to c. 1855', *Business History* 38: 64–83.

1997. 'Towards Financial Integration: The Development of English Joint Stock Banks in London and the Provinces, 1826–1860', in U. Olsson (ed.), *Business and European Integration*, pp. 316–31. Göteborg.

Nishimura, S. 1971. *The Decline of Inland Bills of Exchange in the London Money Market 1855–1913.* Cambridge.

O'Grada, C. 1991. 'Reassessing the Irish Pound Report of 1804', *Bulletin of Economic Research* 43: 5–19.

Ollerenshaw, P. 1987. *Banking in Nineteenth-Century Ireland: The Belfast Banks, 1825–1914.* Manchester.

1988. 'The Development of Banking in the Bristol Region, 1750–1915', in C. Harvey and J. Press (eds.), *Studies in the Business History of Bristol*, pp. 55–82. Bristol.

Opie, R. G. 1962. 'Western Germany', in Sayers 1962b: 53–123.

Pressnell, L. S. 1956. *Country Banking in the Industrial Revolution.* Oxford.

Reed, M. C. 1975. *Investment in Railways in Britain, 1820–1844.* Oxford.

Reed, R. 1983. *National Westminster: A Short History.* London.

Saunders, T. 1928. *Stuckey's Bank.* Taunton.

Saville, R. 1996. *Bank of Scotland: A History 1695–1995.* Edinburgh.

Sayers, R. S. 1957. *Lloyds Bank in the History of English Banking.* Oxford.

1962a. 'Norway', in Sayers 1962b:298–316.

1962b. (ed.), *Banking in Western Europe.* Oxford.

Shannon, H. A. 1930–3. 'The First Five Thousand Limited Companies and Their Duration', *Economic History* 2: 396–419.

1932–3. 'The Limited Companies of 1866 and 1883', *Economic History Review* 4: 290–316.

Simpson, N. 1975. *The Belfast Bank 1827–1970: 150 Years of Banking in Ireland.* Belfast.

Stuart-Jones, F. 1975. 'The First Joint Stock Banks in Manchester 1828–1836', *South African Journal of Economics* 43: 16–36.

1978. 'The Cotton Industry and Joint Stock Banking in Manchester 1825–1850', *Business History* 20: 165–83.

Thomas, S. E. 1934. *The Rise and Growth of Joint Stock Banking,* vol. I, *Britain to 1860.* London.

Thomas, W. A. 1973. *The Provincial Stock Exchanges*. London.

Toft, K. S. 1970. 'A Mid-Nineteenth Century Attempt at Banking Control', *Revue Internationale d'Histoire de la Banque* 3: 149–67.

Wilson, J. S. G. 1962. 'France', in Sayers 1962b: 1–52.

   1986. *Banking Policy and Structure: A Comparative Analysis*. London and Sydney.

Withers, H. 1933. *National Provincial Bank 1833 to 1933*. London.

Ziegler, D. 1990. *Central Bank, Peripheral Industry: The Bank of England in the Provinces, 1826–1913*. Leicester and London.

5 Banking in Europe in the nineteenth century: the role of the central bank

Forrest Capie

Introduction

At the heart of any discussion of central banking is the issue of the lender of last resort. It is an issue that has been the cause of a certain amount of confusion in the study of monetary and financial history. Central banks have two main functions. One is macro, the preservation of price stability; the other is micro, the preservation of financial market stability. It is the latter though that really defines central banking. It is the peculiar position of the monopoly note issuer and holder and provider of the ultimate means of payment that allows, almost obliges, the institution to behave as the lender of last resort.

There is, nevertheless, disagreement as to how the role should be defined, and some debate as to how it should operate. This chapter may appear a little Anglocentric, for it argues that the role is quite well defined in the literature on English monetary economics in the nineteenth century; and further, that the particular institutional arrangements that evolved in England in the nineteenth century were ideal for its execution. The Bank of England was a fully fledged central bank acting as a lender of last resort by the 1870s, coming to the rescue of the market in an anonymous fashion through the buffer of the discount-houses.

If this is accepted, then it follows that the Continental European counterparts did not become fully fledged central banks until at least the end of the nineteenth century and in most cases probably not until the beginning of the twentieth century. This has implications for the stability of the respective systems and also for comparisons of the Anglo-Saxon and European banking systems.

The chapter first provides some views on the definition of 'lender of last resort', and then sets out the 'classical' position on the subject as found in the writings of Henry Thornton and Walter Bagehot. It then offers a revised definition derived from these writers, and describes very briefly how the system evolved and operated in England. We add some thoughts on how it was aided by the peculiar and somewhat accidental advantage of being able to act with anonymity. We turn next to some consideration of the Continental European experience and make some contrasts. Finally, we conclude that fully fledged central banking came to the Continent only in the twentieth century.

Definition

The term central banking conveys somewhat different things to different people, even if there are large areas of agreement on the essential functions and character. It is not, for example, contentious to say that a central bank is the government's bank, that it acts as banker to the commercial banks, and that the chief objective is the maintenance of the value of the currency. But the institutions that we know as central banks have evolved over a long period and acquired, or developed and extended, their functions according to circumstances and the economic and political environment in which they have found themselves.

It is worth recalling the essential features of their origin and development. A common statement in economics textbooks is that the Riksbank (1668) was the world's first central bank. But there was no concept of central banking at that time. Central banking in any meaningful sense is a nineteenth-century concept. Some like to see the origins lying in the acquisition of the right to monopoly of note issue, and there is a case to be made for this, or at least that it is an important element in the make-up of a central bank. Others have emphasized what is often seen as the key function, the lender of last resort. As we have remarked, this will be the central focus of this chapter. Others such as Goodhart have drawn attention to the potential conflict of interest that exists if the 'central bank', the institution set up by government, given the monopoly of its business and a generally privileged position in the monetary system, continues to do a substantial amount of commercial business. The conflict of interest arises since, if the commercial banks get into difficulties, there is an incentive for the central bank to allow them to fail or at least to suffer, and to capture more business for itself. This is the antithesis of the last resort role.

Modern dictionaries of economics frequently see the lender of last resort function as synonymous with central banking, sufficient in itself to define central banking. But what exactly is meant by the lender of last resort? Much has been written on the question. There are two principal views on the issue. The first is that it means the bail-out of an individual institution; the second that it should be taken to mean the rescue of the market as a whole – the provision of liquidity to allay widespread panic. Can these two views in practice be separated? The second also involves the bank declaring its position to the market, what is known today as pre-commitment.

We pursue this issue here first as it is captured in the writings of the two most distinguished contributors to the subject in the nineteenth century, Henry Thornton and Walter Bagehot. The justification for this is that England industrialized first and became the earliest example of an industrial economy with a modern banking system and hence the birthplace of monetary economics.

The classical position

Henry Thornton has been described as the father of the modern central bank. Thornton's classic monograph *Paper Credit* (1802) is the source of his principal ideas. Joseph Schumpeter called it the Magna Carta of central banking.

The essence of central banking for Thornton is contained in the following quotation:

To limit the amount of paper issued, and to resort for this purpose, whenever the temptation to borrow is strong, to some effectual principle of restriction; in no case, however, materially to diminish the sum in circulation, but to let it vibrate only within certain limits; to afford a slow and cautious extension of it, as the general trade of the kingdom enlarges itself; to allow of some special, though temporary, encrease in the event of any extraordinary alarm or difficulty, as the best means of preventing a great demand at home for guineas; and to lean to the side of diminution, in the case of gold going abroad, and of the general exchanges continuing long unfavourable; this seems to be the true policy of the directors of an institution circumstanced like that of the Bank of England. To suffer either the solicitations of merchants, or the wishes of government, to determine the measure of the bank issues, is unquestionably to adopt a very false principle of conduct. (1802: 259)

This is a remarkably clear statement given its date, and the state of development in the money market. It describes the ideal daily operation of a central bank. But how should the lender of last resort behave in a crisis? Thornton accepted the danger of the failure of one bank leading to the spread of fear and possibly panic and the failure of many banks – a common occurrence in the England he was describing, that of the late eighteenth century when there were hundreds of small banks. 'If any one bank fails, a general run upon the neighbouring ones is apt to take place, which if not checked in the beginning by a pouring into the circulation a large quantity of gold, leads to very extensive mischief' (1802: 180).

The remedy for such an occasion was for the Bank to provide liquidity: 'if the Bank of England, in future seasons of alarm, should be disposed to extend its discounts in a greater degree than heretofore, then the threatened calamity may be averted through the generosity of that institution' (p. 188). Thornton even allowed that several institutions could fail but that the central bank may nevertheless not feel the need to save them:

> It is by no means intended to imply, that it would become the Bank of England to relieve every distress which the rashness of country banks may bring upon them: the bank, by doing this, might encourage their improvidence. There seems to be a medium at which a public bank should aim in granting aid to inferior establishments, and which it often must find it very difficult to be observed. The relief should neither be so prompt and liberal as to exempt those who misconduct their business from all the natural consequences of their fault, nor so scanty and slow as deeply to involve the general interests. These interests, nevertheless, are sure to be pleaded by every distressed person whose affairs are large, however indifferent or even ruinous may be their state. (p. 188)

Thornton's view of the lender of last resort was one that placed the emphasis on responsibility to the market and not to an individual institution. The central objective is to prevent the collapse of the money stock. This is what we take to be the classic position.

Bagehot was the great developer and expounder of these views in the nineteenth century. He first wrote on this subject in 1848 in the first article that he published: 'The Currency Problem'. He was writing first of all about the previous year's financial crisis and commenting inevitably on the Act of 1844. His article is remarkable for one so young and is worth quoting at length.

> The currency argument is this: It is a great defect of a purely metallic circulation that the quantity of it cannot be readily suited to any sudden demand; it takes time to get new supplies of gold and silver, and, in the meantime, a temporary rise in the value of bullion takes place. Now as paper money can be supplied in unlimited quantities, however sudden the demand may be, it does not appear to us that there is any objection on principle of sudden issues of paper money to meet sudden and large extensions of demand. It gives to a purely metallic circulation that greater constancy of purchasing power possessed by articles whose quantity can be quickly suited to demand. It will be evident from what we have said before that this power of issuing notes is one excessively liable to abuse because, as before shown, it may depreciate the currency; and on that account such a power ought only to be lodged in the hands of government ... It should only be used in rare and exceptional circumstances. But when the fact of a *sudden* demand is proved, we see no objection, but decided advantage, in introducing this new element into a metallic circulation. (Bagehot 1986: 267)

That is one of the clearest statements on the need for liquidity and the form its provision should take. The English banking system was continuing to evolve, sometimes in ways that Bagehot did not entirely approve of. He would rather there had been no central bank and that competition prevailed, but accepted that the system that had emerged had to be lived with:

I have tediously insisted that the natural system of banking is that of many banks keeping their own cash reserve, with the penalty of failure before them if they neglect it. I have shown that our system is that of a single bank keeping the whole reserve under no effectual penalty of failure. And yet I propose to retain that system, and only attempt to mend and palliate it. (p. 310)

He did, nevertheless, refer to the quarter century since 1844 as a period 'almost marvellous in its banking development' (p. 3).

Before 1870 there had been no consistency in the behaviour of the Bank. Sometimes it came to the rescue of the market and sometimes it did not. Sometimes it bailed out insolvent institutions and at other times it did not. In the context of these developments Bagehot set out his views first in the pages of *The Economist*, of which he was editor in the middle decades of the century, and then in *Lombard Street* (1873). It was in the latter that Bagehot set out what is taken to be his definitive position.

Where in Thornton's time of writing there were no joint-stock banks, by 1870 when Bagehot embarked on *Lombard Street* there were many such banks and they were beginning to dominate the system. The risk of panic was clearly increased if a large joint-stock bank collapsed: 'no cause is more capable of producing a panic, perhaps none is so capable, as the failure of a first-rate joint stock bank in London' (Bagehot 1873: 251). Following Thornton though, the solution was the same:

A panic, in a word, is a species of neuralgia, and according to the rules of science you must not starve it. The holders of the cash reserve must be ready not only to keep it for their own liabilities, but to advance it most freely for the liabilities of others. They must lend to merchants, to minor bankers, to 'this man and that man,' whenever the security is good. In wild periods of alarm, one failure makes many, and the best way to prevent the derivative failures is to arrest the primary failure which causes them. (pp. 51–2)

This is open to some interpretation, and there is some ambivalence over individual institutions as against the market as a whole. He goes on:

That in a panic the bank, or banks, holding the ultimate reserve should refuse bad bills or bad securities will not make the panic really worse; the 'unsound' people are a feeble minority, and they are afraid even to look frightened for fear their unsoundness may be detected. The great majority, the majority to be protected, are the 'sound' people, the people who have good security to offer. (p. 188)

This brings the emphasis back to the security on offer and thus to the market as a whole. But in addition Bagehot argued that these large joint-stock banks should provide more information about their activities so that the sound might be separated from the unsound.

Supposing that, owing to defects in its government, one even of the greater London joint stock banks failed, there would be an instant suspicion of the whole system. One *terra incognita* being seen to be faulty, every other *terra incognita* would be suspected. If the real government of these banks had for years been known, and if the subsisting banks had been known not to be ruled by the bad mode of government which had ruined the bank that had fallen, then the ruin of that bank would not be hurtful. The other banks would be seen to be exempt from the cause which had destroyed it . . . Scarcely anyone knows the precise government of any one; in no case has that government been described on authority; and the fall of one by grave misgovernment would be taken to show that the others might as easily be misgoverned also. (p. 250)

These two writers, Bagehot and Thornton, provide the classic view of the essence of central banking. The ideal form of the lender of last resort was that there should be no individual bail-out, but rather that the Bank should discount good-quality paper irrespective of where it came from.

A derived definition

Some of these quotations cited above are of course open to different interpretation, and especially so since the monetary and banking systems were undergoing continual change. Not surprisingly, there continues to be some disagreement over the precise meaning of the lender of last resort. It is clearly not easy to date the function, as it was something that was groped towards. The issue can perhaps be illuminated in the following way. Any commercial bank may on occasions extend its lending to some customer even if, or particularly if, that customer is in serious danger of default. They may do this for more than one reason. It could be that allowing that customer to fail would have knock-on effects and that other customers would fail. Saving the first, at some cost, may save many others and reduce the net cost. Or it could be that by demonstrating their commitment to a firm in distress their reputation in the business community would be enhanced and that more good business would be attracted to offset the potential loss of the default. In the same way a central bank in the making could come to the rescue of one of its customers (a bank) who was temporarily illiquid or even insolvent. Our argument is that such a rescue is analogous to the commercial bank, simply good business practice. If we were to take this as a measure of the last resort function then the Bank of England became such a lender in the eighteenth century. Furthermore, no central bank could pre-commit itself to coming to the rescue of any individual bank that was confronted with liquidity problems. That would result in serious moral hazard.

A more reasonable position would seem to be that a central bank assumes the function of lender of last resort when it accepts responsibility for the banking system as a whole and that that should override any residual concern with its own profitability. Thus it is the appreciation of how they should behave in a crisis, rather than any individual act of rescue, that should date the acceptance of the role. The latter, a rescue, is easy to date. The former is more difficult. For example, if a central bank had a keen appreciation of what it should do and how it should do it, it is conceivable that it could be acting constantly to avert crises, and that no such crisis would ever appear.

Anonymity

It is possible that a crucial element in this story is that anonymity is of fundamental importance in the execution of the lender of last resort function. The lender of last resort supplies funds to the market in times of need. It does not supply individual institutions. In its proper form it should not engage in bailing out firms of any kind, be they banks or non-banks. Therefore, if the operation could be carried out anonymously it would be ideal.

The mechanism can be thought of as the central bank with a discount window which is of frosted glass and is raised just a few inches. Representatives of institutions could therefore appear at the window and push through the paper that they wanted discounted. The central banker would return the appropriate amount of cash, reflecting the going rate of interest. The central banker does not know, nor does he care, who is on the other side of the window. He simply discounts good-quality paper – or lends on the basis of good collateral. In this way institutions holding good-quality assets will have no difficulty in getting hold of the funds they need. Institutions with poor-quality assets are likely to suffer. In times of panic the interest rate will rise.

By something of a happy accident this was in effect the system that developed in England. At the beginning of the nineteenth century the Bank of England monopoly aroused the ire of the banking community. Such was the antipathy between the Bank of England and the new joint-stock banks that they preferred to keep a distance between each other. Discount brokers emerged who conveniently transacted business between them. These discount brokers gradually acquired the capital base to finance their own portfolios and by the third quarter of the nineteenth century had developed their modern form of the discount-house.

When the commercial banks were under pressure in a liquidity squeeze their first line of defence was to call in their loans to the discount-houses and this in turn sent the discount-houses off to the Bank of England where they had special access. If the commercial banks had to cash in bills they would do this at the discount-houses and the latter would in turn take them to the Bank. In this way the central bank never needed to know where the great bulk of the demand was coming from. It is our point that where it comes from is largely an irrelevance. Good bills get discounted.

In practice of course we know that individual institutions did take bills directly to the Bank, and borrowed on good security from the Bank when pressure developed. These were in the main its own customers, and when they were not, the Bank was simply providing an additional means of supplying funds (Ogden 1991).

It is interesting to speculate that some confusion in the discussion over the nature of the lender of last resort function may have arisen from too cavalier a treatment of this model. Central banking was more advanced in Britain than in other countries, and the British model of central banking was often adopted elsewhere. But the actual mechanism did not exist elsewhere. Thus a key feature of the British system, its inbuilt protective device for anonymity, was ignored. This meant that in most other countries the institutions themselves went to the 'central bank' and anonymity was lost. Difficulties were exacerbated when the government's bank and the commercial banks were in competition for commercial business. This seems to have been ignored in the literature, and it may be that it is this that has allowed the confusion over bailing out to develop as it has.

The case of England

The history of the Bank of England is quite well known and easy to summarize and place in the context of the framework outlined above. Founded in 1694, it was the government's bank from that date on. Joint-stock banking was prohibited but a vigorous banking system developed in the next 100 years. The phrase 'lender of last resort' entered the language at the end of the nineteenth century but, as we have argued, the Bank was not such a lender at that time. It did begin to acquire the monopoly of note issue with the 1844 Act, though in effect the monopoly had to wait until the 1870s.

It was also in the 1870s that the Bank accepted that its public responsibility greatly outweighed its pursuit of profit and it became the lender of last resort. There is no explicit statement to this effect but following the exhortation of Bagehot first in *The Economist* in the 1860s, and then more persuasively in *Lombard Street* (1873), it seems the Bank accepted. Its commercial business continued but was not significant.

In the century after 1870 there seemed to be ample demonstration that the British financial, and particularly banking, system was enormously stable and that this stability was due in some good part to the operations of the Bank of England. The value of the currency was maintained, apart from wartime experience, for most of that period. More significantly, there were no financial crises in the period. Where crises had been periodic before 1870 there were none after that date. Admittedly that requires a little more elaboration. But following Schwartz's definition of a financial crisis – something that threatens or actually produces a collapse in the money stock – seems sensible. There will be occasions when banks, like other firms, fail, but that does not constitute a financial crisis. Exceptions may be taken to this definition but it does seem to provide the most useful approach, in that it allows some harder assessment of a crisis, in terms of cash and reserve ratios.

There were occasions in this period after 1870 when there was the appearance of crises and some of these have been described as crises. For example in 1878 the City of Glasgow Bank failed and that had some repercussions in the banking sector, even if these were not serious. An examination of the public's currency/deposit ratio shows no rush to cash. Neither did the banks build up or lose their reserve/deposit ratio. (We note here that Collins (1989) takes a different view of this episode and that we simply disagree over the definition.) The Bank of England did nothing to help, and rightly so, since the Glasgow Bank was corruptly run. The approach is useful again in describing the events of 1890 – sometimes called 'the Baring Crisis' – and correctly so since there was a crisis for one bank but not for the system. Baring's did indeed fail and was reconstituted. The Bank of England participated in that it organized a 'lifeboat', but it did not bail out an overstretched bank.

In other years, when there were crises around the world, which were generally transmitted by means of the fixed exchange-rate system, they nevertheless did not appear in Britain. The same is true of the interwar years when again British banking was enormously stable. There was a crisis in 1931 but it was an exchange-rate crisis. No banks failed, even if there was a little fudging of that issue. And generally speaking, bank profits were not badly dented. This contrasted starkly with most of the rest of the world, with one or two exceptions such as Canada and the Netherlands.

Furthermore, it has been shown that for the years after 1870 the Bank of England acted to avoid panics and did so very successfully (Ogden 1991). Of course there were other factors in the British experience that contributed to stability. The most important was the structure of the banking system. It was increasingly a thoroughly branched system that allowed banks considerable diversification. At least in the years before 1914 this stability did not depend on the cartel which had barely come into being at that date. Separating the respective contributions of these factors is a task yet to be tackled. Structure may well turn out to have been the more important but the stabilizing presence of a trusted central bank must have made its own important contribution.

Banking in Europe

How then does all of this English/British experience compare with Europe? The contrast between English and Continental European banking is striking. The principal distinguishing feature is that much of Europe's banking was characterized by the universal bank, the large institution that embraced both commercial and investment banking functions. The most persuasive explanation for the different structures derives from Gerschenkron's thesis on the need for such institutions, given the relatively backward state of industrialization. The universal banks developed close relations with industry and are said to have promoted long-term investment which in turn was good for economic growth. The high points were found in Austria and Germany but in different degrees in several other central and south-eastern European countries.

Much of the core of this thesis has been under challenge recently and many of the supposed benefits have been played down or in some instances rejected altogether. But this is beside the point for our particular purpose. The point to make here is that these systems were generally highly concentrated from an early date, with very large banks. Further, the banks that became central banks were often established in order to promote commercial banking. When this is combined with the fact that the institutions that became central banks were frequently established at later dates in the nineteenth century, this meant that in many ways they were competitors of commercial banks and that in some cases at certain times the government banks were at some disadvantage.

Furthermore, if two or three banks dominated the market the problem of distinguishing between the individual institution and the market as a whole, when exercising the lender of last resort function, would have been greater. And the further point to hold in view is that the 'ideal' fashion of treating the market in an anonymous way as did the Bank of England was not a feature of European financial systems. It is important therefore at this point to stress that these two 'models' of central banking are very unlikely to have much in common.

But perhaps the most important point to make is one on commercial rivalry. Goodhart (1988) made the point that an obstacle to acting as a lender of last resort was for the government bank to continue commercial business and behave in a profit-maximizing way. As he put it: 'It was the metamorphosis from their involvement in commercial banking, as a competitive, profit-maximising bank among many, to a non-competitive non-profit-maximising role that marked the true emergence, and development of proper central banking' (1988: 7).

Where the bank continued to transact commercial business on a significant scale there was a conflict of interest. And if we accept that what defines a central bank is the lender of last resort function, then any impediment to its operation suggests caution in both dating the beginning of central banking in Europe and in treating the institutions that are, often misleadingly, called central banks. In what follows we focus on this particular issue in Continental Europe.

According to one historian of German central banking, 'The Reichsbank, acquiring the personnel and experience of the Bank of Prussia, began as a fully fledged central bank' (Bopp 1953: 2). And yet what does this mean? The Reichsbank was a large commercial bank and the great bulk of its business was with industry. Bopp shows that, while the Reichsbank recognized its public responsibilities, its attitude to profit was ambivalent and that at least for the period 1880–96 it was competing with the larger commercial banks by discounting prime bills at preferential rates – often as much as 1.5 percentage points below its official discount rate. It was on occasions lowering its discount rate when, for macro-economic purposes, it should have been raising it. That is to say, it was obliged to maintain the specie stock at a designated level and used its discount rate in order to do this. But the conflict arose when its desire for private business was in opposition to its need to maintain the specie stock. By the beginning of the twentieth century the Reichsbank was using open market operations to influence market rates. That is, by that stage, it was able to force banks to borrow from it and was then able to act as lender of last resort.

Founded in 1816, the Austrian National Bank is amongst the oldest of the institutions that have a more or less continuous history. And of course Austria is usually taken as the most striking example of the universal banking system. The Bank was modelled on the Bank of France and followed to some extent a similar chequered career in the first half of the nineteenth century. It was then that some large banks were established – the Austrian Discount Co. in 1853 and the Creditanstalt in 1855. Throughout the nineteenth century the ANB engaged in a variety of commercial activities. Convertibility was not a serious issue until Austria joined the gold standard in 1891 and it seems (and perhaps not surprisingly) that no open market operations were developed – indeed not until the second half of the twentieth century. It is usually claimed that the Bank acted as a lender of last resort in the crisis of 1873, but this would be to use the term in the way in which we object to. Indeed this particular crisis was essentially a *non-bank* crisis.

The case of the Banque de France is interesting. For while it was established in 1800 and with certain privileges dominated the banking system in the first half of the century, its role was essentially that of an issuing body. It provides an early example of a government bank coming to the aid of a commercial bank, though as we explained above this is not the same thing as being the lender of last resort. However, from the middle of the nineteenth century the principal threat to the Bank came from the growth of large deposit banks whose portfolios were so large that they did not find the need to rediscount bills at the Bank. Plessis shows how the situation 'worsened' up to 1913 and so reduced the role of the Bank further. As Plessis put it, this 'cast doubt on its ability to influence the price of money in the short term since adjusting the discount rate was only really effective when commercial banks needed to make use of the Bank of France at some time' (1994: 11).

Since the Bank then tried to increase its discounting with industrial firms it was competing directly with the banks and making them more determined not to ask for its help. It therefore had great difficulty in achieving recognition as a central bank. Indeed Plessis says the Bank had no intention of taking on the role of lender of last resort before 1914. Nishimura (1995) supports this in his demonstration of the extent of the commercial rivalry that existed between the Bank and the banks in the late nineteenth century.

Much the same kind of story can be told of the Banca d'Italia, although of course its founding date is much later (1893). It was organized as a privately owned joint-stock bank and was indistinguishable from, and competed with, the two other large note-issuing banks, the Bank of Sicily and the Bank of Naples, though their share of the total note issue was comparatively small. Although in appearance it was independent, the state had considerable influence over its discount rate and in fact in 1910 the responsibility for setting the discount rate was transferred to the Treasury Minister. There were financial crises in 1907 and in 1911, in which the Bank was found to be supporting the system but mainly by leading consortia of the commercial banks. Indeed it would seem that even after 1926 when it acquired great privileges the Banca d'Italia continued to function as a private bank.

The National Bank of Belgium was founded in 1850, at which point there were a number of banks in the country, including what is usually claimed to be the first ever commercial joint-stock bank, the Société Générale de Belgique (1822). These banks could all issue notes, accept deposits and make advances, and before 1848 they did so. It was the crisis that broke in that year that prompted the forming of the National Bank which became the sole note issuer, though its charter allowed for the possibility of other issuers being created. The government appointed the

Governor of the Bank who reported to the Ministry of Finance. The principal objective was the maintenance of convertibility, but of almost equal importance was its role as banker to the banks, and it seems that an intention from an early point was that it should act as a lender of last resort. Evidence, however, on how this worked remains limited, but it is one of the earliest such lenders in Europe. Interestingly, when the Bank of Japan was being designed it was the National Bank of Belgium that was used as a model.

Amsterdam and Rotterdam are well known for their sophistication in financial matters. A case could be made for the Amsterdam Wisselbank (1609) being a forerunner of the modern Dutch central bank. But the birth of that bank was in 1814, and business was restricted initially to Amsterdam. New credit institutions appeared in the 1840s and began to deal more with banks (rediscounting) and less with non-banks. The 1863 Act strengthened the Bank's position and gave it a clearer role in note issue and convertibility. It was after 1850 that the Bank's notes had begun to be a larger part of the money supply and as public confidence in these grew so the Bank could try to accommodate the market in times of crisis. The widespread crisis of 1857, with origins in the US, saw the Bank coming to the assistance of the market. Even so, as late as 1900 the Bank did as much lending to the industrial sector as did the rest of the banking sector. It was the 1920s before the Bank lost nearly all these customers, and it accepted that its function was different. Open market operations were not part of the Bank's armoury until the Second World War. But in spite of this the Bank is a strong contender for central bank status before most others in Europe. What damages the case is the extent of commercial rivalry that continued until the First World War, and the absence of any commitment to come to the rescue of the market. It is that that ultimately disqualifies it.

The experience of the Scandinavian countries was remarkably similar. Most of the institutions were founded early and of course the Riksbank was the earliest of all. The Bank of Finland (1811), Bank of Norway (1816) and Danish Nationalbank (1818) are amongst the very earliest of the institutions that we call central banks today. Their histories have strong parallels. The general pattern was that they preceded other banking institutions, the bulk of which tended to come around the middle of the century. The Banks therefore initially carried out commercial banking business, only in the latter half of the century letting that decline and at the end of the century becoming the bankers' bank. In the case of Sweden there was considerable freedom in banking in the nineteenth century, heavily influenced by the Scottish experience before 1844. There was no monopoly of note issue before 1897 and no attempt before that date of behaving as a central bank, that is as a leader of last resort. The Norwegians did have a monopoly of issue and aimed to preserve convertibility into silver. In 1892 an Act remodelled the Bank on the Bank of England and the role of lender of last resort is usually dated from the Bank's participation in the financial crisis of 1899. In Denmark the lender of last resort function is usually dated from 1908.

An interesting feature of the Scandinavian experience is that they had supervisory bodies that were set up separately outside the Banks. This is interesting since supervision/regulation seems to flow more naturally from the lender of last resort function. If the central bank has the responsibility of maintaining financial stability then it will automatically have an interest in the behaviour of the constituent parts and a reasonable desire to both monitor and suggest some guidelines. In the absence of the lender of last resort function this is not a problem.

Both Portugal and Spain established institutions in the middle of the century: Portugal in 1846 and Spain in 1856. The Bank of Portugal was a joint-stock company that operated mainly as a note-issuing commercial bank. It became the state's bank in 1887. It was not until the 1890s that it acquired a monopoly of the note issue. It was not entrusted with a lender of last resort function until World War II, but like others we have noted it did perform some kind of rescue in the crises of the 1870s and 1890s. The Bank of Spain's functions were essentially more of government's bank, note issuer, discounting and commercial lending. Its regulations did not specify its relationship with other banks but it did come to the rescue of some in the crises of 1913 and 1914. It was not in a position to supervise banks before then since its commercial activities made it a competitor.

Summary

In summary, Continental European banks, while mixed across a number of different functions, exhibit strong similarities when it comes to the operation of this basic function of lender of last resort that is the focus of this chapter. In almost all European countries there were, from an early date (early in relation to their industrial development), relatively large joint-stock banks and these competed with the government's bank. The latter's function was essentially the preservation of the value of the currency – metal convertibility. This could conflict with its pursuit of commercial business, and its role as banker to the other banks. As we noted, there were occasions when European banks moved their discount rate in a direction that appeared to be at odds with the preservation of the value of the currency. More research is required on these episodes with a view to ascertaining what pressures were found in the foreign exchange markets and how these were dealt with. But the main point to make is that there were a number of impediments to the proper functioning of a central bank, impediments that did not disappear in the main until the twentieth century.

BIBLIOGRAPHY

Bagehot, W. 1873. *Lombard Street*. London.
　　1986. *The Collected Works of Walter Bagehot*, ed. Norman St. John Stevas. London.
Balderston, T. 1992. 'Universal banks', in Peter Newman, Murray Milgate and John Eatwell (eds.), *The New Palgrave Dictionary of Money and Finance*, pp. 732–5.
Bopp, K. R. 1944. 'Central Banking at the Crossroads', *American Economic Review* 34: 266–77.
　　1953. *Reichsbank Operations 1876–1914*. Philadelphia.
Bordo, M. D. 1984. 'The Lender of Last Resort: Alternative Views and Historical Evidence', *Federal Reserve Bank of Richmond Economic Quarterly* 76(1): 17–23.
Cameron, R. 1967. *Banking in the Early Stages of Industrialisation: A Study in Comparative Economic History*. Oxford.
Capie, Forrest, Goodhart, Charles, Fischer, S. and Schnadt, Norbert (eds.) 1994. *The Future of Central Banking: The Tercentenary Symposium of the Bank of England*. Cambridge.
Capie, Forrest and Wood, G. E. 1995. 'A European Lender of Last Resort? Some Lessons from History', in J. Reis (ed.), *International Monetary Systems in Historical Perspectives*, pp. 209–30. New York.
Capie, Forrest and Wood, G. E. (eds.) 1991. *Unregulated Banking: Chaos or Order?* London.
Collins, Michael 1989. 'The Banking Crisis of 1878', *Economic History Review* 42: 504–27.
　　1993. *Central Banking in History*. London.
Goodhart, C. A. E. 1988. *The Evolution of Central Banks*. Cambridge, Mass.
Kindleberger, Charles and Laffargue, Jean-Pierre 1982. *Financial Crisis: Theory, History and Policy*. Cambridge.
Nishimura, S. 1995. 'The French Provincial Banks, the Banque de France, and Bill Finance, 1890–1913', *Economic History Review*.
Ogden, T. 1991. 'An Analysis of the Bank of England's Discount and Advance Behaviour 1870–1914', in J. Foreman-Peck (ed.), *New Perspectives in the Late Victorian Economy*. Cambridge.
Plessis, A. 1994. 'The Changing Role of the Banque de France from the Beginning of the Twentieth Century to the 1950s', in Youssef Cassis, Gerald D. Feldman and Ulf Olsson (eds.), *The Evolution of Financial Institutions and Markets in Twentieth-Century Europe*, pp. 9–19. Aldershot.

Schumpeter, Joseph A. 1954. *History and Economic Analysis*. London.

Schwartz, Anna J. 1986. 'Real and Pseudo Financial Crises', in Forrest Capie and G. E. Wood (eds.), *Financial Crises and the World Banking System*. London.

Thornton, H. 1802. *An Enquiry into the Nature and Effects of the Paper Credit of Great Britain*. London.

Tilly, R. 1967. 'Germany 1815–1870', in R. Cameron (ed.), *Banking in the Early Stages of Industrialisation*. Oxford.

1989. 'Banking Institutions in Historical and Comparative Perspective: Germany, Great Britain and the United States in the Nineteenth and Early Twentieth Century', *Journal of Institutional and Theoretical Economics* 145: 189–209.

1992. 'An Overview of the Role of Large German Banks to 1914', in Y. Cassis (ed.), *Finance and Financiers in European History, 1880–1960*. Cambridge.

Toniolo, G. (ed.) 1988. *Central Banks' Independence in Historical Perspective*. New York.

6   Public policy, capital markets and the supply of industrial finance in nineteenth-century Germany

Richard Tilly

The evolution of financial institutions in nineteenth-century Germany, as in other times and places, reflected politics and the role of the state, and not just neoclassical market forces. The way in which state actions and politics interacted with financial institutions, however, depended upon the historical sequence of events, i.e. it was path dependent. Generalizing about the relationship between that evolution and state politics, therefore, requires a specifically historical approach. With that idea in mind, this chapter examines just one specific sub-set of Germany's financial history: intermediation of industrial finance via the capital market in the period from around 1880 to 1913. The German case is of particular interest today, for in a sense it represents one side of the debate about the relative merits of financial systems dominated by large universal banks exercising considerable economic power – the German case – and those financial systems characterized by highly competitive financial markets. And the positive role of Germany's 'great banks' in the pre-1914 period has been often stressed.

The story told here begins with a brief survey of the influence of government policy since around the middle of the nineteenth century, paying particular attention to the role of company law and the security exchanges. It then turns to the question of the capital market's performance and attempts to assess how well that market mobilized finance for industry in the period. In so doing it utilizes recent estimates of the 'spread' of returns on newly issued industrial securities. A few comments on the general theme of the role of government in shaping financial systems and on comparison of 'financial systems' form the chapter's conclusion.

I

In spite of relatively low levels of per capita income, the early stages of German industrialization – say, up to the 1840s – were marked by a substantial accumulation of financial capital, as indicated by falling rates of interest and capital exports. And even the 1850s and 1860s produced little evidence of a secular shortage of financial capital, for the large issues of railway and other securities of those years found ready buyers in Germany's nascent capital markets. To put the matter somewhat differently: those young capital markets do not seem to have been limited primarily by an inadequate supply of funds (Borchardt 1961). Attention therefore shifts to the demand side.

One important demand influence stemmed from government policy. The role of government borrowing is so obvious that it hardly requires further attention here (see Ullmann 1986; Tilly 1966). Suffice it to say that the major shifts in government financial demands – the vast increase of the Napoleonic War period, the secular decline of the following decades, and the upward surge of the 1850s and 1860 associated with railway loans – left their mark on both the size and the structure of the German financial sector (Brockhage 1910; Gebhard 1928; Ullmann 1986). It should be emphasized that the increased government borrowing of the Napoleonic era was accompanied by a qualitative change: funded public debt which was based on a central government's legal obligation to pay, and which could now be bought and sold in small lots, replaced the personal debts of princes and the claims on quasi-feudal kinds of assets related hereto. Private bankers versed in the techniques of placing and trading in public debt emerged as important financial intermediaries; and with their emergence the circle of interested investors also widened. Nevertheless, as noted in the introduction to this volume, the largest German state, Prussia, stopped short of a full 'financial revolution'. Its heavy borrowing had seemed to make the monarchy dangerously dependent upon the country's growing bourgeoisie – which, in turn, called for parliamentary controls over state spending.[1] The government response, however, was retrenchment and debt retirement, in a word a return to parsimony as a credible commitment to financial soundness rather than popular consent. Prussia's financial position did seem to improve thereafter, and debt retirement released resources for other purposes – capital export and eventually railways.

In addition, government sought to control private demands for capital. Of particular interest was the policy towards the creation of private business corporations. Until the 1870s business incorporation represented in most German states a privilege only granted for specific purposes (related to 'public welfare'); and few such corporations came into existence (Bösselmann 1939). This conservative policy, however, probably did not become a restraining influence on the demand for industrial finance until the 1840s, when railway building vastly increased the utility of concentra-

Table 6.1 *Numbers of business incorporations and initial equity capital raised, 1826–1907 (in millions of marks).*

	1826–50		1851–70		1870–4		1875–86		1887–1907	
	No.	Capital	No.	Capital	No.	Capital	No.	Capital	No.	Capital
Railways	26	(264)		(1722)		(778)			121	
Banks	4	(22)		(95)	103	(838)			273	
Industry	25	(47)		(430)		(1500)			2230	(3390)
Total	102	(638)	295	(2405)	857[a]	(3307)	1059	(967)	2621	(3458)

Note:
[a] Passow (1922) gives 1018 for Germany as a whole in these years. Excludes GmbH.

tions of capital – not only in railways but also in heavy industry – and the limited liability and continuity which came with incorporation. The historical literature contains abundant, if unsystematic, evidence suggesting a growing gap between applications for incorporation rights and the number of such corporations approved by governments (Bösselmann 1939; Böhme 1966; Martin 1969; Blumberg 1960; Tilly 1966).

Nevertheless, though restrictive, government policy loosened, and approvals of incorporation applications rose sharply in the 1850s; and the great economic boom of the 1850s was in part an incorporation boom related to investment in heavy industry. According to Hoffmann's estimates for Germany as a whole, indeed, capital raised by private corporations rose in these years from a value corresponding to about 10% of estimated net investment to one of over 50% of the latter (Hoffmann *et al.* 1965, table 42 and 239; Blumberg 1960; Rosenberg 1934; Spree 1977). In fact, the experience of the 1850s and 1860s, in particular the evidence of entrepreneurial demand for incorporation rights, probably led the way to the free incorporation law of 1870 (Prussia) and eased the boom and bust which followed in the 1870s. This period, one should recall, was also marked by the still-ascendant ideology of economic liberalism, which in this case called for the withdrawal of the state bureaucracy from decision-making about incorporation rights for private business – on the grounds that such powers no longer reflected superior information and could even be misleading to potential investors.[2] Table 6.1 reports a typical statistical description of the period. The watershed character of the 1870s is unmistakable. I return to that point below; but first a word on the banking component of corporation history is needed.

Readers should note that commercial banks accounted for a more than negligible share of corporate business growth in this period. Most of these banks were 'universal banks', i.e. institutions which combined short-term commercial with long-term investment banking activities and which were accordingly predestined to become important actors in the German capital markets. Loosening of incorporation laws thus indirectly loosened restraints on banking and capital market growth. In one respect, however, government controls over banking remained very important: the issue of bank-notes was a privilege increasingly monopolized by state-run institutions, most importantly by the Prussian Bank (which was founded in 1846 as a private corporation but which was strictly under state control). This, too, was related to government debt policy. For in Prussia, because of the 1820 debt ceiling law, the government felt constrained to hold the line on paper money issues and, moreover, feared that any increase in the debt of its royal banks – there were two such institutions – could be viewed as a violation of that law. This was the reason for choosing the legal form of joint-stock company for the new bank of issue. Nevertheless, worries persisted, and the Prussian Bank followed a conservative course. It was only when privately chartered banks of issue operating in neighbouring German states expanded their note circulation in Prussia in the 1850s that the Prussian Bank shifted to a high-growth policy. The ephemeral growth phase for German private banks of issue thus ended abruptly in 1856, as the Prussian state responded with two measures – a ban on the use of non-Prussian bank-notes in Prussia and a large increase in the statutory ceiling on the note circulation of the Bank of Prussia. By the 1860s the Prussian Bank dominated the Germany-wide note circulation. And in 1875 it became the basis for the new national central bank, the Reichsbank, also a state-controlled institution. This meant that commercial banks increasingly sought and realized their comparative advantage in the less liquid section of the financial sector, an orientation which was reinforced by the Prussian Bank's – and later the Reichsbank's – willingness to serve as a lender of last resort in times of crises (e.g. 1866). Those banks thus became more willing to bear the risks of capital market transactions than would have otherwise been the case (Tilly 1986, 1989).

The impact of the 1870s as historical experience deserves special emphasis here. A strong upswing of the German economy began in the late 1860s, but its interruption by the outbreak of the Franco-Prussian war in 1870 only lent it enhanced impetus when it resumed in 1871 (Spree 1977). This political force – a dampening influence quickly turning into a euphoric one – helps to explain the extraordinarily strong boom of the early 1870s and, no doubt, the severity of the collapse which followed in 1873 as well. Part of the explanation, however, also had specific institutional roots. For one thing, in 1870 free incorporation laws came into force, and the predictable result was an enormous increase in the creation of new corporate business firms. The other important influence derived from the founding of the German Empire. For the new central government, the *Reich*, was seen as the future repository of regulatory powers over the currency and central banking. These powers had hitherto belonged to the individual German states, so that the new situation was marked by a weakening of the central banking controls. At the same time, finally, reparation payments by the French (the famous 'Fünf Milliarden') greatly increased the flow of liquidity into the financial system. Since many of the new private corporations were banks, it is not surprising that the money supply went up sharply at this time while real interest rates fell. From 1873 on, this process reversed itself: the money supply contracted and real interest rates rose. The procyclical behaviour of the banks of issue accentuated those swings.[3] But more important, many of the newly founded business corporations went under, quite a few of them commercial banks, and many more were in deep financial trouble.

The counterpart to the financial difficulties of business corporations was the plight of investors. Few would have lost as much as is implied by the sharp fall in share prices (between 1872 and 1873) of nearly 50% which historians often cite (Gömmel 1992). But one contemporary study (van den Borght 1883) showed that corporate shareholding in this period offered at best an uncertain path to financial success. Its estimates of returns over the 1871–83 period can be recast into the form of an annual rate of return discounted back to the time point of initial outlay. The results are shown in Table 6.2, differentiated across branches and between survivors and all enterprises (for which records are available). Even an investor who had picked only survivors would have done better by investing in government bonds. Those results, contrasted with the euphoric expectations of the early 1870s – as recorded, for example, in the contemporary financial press – give an impression of the shock administered to investors in these years.[4] This was not simply momentary financial distress on top of a basically sound 'real' economy, for a deep depression affecting many sectors of the economy followed the crisis of 1873.[5]

Given the results, mounting public criticism of the institutional arrangements in the German capital market seems understandable. Demands were made for government investigation and institutional reforms. These were part of a more general shift in public sentiment towards economic matters in Germany, what the historian Hans Rosenberg (1967) termed 'the discrediting of economic liberalism'. The two products of that shift which are of interest here concerned (a) company law and (b) the Bourse, or securities exchange.

Table 6.2 *Rate of return on equity investment,*
1871–83 (in % per year).

	Survivors	All
Railways	4.36	–
Mining and metal production	4.90	4.4
Metal working	−4.71	−25.9
Engineering	0	−8.3
Textiles	−0.4	−4.54
Breweries	3.00	1.35
Construction	−7.80	−23.0
Banks	6.13	5.26
Average, entire sample	4.41	2.61
N	294	489

Source: van den Borght 1883 and author's calculations.

The belief that the free incorporation law of 11 June 1870 had eased fraudulent business dealings and especially the exploitation of passive investors by insider promoters was an input which went into the debate of the 1870s and 1880s (see Schubert and Hömmelhoff 1985). For a number of reasons (irrelevant here), a new law was long in coming; but eventually, in 1884, it was enacted. Perhaps the new law's most important feature was its strengthening of suppliers of capital relative to company promoters and managers. It did this by strengthening the supervisory board (*Aufsichtsrat*) at the expense of managers. Supplementary measures included an increase in the minimum denomination of shares companies could issue to 1000 marks, severe penalties for managers' failure to disclose information concerning their private business activities, and various other restraints on managerial autonomy, most importantly the provision for a supervisory board consisting of shareowner representatives with powers to appoint and fire company executives. One of the (probably unintended) results of this legislation was to strengthen the role of the larger universal banks already in business. For one thing, the increased minimum share size (and minimum capital for tradable shares of one million marks) gave banks already operating an advantage over potential entrants (since there were economies of scale in marketing shares). Moreover, thanks to the absence of restrictions on proxy voting on shares deposited with those banks, the latter tended to dominate the shareholders meetings – which elected the supervisory boards and decided strategic issues. But although this most probably facilitated concentration in banking and enhanced 'bank power', an important result of the 1884 law was an improvement in the quality of information available to the actual and potential shareholders of business corporations. It did not obviate the need for additional monitoring devices, e.g. those applied by the commercial banks, but it augmented, rather than substituted for, such devices. I do not think it far fetched to see the law of 1884 as a means for reducing informational asymmetry between business corporations and their supplies of capital. In that connection it is interesting that the prestigious London *Economist* devoted a number of articles to the law, applauding most of its provisions – mainly because of their information-enhancing effects (though they did not use the term) – and recommending similar legislation for Britain (*The Economist* 9 and 16 Feb. 1884; see also Tilly 1988 and Reich 1979).

Germany's security exchanges stood out as a second major target of the political reaction against economic liberalism. Here, too, policy measures had the unintended result of favouring the large universal banks. Direct regulatory steps were long in coming, however. For one thing, the security exchanges were traditionally self-governing bodies and they themselves initiated some reforms. Thus the Berlin Bourse tightened up admission requirements and introduced mandatory prospectuses for officially listed securities in 1881–2 (Loeb 1896; Tilly 1992; Gömmel 1992). For another, indirect measures such as the stamp tax on security transactions introduced in 1881 may have satisfied some critics (and it certainly stimulated a powerful counteraction on the part of defenders of the exchanges) (see, for example, *Deutsche Ökonomist*, 1883: 3, 27, 44, etc.). In subsequent years the tax was increased. One of its results, as anticipated above, was to strengthen the larger universal banks, particularly those with Berlin headquarters, for they were major traders of securities and could match buy and sell orders outside of the exchange – and thus avoid the tax. Clear losers were the smaller private bankers. In any case, the greatest shift – and direct regulation – first came in the 1890s, culminating in the Bourse Law of 1896. The political climate which led up to the securities exchange law and its immediate results have been well studied (Gömmel 1992; Meier 1992; Schulz 1994). The most important results were the following:

(1) a ban on futures trading in most industrial shares;
(2) institutionalization of official brokers (*Kursmakler*) and the system of 'unified prices' as a norm;
(3) two important changes affecting the admission of securities to trading:
    (a) a prospectus describing the financial status of security issuers became mandatory, and the intermediating bankers were made

liable for damages related to misleading or false information therein;

(b) a lag of one year between a company's founding and introduction of its shares to exchange trading became mandatory.

The literature is clear in its judgement of the measures (1) and (3b): they strengthened the large universal banks and thus accelerated concentration in the banking sector (adding to the effects of taxation already mentioned) (e.g. Riesser 1910). On the other hand, some contemporary and historical studies have stressed the informational improvements brought by the reforms. Both changes (2) and (3a) could be said to have improved the quality of information reaching the ultimate investors and thus enhanced their confidence in transactions on the exchanges (Schulz 1994). The law of 1896 was later modified (e.g. in 1908), but it probably did contribute, on balance, to a strengthening of the large universal banks as intermediaries of industrial finance relative to the Bourse. Nevertheless, it would be misleading to regard the Bourse as no more than a subsidiary of the banks. An important competitive arena, where capital market information – which transcended the insider information possessed by the 'great banks' – was generated and became generally accessible. 'Proving' that point, of course, is another matter. Some relevant pieces of evidence are discussed in the next section.

Before proceeding, however, I summarize this section as follows. Marked shifts in government policy stances and policy measures took place over the nineteenth century. The state's treatment of banks of issue, then company law and security exchange regulation, all helped shape the historical development of the German capital market. That result represented neither the triumph of 'the market' nor that of the institution 'great banks', but a combination of the two. It corresponded to a particular balance of power and interactions between financial markets and the hierarchy operated by those 'great banks'. It now remains to be seen whether that balance facilitated the development of a capital market in Germany which was able to satisfactorily meet the country's demand for industrial finance.

II

The question posed at the end of the previous section is an important one, though difficult to answer. One way of responding to it is to undertake comparative history and to attempt to determine whether Germany's capital market did significantly more or less for the financing of industry than the capital markets of other, comparable countries. For the sake of convenience, I take Great Britain as a basis for comparison (which means,

Table 6.3 *Average annual industrial investment and industrial new issue activity in Germany and the United Kingdom, 1882–1913 (in millions of pounds and marks).*

	United Kingdom		Germany	
	Fixed investment[a]	New issues[b]	Fixed investments[c]	New issues
1882–5	23	15.5	480	100
1886–90	21	22.8	1110	212
1891–5	27	16.4	398	123
1896–1900	49	51.9	2299	667
1901–5	60	27.2	802	440
1906–10	51	32.4	1918	815
1911–13	53	28.3	3191	967

Notes:
[a] Gross investment in millions of pounds sterling
[b] Category 'Capital created' (of IMM)
[c] Net investment in millions of marks
Sources: Investment:
UK: Feinstein 1972.
Germany: Hoffmann *et al.* 1965.
New Issues:
UK: *The London Economist; and Investor's Monthly Manual,* 1882–1913.
Germany: Kleiner 1914, Tilly 1984.

in effect, a comparison of London and Berlin). Table 6.3 introduces some relevant data: new issues of industrial securities in relation to estimated net investment (in industry and mining). By sheer weight of new issue activity (taking the pound equal to around 20 marks), the comparison of trends clearly favours Germany (see also Figure 6.1).

Such a comparison may be misleading, to be sure, since Britain's capital market financed a much larger share of foreign investment than did Germany's: over the 1880–1913 period the former's share averaged to slightly over 50%, the latter's to about half that (26–27%).[6] A comparison of the sectoral distribution of new domestic issues might be more to the point. Table 6.4 offers such a comparison, including data on rates of growth in the different sectors. It is slightly favourable to Germany in the sense that new issues there were concentrated in a few high-growth sectors, in Britain less so.[7] However, it is important to focus upon one obvious reason for this difference. The institutional reforms of company law and the security exchanges discussed in the previous section led, on balance, to a much more selective use of the corporate business form in Germany than was typical in Britain in the period observed. With an average number of 4000 to 5000 incorporations per year, Britain was

Table 6.4 *Sectoral rates of growth and distribution of new issues.*
(a) Germany, 1880–1913 (in %)

| Branch | Rates of growth | | Share in portfolio | |
	Mean	Standard deviation	Including sector 12	Excluding sector 12
1 Mining	4.13	4.41	5.3	6.8
2 Quarrying	4.30	8.58	1.2	1.5
3 Metals	5.65	7.64	15.8	20.4
4 Engineering	6.01	6.34	10.5	13.5
5 Chemicals	5.98	3.85	4.8	6.2
6 Textiles	2.52	8.11	2.1	2.7
7 Wood and leather	3.62	7.75	2.2	2.9
8 Food and drink	2.81	3.91	3.2	4.2
9 Utilities	9.80	10.37	16.6	31.4
10 Construction	4.22	7.17	2.5	3.2
11 Transportation	5.63	3.19	10.5	13.4
12 Trade, finance and insurance	3.50	2.27	23.8	–
13 Miscellaneous portfolio	2.73	2.33	2.2	2.9
14 Portfolio, mean			5.51	5.96
15 Portfolio, standard deviation			3.09	

(b) UK, 1882–1913 (in %)*

| Branch | Rates of Growth | | |
	Mean	Standard deviation	Share in portfolio
1 Mining			3.33[a]
2 Quarrying	2.31	7.28	2.00[b]
3 Metals	2.55	9.05	1.43[a]
4 Chemicals	3.63	8.71	4.31
5 Engineering	3.00	9.84	10.60
6 Textiles	1.52	9.33	4.82
7 Food and drink	1.38	4.36	20.71
8 Gas, electricity and water	4.86	3.89	5.16
9 Paper	5.04	10.78	1.76
10 Transport and communications	2.74	2.44	26.60[c]
11 Distribution	2.16	4.00	1.28
12 GDP	2.00	2.64	18.00[d]
13 Portfolio	2.45	8.20	100

Notes:
* Actually covers years 1882–1905, 1907 and 1910–12
[a] Data on new issues of mining and metal production enterprises were merged as originally collected. Here they are assigned to coal and iron and steel as in the 1907 production census: 3:1
[b] As in note 1 with 1907 weight = 13/126 for coal mining
[c] Includes 'Docks and shipping'
[d] Category 'Other' in 'Capital created' statistics of IMM
Source: Tilly 1984, and text.

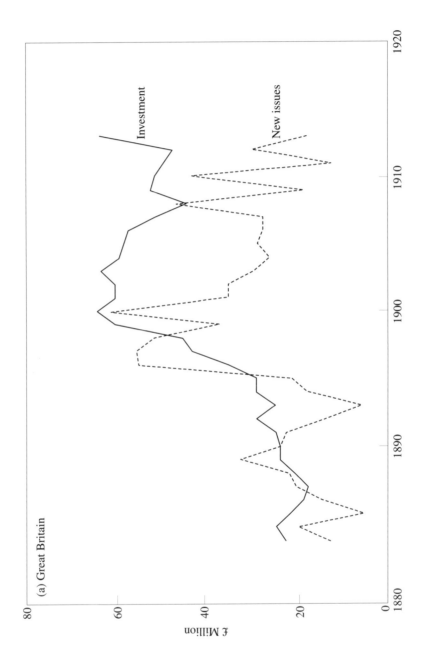

(a) Great Britain

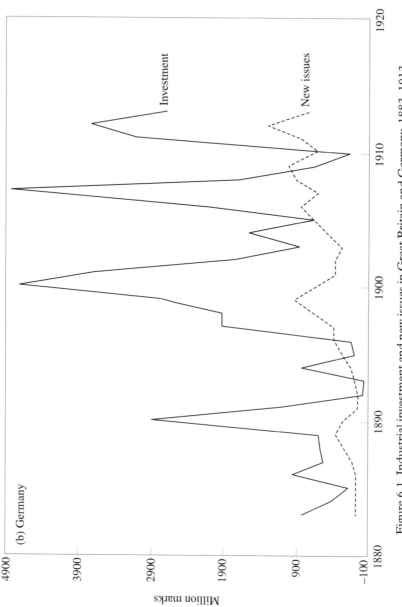

Figure 6.1 Industrial investment and new issues in Great Britain and Germany, 1883–1913

ahead of Germany by a factor of about 10; and the share of incorporated businesses which ever entered the organized capital market (by marketing shares there) was perhaps one fourth as large as in Britain (about 3% as compared with 14%).[8] Enterprises 'in' the German capital market were 'samples' from a population that differed from their British counterparts. Thus, even this comparison suffers from the basic 'identification problem', namely from the fact that Germany's superior performance could have resulted from a different, possibly more dynamic, demand for domestic industrial finance. That motivates the search for additional standards of capital market comparison.

I turn, then, to capital market pricing. Price behaviour is relevant here, since wide swings in security prices imply, *ceteris paribus*, less liquidity for security holders and, hence, higher costs of finance to issuers. In addition, wide spreads of returns on securities – both across different types of securities and as between ultimate buyers and sellers – indicate market imperfections which affect, just as they reflect, the ability of capital markets to mobilize finance efficiently. More specifically, the higher costs of intermediation represented by wide spreads imply, *ceteris paribus*, higher costs of finance to industry.

A comparative look at the long-run behaviour of security prices in Britain and Germany (i.e. London and Berlin) is a useful starting point. Figure 6.2 depicts a pattern for realized rates of return (which are dominated by price fluctuations). It suggests that the London market was less volatile in aggregate than its Berlin counterpart, but that this difference shrank over time and mainly because the volatility of returns in the Berlin market declined so markedly. This improvement characterized the overall structure of returns in the Berlin market. Figure 6.3 compares the standard deviation across the average annual rates of return for sixteen security groups in Berlin with predicted values from a regression of the following form: StdDev (t) = 3.987 + 0.826 Mean Returns (t) − 0.002 TIME. The independent variables are significant at the 1% level. The downward trend in volatility and growing convergence are unmistakable. Examining sectoral differences in returns in both capital markets, moreover, does not alter the impression of convergence and near equivalence (Edelstein (1982) and Tilly (1992) find very little evidence of inefficiency – in the sense of significant sectoral differences in returns not explained by volatility differences). That is significant, I believe, for given the widespread opinion among economic historians (Edelstein 1982; McCloskey 1982; Kennedy 1987) that there was no more efficient capital market in the world than London's at the end of the nineteenth century, and given the large share of relatively volatile industrial shares in the Berlin market, the almost negligible differences between the two imply that Germany's

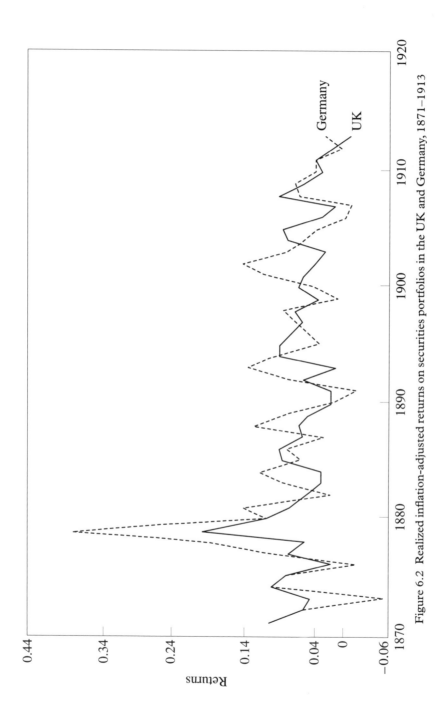

Figure 6.2 Realized inflation-adjusted returns on securities portfolios in the UK and Germany, 1871–1913

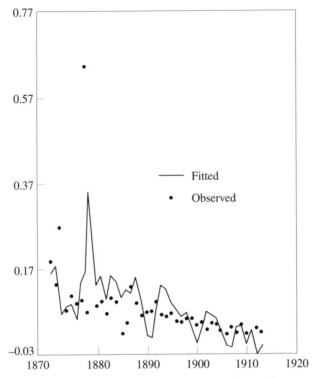

Figure 6.3 Standard deviation among sixteen German
security classes, 1871–1913

principal capital market was, by international comparative standards, a
well-functioning one, one which went a good way towards meeting the
demands for industrial finance placed upon it.

That conclusion also anticipates the judgement of this last section of
the chapter – which takes up the question of the 'spread' of prices of
newly issued industrial shares, i.e. the difference between that received by
the issuer and that paid by the ultimate investor. That difference, as indicated above, corresponds to the costs (including profits) of intermediation of industrial finance. In a typical case the industrial firm which
wished to raise capital approached its own bankers, who then responded –
either alone or in concert with other banks – with an offer. These offers
involved much detail, but the crucial point was the issue price they recommended. Since bankers' gains depended on the spread between the
price negotiated with the issuing firm and that realized in the market,
bankers bargained hard for a low price, industrial firms for a higher one.
Sometimes the parties negotiated a fixed commission based on the

nominal value of the issue, but the fixed price contract – which left most of the risk and possible gain to the bankers – seems to have been the typical arrangement. The standard costs of each issue involved the costs of printing and distributing the prospectuses, printing and registering the shares, taxes, and a few other items. They were usually borne by the issuing industrial firms, but they were to some extent negotiable, and in many cases bankers proved willing to assume all costs in exchange for a favourably low issue price. Quite frequent was the practice of negotiating a fixed price with a bank syndicate, the syndicate then offering existing shareholders first choice on a pro rata basis and at a slightly higher price.[9]

Estimates of the spread on industrial issues are thus highly dependent on the available security price information. Two such measures are utilized here. The first of these is based on those relatively few cases in which companies supplied information on both the price and volume of issue and the total net proceeds. The difference between the two represents the issue costs. These costs, taken as a percentage of total net capital raised, is the measure, 'Spread I' of Table 6.5. The second indicator ('Spread II') corresponds to the difference between the price bankers paid and the price offered old shareholders – as a percentage of the former. This might be said to reflect the relative bargaining positions of issuing firms and banks. In any case, it does reflect bankers' gains and, moreover, is frequently mentioned in the sources. A third measure of spread was calculated, based on the difference between the fixed price negotiated with bankers and an estimate of the average price prevailing in the month or quarter immediately following the date of issue. This estimate, however, contained too many gaps and has been left out of Table 6.5.

Table 6.5 summarizes the estimates, adding to them information concerning the size of the issue, capitalization and age of issuing firm, and status of the intermediating bankers. The range of estimates is quite large, from about 4% to 25%. The measures are not of equal relevance, however. The prices and profits realized by bankers are not measures of the cost of capital to issuing firms, though they are related to them. Independent estimates of bankers' profits, based on syndicate reports in the archives, suggest a range from 3% to 6 or 7%.[10] That is, the relevant range is between roughly 4% and 7%. It is necessary to point out that bankers may have accepted a low price (or spread) in exchange for other longer-term advantages. For example, the four bankers who intermediated the issue of 12 million marks of new shares (in connection with the acquisition of coal mining properties) for the Harpener Mining Company in 1889 demanded as a quid pro quo the exclusive rights to all of the company's financial business for the next ten years and corresponding representation on its supervisory board.[11] Note, however, that the advantage of smaller 'up-front' charges for industrial firms may have out-

Table 6.5 *Two measures of investment banking spread on the issue of German industrial securities, 1885–1913.*

Indicator	Spread I		Spread II	
	Mean	StdDev	Mean	StdDev
Banker price[a]	143	26	145	40.7
Shareholder price			154	40.9
Estimated market price				
Year-end price			184	66
Spread	0.048	0.024	0.063	0.069
Value of issue[b]	5.0	8.5	2.1	2.7
Enterprise capital[c]	12.2	14.7	10.6	17.9
Enterprise age[d]	26	32	20	13
Banker status[e]	1.46	0.8	1.2	0.8
Sample size		16		25

Notes:
[a] See text
[b] Nominal (par) value in millions of marks
[c] In millions of marks
[d] In years
[e] Prominent banks = 2, middling banks = 1, small banks = 0

weighed any losses imputable to the longer-term concessions they made to the banks (see Calomiris 1992 for a similar argument).

Are those costs 'high' or 'low'? Only comparative standards can furnish an answer. International comparison is one possibility. According to recent estimates by Charles Calomiris (1992), German spreads were significantly lower than in the US. His estimates are not completely comparable with those presented here, mainly because of the sparseness of the pre-1914 American data. Nevertheless, his finding that German spreads were less than half of the American ones (8% as compared to 18%) conforms to our results. For Great Britain some of the scattered evidence on underwriting and issue costs has been summarized by Cottrell (1980: 115, 131, 185–6; but see also Edelstein 1982: 50–65). He suggests a figure of from 1% to 5% of nominal share prices as a typical range for relatively large and established industrial enterprises. That would be roughly comparable to the German estimates reported here, though the character of the enterprises and sectoral distribution will have differed (see Tilly 1984). This was not quite the view, I should add, of Lavington's older study of the English capital market. He cited average charges of between 1.5 and 2% as roughly typical for bond issues in both countries. For industrial shares, however, Lavington cited much higher

Table 6.6 *Structure of new industrial security issues in London and Berlin, 1883–1913 (share of ordinary shares in total in %).*

Year	London		Berlin	
	OS	Total in £ thousands	OS	Total in DM millions
1883–6	61	53,011	51	376.8
1887–9	56	75,116	80	719.7
1890–3	72	74,621	38	460
1894–1900	47	298,706	76	3741.3
1901–3			51	1105.6
1904–6	22	36,539	76	1161.5
1907–8			64	1500.4
1909–13	19	66,882	70	1302.4
Weighted average:				
1883–1913	40		73	

spreads – from a minimum of 2.5% to as much as 25%, even 50%! And he suggested that German charges were likely to be lower (Lavington 1921: 218–19). Once again, however, true comparison across national capital markets really requires standardization for the character of the real investment financed. One additional supporting point deserves mention here: the spread data discussed above relate to ordinary shares (or common stock). Comparison among new issues in the London and Berlin markets over the 1880–1913 period reveals, in fact, that ordinary shares were far more important in Berlin than in London. Table 6.6 summarizes the relevant information. This suggests that the German capital market – here represented by Berlin – developed more adequate facilities for the finance of equity capital than did Great Britain. Therefore, though exact figures are lacking, it seems likely that risky industrial investment played a larger role in the German capital market in the period than in Britain. That supports the hypothesis that German industrial spreads were lower than British ones. Thus, it seems justifiable to argue that German institutional arrangements for the supply of industrial finance were, by international comparative standards, more than adequate.

Conclusion

The purpose of this concluding section is to summarize the chapter's findings in the light of the larger themes it hoped to address. It runs the risk of being repetitive, but may have the virtue of illuminating certain relationships which the historical description has obscured. The chapter set out to elucidate three general points: (1) the importance of the role played by the state in the shaping of the development of national financial systems; (2) the truly historical, or path-dependent, character of that financial development; and (3) the complexity of comparisons of financial systems. The following paragraphs restate the chapter's historical argument, largely in narrative form, but with an eye to those broader themes.

Governments profoundly influenced the development of financial institutions in Germany. Their need for financial services stimulated the joint growth of banking institutions and an organized capital market, especially in the early decades of the nineteenth century. As private demands for finance began to mount in the 1830s, governments responded with a variety of attempts to regulate both those demands and the organizations available to supply them. Many avenues of influence linked government with the evolving financial system. An important one mentioned, but not discussed here, concerns the state's demand for finance – both directly as a user of private savings and indirectly as motivation for regulatory measures. Instead, this chapter focuses on just three avenues of such influence: state controls over the money supply and especially the issue of paper money (bank-notes); government regulation of company law and especially incorporation rights; and public controls over the security exchanges (Bourse).

The first of these – government controls over the money supply – received only brief treatment here (they are dealt with in greater detail in other publications) (Ziegler 1993; Tilly 1989). They became important in the 1840s, and gradually drove commercial banking experiments away from concentration on short-term commercial credit and payments transactions and towards the riskier, longer-term, field of industrial and investment banking. The ongoing, cumulative investment of public resources in the central bank of issue and its interregional payments system generated economies of scale, public revenues, ties of interdependence (between central bank and commercial banks) and also politically potent vested interests, which, *in toto*, made the system, with its division of labour between universal banks on the one hand and a strong central bank of issue on the other, in a sense irreversible.

The second set of measures encouraged at first (in the phase of relaxation into the 1870s) the emergence of industrial corporations and of corporate banks catering especially to the needs of large-scale enterprises, then, since the crisis of the 1870s, concentration among industrial enterprises and the strengthening of the larger universal banks at the expense of their smaller, locally based rivals (private and corporate). The law of

1884 probably had a net positive effect on industrial finance by improving the flow of information on industrial enterprises to ultimate investors. However, it also contributed to concentration in industry and in banking, partly because it made monitoring of large-scale enterprises by the larger banks easier. The third set of policy measures produced changes in the operations of the security exchanges and with effects very similar to those of regulation of corporations: they improved the flow of information about investment opportunities to private investors, but they especially favoured the larger universal banks as intermediaries relative to the open security markets and to smaller banks. That is, they also contributed to concentration in banking. In and of themselves, those were irreversible effects in the sense that enterprise concentration is less easy to undo than to permit. However, both of these policy sets were part of, and consistent with, the changes in the predominant economic ideology among policy-makers since the 1870s: the shift to the view which assigned low priority to maintaining competitive markets and which showed a marked preference for ordered, cooperative arrangements (such as cartels). Banking concentration was not seen as a 'bad' *per se*, and no measures were undertaken to correct it. This strengthened the unidirectional character of the shifts described.

Nevertheless, competition among banks retained sufficient vitality and capital market institutions remained sufficiently strong to ensure that gains of specialization and economies of scale in finance were passed on to users of the capital market, at least in part. The creation of virtually nation-wide branch banking systems by the largest banks (*Konzerne*) did not represent pure gain in market power, partly because of continued, indeed intensified, competition 'among the few' giants, and partly because the branching movement itself was a response to the expansion of supra-regional networks of public savings banks and credit cooperatives, that is, to competition for savings. In addition, as industrial enterprises continued to grow, the largest among them became quite independent of the 'great banks', which meant that monitoring of those enterprises by the banks on behalf of investors became less valuable for the latter. This strengthened the capital market relative to the larger banks. Thus enhanced competition in the financial sector lay behind the declining rates of return and declining investment spreads – which reflected falling costs of using the capital market – discussed earlier.

That last point leads to consideration of the third general theme mentioned above: the complexity of 'system comparison'. The question has relevance for current discussions of the relative merits of universal and specialized banking or, more generally, for the comparative analysis of 'bank-oriented' and 'market-oriented' financial systems. The Anglo-

German comparison of this chapter pitted a capital market dominated by a few large players ('great banks') against the broader-based London market with its many smaller-sized actors. At one level the comparison could be said to favour Germany since the costs of industrial finance were probably lower (and certainly not higher) than those evident in the British capital market, while the share of risky industrial takers of capital was doubtless higher in Germany. Moreover, in the 'regular' banking business not covered by the explicit comparison, the share of risky industrial customers will have been a good deal higher in Germany than Britain. It is most unlikely that British industry was better served by this segment of the financial system than Germany's. At another level, to be sure, the comparison is fallacious: London can be said to have served an economy quite different in structure from that served by Berlin. It was mainly for this reason that the London capital market was embedded in a different financial system, with a different kind of commercial banking, a different system of business law, a securities market with different trading rules from those surrounding the Berlin capital market. That is, the universal banks differed from specialized banks in part because they were 'locked into' and integral parts of a much different institutional environment. That is one aspect of their complexity making system comparison difficult. The other important aspect concerns their changeability over time. Both 'systems' were changing in the period observed here (between 1870 and 1914). British finance was becoming more global, commercial banks more powerful relative to the rest of the London financial world; and at the same time German finance was becoming more market orientated, industrial enterprise more independent. The extent to which the 'success' of the German system in the period depended upon its powerful universal banks, to what extent on its vigorously developing financial markets, remains just as unsettled as the question of the extent to which the system's basic characteristics changed during these same years. These represent challenges for further research.

NOTES

1 This is the place to mention the Prussian Edict of 17 January 1820, which made any further increase in the government debt dependent upon approval of an 'estates general' (*Vereinigte Provinzialstände*). That is, the Prussian state offered, in effect, parliamentary controls over future spending and borrowing. The promise was offered to counter criticism of the high level of government debt which was made public at this same time.

2 The political bases of the free incorporation law of 1870 are discussed in Böhme 1966. For an interesting commentary on the 'results' of that law seen

from the perspective of a Prussian official (probably Ernst Engel, then head of the Prussian statistical office), see 'Bestimmungen über Aktien-Gesellschaften', in Deutsches Zentral-Archiv, Rep. 120, II a, Report of 28 October 1876, esp. p. 5b.

3 In real terms the money supply rose by 7.6% (note circulation by 27%) and the discount rate fell by 4.7%, 1871–3; and from 1873–6 the former fell by about 2% (note circulation by 30%) and the latter rose by 1.7%. See Sprenger 1982 and Tilly 1973.

4 The fact that 'Banks' did fairly well in this sample deserves further attention. The result is partly a reflection of the heterogeneity of the sample – which includes some banks of issue and mortgage banks as well. See Spree 1977; *Jahresberichte der Ältesten der Berliner Kaufmannschaft* (security exchange reports), 1871–5; also Böhme 1966.

5 As H. Mottek and others have pointed out, the depression of the 1870s was doubtless the most severe one in Germany's nineteenth-century history. (It lasted until 1878–9, longer than Germany's depression in the 1930s.) See Mottek 1966.

6 Edelstein 1982. It is worth mentioning that British domestic new issues are highly correlated with fixed investment in this period, while the German values show no significant connection. However, the much greater variance of the German investment series may be the principal reason for the difference. See also Eichengreen 1982.

7 See Kennedy and Britton 1985 and Tilly 1986 for the argument that an extension of the comparison to include risk as well as returns to investment for the 1880–1913 period is even more unfavourable to the British capital market.

8 A problem of comparability arises here, involving the German 'private' corporations (GmbH) and the British ones. On this see Tilly 1984 and Lavington 1921.

9 The basic sources used here were contemporary publications, the stock exchange manual, *Salings-Börsen-Jahrbuch*, and the business weekly, *Der Deutsche Ökonomist*; in addition, I drew on some archival materials pertaining to placement syndicates. My thanks to the Oppenheim Bankhausarchiv (OHA) and its director, Frau Gabriele Teichmann, for facilitating the use of these materials.

10 These cover industrial and bank issues over the period from about 1880 to 1900 (OHA, Nos. 149, 202, 204, 205, 210).

11 Copies of Sale Agreement and Minutes of Meetings, November and December, 1889, in OHA, No. 210.

BIBLIOGRAPHY

Blumberg, H. 1960. 'Zur Finanzierung der Neugründungen und Erweiterungen von Industriebetrieben in Form der Aktiengesellschaften während der fünf-ziger des 19. Jahrhunderts in Deutschland, am Beispiel der preußischen Verhältnisse erläutert', in M. Mottek *et al.* (eds.), *Studien zur Geschichte der industriellen Revolution in Deutschland*. E. Berlin.

156   *Richard Tilly*

Böhme, H. 1966. *Deutschlands Weg zur Grossmacht.* Cologne.

Borchardt, K. 1961. 'Zur Frage des Kapitalmangels in der ersten Hälfte des 19. Jahrhunderts in Deutschland', *Jahrbücher für Nationalökonomie und Statistic* 173:401–21.

Bösselmann 1939. *Die Entwicklung des deutschen Aktienwesens im 19. Jahrhundert.* Berlin.

Brockhage, B. 1910. 'Zur Entwicklung des preussisch-deutschen Kapitalexports', in Gustav Schmoller and Max Sering (eds.), *Staats- und socialwissenschaftliche Forschungen* 148. Leipzig.

Calomiris, C. 1992.'The Costs of Rejecting Universal Banking: American Finance in the German Mirror, 1870–1914'. Unpublished conference paper. Cambridge, Mass.

Cottrell, P. 1980. *Industrial Finance, 1830–1914: The Finance and Organization of English Manufacturing Industry.* London.

Edelstein, M. 1982. *Overseas Investment in the Age of High Imperialism: The United Kingdom, 1850–1914.* London.

Eichengreen, B. 1982. 'The Proximate Determinants of Domestic Investment in Victorian Britain', *Journal of Economic History* 42: 145–78.

Feinstein, C. 1972. *National Income, Expenditure and Output of the United Kingdom, 1855–1965.* Cambridge.

Gebhard, H. 1928. *Die Berliner Börse von den Anfängen bis zum Jahre 1896.* Berlin.

Gömmel, R. 1992. 'Entstehung und Entwicklung der Effektenbörse im 19. Jahrhundert bis 1914', in H. Pohl (ed.), *Deutsche Börsengeschichte.* Frankfurt a.M.

Hoffmann, W. *et al.* 1965. *Das Wachstum der deutschen Wirtschaft seit der Mitte des 19. Jahrhunderts.* New York, Heidelberg, Berlin.

Kennedy, W. P. 1987. *Industrial Structure, Capital Markets, and the Origins of British Economic Decline.* Cambridge.

Kennedy, W. P. and Britton, R. 1985. 'Portfolioverhalten und wirtschaftliche Entwicklung im späten 19. Jahrhundert. En Vergleich zwischen Grossbritannien und Deutschland. Hypothesen und Spekulationen', in Tilly 1985: 45–89.

Kleiner, H. 1914. *Emissionsstatistik in Deutschland.* Berlin and Stuttgart.

Lavington, F. 1921. *The English Capital Market.* London.

Loeb, E. 1896. 'Kursfeststellung und Maklerwesen an der Berliner Effektenbörse', *Jahrbücher für Nationalökonomie und Statistik* 3:11.

McCloskey, D. 1982. 'Comment on Kennedy and Phillips', *Journal of Economic History* 42: 117–18.

Martin, P. C. 1969. 'Die Entstehung des preussischen Aktiengesetzes von 1843', *VSWG* 56: 499–542.

Meier, J. C. 1992. *Die Entstehung des Börsengesetzes vom 22. Juni 1896* (Studien zur Wirtschafts- und Sozialgeschichte 9). St Katharinen.

Mottek, H. 1966. 'Die Gründerkrise', *Jahrbuch für Wirtschaftsgeschichte* 1: 51–128.

Passow, R. 1922. *Die Aktiengesellschaft, eine wirtschaftswissenschaftliche Studie.* Jena.

Reich, N. 1979. 'Auswirkungen der deutschen Aktienrechtsreform von 1884 auf die Konzentration der deutschen Wirtschaft', in J. Kocka and N. Horn (eds.), *Recht und Entwicklung der Grossunternehmen im 19. Und frühen 20. Jahrhundert.* Göttingen.

Riesser, J. 1910. *Die deutschen Grossbanken und ihre Konzentration im Zusammenhang mit der Entwicklung der Gesamtwirtschaft in Deutschland.* Jena.

Rosenberg, H. 1934. *Die Weltwirtschaftskrise, 1857–1859.* 2nd edn 1974. Göttingen.

1967. *Grosse Depression und Bismarckzeit.* Berlin.

Schubert, W. and Hömmelhoff, P. 1985. *Hundert Jahre modernes Aktienrecht: Eine Sammlung von Texten und Quellen zur Aktienrechtsreform 1884 mit zwei Einführungen.* Berlin.

Schulz, W. 1994. *Das deutsche Börsengesetz. Die Entstehungsgeschichte und wirtschaftlichen Auswirkungen des Börsengesetzes von 1896.* Frankfurt a.M.

Spree, R. 1977. *Die Wachstumszyklen der deutschen Wirtschaft, 1840–1880.* Berlin.

Sprenger, B. 1982. *Geldmengenänderungen in Deutschland im Zeitalter der Industrialisierung (1835 bis 1913).* Cologne.

Tilly, R. 1966. *Financial Institutions and Industrialization of the Rhineland, 1815–1870.* Madison.

1973. 'Zeitreihen zum Geldumlauf in Deutschland, 1870–1913', *Jahrbücher für Nationalökonomie und Statistik* 187: 330–63.

1984. 'Zur Finanzierung des Wirtschaftswachstums in Deutschland und Grossbritannien 1880–1913', in E. Helmstädter (ed.), *Die Bedingungen des Wirtschaftswachstums in Vergangenheit und Zukunft.* Tübingen.

1986. 'German Banking, 1850–1914: Development Assistance to the Strong', *Journal of European Economic History* 15: 113–52.

1988. 'Unternehmermoral und -verhalten im 19. Jahrhundert. Indizien deutscher Bürgerlichkeit?', in J. Kocka (ed.), *Bürgertum im 19. Jahrhundert.* Munich.

1989. 'Banking Institutions in Historical and Comparative Perspective: Germany, Great Britain and the United States in the Nineteenth and Early Twentieth Century', *Journal of Institutional and Theoretical Economics (Zeitschrift für die gesamte Staatswissenschaft)* 145.

1992. 'Der deutsche Kapitalmarkt und die Auslandsinvestitionen von 1870 bis 1913', *Ifo Studien. Zeitschrift für empirische Wirtschaftsforschung* 38(2): 199–225.

Tilly, R. (ed.) 1985. *Beiträge zur quantitativen vergleichenden Unternehmensgeschichte.* Stuttgart.

Ullmann, H.-P. 1986. *Staatsschulden und Reformpolitik: die Entstehung moderner öffentlicher Schulden in Bayern und Baden, 1780–1820.* 2 vols. Göttingen.

van den Borght, R. 1883. *Statistische Studien über die Bewährung der Actiengesellschaften.* Jena.

Ziegler, D. 1993. 'Zentralbankpolitische "Steinzeit"? Preussische Bank und Bank of England im Vergleich', *Geschichte und Gesellschaft* 19: 475–505.

7   The role of banks and government in Spanish economic development, 1850–1935

Gabriel Tortella

Introduction[1]

Spanish economic growth was notoriously slow in the nineteenth century and accelerated perceptibly in the twentieth. All in all, however, there is a certain continuity in modern Spain's process of economic development. From the mid-nineteenth century to the 1970s, the long-term trend of the Spanish economy has been one of accelerating economic growth. Rather than increasing continuously, however, Spain experienced three successive periods of expansion at increasing rates. These periods were as follows. After several decades of no growth at all (or even possibly decline) in the early decades of the nineteenth century, national income per head started expanding, very slowly at first, in the 1840s. Around the turn of the century the rate of growth increased again (from about 0.5% to about 1%). Between the mid-1930s and the mid-1950s there was a dramatic interruption in the growth process that had started a century earlier. From the mid-1950s to the mid-1970s the Spanish economy reached the fastest growth rates in its history (around 5% on average). Since the 1970s there has been a stop-and-go pattern: there was a serious slowdown to the mid-1980s, rapid growth in the late 1980s, and a new slowdown in the early 1990s.[2]

One can find explanations for these discontinuities. In the 1840s Spain started to put its economic house in order after the Napoleonic wars, the colonial wars which ended in the loss of its overseas empire in 1824, and the first Carlist civil war (1833–9). All this involved a slow and painful reconversion from a cumbersome, declining empire into a backward nation on the European periphery, and brought about a protracted process of social modernization: political reform, redefinition of land-ownership, tax and monetary reform, revamping of the education system, building of a railway network, etc.

Around the turn of the century a new discontinuity occurred which permitted a shift of economic gears and a faster rate of growth for the next three decades. This discontinuity took place at the time of a new colonial crisis, which culminated in the Spanish–American war over Cuba and the

Philippines in 1898. The war ended in Spain's defeat and the loss of the remnants of its overseas empire. War and defeat caused a new wave of political–economic reforms which permitted the subsequent acceleration of growth, most noticeably during the First World War and the 1920s.

The third great discontinuity, that extending from the 1930s to the 1950s, needs little explanation: the effects of the Depression (although milder in Spain than in most European countries), the civil war and the disastrous economic policies of early Francoism caused a twenty-year-long interruption of growth, almost unique by European standards. In spite of the upheavals and destructions of the Second World War (which, although it affected most of the European Continent, did not touch Spain), Western Europe's recovery from them was much faster than Spain's recovery from the ravages of its civil war.

The very rapid growth of the 1950s and 1960s must be understood as a consequence of several factors acting upon the Spanish economy: first and foremost, the pull of European recovery after the war and rapid economic development thereafter; second, the belated recovery of the Spanish economy; and third, the beneficial effects of gradual liberalization by the successive Franco governments after 1951.

This chapter considers the factors in the second discontinuity, namely that around the turn of the nineteenth century to the twentieth. The factors involved were several, and their relative weight is difficult to assess.

Traditionally historians have paid attention to tariff policies, and viewed the acceleration of the early twentieth century as a consequence of the protectionist tariff of 1891. Thus Tamames, in a recent edition of his well-known manual (1990: 221), states the following: 'The new industry catering to domestic demand could only start its development . . . thanks to tariff protection . . . Industrial protectionism was definitively established in Spain in 1892 and from then on industrialization never stopped progressing.'[3]

Jürgen Donges expressed the same idea when he said that the 'system of protection acted as the catalyst in the start of the industrialization process' (1976: 25–6). However, more recent work is less sanguine about the positive effects of protectionism in the Spanish case. Prados de la Escosura (1988: esp. ch. 5) has shown that foreign trade was one of the most dynamic sectors of the Spanish economy in the nineteenth century. Tena (1988, 1989, 1992) has shown the distorting effects of protection in the early twentieth century. Fraile, in a study on the iron and steel and the textile industries in the early twentieth century, concluded that 'the effect of prohibitionist protection on Spanish industry during the first half of the twentieth century was backwardness relative to Europe' (1991: 216). Possibly even more convincing is Carreras' index of industrial production, which, according to its own author, shows that 'There is no discontinuity in the pace of [Spanish] industrial growth around 1900, nor around 1890, or 1906 [the date of a new protective tariff] . . . [W]hat obtains in the ninety years prior to the [Spanish] civil war . . . is a long period of growth, sometimes faster, sometimes slower, which suggests that Spain has a long industrial tradition' (Carreras 1987: 284).

A more recent estimate of the index of industrial production of Catalonia, Spain's leading industrial region and the one which supposedly benefited most from tariff protection, also shows, according to its author, that, up to 1935, 'Catalan industrialization progressed without sudden jumps, that is, without accelerations of great intensity' (Maluquer de Motes 1994: 66). In fact, as already mentioned, the jump in national income growth is only perceptible after 1914.

In view of all this, a search for other explanations of the second discontinuity seems advisable. This chapter will contend that a more decisive shift may have occurred around 1898, when Spain was defeated in the Spanish-American war and lost the last remnants of its overseas empire. A chain of events developed during those years which substantially modified Spain's financial system and which contributed to the relatively fast process of growth which took place during the decades before the Spanish civil war. I would summarize this chain of events as follows.

The colonial war in Cuba, which started in 1895, put a strain on the financial resources of the metropolis. Military expenditures weighed heavily on a government budget which was already in chronic deficit. The shortfall was covered by increased bank-note issues by the Bank of Spain; aside from a sudden increase in the public debt outstanding, the rapid expansion of the money supply caused a bout of inflation and a fast depreciation of the peseta which was on a fiduciary (silver) standard. The end of the war in defeat provoked widespread revulsion against establishment politicians and a deeply felt 'regeneration' movement. Economically this was translated into a serious stabilization plan (the *Plan Villaverde* of 1899) which produced the only ten-year series of budget surpluses in Spain's history. Among the consequences of this change in economic policy were a sharp appreciation of the peseta and an inflow of foreign capital. Capital imports were favoured by two factors: first, renewed confidence in the peseta, which by 1912 had recouped practically all its losses in the 1890–8 period; and second, the repatriation of capital from Cuba and Spanish America after the defeat. A substantial part of this capital was channelled into the foundation of new banks or the reorganization of old. Thus a much stronger banking system developed in Spain in the first decades of the twentieth century.

The existence of this new banking system permitted increased specialization: the Bank of Spain evolved towards the figure of a modern central
bank, and its relationship with private banks acquired original characteristics derived in part from the fact that the Spanish monetary system was
fiduciary, and also from the renewed financial needs of the government.
This relationship allowed the largest banks to practise 'mixed banking' in
the style of the German 'universal banks' or the Italian *banca mista*, and
favoured a Gerschenkronian industrial 'spurt' in the 1920s.

The nineteenth century

Regarding the matters dealt with in this chapter, the Spanish nineteenth
century was characterized by persistent budget deficits and by the weakness of the private banking sector. In spite of a surge in new bank foundations in the late 1850s and early 1860s, which brought the number of
institutions from five in 1855 to the vicinity of sixty ten years later, the
sector remained weak. Expansion was followed by a sharp contraction in
the mid-1860s, when the number of banks was greatly reduced, and so
were their assets. By 1874 the paid-up capital of the Bank of Spain was
about half of total paid-up capital of incorporated banks (and this
includes the capital of the recently founded Banco Hipotecario, the
official mortgage bank), and the proportion was even higher for demand
deposits (Tortella 1974: 263, 490–2). This situation remained for the rest
of the century, even though the number of private banks expanded somewhat after 1874: by 1899 the Bank of Spain's proportion within total
paid-up banking capital was about 40%, whereas its share of demand
deposits had grown to 75%. The hegemony of the Bank of Spain was
undoubtedly helped by the fact that it was vested with the monopoly of
bank-note issue in March 1874 (Tortella 1974: 329–30, 490–2; 1977:
table I-1 and 541–6).

A remarkable but short-lived expansion of the Spanish banking system
had taken place after 1856. In January of that year two banking laws were
issued (one on banks of issue, the other on 'credit companies'). The
Banks of Issue Law established what may be called a 'plurality of issue'
system, which meant that 'in each town only one note-issuing institution
w[ould] be permitted'. The *Credit Companies Law* was intended to favour
the establishment of incorporated business banks: it was especially aimed
at inviting the entry of branches of the large French credit companies, the
Rothschild House of Paris and the Crédit Mobilier Français of the
Péreire brothers. In ten years some sixty new banks opened in Spain,
most of them in Madrid and Barcelona, but the rest scattered throughout
the country. Of these sixty corporations, about twenty were banks of issue

and the rest credit companies. This was a remarkable growth, since in 1855 there were no more than five banking corporations. However, this rapid development concealed serious structural weaknesses, foremost among them a dangerous concentration of assets: loans to railway companies and government bonds made up most of the banks' investments.

From 1856 to 1874 the Spanish banking system was composed of four main groups: (1) *banks of issue,* which numbered about twenty in 1864; they were chartered by government decree at the rate of one per city, and granted the local monopoly of issue; the Bank of Spain was the bank of issue in Madrid; (2) *private corporate banks* ('credit companies', according to the legal expression), which also needed government authorization but were not subject to numerical limitation; (3) *unincorporated private banks* or merchant capitalists, which were subject only to the very liberal regulations concerning merchants and traders; except for a few prominent houses, our knowledge of this group is necessarily spotty (García López 1987; Otazu 1987; Tedde 1974);[4] and (4) *savings banks,* whose combined deposits grew rapidly in the last quarter of the nineteenth century, but whose financial import remained marginal until well into the twentieth century (Tedde 1991; Titos 1991).

Railway construction was very active during these years, but when in 1864 it became obvious that receipts from railway traffic did not even cover operating costs in most companies, a good number of these were forced to suspend payments, and the consequences for banks were the logical ones: many suspended payments also and in a few years most of them were forced to close, leaving many millions in unpaid debts. There was a grave financial crisis in 1866 and a political revolution in 1868. The number of banks was greatly reduced. In early 1874 there were not more than fifteen, most of them banks of issue; the credit companies, the ones that had invested most heavily in railways, disappeared almost as fast as they had come. The only important one surviving was the Crédito Mobiliario Español, the first and largest of those founded in 1856.

The number of banks was further reduced after the Bank of Spain became the issuing monopolist, as most of the old institutes of issue chose to merge with the central bank. The growth of the private banking system during the last quarter of the twentieth century was slow: the most important banks during this period were three old banks of issue which had refused to merge with the Bank of Spain (Banco de Barcelona, Banco de Santander and Banco de Bilbao), plus a few others mostly located in Catalonia, the Basque country and Madrid, notably the Crédito Mobiliario.

The vesting of the monopoly of bank-note issue in the Bank of Spain in 1874 was due to the government's need for financial support. The government had been running almost continuous budget deficits since

1850 (when budget statistics started to be published regularly), and probably for many years before. The Bank of Spain had been created (originally in 1782 under the name of Banco Nacional de San Carlos; refunded in 1829 as Banco Español de San Fernando; and rebaptized Banco de España in 1856) first and foremost as the financial supporter of the government (Tortella 1977: ch. 2). In the 1860s the size of the budget deficit had become very large: in the late sixties the deficit was about one third of total government revenues, and public debt outstanding was growing alarmingly. In 1870, public debt payments reached 53% of total budget expenditure (Comín 1987). At that time the Spanish government was having serious financial difficulties and had recourse to desperate measures to solve its day-to-day problems, such as putting up for sale the rights to exploit the Rio Tinto pyrite mines and exchanging bank charters for loans. The Banco Hipotecario was chartered in 1872 in exchange for a 100 million peseta loan,[5] after long negotiations mainly to overcome the opposition of the Bank of Spain. Two years later the bargaining with the Bank of Spain was again long and protracted, this time because the government was loath to grant the bank an outright national monopoly of issue. The reasons for this reluctance were, on the one hand, that the government was professedly liberal in economics and in politics and, on the other, that granting such monopoly at the time was an infringement upon the rights of other banks of issue. On the occasion, however, the Bank had the upper hand, and the monopoly was granted over the justified complaints (and useless legal procedures) of the other banks of issue and in exchange for a loan of 125 million pesetas. But this was not the only time the Bank of Spain came to the rescue of the government during the last quarter of the nineteenth century.

After becoming the sole authorized issuer of bank-notes the Bank made good use of its privilege at the same time as it lent generously to the government. The main activity of the Bank became the 'monetization of the public debt': the Bank loaned to the government; and the public, in accepting its notes, loaned to the Bank. The composition of the money stock underwent a marked shift during these years. Although Spain was nominally on a bimetallic standard, in 1883 the Bank decided to redeem its notes only in silver, for fear of running out of its stock of gold. Thus gold in fact ceased to circulate: silver and notes became the only currency, with deposits about one third of the money supply by 1900. Thus in fact Spain never adopted the gold standard; it went from bimetallism to a *de facto* silver standard; and since silver depreciated substantially in the last quarter of the nineteenth century, the intrinsic value of its coins was substantially below their facial value; its standard, therefore, was actually fiduciary.[6]

Figure 7.1 shows the close parallel between yearly increases in the

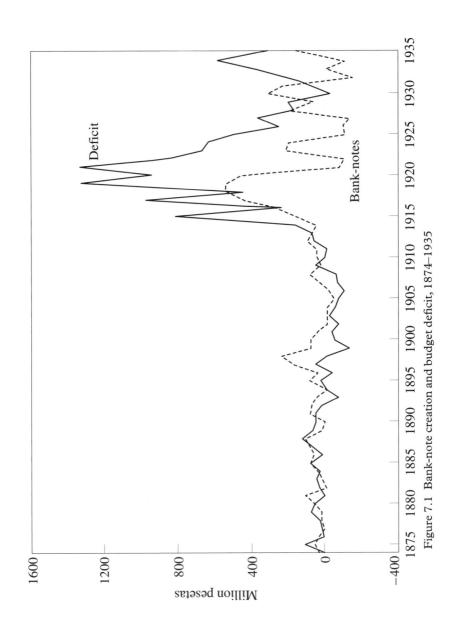

Figure 7.1 Bank-note creation and budget deficit, 1874–1935

volume of bank-notes in circulation and government budget deficits up to the inception of World War I.[7] Statistical correlation as measured by the adjusted R^2 is not very high for these years (0.229) because there are variations in year-to-year leads and lags; but the similarities in the volumes involved and the shapes of overall fluctuations are remarkable and seem to me to be convincing proof of the close dependence between the yearly issuing of bank-notes by the Bank of Spain and the financial needs of the government during the late nineteenth century. After the beginning of the Great War, correlation was not only low but practically non-existent (adjusted $R^2=0.005$), for reasons which we will see later.

Inflation and stabilization (1890–1914)

In spite of being on a fiduciary standard, the Spanish monetary system behaved in a rather conservative way during this period. The growth of the money supply was moderate, and so was its main component, bank-notes in circulation. As a matter of fact, for the 1875–1913 period the growth of the money supply in Spain was much lower than that in countries on the gold standard, such as the United States, France or England (Tortella 1974: 468–9). The reason for this was extreme caution on the part on the authorities, who were torn between their desire to establish gold convertibility and their fear of losing the specie in the vaults of the Bank of Spain.

There were two periods, however, when money in circulation increased very rapidly, and both periods coincided with wars: 1895–8 and 1914–20. The expansion during the First World War, serious though it was, escaped the control of the authorities, being largely the consequence of the hostilities beyond Spain's borders. Furthermore, owing to the country's neutrality, its balance of payments turned very favourable mainly as a consequence of the increase in its exports and the fall in its imports. Thus sudden commercial surplus was chiefly responsible for the increase in prices, but it also had two effects that were considered highly desirable: first, it produced a substantial inflow of gold; and second, the peseta appreciated considerably relative to gold and to the main foreign currencies.[8]

The earlier inflationary period, however, was different. The war that caused it was domestic or, more properly, colonial: the war of Cuban independence. The rebellion started in February 1895; Spain tried to suppress it and became increasingly mired in the conflict. The government attempted to insulate the peninsular population from the war by not increasing taxes and instead having recourse to credit from the Bank of Spain to finance war costs. Bank-notes in circulation more than doubled

between 1890 and 1898, and two thirds of this increase took place during
the war years (1895–8). In 1891 the maximum volume of bank-note
circulation was established at 1,500 million pesetas; this limit was being
approached by 1898, so a decree was issued raising it to 2,500 million.
Prices correspondingly shot up. The price index (1913=100) went from
75.2 in 1894 to 90.5 in 1898. Although at this time international prices
were recovering after the 'great depression' of the late nineteenth century,
Spanish inflation was acute, and the peseta was not backed by gold: its
rate of exchange worsened considerably. Thus in 1890 the peseta hovered
at an exchange rate of around 26.3 pesetas per pound sterling; in May
1898 the rate was at 49.2 pesetas, almost double its original or theoretical
parity of 25 pesetas per pound sterling.[9] This depreciation had a strong
negative effect on public opinion, and was viewed as part and parcel of the
humiliation of military defeat in the Spanish-American war and the end
of the Spanish colonial empire, in the sad episode known in Spanish
history and literature as 'the disaster'.

The new fiscal and monetary policies

'The disaster' caused long-lasting revulsion in Spanish society. 'As with
the Crimean war in Russia, the humiliation of defeat in 1898 forced
Spaniards to self-examination . . . At the turn of the century regeneration
was a theme essayed by all' (Carr 1966: 473). A whole literary generation
was defined by its reaction to the shock (the 'generation of 98'), and tor-
rents of ink were poured to define the formula for the regeneration of
Spain.

The main positive reaction to 'the disaster' was the *Plan Villaverde*,
devised by Raimundo Fernández Villaverde, Finance Minister in the
Silvela cabinet (March 1899 to October 1900), and later several times
Prime Minister and again Finance Minister.

His recipe for regeneration – like all others he was a regenerationist of a
kind – 'was a sound, conservative economy which would save the country
from the humiliation of a depreciated currency or the repudiation of the
National Debt. Taxation and rigid economy would "liquidate the disaster" by paying off a debt which, after the war, ate up 60 per cent of the
budget . . . Villaverde was indubitably successful in his immediate aims:
the reduction of the debt and the fight against post-war inflation' (Carr
1966: 479).

Villaverde's plan was three-pronged: budget surplus, tax reform and
debt reduction. Its crowning achievements were three-pronged also:
reduction in bank-note circulation, price stability and rise in the peseta
rate of exchange. Budget surplus was the keystone of the plan; it was

attained by a series of changes (no radical fiscal reform) in the tax system which brought about a substantial surge in revenues, and by a revamping of the public debt structure which in fact amounted to a partial repudiation (Solé Villalonga 1964: 41 note 2). It was skilfully managed, however, and provoked no bondholders' revolt, although it produced indignation in some circles.[10] The result of the increase in revenue and the fall in expenditures consequent upon debt reduction was a long series of budget surpluses (from 1899 to 1908, ten in a row). These surpluses were used to redeem public debt bonds in the possession of the Bank of Spain, which had been using them as high-powered money. The Bank was thus induced to curtail its bank-note issue: the money supply underwent a sharp contraction from 1899 to 1907, and a gradual increase afterwards so that by 1914 its total volume was about the same as it had been in 1898. As a result, the price level steadied and the pound–peseta exchange rate improved, especially after 1904 (Figure 7.2). Villaverde's aims had been attained, and his financial principles lingered for many years.

Carr does not consider this to have been an unmixed blessing: 'He and his successors did not see that, though disinflation might be defended as an immediate remedy, it did not favour growth' (1966: 479). The evidence, however, shows this to have been a period of moderate growth and substantial structural change. Industry diversified: food industries were modernized (sugar, preserves, olive oil, wine) and heavy industry, hitherto non-existent, started developing (iron and steel, cement, heavy chemicals). Agriculture was also (partially) modernized, and the basic diet clearly improved in spite of unprecedented population growth. All this was possible thanks to increased investment, stimulated by financial and political developments. The supply of loanable funds increased owing to a series of factors. Capital was repatriated from the lost colonies. Some of this capital was used to establish new banks, notably the Banco Hispano Americano (Tortella 1995), and possibly also the Banco de Vizcaya. There were also renewed waves of foreign investment induced by growing confidence in the Spanish economy and the stability of its currency (Broder 1976, 1981). In 1902 the Banco Español de Crédito was founded, largely with French capital, under the aegis of the Banque de Paris et les Pays Bas (Paribas), with the old Crédito Mobiliario Español as its nucleus. The idea of revamping the Crédito Mobiliario had been mooted in Paribas already in the mid-1880s, and shelved, to be revived when the conditions seemed right.[11] Spaniards also gained confidence in their economy, and took advantage of the stronger peseta to purchase foreign-owned Spanish companies (Tortella 1983, 1987, 1993). Finally, the increasing flow of emigrants sent home a swelling current of remittances which no doubt contributed to capital formation (García López

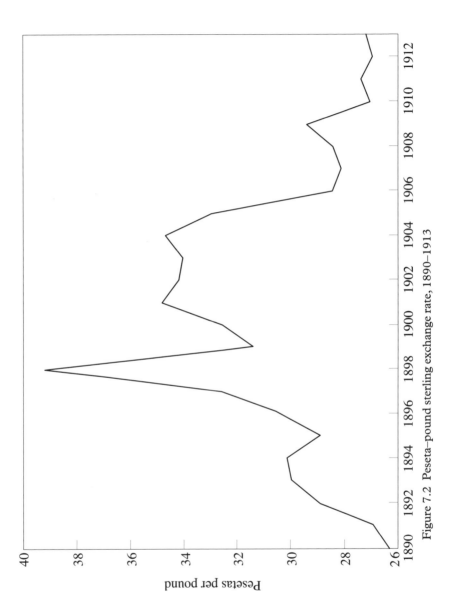

Figure 7.2 Peseta–pound sterling exchange rate, 1890–1913

1992; Sánchez Alonso 1995). On the demand side, investment was no doubt favoured by a decrease in interest rates. The Bank of Spain lowered its rates to facilitate the government's operations in public debt bonds, and the success of those operations brought about a decrease in long-term rates (Tortella and Jiménez 1986: 17–18). Entrepreneurial attitudes also changed: after centuries of indifference or even hostility towards economic activities, the Spanish nobility, following the example of a king who devoted a substantial share of his time to informed investment in the stock exchange, increasingly paid attention to business; businessmen's associations started to be formed and to play an active part in politics (Gortázar 1986; Cabrera 1983; Rey 1992). Of course bankers, especially those leading mixed banks, also doubled as entrepreneurs in typical Cameronian fashion, promoting new firms, sitting on their boards, and in general contributing a factor (entrepreneurship) in very short supply (Cameron 1994; Tortella 1994: ch. 8).[12]

The mixed banks and the new industry

After ten years of observing Villaverde's discipline, Spanish politicians returned to budget deficits in 1909, the immediate reason being the increase in military expenditure due to the war in Morocco and the 1909 political crisis known as 'the tragic week' (Comín 1988: ch. 4, esp. 631–3; Ullman 1968). Deficits, however, remained small until 1914. As Comín 1988: 621 has pointed out, the inflation produced by the First World War was the cause of the increase in public expenditure, owing to greater 'monetary costs of the services which the state supplied'. Revenues did not grow in proportion: the size of the deficit consequently shot up (see Figure 7.1). Whereas in 1909 the deficit had been 0.5% of national income, in 1915 it was 4.9%, and the average for the 1914–23 period was 3%.

How were these deficits financed? Figure 7.1 shows there was an increasing gap between increments in fiduciary circulation and deficits. In fact, most of the rise in fiduciary circulation was due to an expansion of credit to the private sector, permitted by an increase in the Bank's gold reserves and by legislation raising the maximum bank-note circulation allowed. There was pressure from the government and the public for the Bank to expand its credit facilities, especially during the Great War.[13] Furthermore, the quantity of public debt bonds in the Bank's portfolio, which had decreased substantially during the early years of the century (from some 1.5 to about 0.6 million pesetas), did not vary during the years of great deficits and great increases in public debt outstanding. The short-term operations with the Treasury also maintained a virtually con-

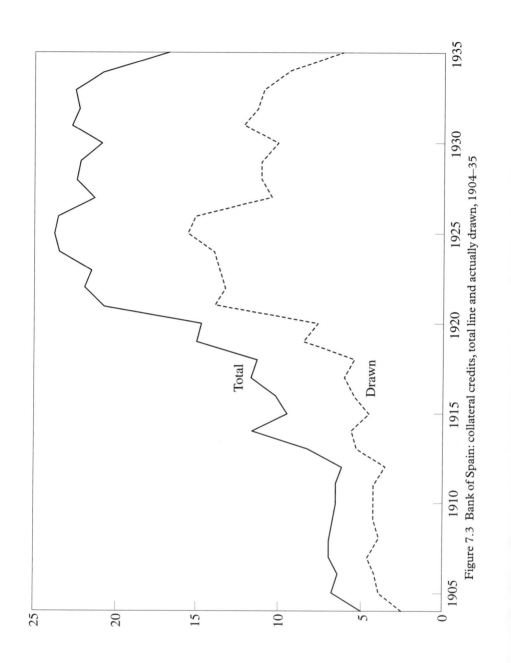

Figure 7.3 Bank of Spain: collateral credits, total line and actually drawn, 1904–35

stant volume during these years (Martín Aceña 1985: 93–7; Comín 1988: 645–69).

The answer to the above question lies in the greater role played by the private banking sector. There is evidence that the recently created large banks, together with a few of the old institutions, became active purchasers of government bonds, and that there was a tacit understanding with the Bank of Spain that this institution would grant credits almost automatically when these bonds were submitted as collateral. Figure 7.3 shows this type of credit (collateral credits) increasing after 1912, almost coinciding with the return of budget deficits (compare with Figure 7.1). Soon this method of financing the deficit (known by Spanish scholars as *indirect monetization of the debt*) became institutionalized. As the Bank of Spain divested itself of government bonds in the early years of the century, the private banks were probably invited to acquire this type of paper. Glimpses into the portfolios of private banks for these years are rare; but I can at least provide one example. On the occasion of suspension of payments by the Banco Hispano Americano in 1913 this bank published the list of its holdings: 52% of the bank's portfolio was made up by Spanish government debt bonds (Tortella and García Ruiz n.d.: 52). After 1921 the recently created Supreme Banking Council (Consejo Superior Bancario) published aggregated data of its affiliated banks; these data show that the aggregate portfolio of affiliated banks (practically all of Spanish incorporated banks) was around 15% of total assets in the 1920s and 1930s. Of this portfolio around one third (a decreasing proportion) was discounted bills, and the remainder stocks and bonds (about 40%, and increasing, the proportion of government bonds; about 25% the proportion of industrial securities).[14] Within total assets, all securities went from 9.3% in 1923 to 13.3% in 1934, and public debt bonds from 6.0% to 8.7% in the same period. The trend endured, for in 1959 government bonds made up 22.6% of total assets, and industrial securities 7.2%.[15]

From early on these government bonds were used by the banks to obtain lines of credit from the Bank of Spain. Possibly at the government's behest, the Bank did all it could to facilitate these operations whereby the Bank opened a current account for the total amount of the line of credit (*disponible*), with the agreement that only the quantity actually withdrawn (*dispuesto*) would be liable to interest. These operations probably started in 1902, when the Bank's statutes were modified in order to 'widen its genuinely mercantile sphere, as well as to devote itself to new operations', and a law and an agreement between the government and the Bank were issued which regulated the relationships between the two institutions and determined that the interest levied on loans with government bonds as collateral would be jointly fixed by the Bank and the Finance Ministry.[16]

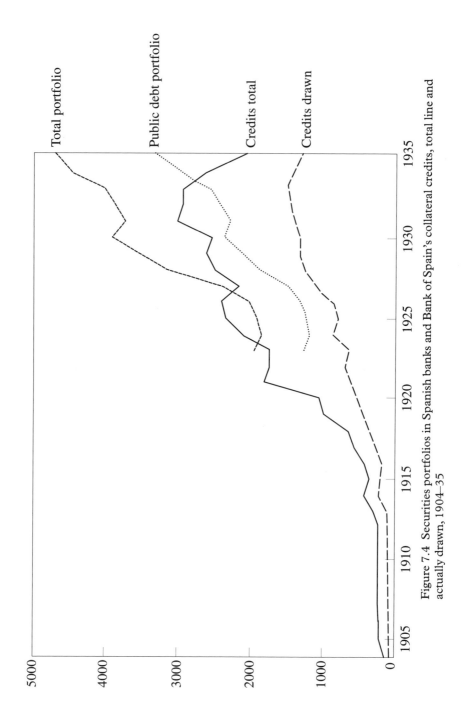

Figure 7.4 Securities portfolios in Spanish banks and Bank of Spain's collateral credits, total line and actually drawn, 1904–35

The collateral backing these operations was divided into public debt bonds and industrial stocks and bonds. In 1908 the share of public debt was 60%; in 1910, 70%; and around this figure it stood until 1913, the last year for which the Bank of Spain's reports supply this information.

It is obvious that the government was interested in promoting these operations, since they eased the placement of its bonds. In 1902 this was necessary because of the new issues of public debt, which the Bank of Spain was not allowed to purchase. Later on the government seems to have lost interest in them, since the succession of budget surpluses obviated the need to issue public debt. The Bank repeatedly complained that a government tax prevented the growth of these loan accounts. Figure 7.3 shows that their share in the Bank's balance sheet stagnated until 1913. The situation changed again during the First World War. The government did not want to have recourse to the Bank of Spain once more to finance its deficits; therefore, it had to make its bonds attractive to private lenders. As a consequence it allowed the Bank to waive the tax, then prodded it to decrease the interest rate it charged, so that in fact from 1917 onwards the rate was below the yield of the bonds. This was clearly explained to the Bank's shareholders: 'As the Board considered it opportune and convenient to reduce the interest rate in operations guaranteed with certain securities as collateral, it begged the Minister of Finance for authorization to reduce to 4% the interest on loans and credits on bonds, and obtained approval by Royal order of 12 March [1917].'[17]

This explains the banks' reliance on public debt bonds, and the high proportion of them they kept in their vaults. It also explains the resilience of Spain's mixed banks. In addition to public debt bonds, Spanish banks also held a considerable amount of industrial securities: about a quarter of their portfolios, as shown above. By combining holdings of public debt bonds with industrial securities they could devote a substantial share of their portfolio to industrial stocks and bonds, knowing that they could always use most of this paper as collateral for a loan from the Bank of Spain in a liquidity crunch. That this was a conscious policy is well known. Bankers considered borrowing on collateral from the Bank of Spain as the counterpart of their industrial promotion.[18] And, as Figure 7.4 shows, the securities portfolio of Spanish banks and the Bank of Spain's collateral credits grew in a parallel fashion during the twenties, although in the short term they fluctuated in opposite directions. The reason for this opposition seems obvious. The banks purchased public debt as a safe investment and as an insurance against bad times. They only used their bonds as collateral when they needed liquidity. Their line of credit at the Bank of Spain was proportional to the amount of bonds pledged. In difficult times (1921, 1924, 1931) they pledged greater quantities of bonds while they stopped purchasing them. The falls in total portfolio holdings in 1924 and 1931 may be due to actual disinvestment or simply to decreases in stockmarket prices. An ongoing statistical analysis (carried out by this author and Stefan Houpt) of the balance sheet statistics published by the CSB supports the above description of the banks' policies. The analysis of preliminary results shows that for most years during the 1922–34 period the banks' cash holdings and their public debt portfolio were negatively correlated.

These arrangements permitted the remarkable expansion of Spain's industry, especially during the 1920s when steel, cement, electricity, construction, public works, shipbuilding, even automobile and aircraft making, developed remarkably, making Spain one of the fastest-growing economies in the interwar period (Tortella 1994: 255–67; Tortella and Palafox 1984; Carreras 1987a; Prados de la Escosura 1995).

An interesting case is that of the Banco Central. Founded in 1919, the Central was a sort of parvenu among the big banks. After a few years of aggressive activity, it suffered a serious setback in 1924–5 when a close associate, the Crédito de la Unión Minera, suspended payments. In fact, the Banco Central during those years was the victim of rash management, which saddled it with securities of coal mining and electricity companies, at a time when energy prices were going down. Then in 1929 it fell into the hands of a swindler who in fact defaulted on an enormous loan. In 1925 the Central was reluctantly rescued by the Bank of Spain, under the pressure of the Prime Minister (then the dictator General Miguel Primo de Rivera).[19] It recovered in 1926–8 and proceeded with an active – although not always wise – policy of industry promotion. So active was this policy by the Banco Central that the volume of its subscriptions of public debt bonds was much below the average for the banking sector as a whole. When its second liquidity crunch came in 1929, the Central's ability to borrow from the Bank of Spain on public debt as collateral was insufficient and it had to rely on rediscounts. Its liquidity problem was so acute that, before granting credit to a customer, the Central's board, as a matter of routine, checked with the Bank of Spain to make sure the credit instrument could be rediscounted.[20] Although the Central was not a typical mixed bank, in that it was newer and its policies were less prudent, this seems to be a good illustration of the reliance of mixed banks on the Bank of Spain.

This became even clearer in the spring and summer of 1931. The banking situation in Spain was extremely serious: to the generalized European banking panic of that same period, a domestic political crisis was added.

The proclamation of the Republic [on 14 April 1931] had in itself caused a grave financial crisis in Spain. Wealthy Spaniards had immediately begun to transfer their capital to foreign banks, and the international financial community reacted skeptically to the new regime. (Jackson 1967: 78)

All in all, between 30 March and 30 September [1931] demand and savings deposits decreased by about 1,300 million pesetas, which was equivalent to a sudden reduction by 20 percent. The magnitude of the crisis can be better understood if we take into consideration that [the Spanish] percentage of reduction was greater than that experienced by American banks during the same period. [. . . But this] abrupt reduction in demand and savings deposits did not bring about a chain of bankruptcies of credit institutions. (Martín-Aceña 1983: 615–17)

As Martín Aceña points out, this was due to two factors. First, the Bank of Spain, at the behest of the government, followed a Bagehotian policy of lending freely at increased rates. And second, the mechanism of automatic granting of collateral credits gave Spanish banks considerable leeway. In its 1932 report the Bank felt it had to explain the 'surprising fact' that 'national wealth has been able to surmount the difficulties of the present moment, not totally alien, certainly, to the world economic disturbance'. On the one hand, discount and other rates were increased, but not those charged on credits in operations guaranteed by public debt bonds. On the other hand, '[a]t the behest of Messrs the Ministers of Finance, based upon reasons of public interest, the [Bank's] Council agreed to grant several operations of an extraordinary character'. Also strategic must have been the fact that the Ministry of Finance issued two decrees during the month of May raising the fiduciary circulation ceiling, first to 5,200 million, then to 6,000 million. This was an unequivocal sign that the government and the Bank were not afraid to increase bank-note circulation in order to follow a liberal lending policy.

The Banco Central clearly benefited from these policies. Its deposits had been falling since 1929; between 15 July 1929 and 15 July 1931 combined demand and savings deposits had been reduced by more than 50%. Its situation was so desperate that its president took an unusual step: he asked the Bank of Spain to rediscount the Central's entire portfolio, pledging *all* its assets in guarantee. In an even more unusual decision, the Bank of Spain accepted that proposal, and even thanked the Central, whose 'behavior . . . constituted a precedent which was all the more plausible as there are some Banking Institutions to whom [the Bank of Sapin] will be obliged to ask for guarantees similar to the ones [the Central] is offering on its own and without any compulsion'.[21] The Bank was really willing to help. The Central survived and after the Spanish civil war it became one of the most solid of the big mixed banks.

The catastrophe was thus avoided. After 1931 confidence returned. By the end of 1935 total combined bank deposits were almost 40% higher than in 1931. In October 1932 the Bank of Spain started a gradual lowering of its interest rates. Given the depressed conditions, however, and probably remembering the difficulties of 1931, the banking sector as a whole, and especially the big mixed banks, the Central included, limited their industrial portfolio and went on purchasing public debt bonds and reinforcing their cash holdings. With the benefit of hindsight this seems a rational policy.

Conclusions

For reasons which have been studied elsewhere (Sardá 1948: 151–210; Tortella 1974: 475–81; Martín Aceña 1994), Spain was one of the few European countries that never adopted the gold standard. This posed some serious problems, mainly derived from the fact that this monetary disparity contributed to isolating its economy, but it had some compensating aspects. Among the advantages of a *de facto* fiduciary standard was that it gave the government and the Bank of Spain a freer hand in monetary policy. It also permitted the development of a *sui generis* relationship between the Bank of Spain and the private banking sector, in which the former, although certainly not playing the role of a central bank in the orthodox sense, could become a little less dependent on government finance than it had been in the nineteenth century and could play, however reluctantly, the role of lender of last resort.

The development of this *sui generis* relationship between the central bank and the large universal banks, with the explicit support of the government, permitted an expansion of credit which decisively contributed to the beginning of an industrialization process in Spain. Manufacturing diversified and the bases of a capital-goods industry were established during the first decades of the twentieth century thanks largely to the expansion of bank credit. While the output of the food industries expanded at an average rate of 1.9% and that of the textile industries at a rate of 0.8% between 1900 and 1930, the output of the capital-goods industries (metal transformation and machinery) grew at a rate of 4.0% in the same period. The weights of those sectors within the total index of manufacturing value added between 1913 and 1929 went from 14.2% to 20.2% for capital goods, from 41.6% to 34.5% for food and from 17.6% to 16.4% for textiles. All in all, the growth of Spanish national income was one of the fastest in Europe during the 1913–29 period (Prados de la Escosura 1995: tables 4 and 12).[22]

These unconventional monetary and credit arrangements also explain the 'surprising fact' that the Spanish banking sector, heavily loaded with industrial securities, emerged relatively unscathed from the Depression, unlike other 'mixed' banking systems, such as the German, the Austrian or the Italian.

Whether this Gerschenkronian path was the only possible or there were better alternatives is another question.

NOTES

1 The author thanks the Spanish Ministry of Education, the Real Colegio Complutense of Harvard University and the Banco Central Hispano for their support; Charles Calomiris, John Coatsworth, Brad DeLong, Claudia Goldin, David Landes, Jeffrey Williamson, Alan Dye and members of the Barnard-Columbia Economic History Workshop for their helpful comments; and Stefan Houpt for his cooperation. The sole responsibility for errors is his. The series on which the graphs are based are available from him on request.

2 The most recent estimates of Spanish GDP are by Prados de la Escosura (1995).

3 My translation. Unless otherwise indicated, all translations are mine.

4 A good description of the Madrid private bankers in 1871 is in Archive of the Crédit Lyonnais, Paris, Paquet CEES 73.247, folder 'Banques'.

5 The approximate equivalent of the peseta at the time was 25 pesetas per pound sterling.

6 By 1900 the intrinsic value of a 1 peseta coin was 45 *céntimos*. Cf. Tortella 1974: 481.

7 Deficits have been given a positive value, surpluses negative.

8 Gold reserves in the Bank of Spain stood at 674.1 million pesetas in 1913 and at 2,315.0 million in 1918; cf. Bank of Spain, *Memorias*. The peseta, which exchanged at 26.1 per pound sterling in July 1914, exchanged at 17.4 in July 1918; cf. Martínez Méndez 1983: 564.

9 *Información Comercial Española* February 1960: 74–5. See Figure 7.2, which gives annual averages.

10 The British Council of Foreign Bondholders tried to organize some concerted action against this debt reform with the French holders of Spanish debt, apparently without success. See letter of James P. Cooper, Secretary of the British Council, to the managers of Paribas (9 June 1899) in Archive Paribas (Association pour l'Histoire du Paribas, Paris), Conteneur 64, Dossier 16, 'Crédits en Espagne'.

11 Archive Paribas, Conteneur 63, Dossier 10, 'Banque espagnole de crédit', and Dossier 14, 'Banques diverses'.

12 The examples are numerous, but perhaps the clearest cases of bankers-entrepreneurs would be Valentín Ruiz Senén of the Banco Urquijo, the brothers Francisco and José Luis Ussía y Cubas, of the Banco Central, and José Gómez-Acebo y Cortina, of the Banco Español de Crédito. (Except for Ruiz Senén, the others bore recent titles of nobility.)

13 'The Council of Government of our Establishment, conscious of the serious situation created [by the war], understood that its main duty, as a National

Bank, was to provide all its help and support to the most important banking institutions as much as to Savings Banks and to the most modest industrialists, merchants, and property owners deserving credit'; 'At the behest of the Minister of Finance, which the Council immediately seconded, in its ardent desires to contribute to the expansion of credit, thereby satisfying the general strivings of the country, the Bank has shown itself determined to facilitate the export trade of Spanish products, the importation of raw materials necessary to manufacturing, and to alleviate the situation of some agricultural areas which could not give vent to their products as a consequence of the European war.' Bank of Spain, *Memoria*, 1916, 1917.

14 Calculated from Consejo Superior Bancario figures as published by *Anuario Financiero y de las Sociedades Anónimas de España*.

15 Calculated from Martín-Aceña and Pons 1994: table 5.

16 Bank of Spain, *Memoria*, 1903. The Bank started listing them on its balance sheet in 1904.

17 The nominal rates of those bonds, whose enumeration ensued, were 4% and above. As they were usually bought at a discount, they produced a positive yield even if they were pawned. As the loans were automatic for banks in good standing, the bonds were in effect like interest-bearing cash. Cf. Bank of Spain, *Memoria*, 1918.

18 For instance, Luis de Usera, who was President of the Banco Hispano Americano from 1968 to 1983, and effective manager since 1959, reported that the Hispano Americano, the most commercial of the big banks, never had to have recourse to borrowing on collateral from the Bank of Spain. This he considered to be the preserve of industrial banks such as the Central, the Bilbao and the Vizcaya. (Interview with the author, 24 March 1994.)

19 Martín-Aceña 1984: 85–6; Bank of Spain, *Actas Consejo*, 1, 2, 11 and 13 March 1925; Banco Central, *Actas Consejo*, 11 and 12 March 1925.

20 Banco Central, *Actas Consejo*, 31 August 1929; *Actas Comisión*, 17 August 1929, 12 December 1930, for example.

21 Banco Central, *Actas Consejo*, and *Actas Comisión*, 11 and 18 July 1931, respectively.

22 The sectoral growth rates have been calculated from this work's Appendix, Table B.3.

BIBLIOGRAPHY

Documents

Anuario Financiero y de las Sociedades Anónimas de España.
Archive of the Crédit Lyonnais, Paris.
Archive Paribas, Association pour l'Histoire du Paribas, Paris.
Banco Central, *Actas Comisión* (reports of committee meetings – this was the board's committee, a smaller body meeting more frequently).
Banco Central, *Actas Consejo* (reports of board meetings).
Bank of Spain, *Actas Consejo* (reports of board meetings).
Bank of Spain, *Memorias* (reports to shareholders, printed).

Works cited

Anes, G., Rojo, L. A. and Tedde, P. (eds.) 1983. *Historia económica y pensamiento social: estudios en homenaje a Diego Mateo del Peral*. Madrid.

Bordo, Michael D. and Capie, Forrest 1994. *Monetary Regimes in Transition*. Cambridge.

Broder, Albert 1976. 'Les investissements étrangers en Espagne au XIXe siècle: méthodologie et quantification', *Revue d'Histoire Economique et Sociale* 54, 1: 29–62.

1981. 'Le rôle des interêts économiques étrangers dans la croissance de l'Espagne au XIXe siècle, 1767–1924', doctoral dissertation, Université de Paris I.

Bustelo, Francisco and Tortella, Gabriel 1976. 'Monetary Inflation in Spain, 1800–1970', *Journal of European Economic History* 5: 141–50.

Cabrera, Mercedes 1983. *La patronal ante la II República: organizaciones y estrategia (1931–1936)*. Madrid.

Cameron, Rondo 1994. 'Bankers as Entrepreneurs', in Klep and Van Cauwenberghe (eds.), pp. 411–17.

Carr, Raymond 1966. *Spain, 1808–1939*. Oxford.

Carreras, Albert 1984. 'La producción industrial española, 1842–1981: construcción de un índice anual', *Revista de Historia Económica* 2: 127–57.

1987a. 'La industria: atraso y modernización', in J. Nadal, A. Carreras and C. Sudrià (eds.), *L'economía española en el siglo XX: una perspectiva histórica*, pp. 280–312. Barcelona.

1987b. 'An Annual Index of Spanish Industrial Output', in Sánchez-Albornoz (ed.), pp. 75–89.

Comín, Francisco 1987. 'Perfil histórico de la deuda pública española', *Papeles de Economía Española* 33: 86–119.

1988. *Hacienda y economía en la España contemporánea (1800–1936)*, 2 vols. Madrid.

Donges, Jürgen B. 1976. *La industrialización en España: políticas, logros, perspectivas*. Vilassar de Mar, Barcelona.

Estadísticas Históricas de España: Siglos XIX–XX (coordinación de Albert Carreras). Madrid.

Fraile, Pedro 1991. *Industrialización y grupos de presión: la economía política de la protección en España, 1900–1950*. Madrid.

García López, José Ramón 1987. *Los comerciantes banqueros en el sistema bancario español: estudio de casas de banca asturianas en el siglo XIX*. Oviedo.

1992. *Las remesas de los emigrantes españoles en América: siglos XIX y XX*. Gijón.

Gortázar, Guillermo 1986. *Alfonso XIII hombre de negocios: persistencia del Antiguo Régimen, modernización económica y crisis política, 1902–1931*. Madrid.

Jackson, Gabriel 1967. *The Spanish Republic and the Civil War, 1931–1939*. Princeton, NJ.

Klep, Paul and Van Cauwenberghe, Eddy (eds.) 1994. *Entrepreneurship and the Transformation of the Economy (10th–20th Centuries): Essays in Honour of Herman Van der Wee*. Leuven.

Maluquer de Motes, Jordi 1994. 'El índice de la producción industrial en

Cataluña. Una nueva estimación (1817–1935)', *Revista de Historia Industrial* 5: 45–71.

Martín Aceña, Pablo 1983. 'La crisis financiera española de 1931 y la política monetaria del primer gobierno de la República', in Anes, Rojo and Tedde (eds.), pp. 611–48.

1984. *La política monetaria en España, 1919–1935.* Madrid.

1985. *La cantidad de dinero en España, 1900–1935.* Madrid.

1994. 'Spain during the Classical Gold Standard Years, 1880–1914', in Bordo and Capie (eds.), pp. 135–72.

Martín Aceña, Pablo and Pons, María, A. 1994. 'Spanish Banking after the Civil War, 1940–1962', *FHR* 1(2): 121–38.

Martínez Méndez, Pedro 1983. 'Nuevos datos sobre la evolución de la peseta entre 1900 y 1936', in Anes, Rojo and Tedde (eds.), pp. 561–610.

Otazu, Alfonso 1987. *Los Rothschild y sus socios españoles (1820–1850).* Madrid.

Prados de la Escosura, Leandro 1988. *De imperio a nación: crecimiento y atraso económico en Espana (1780–1930).* Madrid.

1995. *Spain's Gross Domestic Product, 1850–1993: Quantitative Conjectures,* Universidad Carlos III de Madrid, Working Papers, 95–105.

Prados de la Escosura, L. and Zamagni, Vera (eds.) 1992. *El desarrollo económico en la Europa de Sur: España e Italia en perspectiva histórica.*

Rey Reguillo, Fernando del 1992. *Propietarios y patronos: la política de las organizaciones económicas en la España de la Restauración (1914–1923).* Madrid.

Riis, Thomas (ed.) 1993. *A Special Brew . . . : Essays in Honour of Kristof Glamann.* Odense.

Sánchez-Albornoz, Nicolás (ed.) 1987. *The Economic Modernization of Spain, 1830–1930.* New York.

Sánchez Alonso, Blanca 1995. *Las causas de la emigración española, 1880–1930.* Madrid.

Sardá, Juan 1948. *La política monetaria y las fluctuaciones de la economía española en el siglo XIX.* Madrid.

Solé Villalonga, Gabriel 1964. *La deuda pública española y el mercado de capitales.* Madrid.

Tamames, Ramón 1990. *Estructura económica de España,* 19th edn. Madrid.

Tedde de Lorca, Pedro 1974. 'La banca privada española durante la Restauración (1974–1914)', in Tortella (ed.), pp. 217–455.

1991. 'La naturaleza de las Cajas de Ahorros: sus raíces históricas', *Papeles de Economía Española* 46: 2–11.

Tena Junguito, Antonio 1988. 'Importación, niveles de protección y producción de material eléctrico en España (1890–1935)', *Revista de Historia Económica* 6: 341–71.

1989. 'Comercio exterior', *Estadísticas Históricas de Españo: Siglos XIX–XX,* pp. 329–61.

1992. 'Protección y competitividad en España e Italia, 1890–1960', in Prados de la Escosura and Zamagni (eds.), pp. 321–55.

Titos Martinez, Manuel 1991. 'La respuesta histórica de las Cajas de Ahorros a las demandas de la sociedad española', *Papeles de Economía Española* 46: 12–38.

Tortella, Gabriel 1977. *Banking, Railroads, and Industry in Spain 1829–1874.* New York.

1983. 'La primera gran empresa química española: La Sociedad Española de la Dinamita (1872–1896)', in Anes, Rojo and Tedde (eds.), pp. 431–53.

1987. 'La implantación del monopolio de los explosivos en España', *Hacienda Pública Española* 108–9: 393–409.

1993. 'Foreign Entrepreneurship and Capital in Spain: From the Sociedad de la Dinamita to the Unión Española de Explosivos, 1872–1903', in Riis (ed.), pp. 391–404.

1994. *El desarrollo de la España contemporánea: historia económica de los siglos XIX y XX.* Madrid.

1995: 'The Hispanic American Connection in the Banco Hispano Americano of Madrid', in *Wirtschaft, Gesellschaft, Unternehmen: Festschrift für Hans Pohl zum 60. Geburtstag,* 2 vols., pp. 1179–85.

Tortella, Gabriel (ed.) 1974. *La Banca española en la Restauración: I Política y finanzas.* Madrid.

Tortella, Gabriel and García-Ruiz, J. L. n.d. *Una historia de los bancos Central e Hispanoamericano, 1901–1991: noventa años de gran banca en España.* Madrid.

Tortella, Gabriel and Jiménez, J. C. 1986. *Historia del Banco de Crédito Industrial.* Madrid.

Tortella, Gabriel and Palafox, Jordi 1984. 'Banking and Industry in Spain, 1918–1936', *Journal of European Economic History* 13(2): 81–111.

Ullman, Joan Connelly 1968. *The Tragic Week: A Study of Anticlericalism in Spain, 1875–1912.* Cambridge, Mass.

8 Central banking and German-style mixed banking in Italy, 1893/5–1914: from coexistence to cooperation

Peter Hertner

Nineteenth- and early twentieth-century central banking is certainly not one of the most neglected topics in historical research. Within that framework, however, the various aspects of relationship between banks of issue and commercial banks have attracted less attention, probably because source material referring to this particular problem is not abundantly available.

This chapter will essentially be based on the correspondence of Bonaldo Stringher, head of the Bank of Italy from 1900 until his death at the end of 1930. Several thousand letters, memos and printed documents had then been handed over by the Bank to the Stringher family which, in 1985, made these papers available to the public by depositing them in the historical archives of the Bank of Italy.[1] At least for the part which covers the pre-1914 period, this seems to be one of those rare cases where such documents – most of them private or semi-official letters – written or received by the leader of an important bank of issue have been preserved. Together with these papers, sources from the historical archives of the Banca Commerciale Italiana, certainly one of the richest banking archives on the European Continent, will be used.[2]

This chapter will, of course, not be able to draw a complete picture of the manifold relations between the Bank of Italy and the two major Italian commercial banks, Banca Commerciale Italiana and Credito Italiano, between the middle of the 1890s, when all three of them had been founded, and the outbreak of World War I. Its aim is much more modest: to find out, by looking at Stringher's correspondence, how 'practical men' – central and commercial bankers – judged the relationship between the two spheres. Their views could reach from benign neglect to confrontation or cooperation. Their opinion could be influenced by the existing set of institutional regulations, by the then accepted wisdom in the field of monetary policy, or by the momentary vicissitudes of the business cycle, though possibly by all three factors together. In comparison, the character and personal views of the actors, those central and commercial bankers, played an all but negligible role. The conclusions of this short chapter will be highly 'impressionistic', illuminating some aspects and leaving others in the dark. The outcome will necessarily be also quite subjective since it will reflect above all the views of those directly involved.

Let us start by characterizing briefly the institutions involved and the principal persons acting on the scene. Subsequently we shall try to distil some of these actors' opinions on specific problems of the relationship between banks of issue and commercial banks, out of the mass of letters contained in Stringher's correspondence and in some other contemporary documents.

The institutions

The Bank of Italy

As a bank of issue the Bank of Italy (Banca d'Italia), founded in 1893, was rather a late-comer in this country. Whereas in many other sectors Italy, unified in 1859/60, adopted a strictly centralized administrative structure, currency issue remained decentralized. There were no less than six banks of issue from 1870 onwards, the most important being the Banca Nazionale nel Regno d'Italia, successor to the corresponding Piedmontese institution. The Banca Nazionale and its sister institutions were constantly torn between their public role as issuing banks and their interest in making the highest profit possible for their private shareholders; this, however, was not at all an Italian specificity but was a well-known dilemma which applied to more or less all nineteenth-century banks of issue. More specific was the role of the Italian issuing banks as direct lenders to the private sector, particularly in the south of the country where the development of commercial banking was still far behind (Sannucci 1990). At the end of the 1880s the Banca Nazionale ran into difficulties with increasing outstanding credits granted to the infant heavy industry, and by trying to help a number of commercial banks which had more or less immobilized their assets in urban real estate ventures (Confalonieri 1974: 89ff). On top of all this came the Banca Romana scandal that surfaced at the beginning of 1893. The Rome-based Banca Romana had been the issuing bank for Latium, the remaining bit of the papal state after 1860. The bank and its issuing privilege had survived the annexation of Rome by the Kingdom of Italy in 1870. Now in early 1893, after a careful investigation by a governmental commission, it turned out that 91% of Banca Romana's assets were illiquid and that the bank's directors had committed a criminal offence by permitting an additional number of bank-notes with double numbering to be printed (Vitale 1972, III).

Faced with such a situation, the government finally decided to liquidate the Banca Romana; practically at the same time it forced the Banca Nazionale and the two Tuscan issuing banks to merge into a still-to-be-founded Banca d'Italia. This new bank of issue came into being as a consequence of the law of 10 August 1893 which reordered and re-regulated the entire issuing sector and its privileges (Corbino 1934: 343ff). The existing equilibrium of power in the national parliament did not allow for the creation of a truly central bank with a monopoly of currency issue. Thus the two southern banks, Banco di Napoli and Banco di Sicilia, remained on the scene as banks of issue until 1926. Their position was, however, much weaker: the currency contingent granted to both of them by the new law amounted to only slightly more than a quarter of total circulation (Negri 1989). Therefore monetary policy seems to have been always firmly in the hands of the Bank of Italy; the discount rate, for example, was normally decided between this bank's Director General and the Treasury (Ciocca 1978: 180ff). The shares of the new Bank of Italy were distributed among the shareholders of the three merged banks of issue; additional capital was offered to them at option. As well as the annual meeting of the Bank's shareholders, a Superior Council was established. It was elected in the following manner: 'The administrative council of each branch (*sede*) appoints two councillors from its midst. Five additional councillors are chosen by the general assembly of the shareholders from the midst of the remaining members of the administrative councils of the main offices or branches' (Ferraris 1911: 226). This Superior Council elected the Director General with a two thirds majority. The election had in any case to be confirmed by the government (Wilmersdoerffer 1913: 166). The new Bank of Italy had to liquidate the heavy legacy of the Banca Romana and the three issuing banks which had merged into it. During its first years of existence these immobilized assets amounted to almost two thirds of its total assets, and the Bank was given ten years to complete the entire liquidation process. It turned out very soon that more time was needed for winding up these illiquid holdings, and thus two years later parliament extended the ten-year limit to fifteen years.

Faced with such a formidable task, the Bank of Italy had, during this first period, to pursue a very careful policy in order gradually to gain sufficient strength and standing. Monetary expansion was strictly limited since a fixed maximum circulation of notes had to be guaranteed by a 33% cover of gold and silver (of which at least three-quarters in gold) and by a 7% cover of 'foreign bills of exchange on firms of the first order, recognized as such by the Minister of the Treasury' (Canovai 1911: 122). In 1897/8 this latter quota was extended to 11%; since 1895 it could include also 'treasury bonds of foreign states with a normal metallic circulation, and also certificates of deposits of money with foreign banks and bankers who were correspondents of the Italian treasury' (Canovai 1911: 123). These specific measures certainly helped to improve the Bank's profit situation, but they were also – as Tito Canovai, General Secretary of the Bank of Italy, stated in a publication of the US National Monetary Commission in 1911 – 'of monetary utility, since [they] allowed the banks to have a part of their funds in foreign countries, which might serve as a powerful protection in case of monetary disturbances and high rates of exchange. From this point of view, Italy introduced into its banking legislation a provision already tried to advantage in other countries, such as Germany, Austria-Hungary, Russia, Switzerland, Holland, Belgium and Spain' (Canovai 1911: 122ff). If circulation went beyond the upper limit fixed for each of the three issuing banks, coverage had to be supplied by a 100% metallic base or the banks had to pay – on top of the 1% circulation tax due for all issued bank-notes beyond the metallic reserve[3] – 'an extraordinary tax corresponding to double the discount rate on the excess of circulation and the deficit of metallic reserve' (Canovai 1911: 123). Not even a year later this prohibitive 'extraordinary tax' was lowered to two thirds of the discount rate if a prescribed limit to the excess of circulation was respected, 'and could further exceed the circulation by a like amount, on condition of paying a tax equal to the discount rate', the metallic reserve remaining in any case 'in the ratio of 40%' (Canovai 1911: 139).

In the meantime, and despite the successful reordering of the issuing banks' sector, the two major commercial banks of the country, Credito Mobiliare and Banca Generale, had to be closed down at the end of 1893 and at the beginning of the following year. On 23 January 1894 the lira's convertibility was offically suspended: *de facto* this had been the situation already since the end of the 1880s when the lira had started again to be traded at a discount (Manacorda 1993: 149ff). Interestingly enough, Italy did not go back to convertibility until the outbreak of the First World War. As it seems, such a move was not even considered when the country's financial and monetary situation had greatly improved and when the lira's discount had, in 1902, disappeared for the first time since the middle of the 1880s (Corbino 1938: 391).[4] The country's improved conditions after 1900 would undoubtedly have allowed the resumption of convertibility, since Italy had managed to double its metallic reserves between 1900 and 1906[5] – they grew effectively by 109% during that period – and could increase them by another 39% from then until 1913, whereas note circulation was augmented only by 36% during the first and by 42% during the following period (Confalonieri 1982, I: 102). One can only assume that Italy's 'political class' had been busy resolving other issues it regarded as of the utmost importance during those years which could have allowed the return to convertibility, i.e. roughly the quinquennium 1903–7, these issues being above all the nationalization of the railways in 1905 and the conversion of the so-called 'rendita 5%', the most important part of non-redeemable public debt, in 1906. With economic stagnation after 1907 and the rapid growth of public spending starting shortly aftewards, the window of possible convertibility had been closed again.[6] Fratianni and Spinelli believe that Italy's monetary experience 'on the whole was not different from what it would have been had she adhered to the standard throughout, particularly from 1900 to 1913'. Despite its conspicuous abstinence from convertibility Italy, according to these two authors, 'was guided by the norm of the gold standard' (Fratianni and Spinelli 1984: 408). Looking at 'the geography of the gold standard' and taking 1908 as a benchmark, Italy found itself therefore in a group with economically more backward nations like Spain and Greece whereas practically all other European countries had by then adopted convertibility (Eichengreen and Flandreau 1994: and table 2).

Renunciation of convertibility, by sheer necessity in 1894 and from 1902 onwards possibly by benign neglect,[7] meant of course that the principal reason for changing the discount rate in the framework of the classical model of the gold standard, namely the defence of the country's gold reserve, did not play any role. Theoretically, by increasing the rate, the banks of issue could attract money from abroad and restock their metallic reserves, but during the first years after 1893 this mechanism does not seem to have worked to any extent since foreign investors had to calculate the risks connected with the lira's changing quotations (Confalonieri 1975: 144ff). There were, however, other reasons for using the discount rate as a policy measure. Luigi Einaudi, one of the major Italian economists of that period, wrote in 1910 that, in the absence of convertibility and with the metallic reserves not running any risk of being drawn out of the country, there had to be 'other brakes' if one did not want to let the banks of issue 'print their notes without any limits and discount their bills at a moderate but still profitable rate for them given the minimal price of note printing'. According to Einaudi the 'brakes' in the system were the severe coverage requirements of the 1893 Banking Law. Under these circumstances it was above all the task of discount rate policy to keep circulation within the allowed limits (Einaudi 1960: 151).[8]

Some quite peculiar institutional aspects characterized discount policy within the Italian context. Already in 1866, when the lira's convertibility had been suspended for the first time, the government had decreed that from now on changes of the discount rate to be applied by the individual banks of issue had to be approved by the Ministry of Finance (Pecorari 1994: 37ff). This rule was again inserted into the already mentioned law of 1893 which regulated the entire issue bank sector. As Canovai put it, 'the discount rate was to be the same for the three banks [of issue] and could not be changed without the permission of the Government. They could, however, discount at a rate [of] 1 percent below the official rate paper presented by people's banks[9] and institutions of discount and agricultural credit, organized to serve as intermediaries between the small trade and the banks of issue' (Canovai 1911: 121ff). This co-called *tasso di favore* – one could translate it as 'preferential rate' – served for rediscounting, and there was an upper limit established for each of the three banks of issue. In 1895 the issuing banks were allowed to discount a third type of paper 'at a rate below normal'. This referred to 'bills of not more than three months currency, presented and guaranteed by banking and commercial firms of the first order . . . [This] minimum rate of discount was to be fixed every three months by the decree of the minister of the treasury and could not go below $3\frac{1}{2}$ per cent' (Canovai 1911: 145). In 1903 the three-month term for changing the discount rate was reduced to one month, but only on 31 December 1907, at the end and certainly as a result of the most dramatic economic and financial crisis since 1893/4, was a less cumbersome procedure introduced by a law allowing for rate changes at any time if necessary (Confalonieri 1975: 164). The same law reduced the lower limit of the minimum rate to 3%, a measure welcomed by the Bank of Italy in its annual report for 1907 where the Bank considered this to be of some help 'against eventual inordinate moves of the speculation banks[10] which are provided with other compensatory means for securing their level of profit' (Banca d'Italia 1908: 9). This minimum rate of discount was widely applied by the issuing banks: in 1898 the Bank of Italy used it for 77% of all its discounts, in 1900 – a difficult year – for only 18%, but between 1903 and 1906 this share stood in almost every year slightly above 50% (Banca d'Italia 1908: 163 note 3). Whereas the minimum rate of discount was varied several times in certain years, the official rate, applied to customers of lesser 'quality', remained fixed at 5% during no fewer than thirteen years, from November 1894 until October 1907 (Banca d'Italia 1908: 161). It changed eight times during the following seven years, until August 1914, but the other two rates, which had been changed twenty times during the previous period, were altered twenty-six times between October 1907 and the outbreak of the Great War (Confalonieri 1982, I: 109). In practice and from day to day the banks of issue applied, within the spread between the official and the minimum rate of discount, a whole set of rates – up to nine or ten different ones – to their customers according to their presumed 'quality' (Ciocca 1978: 198).

The relatively more frequent changes of the discount rates after 1907 must be seen as a response to a more difficult general economic environment. In particular they reflect the fact that, as already mentioned, note circulation increased, between 1907 and 1913, by 42.3% whereas metallic reserves grew only by 39.1%. In itself this was not yet alarming since coverage remained quite high – it lay constantly around 70% until the outbreak of World War I (Ciocca 1978: graph on 204) – but the years from 1911 until 1914 saw more than one moment of political and financial crisis in Europe and from October 1911 until October of the following year Italy was at war with the Ottoman Empire over Libya. Low economic growth and an increase of about 50% in public spending – above all for infrastructure and armaments – between 1907 and 1913 put the balance of payments under strain and influenced the exchange rate of the lira which was again traded with an albeit relatively small discount starting in 1909 (Corbino 1938: 406ff; Confalonieri 1982, I: 37ff, 55ff).

The Bank of Italy's increased level of activity probably reflected also a higher degree of independence which it had reached in the meantime. At the end of 1906 the Bank was finally able to declare definitively closed the account of illiquid holdings. About half of them had been sold or written off by the end of 1900. A booming real estate market and the transfer of part of the remaining holdings to two separate real estate companies, founded on purpose, made it possible that the Bank, during the following six years, could 'liberate itself gradually from activities which were not proper to its functions' (Banca d'Italia 1907: 26). Its Director General, Stringher, could proudly state in 1907 that, 'helped by the growth and the healthy and organic development of all the economic forces of the country which, in a few years only, gave splendid proof of their strength, the Bank has managed to cure its sufferings' (Banca d'Italia 1907: 57). Only now was it possible to ask for a less vexatious legislation and to increase gradually the dividend payments to the shareholders without being accused of wasting the Bank's resources (Ciocca 1978: 184; Bonelli 1991: 62ff).

Like their predecessors before 1893, the three banks of issue counted among their customers other (non-issue) banks and a considerable number of industrial firms and private individuals. Their possibilities to do business with these different partners were, apart from discounting their bills of exchange, rather limited: contango business was, for instance, forbidden to the banks of issue, as was the granting of loans on real estate, and they were not allowed to grant unsecured credits. They could accept deposits but there was an upper ceiling, fixed by law, and the interest the banks of issue could pay on current account deposits was limited to a third of the official discount rate (Ferraris 1911: 244; Ciocca 1978: 188, 190). Apart from this rule, 'private banks – as Canovai told the U.S. Monetary Commission – do not keep their reserve with the Bank of Italy' (Goodhart 1988: 137). The Bank's General Director, Stringher, had deplored this fact already in his annual report for 1907 where he had commented that such deposits would at a moment of crisis allow the Bank to satisfy credit demand without having to expand circulation of bank-notes. 'In a more developed system of issue banks the functions of such deposits would be to provide the biggest part of liquidity during the periods of calm in order to leave to the mass of bank-notes the possibility of providing for extraordinary credit demands when special needs arise, and particularly when there happens to be a crisis . . . The theory of W. Bagehot will certainly be confirmed also with us as time goes on' (Banca d'Italia 1908: 24ff). Three years later Stringher had to come back to the same problem: this time he mentioned explicitly the example of 'those foreign banks of issue who work to a large extent with current account deposits and can thus save on the issue of bank-notes' (Banca d'Italia 1911: 22). Compared with Britain, where London bankers had already started to open accounts with the Bank of England 'during the Napoleonic wars', and increasingly large ones after the crisis of 1825 (Morgan 1965: 7), but also compared with other countries, the Italian case was of course 'unusual' and, at least according to Charles Goodhart, this meant that 'the Banca d'Italia did not, therefore, normally act as a bankers' bank' (Goodhart 1988: 137).

There was in any case, as we shall see below, enough space for competition and eventually also for conflict with the commercial banking sector.

Banca Commerciale Italiana and Credito Italiano

Banca Commerciale Italiana was established at Milan in October 1894, and Credito Italiano at Genoa at the beginning of the following year by practically refounding the ailing Banca di Genova which could date its existence back to 1870. Both banks seemed to bridge a gap which had opened only a few months before when the hitherto leading Italian investment and commercial banks, Credito Mobiliare and Banca Generale, had to close down. To make matters still worse these two failures coincided with the crisis of the entire bank of issue sector, already briefly described.

Banca Commerciale's capital was mainly subscribed by the big Berlin joint-stock banks and by the private banking house of Bleichroeder, also from Berlin and traditionally strong in business with the Italian state. At the beginning almost four fifths of the capital of the new Milanese bank was taken by this German group: the rest went to the Austrian Credit-Anstalt of Vienna and three leading Swiss banks. Credito Italiano had at its start a considerable but less than 50% share of capital subscribed by solid if not first-rate German and Swiss banks (Confalonieri 1975: 3ff; Hertner 1984: 169ff). The German and Austrian shareholders of Banca Commerciale sold out their shares rather fast. In 1895 these had amounted to 74%; six years later their participation was reduced to about 10%. It was only 2.4% in 1914, while at the same time Swiss shareholders owned 20.5% and French shareholders 14% of its capital. From 1899 Banque de Paris et des Pays Bas became a stable partner of Banca Commerciale. During the same period Credito Italiano started close collaboration with several French, Belgian and Swiss banks who regularly took part in its increases of capital. The German share amounted in this latter case probably to less than 1% in 1914 (Hertner 1984: 177ff., 184ff). Despite the gradually shrinking role of foreign capital in both banks, foreign bankers still played an important role on their boards: in 1914 no less than eighteen of the thirty-three members of Banca Commerciale's *consiglio di amministrazione* were foreigners, and the two leading managers of the bank were of German origin. This fact induced public opinion and foreign diplomats to consider the Banca Commerciale a 'German bank', an opinion which by 1914 was certainly quite far from the truth (Hertner 1984: 104). Credito Italiano had a much lower proportion of foreigners on its board, but a considerable part of its upper management nevertheless consisted of Germans, Austrians and Swiss.

The origins of their 'founding fathers' and the make-up of their upper management were certainly strong factors which influenced these two credit institutions to behave according to the German model of 'mixed banking'. It was equally no accident that Otto Joel, the German-born Managing Director of Banca Commerciale, in his correspondence with Edouard Noetzlin of Paribas, named Deutsche Bank as the model that Banca Commerciale should follow (Confalonieri 1976: 73, 77 note 2). Not so much in their territorial expansion within Italy, which came closer to the French model than to the development then going on in Germany, but in their internal administrative structure and above all in their 'industrial policy', the two new Italian banks came quite close to the behaviour of their German counterparts and founders. One can observe clear parallels with the German model in this field. Permanent contact between bank and industrial enterprise via the adoption of the *Hausbankprinzip*, i.e. the principle of exclusive relationship, the importance of current account credit, the presence of bank representatives on industrial firms' boards, and the willingness of the bank to carry an enterprise through difficult periods of its existence, these are all elements which, together with the ratios one can get out of the balance sheets, point to 'a high degree of structural relationship between the two Italian banks and their founders' (Hertner 1991: 349).

It is, of course, much more difficult to assess the concrete importance of these two banks for the process of Italian industrialization,[11] which moved into a decisive phase in about 1897–8, only shortly after the banks had been founded. In 1897 the assets of Banca Commerciale and Credito Italiano taken together amounted to 20.7% of the total assets of all Italian 'ordinary credit banks' (i.e. non-issue joint-stock banks); in 1913 their share had risen to 48.7% (Hertner 1984: 132). This growing degree of concentration could, of course, be taken as an indicator of success; it does not, on the other hand, tell us anything about the role of these two banks in the process of capital allocation. Thanks to the detailed studies of Antonio Confalonieri, we are now well informed about their truly important role in financing industrial branches which then sprang up on, at least for Italy, a new scale, such as iron and steel, engineering, electricity production and distribution, automobile construction and sugar beet refining (Confalonieri 1975, 1976, 1982). There was also an increasing engagement in a sector as traditional as cotton textiles where, at least in part, the family enterprise ceded to joint-stock firms after 1900 and where the two banks supported this process of transformation by launching the new firms on the stock exchange and financing them continually afterwards (Hertner 1984: 196).

The principal persons involved: Stringher, Mangili, Joel

Institutions are administered by individuals and/or by groups of individuals. Since this chapter sets out to present the opinions of the principal actors on a specific problem, i.e. the relationship between a central bank – or rather in this specific case a quasi-central bank – and the two principal commercial banks, it seems appropriate to offer short accounts of these people before confronting the reader with their particular views.

Bonaldo Stringher (1854–1930) was Director General – from 1928 onwards Governor, after the new title had been created – of the Bank of Italy from December 1900 until his death in December 1930 (for the following, see Bonelli 1985: *passim*). Before being promoted to the top of Italy's major bank of issue Stringher had served as a state official for twenty-five years. He was born in Udine, in the northeastern corner of the Kingdom of Italy, into a family of the local *petite bourgeoisie*. Like most people coming from nineteenth-century border regions, Stringher was a man of rather strong national convictions. He received his formal education in a commercial high school at Udine and then went on to the 'Superior School of Commerce' in Venice. At the age of 21 he was called to a post in the statistical department of the Ministry of Agriculture, Industry, and Trade in Rome, where he started regularly to publish articles on problems of social policy, monetary questions and banks of issue. Very early on he became a close collaborator of various ministers; in 1883 the government appointed him as secretary of the National Monetary Commission. He took part in a series of international conferences on monetary and commercial problems. In 1884 he became head of department in the Ministry of Finance and then participated in the preparation of the protectionist Italian tariff of 1887. Four years later he acquired the *libera docenza* in public finance and fiscal law and started to give lectures on comparative tariff legislation at the University of Rome. In 1891 he again became Secretary General of a committee of parliamentarians and high officials which had to make proposals for the imminent renewal of several commercial treaties. Transferred to the Treasury in 1892, where he played an important role in the preparation of the banking law of the following year, Stringher was then appointed at the end of 1893 – at age 39 – General Director of the Treasury. In this new position he had, among other things, to prepare and to control the ongoing legislative projects referring to the banks of issue. In 1898 he left this Ministry and was appointed a member of the State Council, this being about the highest position a state official could hope to achieve. In the summer of 1900 he stood for election to the House of Deputies in his native region of Friuli. He was elected and was immediately nominated Under-Secretary of State to the Treasury. When Giuseppe Marchiori, Director General of the Bank of Italy since 1894, died in November 1900, Stringher was at once considered to be the 'natural candidate to his succession' (Bonelli 1985: 94).

During his years at the top of the Bank of Italy Stringher united the qualities of a highly experienced bureaucrat with an undisputed technical knowledge. He clearly saw the priorities necessary for transforming the Bank of Italy into '*the* Italian bank of issue' (Bonelli 1991: 113) within a realistic span of time, and he was successful. What he lacked – and, given his origins and his ensuing *cursus honorum*, it would be quite unfair to blame him for this deficiency – was international experience. Compared with the views of his principal interlocutors, the leaders of the big commercial banks, Bonaldo Stringher's horizon seemed to remain restricted mainly to the national environment. Once he had become the leader of the Bank of Italy he saw the Bank as 'a solid instrument of the country's economic activity' whose moral prestige was supported not only by its own standing but also 'by the benevolent assistance of the public powers', i.e. state and parliament. This assistance could not be refused if the Bank 'stayed within the limits set by the laws and the decrees through which it is

governed' (Banca d'Italia 1901: 46). This was not just an official statement produced for public use; it probably also reflected quite well the
intimate convictions of this public servant *par excellence*.

One of the principal correspondents of Stringher between 1900 and
Italy's entry into the First World War in 1914 was Cesare Mangili
(1852–1917), heir to a Milanese shipping company established in 1816
and with agencies – after 1900 – in various German, Swiss and northern
Italian towns and cities (see, for the following, Società Innocente Mangili
1917; Bonelli 1991: 847, 857). He had already played an important role
within the Milanese Chamber of Commerce and as a *reggente* of the Bank
of Italy's Milan branch when he became a member of the Bank's Superior
Council in 1898. In 1903 he was elected president of this Council. At the
end of 1905 he was appointed to the Kingdom's Senate and left the Bank
because an article of the 1893 banking law 'stipulated that members of
Parliament could not fill any office, with or without remuneration, in the
banks of issue' (Canovai 1911: 127). A few months later, in March 1906,
Mangili joined the board of the Banca Commerciale Italiana, a step
which was strongly resented by Stringher but justified by Mangili who
claimed that this new position would offer him the possibility to act as a
mediator between the competing commercial banks.[12] The following year
Mangili became president of the Banca Commerciale's board and he
remained in office until the spring of 1916, when he had to resign because
he was accused of trading with the enemy and in any case of having been
too close to the German and Austrian founding banks of the Banca
Commerciale, an absurd reproach if one thinks of Mangili's well-known
francophile attitude and his strong personal links with his colleagues at
Paribas.

Mangili was an energetic businessman and an excellent organizer who
systematically cultivated the network of friends and acquaintances built
up in decades of intense activity (see above all Pino Pongolini 1994:
xxivff). From the point of view of Banca Commerciale he was, as its director Otto Joel noted in 1907, 'a true and great acquisition for us'.[13]
Mangili's correspondence with Bonaldo Stringher is particularly interesting because during the early years it reflects, all in all, the position of
the Bank of Italy of which Mangili was, as we have seen, councillor and
president. When he later moved on to Banca Commerciale he became, on
some occasions, a competitor, on others someone with whom the major
bank of issue had to collaborate. To show how this relationship evolved
over time should be quite revealing.

The third principal actor in our story is Otto Joel (1856–1916), born in
Danzig of a German family of Jewish origin and, together with his similarly German-born colleague Weil, leading manager of the Banca

Commerciale Italiana from its foundation in October 1894 until June 1915 when he had to give up for health reasons. The true cause of his withdrawal was, however, that his position within the bank had become extremely precarious in the wake of heavy attacks launched against him by a chauvinist public shortly before and after Italy's entry into the War on the side of the Allied Powers. He had been awarded Italian citizenship in 1910, but the political climate of these months had become so over-heated that it was certainly also in the interest of the Banca Commerciale itself when Joel left the limelight of public attention and became one of the bank's vice-presidents. He died shortly afterwards in April 1916 (on this, and also for the following, see Hertner 1984: 90ff; Confalonieri 1982, I: 532ff).

Joel had been in Italy, apparently for health reasons, since the age of fifteen, his stay being interrupted only by a three-year apprenticeship in a Frankfurt bank. In 1886 he had obtained the post of deputy manager in the Milanese branch of the Banca Generale, then the second largest commercial bank of the country. In 1889 he became the leading manager of the Genoa branch of the same bank, and in the autumn of 1893, three months before Banca Generale had to close down, he was named head of its inspectorate. He must have shown quite early the qualities of an outstanding banker – prudence combined with the ability to weigh adequately the risks involved in profitable business – and he was, of course, at home in two worlds of banking, German and Italian. He was known to the Berlin bankers well before they decided to found Banca Commerciale in October 1894, and when they offered the jobs to him and to his colleague Weil, who had also been employed in Italian banks for a long time, it must have been for them almost an obvious choice.

Once Stringher was installed at the Bank of Italy, Joel became one of his most important correspondents; they also met rather frequently, Joel's fragile state of health permitting. In a letter to Mangili written in 1903, Joel was characterized by Stringher in the following way: Stringher believed he knew Joel's 'Teutonic shortcomings, but I esteem the achievements and the intellect. In my positions as General Director of the Treasury, as Under-Secretary of State and as Director of the Bank [of Italy] I have found Joel to be always loyal in his relationship with me. He is certainly much better than other gentlemen whom we know.'[14] Anticipating what will be illustrated below, one might as well agree with Confalonieri when he comes to the conclusion that 'despite formal politeness and despite the fact that they esteemed each other for their technical expertise there never existed real confidentiality between the two of them, and on Stringher's side there was a good deal of distrust' (Confalonieri 1982, I: 138, note 1).

Banks of issue and commercial banks: coexistence, confrontation, cooperation

To start with, it might be a good idea to present some programmatic statements coming from our principal actors as to the role of banks of issue on the one hand and commercial banks on the other.

When Stringher presented his first annual report in March 1901 after having arrived at the Bank of Italy only in December of the preceding year, he explained quite clearly the role of the institution he was now guiding: 'The Bank must become the moderator of the Italian financial organism and promote combined actions of the various credit institutions. It must keep in mind that excessive rivalries and the bitterness of competition among these lead to ruinous consequences . . . The Bank of Italy, on the other hand, cannot but fight against what, on the pretext of caring for the public interest, pushes towards an unsound speculation' (Banca d'Italia 1901: 46ff). Mangili, in a letter of December 1902 when he was not yet President of the High Council of the Bank but one of its normal members, underlined that the Bank of England and the Banque de France were the two models which the Bank of Italy would have to emulate. 'It will always have to side with the government because it practises a prerogative of the state via the right of issue.'[15]

The most exhaustive declaration came, perhaps, from Joel who, in a letter to Stringher of 2 May 1905, went back into the past in order to dissipate the doubts of the Bank of Italy's Director General on the recent development of the country's capital markets:

I have looked around, but I must confess that in the field of banking I do not see the danger of those extremely dangerous trips back into a not too distant past. My recollection of the awful years from [18]90 until [18]94 is still too fresh not to tell me that the actual period is in almost all respects quite different. Catastrophe was then inevitable since for more than a decade masses of fictitious securities had been created and because the private banks, helped and seduced by a policy which had completely falsified the role of the banks of issue, snatched from each other the operations which could be settled only in the long run and with difficulty. Thus they immobilized not only their own capital but also almost their entire deposits . . . The private credit institute must be the complement to the bank of issue. It is able, with its greater elasticity and flexibility, to enter into a lot of combinations which would not be proper for the other one; in a certain way it is able to act as its intermediary or as its buffer. It should, according to my opinion, accomplish this mission not only in the big places where capital and credit are abundant, but perhaps, and also more usefully, in the less developed provincial towns. The bank of issue remains, on the contrary, always the true, the supreme regulator of credit which, with the rigidity of its principles . . . shows the way also to the most powerful of the commercial banks . . .[16]

It was probably inevitable that harmonious statements of that kind had to clash with the harsh realities of everyday life. The Bank of Italy had, as we have seen, to dismantle gradually its heavy burden of illiquid assets, but it also had its private shareholders who wanted to see their capital sufficiently remunerated. In a letter to Stringher of August 1902 Mangili put this into rather realistic terms: 'It must be our policy to gain time and to set aside the largest possible amounts without the shareholders losing their patience.'[17] The problem of sufficient profitability – typical of nineteenth-century banks of issue organized as joint-stock companies with private shareholders (cf. for the case of the Bank of England Sayers 1986: 17ff; Ziegler 1990: 29ff) – put the Bank of Italy's leaders under constant strain, particularly during the difficult first decade of its existence. Complaints concerning the small volume and the unsatisfactory quality of Italian commercial paper were recurrent: 'The fundamental misfortune from which we suffer is the fact that our country does not offer enough suitable fuel for our big locomotive, i.e. it does not produce a sufficient and healthy portfolio which could be liquidated for our consumption' – this is what Mangili told Stringher in July 1904.[18] A year before, Mangili had discussed the matter with Minister of the Treasury Di Broglio, complaining that the Bank of Italy lacked the bills of exchange portfolio 'possessing the requirements for being admitted by a bank of issue, and that as a consequence we have to accept signatures coming from non-merchants, farmers etc. etc.'. 'I told him also [so Mangili in his report to Stringher on his talk to the Minister] that the best and truly commercial portfolio is being absorbed by the private banks and the savings banks which are not obliged to respect the unchanging rates of discount.'[19] Complaints of this sort were quite frequent in 1904/5 when interest rates had gone down considerably and the banks of issue had serious problems of 'following the market', but they can be observed also as late as in 1913 when the instruments of intervention at the disposal of the Bank of Italy had been improved by ongoing legislation (Ciocca 1978: 187ff).

Discount policy as it was ruled by the banking law of 1893 and as we have described it above discriminated against the banks of issue as far as their acquisition of a good portfolio was concerned. This changed, at least partially, with the introduction of the minimum rate, the so-called *sconto ridotto*, in 1895 which should have somewhat improved their competitive situation *vis-à-vis* commercial banking (Bonelli 1991: 20, 72ff, 532 note 3). The problematic side of the relationship between the Bank of Italy and the two new commercial banks founded in 1894/5 had surfaced rather quickly in this field. In July 1895, a few months before the minimum rate was introduced by decree, Banca Commerciale, which had started its operations only in December of the previous year, stated quite clearly in a letter to the Bank of Italy in which it had asked before that its branches be admitted to the Bank of Italy's preferential rate of discount: 'Your Excellencies will understand that a bank like ours will discount only bills with a very short currency if it does not at all prefer to have them cashed in by its own correspondents . . .'[20] It has been said that the big commercial banks did not rediscount[21] and did not regularly maintain balances at the Bank of Italy, and that their relations with the latter were only occasional (Bonelli 1991: 92). The refusal of having its commercial paper rediscounted by the banks of issue is confirmed for Banca Commerciale by a letter which the bank wrote in November 1914 to the newspaper *Giornale d'Italia* which had published an article by the prestigious economist Maffeo Pantaleoni who was then leading a nationalist press campaign against the allegedly 'German' Banca Commerciale. In this letter the bank asked the editor of the newspaper to rectify some of the claims made by Pantaleoni and stated, among other things 'As to our [bank], because of the importance of the capital which has been put at its disposal, it does not fall back on rediscounting in normal times. The reason for this lies in the necessity to keep the money of its depositors in assets of prompt and easy liquidity, i.e. mostly in the form of bills of exchange, since these are the classical means by which, in the case of extraordinary circumstances, extraordinary demands for payments can be met.'[22] The refusal to rediscount bills with the banks of issue, and this meant of course first of all with the Bank of Italy, could be explained by the fear of Banca Commerciale and Credito Italiano of becoming dependent on these institutions which were also their competitors and which could thus gain insight into the names, the quality and the structure of their portfolios. Only on quite exceptional occasions – the crisis of 1907 or the outbreak of World War I, when Italy stayed neutral until May 1915 – did they fall back on the major issuing bank for rediscounting (Gigliobianco 1990: 321ff). In some cases they preferred to rediscount with 'lesser' partners, as Banca Commerciale seems to have done with the Turin branch of the Banco di Napoli around 1908 (Gigliobianco 1990: 322) or as Credito Italiano did with the Milan Savings Bank (Confalonieri 1975: 222). On the contrary, Banco di Roma and Società Bancaria Italiana, the two other – smaller and less solid – 'mixed banks', made intense use of the Bank of Italy's rediscounting facilities (Gigliobianco 1990: 318; see also Bonelli 1971: 32). Rediscounts have been estimated to amount to about 30–40% of the Bank of Italy's bills of exchange portfolio during the last decade before the outbreak of the First World War (Gigliobianco 1990: 316).[23]

Another field where the Bank of Italy felt threatened by the big commercial banks was the accumulation of deposits. Its possibilities were, as we have already seen, quite limited: the interest rates it was allowed to pay were rather low and the overall volume was quite restricted. One can observe an increase in the volume of current account deposits from 138 million lire in 1894 to 149 million in 1897 while the interest rate went down from 1.5% to 0.75%. Starting in 1898 these deposits declined until 1907 from 141 to 64 million lire. Interest was down to 0.5% starting in March 1902. Total current account deposits at the Bank of Italy went up to 87 million lire in 1908, but from then on they diminished rather quickly to 57 million lire in 1912 (Bonelli 1991: 479–81). The official report of June 1913, where these figures were published, tried to explain these movements by the growth of competition exercised by the commercial banks after 1897, but also by variations in risk. This latter one had been rated probably rather highly after 1893/4, when the previously existing two major commercial banks had gone out of business and when the success of the two newcomers – Banca Commerciale and Credito Italiano – was still quite uncertain. Risk was again judged to be considerable during and immediately after the crisis of 1907, and this should explain the (temporary) transfer of accounts to the major bank of issue. But as we have seen above, once the immediate crisis situation seemed to have passed deposits diminished again starting from 1909, and this despite the fact that a new law, passed in the same year, allowed the banks of issue to raise the interest rate on deposits to three quarters of the level permitted to the postal savings bank (Bonelli 1991: 476).

Stringher had already been upset in 1905 when he described, in a letter to Mangili, how the economic situation of the Bank of Italy had been threatened by the decreasing interest rates and by 'the violent competition coming from the commercial banks. Banca Commerciale, which asks for deposits [by offering] 3%, 3.25% and 3.5% [interest] and discounts at 3.5% and 3.75%, ousts everybody and disturbs the markets. Joel is preparing truly bitter days for the Italian economy, and I hope to get the opportunity to say it *in public* and with efficiency!!'[24] There was an allusion to these reproaches in the report which Stringher read to the Bank's shareholders in the annual meeting which took place ten days later (Banca d'Italia 1905: 50), but it remained relatively vague and referred quite generally to 'the growth of competition between the banks' and mentioned 'the danger which the lack of a prudent behaviour in the motions of the stock exchange could one day prepare for national wealth'.

Some years later Stringher came back quite regularly to the deposit question in his annual reports to the Bank of Italy's shareholders. In 1911 he deplored the lack of functional coordination for current account deposits between *the* bank of issue – the other two were not even mentioned – and the commercial banks (Banca d'Italia 1911: 22). A year later he showed himself to be concerned by the risk depositors seemed to run particularly with small and medium-sized banks. He rejected the possibility of changing the existing legislation. Instead he placed his hopes in

a movement in public opinion which would lead to a more efficient control of deposits and to a more modest remuneration paid for them. The initiative could start spontaneously from the bigger commercial banks and from the major savings banks which exercise an indirect influence on the behaviour of the medium-sized and small [credit] institutions by offering them, albeit involuntarily, good arguments for applying high interest rates on deposits and pushing them – through steadily increasing competition – to operations which promise a higher income, but which are also less liquid and maybe less secure. (Banca d'Italia 1912: 11ff)

This appeal obviously did not meet with any success, otherwise Stringher, referring to 'the weak contribution which the Bank receives from current account deposits', would not have been forced to say, in his report for the shareholders' meeting of 1914: 'we only have to repeat the things said in the previous reports', pointing also to the much more satisfactory situation in 'some foreign central banks' (Banca d'Italia 1914: 33; see also Ciocca 1978: 190ff).

The impression which we get from this ongoing confrontation between the biggest bank of issue and the major commercial bank should not, however, mislead us. From the evidence at our disposal it seems that the two camps almost ignored each other until about 1900 and that afterwards there were frequent occasions of contact and active collaboration.

In January 1895, only a few weeks after Banca Commerciale had started to operate, Joel made a courtesy call to Bank of Italy's Director General Marchiori in Rome and offered the services of his new bank for any type of business occurring at Milan.[25] There must afterwards have been 'technical' contacts between the two banks as there already had been before,[26] but Joel's correspondence, which has been preserved complete for the following two years, does not show any traces of ensuing regular contacts between the two leading managers. The reason can probably be found in the Bank of Italy's struggle to become a true central bank, since for the moment it could be considered only 'a gigantic real estate company *in fieri*, with conspicuous interests in industrial finance', as Confalonieri has put it quite adequately (1975: 103). Practically speaking it meant that Marchiori was extremely busy with other problems, i.e. liquidating a maximum of the Bank's blocked real estate and industrial participation holdings and trying to get better institutional conditions from the legislator. Joel, on the other hand, may not have expected too much from an institution which was still struggling to find its true role. He may have remembered his own times at Banca Generale. When this bank had to close its counters on 18 January 1894, he explained in a letter of the same day that 'the new banking law limits the facilities of the Bank of Italy in such a way that no special operation, even if assisted by guarantees, was still possible'.[27] Fortunately Banca Commerciale did not need these 'special operations', but it seems that the Bank of Italy during its first years under the directorship of Marchiori was not considered by Joel to be an interesting partner.

This certainly changed when, after the death of Marchiori in November 1900, Stringher arrived at the top of the major Italian bank of issue. From then on quite a regular correspondence developed between him and Joel who had known each other since at least 1893.[28] Their exchange of letters was particularly intense between 1902 and 1906. Afterwards it was partly replaced by a correspondence which developed between Stringher and Mangili when the latter had become president of the Banca Commerciale's board in 1907. From 1907 Stringher started also to correspond rather frequently with Luigi Della Torre, head of the Milan private bank Zaccaria Pisa, which as a smaller bank was normally allied with Banca Commerciale in consortia and other business.[29]

Stringher used the correspondence with Joel, and later with Mangili, above all in order to collect the latest news on the national and international money and capital markets. In this way he could gather first-hand information on the states of opinion prevailing in the Milan banking scene. These letters furthermore certainly helped him to understand the position of Banca Commerciale itself which at that time was already by far the most important commercial bank in the country. Joel was particularly valuable for Stringher because he had an intimate knowledge of international banking, a field in which the head of the Bank of Italy lacked experience.[30] Joel, on the other hand, profited equally from the exchange of information and opinions with Stringher. He thus became better informed on the current strategies of the major issuing bank and on the government's intentions in monetary and banking matters. He could also pass on his opinions and his bank's points of view to the Bank of Italy, and this was not a negligible fact in a period when there were no official ties between the two systems.

There seems to have been a comparable but not quite so intense correspondence between Stringher and the chief manager of Credito Italiano, Enrico Rava, even if historical research suffers from a large gap between 1901 and 1910 because the letter books of these years have been lost.[31] Stringher was apparently quite an intimate friend of Giovanni Battista Pirelli, Milan industrialist and Vice-President of Credito Italiano from 1904, and this may have brought him into closer contact with Pirelli's bank.[32]

Apart from providing valuable information there were other services which Joel and his bank could render to Stringher. In 1903, when the country's metallic reserve grew by one third (Confalonieri 1975: 181), it was Banca Commerciale that offered foreign exchange to Stringher; in one case it came from the bank's foreign shareholders on the occasion of a capital increase.[33]

Public debt, its issue and placement were another field of competition and coordination between the Bank of Italy and its commercial counterparts. Each was in need of the other: the banks of issue had to prepare the scene for the launching of a new loan by an adequate monetary policy, and the government normally wanted them to participate if not to take the lead in this process. The commercial banks on the other side were needed for placing the newly created securities with the public. If part of the loan was to be placed abroad, foreign commercial banks had to be contacted; this was often done by the national commercial banks who traditionally maintained the best relations with their foreign counterparts. The best example in our context is provided by the well-known *Conversione della Rendita 5%*, the conversion of the principal, non-redeemable part of Italian public debt in 1906 (see Corbino 1938: 342ff; Confalonieri 1975: 62ff; Ballini 1994). The key to a possible conversion of this particular security lay with the Paris capital market, and particularly with the Rothschilds. Luigi Luzzatti, economist and one of the leading statesmen of the period, played an active role in putting this conversion on the agenda of the various Italian governments, starting with his efforts as early as 1899 (Ballini 1994: 297ff). Joel had been consulted by Stringher quite early on the chances of such a conversion and denied these, in the light of the impressions he had personally received when talking to his colleagues in the French banks, at the end of 1902 and during the first months of 1903.[34] Again, in March and April 1903 he kept Stringher informed on Rothschilds' and Crédit Lyonnais' position in this matter.[35] When things seemed to become serious at the beginning of 1904, Luzzatti, Minister of the Treasury since November of the previous year, let Joel know that he would have to negotiate with the German group of banks who were supposed to become part of the international syndicate.[36] During the second half of January 1904 Joel spent two weeks in Rome, mostly in order to discuss the technical details of the planned conversion with Stringher and with the government.[37] At the end of February the whole action was suspended since in the meantime the Russo-Japanese War had broken out and international capital markets would be deeply disturbed, but there were also internal reasons, for instance the imminent nationalization of the principal Italian railways, which would certainly have put some additional strain on the markets.[38]

Even after this temporary stop Joel was asked by Luzzatti to see the Rothschilds in Paris during the following month of March in order to keep in touch with this principal foreign actor who was supposed to have a crucial part in any future attempt to convert the *Rendita*.[39] Only one and a half years afterwards, in June 1906, could the conversion finally be realized (De Cecco 1990: 567ff; Ballini 1994: 332ff). The foreign banks were no longer asked to guarantee the entire operation; they were just requested to grant a credit to the Italian Treasury which would have been used in order to repay only those bearers of the *Rendita* who wanted to be repaid instead of accepting the conversion. Joel had been invited by the Italian government 'to participate actively at all negotiations', and in a telegram to Deutsche Bank he claimed to have 'always energetically defended position of our Berlin group'.[40] The German group of banks had delegated the head of the house of Bleichroeder, Paul von Schwabach, to the final talks in Rome and Paris,[41] but there can be no doubt that Joel – in the triple role as 'lobbyist' of the German group, as expert on the German capital market appointed by the Italian government, and finally as representative of the Banca Commerciale – must have been quite active on front of stage as well as behind the scenes. The French ambassador in Rome, Barrère, commented in a way which was transparently hostile but not totally inappropriate: 'M. Joel est dans cette affaire un agent allemand sans épithète. Il agit non seulement pour la Banque mais pour le Gouv.[ernement] allemand.'[42]

The Bank of Italy as a lender of last resort

On three occasions before Italy's entry into the First World War in May 1915 did the Bank of Italy act as a lender of last resort.

(1) In the autumn of 1907, when the international crisis had hit the Italian economy particularly hard, Stringher's Bank of Italy saved Società Bancaria Italiana (SBI) which was threatened by insolvency. In its race to reach Banca Commerciale and Credito Italiano SBI had disregarded the elementary rules of risk distribution and risk control. Stringher had appreciated the initial rise of SBI, probably because he wanted a third big commercial bank besides the two first-comers. These latter two as well as other banks were pushed by Stringher to participate, under the direction of the Bank of Italy, in an effort to save SBI. Neither Banca Commerciale nor Credito Italiano was enthusiastic, but they could hardly have declined Stringher's urgent request (see Bonelli 1971: *passim*; Confalonieri 1982, I: 12ff; Hertner 1984: 191ff, 235ff). Stringher's initiative was successful, at least in the short run, and a few years later Canovai could comment as follows:

This assistance, very different from the forms of aid that had been afforded twenty years before, showed how effective a safeguard for a country is the existence of a great bank of issue in moments of difficulty and disturbance; and it showed further that the most difficult ordeals can be surmounted and the most severe disasters avoided by comparatively insignificant means, when there is no lack of precise perception of the situation and promptness in meeting it. (Canovai 1911: 175)

Self-praise is not absent in this comment, and it cannot really surprise since Canovai was a high official of the Bank of Italy. But the substance of this 'first touchstone' for the lender of last resort, as Gianni Toniolo calls this act of intervention by the quasi-central bank (Toniolo 1995: 51), must be acknowledged. By successfully avoiding a run on a single bank, in this case on Società Bancaria Italiana, the Bank of Italy in a certain way justified its own existence as a central bank, if one accepts Goodhart's concept (Goodhart 1987).

(2) Less than four years later, in the spring of 1911, another set of problems had to be solved, and again the difficult task of coordination was exercised by the Bank of Italy embodied by its Director General. This time it was not a single firm but an entire industrial sector, iron and steel production, that was in the doldrums. Since 1899, and with the decisive help of Banca Commerciale and Credito Italiano, new integrated steelworks had been built along the coast of the Tyrrhenian Sea, on the isle of Elba, and just opposite it at Piombino as well as at Bagnoli near Naples. They all used coal imported from Britain and iron ore, mostly from Elba. Government subsidies rather than tariff protection and generous financing by the big banks – a conspicuous part of it was mobilized via contango credits – enabled impressive growth rates, but when after a few years most plants started to produce, markets were flooded, prices and profits went down and in a certain way the banks became prisoners of the firms they had helped to create. The situation became gradually more critical from 1908 onwards when the general growth of the Italian economy was reduced and international competition was increasingly felt. 'Our steel industrialists have a characteristic in common: megalomania and a lack of foresight' – that is what Mangili wrote to Stringher in March 1909.[43] This is certainly not the occasion to tell the story in all its details (see in particular Confalonieri 1982, I: 48ff; see also Hertner 1984: 247ff). What should be briefly mentioned is the fact that this was a serious attempt by the banks and by the large firms of the industry itself to 'reorganize' the major part of Italian steel production by forming a sort of 'steel trust'. Finance was provided under the guidance and through the participation of the Bank of Italy by the four major commercial banks and by some of the biggest savings banks in the country. Almost 100 million lire, a considerable sum

for the period, were spent in this exercise in 'industrial policy'. It was not a typical operation of a lender of last resort; the Bank of Italy was rather doing what in other circumstances and also in other countries the respective governments would have done. Stringher pointed out that there was an entire industrial branch with about 250 million lire invested and with tens of thousands employed. Nevertheless he saw himself in this affair 'less than a driver [but] more like a coordinator'.[44]

(3) Toniolo sees August 1914 as the watershed: to him this was the moment when the Bank of Italy became a 'central bank in the modern sense'. According to him this presupposed that it accepted 'full responsibility for the stability of the system subordinating to this its proper interests as a firm' (Toniolo 1995: 50). In his introduction to the collection of documents which show the activities of the Bank of Italy during the First World War the same author has demonstrated quite clearly how these requirements were met at the very beginning of the conflict when Italy was still neutral (Toniolo 1989: 18ff). Two important measures were taken by the Bank on that occasion. A special consortium, the *Consorzio per sovvenzioni su valori industriali*, was created which was to give financial support to the entire economy and not only to specific sectors or firms. The state, pushed by the Bank of Italy, decreed furthermore a moratorium which was extended several times and which prevented runs and kept the markets quite calm. Toniolo's view seems acceptable, even if one has to keep in mind that the War was an absolutely exceptional circumstance and that therefore the Bank's decisions were rather the result of these emergencies than of a development which had had the necessary time for maturing.

A very short conclusion

How would one have to conclude this, as we have said already, rather 'impressionistic' account? Looking at the three types of relationship between 'quasi-central bank' and big commercial banks – no contacts, competition or cooperation – one must recognize that the interests of the commercial banks were quite clear and did not have to change over time: they did what they had to do as private firms in a capitalist economy, and that meant that they had to achieve profit – not necessarily maximizing it in the short run but certainly trying to survive in the long run through steady and positive economic results. Whether they succeeded is another question: the crisis of 1907 and the steel crisis of 1911 gave at least some warnings that there might be a danger of running into a 'systemic risk' if operating in a relatively small and late industrializing economy. The banks of issue had, quite on the contrary, two different interests for which they had to care: the interests of their private shareholders, and we have seen for how long a time these were practically set aside; and also a 'public interest', continually recalled by someone like Stringher who had been a public servant for a long part of his career. We know the end of the story, i.e. how these banks of issue became truly 'public', far from any idea of independence as it is advertised today. Contemporary observers who lived before the First World War did not know the outcome. They were just surprised when they were confronted with the contradictory behaviour of central bankers, partly private and partly public. We ought to know better and try to understand the dilemmas they had to live with.

NOTES

Abbreviations used in the notes

AS BCI Archivio storico della Banca Commerciale Italiana, Milano (Historical archives of the Banca Commerciale Italiana, Milan)

AS BI   Archivio storico della Banca d'Italia, Roma (Historical archives of the Bank of Italy, Rome)

AS CI   Archivio storico del Credito Italiano, Milano (Historical archives of Credito Italiano, Milan)

1 See the inventory edited by Bonelli and Stringher (1990). See also Banca d'Italia 1993: 541.

2 I am most grateful to the Bank of Italy and to Sergio Cardarelli who directs its historical archives as well as to Banca Commerciale Italiana at Milan and to the director of its historical archives, Francesca Pino, for having granted me access to their sources and for having supported my research on so many occasions.

3 In 1898 a law decreed the gradual reduction of this tax to 0.1% in exchange for a participation of the government in the yearly profits of the three banks of issue (Canovai 1911: 154).

4 In this context, Bonaldo Stringher mentioned – in his annual report to the shareholders of the Bank of Italy for the year 1902 – the favourable influence of 'that psychological element' which, quite to the contrary, in other times had contributed to keep the lira at a discount (Banca d'Italia 1903: 8).

5 At the end of 1906 Italy's gold reserves were bigger than those of Britain and Germany and occupied the fourth position in Europe, after France, Russia and Austria-Hungary (Confalonieri 1975: 189).

6 The fact that the Italian Treasury circulated its own notes – their volume amounted to 29% of total Italian note circulation in 1900 and had shrunk to 18% in 1913 – may have contributed to the refusal to go back to convertibility, since part of the gold reserve backing the Treasury notes was used in 1912 in order to get money printed by the Bank of Italy without having to increase the latter's reserves (Corbino 1938: 410, 412).

7 Franco Bonelli talks of 'the ritual request for a return to bank-note convertibility, present in many speeches given by ministers and Members of

Parliament' which never found any real response when monetary issues were discussed in parliament. According to him, the topic remained relevant only in scientific literature and in academic teaching (Bonelli 1991: 13).

8 Marco Fanno (1933: 84ff) mentions the 'indirect' effect of discount policy in a system of 'inconvertible paper money' via price changes, money circulation, balance of payments and exchange rates.

9 These were the so-called *banche popolari*, many of them legally organized as cooperatives (Polsi 1993: 193ff).

10 The term *banche di speculazione* was not necessarily a polemical one. Contemporary economists used it as a synonym for what we would call today *universal banks* (cf. for instance Weber 1922: esp. 4ff).

11 As Federico and Toniolo (1991) underline, this important question still awaits a definitive answer.

12 AS BI, CS: Mangili to Stringher (9/3/1906); Stringher to Balduino (12/3/1906); Stringher to Mangili (16 and 18/3/1906).

13 AS BCI, Carte personali di Otto Joel (PJ) 12: Joel to Eugenio Pollone (11/8/1907).

14 AS BI, CS, 201.1.03.60: Stringher to Mangili (11/10/1903).

15 *Ibid.*, 201.1.02.66: Mangili to Giulio [Prinetti?] (1/12/1902).

16 *Ibid.*, 205.2.02.183: Joel to Stringher (2/5/1905).

17 *Ibid.*, 201.1.02.37: Mangili to Stringher (8/8/1902).

18 *Ibid.*, 201.1.04.65: Mangili to Stringher (1/7/1904).

19 *Ibid.*, 201.1.03.153: Mangili to Stringher (2/4/1903).

20 AS BCI, Copialettere della Direzione Centrale (CpD), vol. 7, fol. 348 (15/7/1895).

21 Joel, in a letter to Stringher of 22 May 1905, underlined that Banca Commerciale 'on principle never rediscounts its portfolio' (AS BCI, PJ 5, fol. 194ff). Enrico Rava, Director of Credito Italiano, told Milan industrialist Giovanni Battista Pirelli in a letter of 28 December 1910: 'You should know on the other hand that we almost never rediscount and that therefore your bills will remain in our portfolio' (AS CI, Copialettere della Direzione Centrale, fol. 447ff).

22 AS BCI, Copialettere del Presidente Cesare Mangili (CpPM), vol. 30, fol. 200 (25/11/1914).

23 Rediscounting by the Bank of Italy was concentrated above all in the northern economic centres like Milan and Genoa. In the South and in Tuscany, where the network of local banks was much less developed, the Bank discounted directly with merchants, industrialists and agricultural entrepreneurs (cf. Gigliobianco 1990: 315ff).

24 AS BI, CS, 201.1.04.135: Stringher to Mangili (17/3/1905).

25 AS BCI, CpD, vol. 2, fols. 338ff: Joel to Marchiori (11/1/1895).

26 There was for instance a correspondence between the barely founded Banca Commerciale and the Bank of Italy referring to the gold deposit which had to be delivered by the Commerciale's founders and which the Bank of Italy would have liked to incorporate, albeit briefly, into its metallic reserve (AS BCI, CpD, vol. 1, fols. 47 (24/10/1894), 101ff (28/10/1894), 192 (7/11/1894)).

27 AS BCI, PJ 2: Joel to Martinengo (18/1/1894).

28 Cf. the two letters by Joel to Stringher, written in October/November 1893

when Joel was employed at Banca Generale and Stringher was a high official of the Treasury (AS BCI, PJ 2, fols. 1ff (19/10/1893), 76ff (22/11/1893)).

29 Cf. the biographical note by Biscione 1989. Della Torre was a member of the Milan Stock Exchange Committee from 1908 until 1911 and informed Stringher on the latest news from the Milan money and capital market (cf. their correspondence during these years in AS BI, CS, 205.3.02).

30 One could not accuse Stringher of lacking *any* international experience since he had participated at a series of international monetary conferences and had been a member of various national committees who were active in the preparation of international trade agreements during the 1880s and 1890s (see Bonelli 1985: 48ff).

31 There are only a few letters in the Stringher Papers which document any personal contacts between Stringher and the leading men of Credito Italiano during the period 1895–1914, especially for the period before 1907. For these earlier years the letterbooks of the *Direzione Centrale* of Credito Italiano have been preserved for the years 1898–1901, but according to these books there was practically no correspondence between this bank and the Bank of Italy (AS CI, Copialettere della Direzione Centrale, vols. 1–7). There are, however, quite a number of letters exchanged between Rava and Stringher in the letterbooks preserved for the period 1910–14 (*ibid.*, vols. 8–12).

32 See the letter written by Stringher to Pirelli in August 1910 where he informed him 'confidentially' on his correspondence with Joel (AS BI, CS, 205.3.01.2: 24/8/1910).

33 AS BCI, PJ 3, fols. 256ff, 273ff: Joel to Stringher (25 and 27/2/1903); 468ff, 476ff (25 and 28/5/1903). AS BI, CS, 201.1.04.13: Mangili to Stringher (10/1/1904).

34 AS BI, CS, 205.2.01.6: Joel to Stringher (11/11/1902); AS BCI, PJ 3, fol. 256: Joel to Stringher (25/2/1903).

35 AS BCI, PJ 3, fols. 353ff, 420ff: Joel to Stringher (17/3 and 10/4/1903).

36 AS BI, CS, 205.2.02.8: Stringher to Joel (8/1/1904).

37 *Ibid.*, 205.2.02.23: Joel to Stringher (12/1/1904); 205.2.02.30: Stringher to Joel (2/2/1904).

38 *Ibid.*, 205.2.02.99: Joel to Stringher (26/2/1904).

39 *Ibid.*, 205.2.02.125 and 205.2.02.128: Joel to Luzzatti (7 and 12/3/1904).

40 Joel to Deutsche Bank (received on 25/6/1906) (document 113 in De Cecco 1990: 550).

41 See the minutes of the meeting of the *Konsortium für italienische Geschäfte* held at Berlin on 25/6/1906 (document 114 in De Cecco 1990: 552).

42 Telegram of 4/6/1906 (quoted in Ballini 1994: 333).

43 AS BI, Consorzio Siderurgico: Mangili to Stringher (14/3/1909).

44 AS BI, Verbali del Consiglio Superiore [minutes of the High Council], anno 1911, reg. 2, p. 164.

BIBLIOGRAPHY

Ballini, Pier Luigi 1994. 'Luigi Luzzatti e la conversione della rendita del 1906', in Pier Luigi Ballini and Paolo Pecorari (eds.), *Luigi Luzzatti e il suo tempo. Atti del Convegno Internazionale di Studio (Venezia, 7–9 Novembre 1991)*, pp. 297–347. Venice.

208   *Peter Hertner*

Banca d'Italia (ad annos), *Adunanza generale degli azionisti tenuta in Roma il giorno* ... Rome.

1993. *Guida all'Archivio Storico.* Rome.

Biscione, F. M. 1989. 'Della Torre, Luigi', in *Dizionario biografico degli Italiani,* vol. 37, pp. 609–11. Rome.

Bonelli, Franco 1971. *La crisi del 1907: una tappa dello sviluppo industriale in Italia.* Turin.

1985. *Bonaldo Stringher, 1854–1930.* Udine.

Bonelli, Franco (ed.) 1991. *La Banca d'Italia dal 1894 al 1913: momenti della formazione di una banca centrale* (Collana storica della Banca d'Italia. Serie Documenti 4). Rome and Bari.

Bonelli, Franco and Stringher, Bonaldo, Jr 1990. *Carte Stringher: inventario* (Quaderni della Rassegna degli Archivi di Stato 62). Rome.

Canovai, Tito 1911. *The Banks of Issue in Italy, with an Article by Carlo F. Ferraris and the Text of the Italian Banking Law* (National Monetary Commission. US Senate, 61st Congress, 2nd Session, Document No. 575). Washington, DC.

Ciocca, Pierluigi 1978. 'Note sulla politica monetaria italiana 1900–1913', in Gianni Toniolo (ed.), *L'economia italiana 1861–1940,* pp. 179–221. Rome and Bari.

Confalonieri, Antonio 1974, 1975, 1976. *Banca e industria in Italia 1894–1906,* 3 vols. Milan.

1982. *Banca e industria in Italia dalla crisis del 1907 all'agosto 1914,* 2 vols. Milan.

Corbino, Epicarmo 1934. *Annali dell'economia italiana,* vol. 4: *1891–1900.* Città di Castello.

1938. *Annali dell'economia italiana,* vol. 5: *1901–1914.* Città di Castello.

De Cecco, Marcello (ed.) 1990. *L'Italia nel sistema finanziario internazionale 1861–1914* (Collana storica della Banca d'Italia. Serie Documenti 1). Rome and Bari.

Eichengreen, Barry and Flandreau, Marc 1994. *The Geography of the Gold Standard* (Centre for Economic Policy Research. Discussion Paper 1050). London.

Einaudi, Luigi 1960. 'Il rialzo del saggio dello sconto', in Luigi Einaudi (ed.), *Cronache economiche e politiche di un trentennio (1893–1925),* vol. 3, pp. 145–152. (First published in the *Corriere della Sera* on 28/10/1910.)

Fanno, Marco 1933. *Lezioni di economia e legislazione bancaria.* Padua.

Federico, Giovanni and Toniolo, Gianni 1991. 'Italy', in Richard Sylla and Gianni Toniolo (eds.), *Patterns of European Industrialization: The Nineteenth Century,* pp. 197–212. London.

Ferraris, Carlo F. 1911. 'The Italian Banks of Issue', in Canovai 1911, pp. 207–55.

Fratianni, Michele and Spinelli, Franco 1984. 'Italy in the Gold Standard Period, 1861–1914', in Michael D. Bordo and Anna J. Schwartz (eds.), *A Retrospective on the Classical Gold Standard, 1821–1931,* pp. 405–41. Chicago and London.

Gigliobianco, Alfredo 1990. 'Tra concorrenza e collaborazione: considerazioni sulla natura dei rapporti fra "banca centrale" e sistema bancario nell'esperienza italiana (1844–1918)', in *Ricerche per la storia della Banca d'Italia,* vol.

1, pp. 295–338 (Collana storica della Banca d'Italia. Serie Contributi 1). Rome and Bari.

Goodhart, C. A. E. 1987. 'Why Do Banks Need a Central Bank?', *Oxford Economic Papers* n.s. 39: 75–89.

1988. *The Evolution of Central Banks*. Cambridge and London.

Hertner, Peter 1984. *Il capitale tedesco in Italia dall'Unità alla Prima Guerra Mondiale: banche miste e sviluppo economico italiano*. Bologna.

1991. 'Foreign Capital in the Italian Banking Sector', in Rondo Cameron and V. I. Bovykin (eds.), *International Banking 1870–1914*, pp. 345–50. New York and Oxford.

Manacorda, Gastone 1993. *Dalla crisi alla crescita: crisi economica e lotta politica in Italia 1892–1896*. Rome.

Morgan, E. Victor 1965. *The Theory and Practice of Central Banking 1797–1913* (1st edn 1943). London.

Negri, Guglielmo (ed.) 1989. *Giolitti e la nascita della Banca d'Italia nel 1893* (Collana storica della Banca d'Italia. Serie Documenti 3). Rome and Bari.

Pecorari, Paolo 1994. *La fabbrica dei soldi: istituti di emissione e questione bancaria in Italia 1861–1913*. Bologna.

Pino Pongolini, Francesco 1994. 'Introduzione', in Banca Commerciale Italiana, Archivio Storico, *Segretaria Generale (1894–1926) e fondi diversi* (Collana Inventari, Serie III, vol. 1), pp. I–LXVII. Rome.

Polsi, Alessandro 1993. *Alle origini del capitalismo italiano: stato, banche e banchieri dopo l'Unità*. Turin.

Sannucci, Valeria 1990. 'Molteplicità delle banche di emissione: ragioni, economiche ed effetti sull'efficacia del controllo monetario (1860–1890)', in *Ricerche per la storia della Banca d'Italia*, vol. 1, pp. 181–218 (Collana storica della Banca d'Italia. Serie Contributi 1). Rome and Bari.

Sayers, R. S. 1986. *The Bank of England 1891–1944*, paperback edition. Cambridge.

Società Innocente Mangili (ed.) 1917. *In memoria di Cesare Mangili nel trigesimo di sua morte. 18 Giugno 1917*. Milan.

Toniolo, Gianni 1995. *Sull'arte del banchiere centrale in Italia: fatti stilizzati e congetture (1891–1947)* (Banca d'Italia. Temi di discussione del Servizio Studi, No. 255). Rome.

Toniolo, Gianni (ed.) 1989. *La Banca d'Italia e l'economia di guerra 1914–1919* (Collana storica della Banca d'Italia. Serie Documenti 5). Rome and Bari.

Vitale, Eligio 1972. *La riforma degli istituti di emissione e gli 'scandali bancari' in Italia, 1892–1896* (Camera dei Deputati. Segretariato Generale, Archivio Storico), 3 vols. Rome.

Weber, Adolf 1922. *Depositenbanken und Spekulationsbanken: ein Vergleich deutschen und englischen Bankwesens*, 3rd edn (1st edn 1902). Munich and Leipzig.

Wilmersdoerffer, Ernst 1913. *Notenbanken und Papiergeld im Königreich Italien seit 1861* (Münchener Volkswirtschaftliche Studien, vol. 122). Stuttgart and Berlin.

Ziegler, Dieter 1990. *Das Korsett der 'Alten Dame': Die Geschäftspolitik der Bank of England 1844–1913* (Schriftenreihe des Instituts für bankhistorische Forschung, vol. 15). Frankfurt am Main.

9   State power and finance in Russia,
1802–1917: the Credit Office of the Finance
Ministry and governmental control over
credit institutions

Boris Anan'ich

The characteristic features of the Russian Empire, a state with autocratic administration that embarked on industrial modernization later than other European countries, were active state intervention in the economic life of the country and strict governmental control over credit institutions. These features were established by the early years of the nineteenth century. They continued for more than a century, into the early twentieth century when Russia's industrialization was well underway. Industrial modernization was accompanied by rapid financial development. This prompted Finance Minister P. L. Bark in 1916 to recommend changes in the Russian state's strict controls over credit institutions to bring them more into line with Western European practices. Nothing came of Bark's initiatives, however, for within a year Russia was engulfed in revolution. In the end, the Czarist legacy of state control over finance probably facilitated the new regime of state finance put in place by the Communist regime that seized power in 1917.

This chapter traces the evolution of state control over the Russian financial system from 1802, when the Finance Ministry was established, to the 1917 revolution. Special attention is given to the Finance Ministry's Credit Office, established in 1824 as an outgrowth of the ministry's department charged with supervising and regulating finance in Russia. The evidence on which the chapter is based is drawn primarily from documents in the Russian State Historical Archives.

Origins of state financial control and the Credit Office

Banking institutions, which appeared in Russia towards the end of the eighteenth century, as a rule originated in the State Treasury. Banks were opened in Moscow and St Petersburg in 1769 to issue bank-notes (called *assignats*). In 1786, these banks were combined into a State Issuing Bank. Also in 1786, a State Loan Bank opened to extend long-term credit to the nobility. In 1817, a State Commercial Bank was established to promote industrial development and to finance trade. Financial operations involving other countries were carried out through court financiers and private family banking houses having international financial contacts.

The Institute of Court Financiers was formed in 1798 by order of Emperor Paul I. It was subject directly to the State Treasurer. This Institute remained in existence until 1811, when it was officially closed, although its operations continued *de facto* until 1861. The gradual decline of its role in international settlements, followed eventually by its abolition, was a direct result of the establishment in 1802 of the Finance Ministry and the development of the Ministry's expertise and effectiveness in organizing the finances of the Russian state (Anan'ich and Lebedev 1991: 144).

Wars during the late eighteenth and early nineteenth centuries caused the national debts of many European countries to grow considerably. Loans became an increasingly integral part of state finances. Governments found it necessary to establish special institutions both to control growth of the national debt and to take steps towards its gradual redemption. Towards these ends, in Prussia the Staatsschulden Tilgungskasse and in France the Caisse d'amortissement were formed. Their counterpart in Russia was the State Commission on Debt Redemption, which was established in 1810 at a time when state finances and monetary circulation were in a deplorable condition because of the Napoleonic Wars.[1] In July 1810, bonds were issued by the State Commission. In addition, the Commission received for sale Treasury lands valued at no less than 200 million rubles. Finally, certain taxes were designated as a source of money for repaying debts and regulating the monetary circulation.

A Council of State Credit Regulation was established in 1817 to inspect and supervise all financial institutions and operations in the country. Tied closely to the Finance Ministry, the Council initially controlled the activities of the Commission on Dept Redemption.[2] In accordance with statutes promulgated in April 1817, however, the Commission on Debt Redemption was placed directly under the authority of the Finance Minister and in fact became a subdivision of the Finance Ministry.

According to the 1817 statutes, the Commission became responsible for all aspects of state debt management. It was not only in charge of negotiating loans, but also responsible for servicing interest, repaying old debts, withdrawing bank-notes from circulation and destroying them, and various other credit operations.

After the Finance Ministry was established in 1802, new subdivisions soon appeared within its structure. These became an integral part of the

Ministry and they also exercised control over all financial operations and banking organizations in Russia. In 1811, it was the Third Department of the Office of the Finance Ministry that became responsible for exercising such controls. In December 1824, the Third Department was reorganized into a Special Office on Credits (the Credit Office).[3] The Credit Office remained the primary supervisor and regulator of finance in Russia until October 1917 when it lost its influence; it was closed down in 1918. During its near century of existence the Credit Office became a powerful instrument the Finance Minister could use to control the administration of the empire's financial system and its international financial relations.

From the time it was established, the Credit Office exercised control over the operations of the Treasury banks and the activities of the Commission on Debt Redemption. All these institutions had to submit annual accounts to the Credit Office. In addition, the Credit Office took over most of the loan and debt management activities that previously had been the responsibility of the Commission on Debt Redemption. Through the 1850s, all payments abroad were usually conducted through court financiers. In the 1840s and 1850s, for example, most of Russia's international payments were made through the private banking firm of Stieglitz and Company. But all of these payments were controlled by the Credit Office, which later gave orders to the State Treasury with regard to settlement of accounts with Stieglitz and Company.

The Credit Office shapes Russia's financial system

Russia's period of significant reforms at the end of the 1850s and the beginning of the 1860s brought about important changes in the financial system of the empire. Treasury banks were either liquidated or reorganized. A commission was formed under the chairmanship of the Director of the Credit Eureka to discuss opening private land banks. The Commission drew up a draft project titled 'Statutes on Private Mortgage Banks or on Mortgage Land Banks'. This first attempt in Russia to work out general banking legislation failed, however. The draft statutes were not even submitted to the State Council for consideration, and in 1861 the Commission was dissolved.[4] The work of shaping Russia's financial system in the second half of the nineteenth century fell instead to the Credit Office of the Finance Ministry.

All matters concerning the establishment of private and public banks were passed on to the attention of the Credit Office. As a result, when public and private credit institutions began to emerge in the 1860s, their draft statutes (essentially charters) were revised each time in the Credit Office before being presented for the approval of the State Council. City public banks were the only exception to the rule of Credit Office control; they were covered by a separate 'Normal Statute' promulgated in 1862.[5]

The charters of financial institutions granted under Credit Office oversight in the 1860s became models for subsequent institutions of this kind. In May 1872, the State Council passed a law that authorized the Finance Minister to approve, according to established patterns, the charters of credit institutions to be opened. Only minor deviations from these established patterns were allowed in each particular case. In the 1870s and 1880s, a number of laws were adopted promoting the expansion of the range of banking services. Legislation of the period, however, did not weaken state control over finance. The state continued to play a major role through the existence and activities of the Credit Office.

The State Bank, established in 1860 on a level with the Credit Office, became another instrument that exercised control of finance and money circulation. The advent of the State Bank coincided with the termination of the Institute of Court Financiers, which had been 'officially' abolished in 1811, but had continued for decades to have some influence on Russia's internal financial development as well as its external financial relations. In the transition, the last court financier, Alexander Stieglitz, was appointed the first director of the State Bank.

Initially, the State Bank was charged with settling international accounts. This allocation of responsibility, however, did not last long. In December 1886–January 1887, by the Emperor's order, the Department of the State Bank engaged in operations abroad was transformed into the International Department of the Credit Office. From then on the Credit Office prepared materials for issuing bonds. Credit Office agents monitored the situation in world money markets and prepared necessary documents for negotiating new loans abroad. Generally, the Finance Minister (either personally or through his agents abroad) conducted preliminary rounds of negotiations with bankers to determine market conditions, and to define the types of loans to be made and the terms of servicing and repaying them, as well as conditions for subscriptions and so on. A report was then drawn up to be presented to the Finance Committee, which discussed problems concerning future loans and worked out a draft of the Emperor's order regulating the loan procedure. The Credit Office played an active part in all the stages of preparing documents for placing a loan, and it was there that projects for converting old loans to new ones and other bond operations were developed. Responsibilities of the Credit Office for placing loans abroad grew considerably in the last decade of the nineteenth century as Russia began to attract foreign capital for the modernization of its economy.

Apart from its involvement with the state loans, the Credit Office actively participated in issuing state-guaranteed foreign bonds of Russian railway companies, an important aspect of economic modernization. The Credit Office not only took part in setting the conditions for the implementation and servicing of the railway loans, but also decided to what extent Russian joint-stock banks should participate in the process.

As the functions of the Credit Office expanded, it became an absolutely original institution in the realm of finance, one that combined not only administrative functions of a governmental nature but also operational functions of both public and private finance. That is, along with administrative tasks of state management in the financial and credit spheres, the Credit Office was involved in issuing bonds, buying hard currencies, and making international financial settlements for the government as well as for numerous public companies. The volume of the Credit Office's business exceeded hundreds of millions of rubles, far in excess of the volume of business of any banking institution.[6]

After instituting its reforms, which included creating conditions for the emergence of new types of banks (land, joint-stock and commercial banks), the Russian government retained its control over them, primarily through the operations of the Credit Office. As Minister of Finance P. L. Bark wrote in 1916, 'historical and everyday experience could not but affect the government policy even in the post-reform era . . . When it allowed the appearance of new private banks the state did not give up its influence on credit matters of which it had made very good use before.'[7]

Around the turn of the century, the role of the Credit Office as the main channel of state control over Russia's financial system continued to increase. The Credit Office, for example, controlled many of the main operations of joint-stock land banks from the moment they came into existence at the beginning of the 1870s. In 1898, special business correspondence requirements were introduced by the Credit Office to control land banks. And in 1901, by order of the Emperor, the Minister of Finance received the right to appoint special representatives of the ministry to supervise the operations of joint-stock land banks to the 'full extent'. In 1902, Finance Ministry control over joint-stock land banks was formalized by means of an Institute of Representatives, a form of public oversight of private financial institutions. When the boards of directors of the banks did not agree with the policy of the representatives, the conflict was to be settled in the Credit Office.

Wide range of Credit Office financial control

The beginning of the 1880s proved to be an important stage in the development of the Credit Office, for during this period its influence on joint-stock and commercial banking institutions grew considerably. During 1883, in connection with the bankruptcy of several city banks, the Bank Statutes of 1862 had to be re-examined. In 1884, a law was passed regulating the liquidation procedure of credit institutions. In accordance with law, the Finance Minister was empowered to form liquidation commissions, which were immediately placed under the supervision of the Credit Office.[8]

In 1885, Russia introduced a 5% income tax. Again, it was the Credit Office that supervised that fiscal operation. Even the Russian mint was within its jurisdiction for a short period of time, from 1875 to 1879. This control then went to the State Treasury, but in 1894 it was given back to the Credit Office. In 1897, when Russia went on the gold standard, the number of Credit Office operations connected with coinage grew. From 1895 to 1909, 1.66 billion rubles were coined, compared with a far lower total of 394 million during the previous fifteen years.[9]

In 1900, the St Petersburg Exchange opened its Stock Department. A representative from the Credit Office was made a member of the Stock Department Council, which was authorized to decide matters related to securities trading. In that way, the government could closely monitor the nascent Russian securities market.

In 1882, a State Mortgage Bank for Peasantry was established, followed in 1885 by a State Mortgage Bank for Nobility. The managements of both banks, as well as that of the State Bank, were under the absolute control of the Credit Office. In the first half of the 1890s, however, new Standing Orders were promulgated for these banks, and through these orders the banks received greater independence in solving their problems directly through the Finance Minister, rather than through the Credit Office as before. Nevertheless, even after the 1890s, the Director of the Credit Office, because he was a member of the State Bank's board of directors *ex officio*, continued to play an important role in managing State Bank affairs.

In 1901, administration of state savings banks was separated from that of the State Bank and the savings banks became separate legal entities. Again, a representative from the Credit Office was placed in one of the savings bank administration departments. The most important questions of savings bank operations were still discussed at State Bank board of directors meetings, with the participation of the Credit Office representative. The Director of the Credit Office along with the State Bank manager reported to the Minister of Finance as to how money in savings banks should be used.

Thus, from the mid-1890s the Credit Office and the State Bank began jointly to carry out a number of important financial operations. They were actively involved in regulating money circulation, currency issues and discount policies. As far as the Banks for the Peasantry and the Nobility were concerned, the Credit Office preserved its position in their affairs and continued to control many of their operations. For instance, these banks together with the Credit Office worked out the conditions for issuing bonds to fund their lending, for servicing and repaying these bond issues, and for the conversion of old liabilities.[10] In the opinion of V. M. Kokovtsov, Finance Minister from 1906 to 1914, by the beginning of the twentieth century the Credit Office had begun to be the link between the State Bank and the Banks for the Peasantry and the Nobility on the one hand, and Russia's private banks on the other.[11]

With the growth of the influence of the Credit Office and the expansion of its functions, private banks became more dependent on it. They came under strict Credit Office control from the moment their charters were approved. Until 1884, inspections of banks could be conducted only by order of the Emperor. A law promulgated in 1884 gave the Finance Minister wide powers to decide bank inspection questions. In the period from June 1883 to January 1910, the Finance Ministry carried out 288 inspections of private credit institutions.[12] By 1904 a 'special record keeping' section was introduced in one of the departments of the Credit Office to supervise credit institutions and to conduct inspections.

The Credit Office always received a great amount of paperwork in the form of financial reports from different credit institutions, the number of which was constantly rising in Russia. Summaries of these reports allow one to gain a glimpse of the extent and growth of Russia's financial system during the industrial upsurge before the First World War. Table 9.1 gives the comparative data for 1910 and 1913, which indicate the rapid pace of financial development in these years.

The Credit Office received annual reports from all these institutions as well as reports of the inspecting commissions, and resolutions of general meetings of share- and stockholders, and of town dumas related to the approval of these reports. In addition, joint-stock banks and their branches were required to submit monthly balance sheets of their enterprises to the Credit Office.

Strict state control, however, did not extend to private bankers' and moneychangers' houses that grew up outside the tutelage and supervision of the state. According to the returns of the Credit Office, their number totalled 300 or 400 in the period before the First World War. All attempts on the part of the government to exercise control over them failed. In 1913, the Credit Office was able to collect information about only 158 private bankers' houses (Anan'ich 1991: 26–36, 153–6).

Table 9.1 *Numbers of different types of credit institutions in Russia in September 1910 compared with May 1913.*

Type of credit institution	1 September 1910	1 May 1913
Joint-stock commercial banks	38	48
Departments of commercial banks	547	603
Mutual credit societies	576	994
Central mutual loan banks	1	1
Joint-stock land banks	10	10
Land banks and societies on special basis	7	7
City credit societies	34	36
Joint-stock pawnbrokers	14	14
City public banks	284	312
City pawnbrokers	91	99
Village banks	7	7
City and industrial savings banks	10	10
Total	1619	2141

Sources: Library of the Russian State Historical Archives. Publications 1105–9; the report of V. M. Kokovtsov to the State Duma on 12 September 1913, p. 9.

Although the control of the Credit Office over credit institutions progressively grew, the Finance Ministry still did not think it sufficient. In September 1910, Finance Minister V. M. Kokovtsov submitted for consideration by the State Duma a bill on increasing the Credit Office staff and the creation within the Credit Office of a special department that would exercise control over private credit institutions. But the bill was recalled by the Finance Ministry for revision. In the spring of 1912, several bankers' houses in St Petersburg went bankrupt. This gave Finance Minister Kokovtsov cause to propose to the State Duma, in September 1913, a new project entitled 'On organization of the private credit institutions and strengthening of the money resources in the ownership of the Special Office on Credit'. The Minister again demanded that the Credit Office staff be increased and that necessary conditions be created for careful and systematic examination of monthly and yearly reports submitted by credit institutions. From his point of view, inspections were supposed not only to ensure proper control over credit institutions' operations and to defend shareholders' interests, but also to promote an improvement of the institutions' activities. Kokovtsov's project got the approval of the State Duma and of the State Council, but the measure never became law because their regular meetings were soon discontinued.[13]

Financial effects of the First World War

The First World War brought alterations in government control policies towards the financial sector. Relations of banks and credit institutions in Russia with their counterparts in Germany and Germany's allies during the war were at the forefront of the government's attention. In November 1914, the Czar issued a decree that forbade any kinds of payments to an enemy's subjects, and in May 1915 another order that prevented enemy subjects from withdrawing their deposits. At the end of February 1917, the Credit Office sent all public and private credit institutions a secret instruction supplemented by a list of credit organizations in neutral countries with which it was necessary to break relations.[14]

At the same time, the war brought about great changes in the Russian banking system. In the course of the war, the role of the joint-stock commercial banks in the economic life of the country grew sharply (see Table 9.2). As far back as the eve of the war, the Finance Ministry pointed to the considerable increase in business of joint-stock commercial banks in granting credit for the grain trade and in financing industrial enterprises. The banks had begun to attend to economic necessities of the country. The credits allocated by commercial banks became of national importance.

To expand their volume of business and to be able to meet the deposit withdrawal demands at critical moments, joint-stock commercial banks resorted to the State Bank credit. For example, in the first months of the war it was only due to the aid provided by the State Bank that commercial banks were able to weather the crisis and to meet depositors' requests to withdraw 207 million rubles.[15]

In periods of economic crisis, large commercial banks participated in consortia headed by the State Bank, whose prime responsibility was regulation of monetary flows. Monetary flows were also under the control of the Credit Office and the government's Finance Committee, with the Credit Office having direct involvement in the placement of external loans. At the same time, many St Petersburg commercial banks took part in Russian groups of consortia that formed in the European market for Russian bonds (Cameron and Bovykin 1991: 257–67, 280–90).

The Credit Office and the State Bank provided the connection between joint-stock commercial banks and the government. These arms of the state became instrumental in the growth of the Russian financial system. But the Finance Ministry expressed concern about the obvious process of concentration of commercial bank capital due to the absorption of small provincial banks by city banks and to mergers of several commercial banks. Finance Minister P. L. Bark wrote in 1916, 'By bringing their

Table 9.2 *The growth in business operations of the joint-stock commercial banks.*

Item	1895	1905	1915
Number of banks	38	39	53
Number of branch banks	99[a]	280	635
Liabilities (million rubles)			
Bank capital	179	307	916
Investment	310	837	2914
Loans	45	55	363
Assets			
Treasury securities	56	120	492
Credit against bills	208	706	1916
Credit against securities	237	281	942
Credit against commodities	23	85	303
Correspondents: Lozo	142	302	1402
Including coverage of unguaranteed securities	37	52	659
Nostro (free bank capital)	40	68	161
Total assets	888	2181	5884

Note:
[a] Besides bank branches abroad and the branches of the Credit Lyonnais in Russia.
Source: Russian State Historical Archives (RGIA) f. 1276; op. 7; d. 1232; 1. 9.

capital together and organizing syndicates, the banks through these forms of activity acquire great financial power which, not meeting any counter-action from equally powerful organizations, give them supremacy and can make the banks the main players in the activities and politics of industry and trade.'[16]

The Finance Ministry did not have the slightest intention of yielding even a small portion of its influence in the financial sphere to commercial banks. Besides, the Finance Ministry had a number of reservations concerning the banks' operations. In the first place, the war gave rise to a new banking practice: banks began to give the State Treasury letters of indemnity against advances to the contractors fulfilling war orders. Joint-stock commercial banks, in other words, acted as guarantors. In case of contractors' failures to deliver, the banks were to return the money advanced to the Treasury. Even though the permission of the Finance Ministry was required for each letter of guarantee, the Finance Ministry eventually concluded that the mediation of banks in financing the war orders had caused a rise in costs and delays in their fulfilment, while the banks themselves received a good commission for the services.

Second, the Finance Ministry was displeased because commercial banks were engaged in trading for their own account, which was contrary to the terms of their charters and which was thought to have a negative impact on trade in general. In contrast to Russian banks, many European banks were allowed to conduct trading operations for their own account, but normally they did not make much use of this power. The Austro-Hungarian banks were the exception. The Finance Ministry explained the growth of own-account trading by banks by noting that Russia, like Austro-Hungary, 'lacked the commercial class which had the capital and which existed in other European countries.'[17] In other words, the banks' trading activities were an indication of Russia's economic backwardness.

Third, the Finance Ministry thought that banks' involvement in financing industrial enterprises was fraught with a threat of future subordination of industrial enterprises to credit institutions. The credit institutions would then be able to exploit industrial enterprises in their own interests regardless of economic needs of the country.

Finally, the Finance Ministry suspected commercial banks of speculative deals in hard currencies, which brought about declines in the value of the ruble. In this connection the Finance Ministry instituted control over all money transfers conducted by private banks and obliged them to inform the Credit Office daily of their currency operations.

All the above-mentioned considerations proved sufficient in the autumn of 1916 to lead to the extension of state control over these banks – an extension of control which, as Finance Minister Bark wrote, was dictated 'by national and state reasons'.[18] The Cabinet of Ministers adopted a resolution authorized by the Czar in October 1916, which gave the Finance Minister the right to take all necessary measures to ensure the strict observance of existing laws and instructions of the Finance Ministry by commercial banks for the period of the war and until one year after the ratification of a peace treaty.

Rethinking state control over the banking system

At the end of 1916, Finance Minister P. L. Bark together with the Director of the Credit Office presented to the State Duma a memorandum 'On the extension of the governmental control over commercial credit banks'. This document did not call for any new laws in the sphere of banking and finance. Instead, it was perhaps the first attempt to analyse the policy of state control over private banks in Russia in comparison with European traditions and practice.

In this report, Finance Minister Bark noted 'a substantial difference between the situation in West European countries and in Russia'. In the West, 'the law does not create special norms for grant [chartered] institutions and does not grant the government the right of intervention and control. In Russia, in contrast, matters of credit are regulated by special norms, and credit institutions are subjected to the supervision of the government, which assumes different forms as far as each of the different categories of credit institutions is concerned.'[19]

In comparing the position of the credit institutions in Russia with the position of their counterparts in Germany, France and England, Bark noted that in all these countries there existed the *laissez-faire* system of opening credit institutions, while Russia's system was state controlled. In Germany, commercial banks were not subject to any inspections or governmental control. The government could only check on activities of savings banks as they conducted their business under the supervision of cities. Governmental control in Germany also applied to joint-stock mortgage banks which came into existence with state permission and which operated according to the special law of 1899. On the whole, however, public control through self-regulation played a conspicuous role in German banking. This control was exercised by the Central Union of German banks and bankers, which in 1910 established a special organ to supervise banking business.[20]

In Bark's opinion, 'the ruling principle in France was the principle of complete non-interference by the state in the sphere of activities of private credit institutions', with the exception of those special cases when they enjoyed special privileges, loans or grants from the French Treasury. In England, control over credit institutions was also exercised in 'its weakest form'.[21] Bark stressed that despite the relative freedom from state control of bank establishments and the highly developed state of commercial legislation, there was a tendency in Western European countries towards increasing public control over banks. But this control was exercised not by the government, but rather by self-regulatory organizations of banks and bankers. In the West, governmental control in some form mainly applied to mortgage credit banks.

Bark attributed Russia's existing system of stringent governmental controls over banking to the country's economic backwardness, its imperfect commercial laws, the sluggishness in its legal proceedings, an insufficiency of public (that is, private self-regulatory) institutions, and the lack of internal inspections in financial institutions.

The Finance Minister abandoned the idea of conducting regular inspections as a measure of effective control over banks. He thought it necessary for Russia to develop other forms of public control by means of self-regulation. He supported the idea, brought up in stock exchange meetings by representatives of business circles, of establishing an Institute of Chartered Accountants in Russia. The Institute could train inspectors for joint-stock companies just as did the Institute of Chartered

Accountants in England and Wales and the Treuhandgesselschaft in Germany.[22]

Bark's late 1916 memorandum to the State Duma reflected a turning point in the government's long-standing financial policy. On one hand, the Finance Ministry tried to strengthen its control over commercial banks, at least in wartime. This was consistent with Russia's long history of state control over finance. On the other hand, Bark's report spoke of the government's readiness to give up traditional methods of control over credit institutions and meet the demands of business circles, that is, to bring the system of control over finance in Russia in line with European norms.

Conclusion

In Russia, state policy regarding credit institutions was not fated to change. Instead, revolution lay in store for the country. The Czarist autocracy and the strictly controlled financial system it created by the end of 1916 had only months to exist. The Credit Office, which continued functioning under the Provisional Government, practically stopped working after the revolution of October 1917. Qualified staff left and the Credit Office dragged through a miserable existence until its demise in 1918. A. E. Akselrod was appointed its director. He made attempts to resume business relations with foreign correspondents of the International Department of the Credit Office, but his telegrams to that effect went unanswered. The only reply Akselrod received came from a Swedish bank in which the Credit Office had small assets.[23]

In the end, the system of Treasury banks and the Finance Ministry Credit Office that had existed in Russia for more than a century, along with the tradition of strict state control over private credit institutions, facilitated for the new political regime a transition to state financing. Russia's transition to less, not more, state control over finance – hinted at in Finance Minister Bark's report of 1916 – would be postponed for many decades, until our own time at the end of the twentieth century.

NOTES

1   The Library of the Russian State Historical Archives. Publications 1105–9. Kokovtsov's report to the State Duma on 20 September 1910, pp. 1–4.
2   The Council of State Credit Regulations gradually lost its influence and was abolished in 1895.
3   Osobennaia Kantselariia po Kreditnoi Chasti.
4   Russian State Historical Archives (RGIA) f. (fund) 583; op. (inventory) 3; d. (file) 1054; l. (folio) 29.

5 *Ibid.*
6 RGIA f. 583; op. 3; d. 1054; l. 6–7.
7 RGIA f. 1278; op. 7; d. 1232; l. 6.
8 RGIA f. 583; op. 3; d. 1054; l. 29.
9 *Ibid.*, l. 15.
10 *Ibid.*, l. 8.
11 *Ibid.*, l. 7.
12 *Ibid.*, l. 27.
13 The Library of the Russian State Historical Archives. Collection of publications 1105–9. Kokovtsov's report to the State Duma on 12 September 1913,
   p. 15; RGIA f. 583; op. 3; d. 1133; l. 1.
14 RGIA f. 583; op. 19; d. 101; l. 1.
15 RGIA f. 1278; op. 7; d. 1232; l. 9.
16 RGIA f. 1279; op. 7; d. 1232; l. 10.
17 RGIA f. 1278; op. 7; d. 1232; l. 11.
18 RGIA f. 1278; op. 7; d. 1232; l. 14.
19 RGIA f. 1278; op. 7; d. 1232; l. 4.
20 RGIA f. 1278; op. 7; d. 1232; l. 4.
21 RGIA f. 1278; op. 7; d. 1232; l. 5.
22 RGIA f. 1278; op. 7; d. 1232; l. 15.
23 RGIA f. 583; op. 3; d. 998; l. 31.

BIBLIOGRAPHY

Anan'ich, B. V. 1991. *Bankirskie doma v Rossii (1860–1914)* (Bankers' Houses in
   Russia 1860–1914). Leningrad.
Anan'ich, B. V. and Lebedev, S. K. 1991. *Kontora pridvoznykh bankirov v Rossii i
   Evropeiskie denezhnye rynki (1798–1811): Problemy sotsialnoi i economicheskoi
   istorii Rossii* (The Institute of Court Financiers in Russia and European
   Money Markets (1798–1811): Problems of the Social and Economic History
   of Russia). St Petersburg.
Cameron, Rondo and Bovykin, V. I. 1991. *International Banking 1870–1914.* New
   York.

10 The origins of banking in Argentina

Roberto Cortés Conde

Introduction

From the perspective of European industrialization, the Argentine case appears as one of a country of new settlement. Rich in natural resources, high in agricultural potential, it early became an important target of periodic waves of European foreign investment and emigration, its development reinforced by booms of exports of primary products.

Taking a fairly long-term view, it was basically a successful developing economy in the nineteenth century. According to Maddison's and Cortés Conde's estimates, it grew more rapidly than most of the industrializers of the 1870–1913 period; and it had in 1913 a per capita income which put it well within the West European league (Maddison 1991: 30; Cortés Conde 1997).

Argentina's development, however, was not merely a reflection of European markets and European capital, but depended very much on its own internal political conditions. Needless to say, financial problems formed an important aspect of those conditions. Nevertheless, the broader, international context of Argentina's development, just outlined, should be kept in mind.

The colonial period

Financial institutions developed late in Argentina. Up until the second half of the nineteenth century there were no discount, deposit or issue banks in the country. Other than the short-lived experiments of the Banco de Descuento (1822–7) and the Banco Nacional (1827–36), the growth of financial institutions started slowly in the 1860s, to reach a real momentum in the 1880s. It was interrupted during the years of the 1890s crisis, reaching a mature stage in the first decade of this century. In spite of the fact that the monetary history of Argentina seems to have been the history of paper money, bank-notes were not known until the nineteenth century, nor were treasury notes (government paper money) – like those that were used during the colonial period in the British colonies of North America.

During colonial times in the Río de la Plata, as in Spain, there was a bimetallic system, with gold and silver pesos (eight reales). The Río de la Plata region was in one of the richest silver mining areas in the world, Potosí. Potosí, in Upper Peru (or Bolivia), was incorporated into the vice-royalty of the Río de la Plata region in 1776. The active commercial activities which took place around the axis that linked Potosí in Bolivia with the Atlantic outlet – the port of Buenos Aires – demanded large amounts of money for transactions. For that purpose silver coins minted in Potosí were used. As throughout the world at that time, silver coins were the main means of payment. When silver was scarce (because of wars or other causes of regional isolation) substitutes were used, such as commodities like woollens and other textiles.

Because commercial transactions were widespread, credit should have been more amply available. The credit which was mobilized in this early period, however, was mainly commercial credit provided by wholesale traders who dealt in trade between Spain and the colonies. This made use of those standard commercial instruments, bills of exchange. But though general in international trade, they were not used on a substantial scale in Argentinian trade until 1820 (and not really very widely until the 1860s). And since bills represent the very beginning of credit markets, one must say that specialized financial intermediaries were not really known in the Río de la Plata before then.

Independence

The revolution in the Río de la Plata that led to the separation from Spain and the establishment of a new government had negative financial and monetary consequences. Upper Peru (Audiencia de Charcas), incorporated into the viceroyalty of the Río de la Plata at the time of its creation, did not recognize the authority of the Buenos Aires government and returned to the jurisdiction of Peru. Located there were the Potosí mines, the main source of silver. The military attempts by the Buenos Aires government to recapture Upper Peru all failed. Consequently the funds at the Caja del Potosí were beyond the reach of the new government. The situation became more serious with the continuous war, which lasted almost a decade. This created a profound monetary and commercial crisis in the interior provinces. It did not much affect Buenos Aires, however, since that region in the meantime had found an outlet for its production in the United Kingdom.

The commercial transactions with the United Kingdom were carried out in pounds sterling, gold or commercial bills of exchange, to be paid in London. Therefore the dearth of money was limited to the interior, to retail trade and to the payment of wages for which silver was used. Silver was needed for military expenditures when there was no possibility of obtaining supplies though confiscations. As occurred at other times and places, quasi-moneys were developed to alleviate the means of payment shortages, but in Argentina in these years their appearance was associated with the need to finance the government. Credit was mainly trade credit provided by the wholesalers in these years. And there were still no specialized financial institutions that discounted bills of exchange.

Some of the government loans of 1818 (some of which were forced loans) were issued to the bearer, and provided that after some specified time (usually a year) this paper would be accepted in payments of taxes (mainly customs duties). In a very limited way, some of these bonds circulated among the public as a very imperfect means of payment. In 1818, a public institution, the Caja Federal de Fondos de SudAmérica, was founded for the purpose of obtaining deposits from the public which were to be lent to the government and which paid interest a little below the market rate. This proved unsuccessful. The government also issued other debts, which would be accepted to pay taxes, many of which served as means of payment. Generally speaking, then, until the third decade of the nineteenth century, there were no specialized financial institutions operating in the Río de la Plata and the currency consisted mainly of silver coins (the Spanish pesos of eight reales, in this case minted in Bolivia and later known as Bolivianos).

The first discount and issue bank: Banco de Buenos Aires

The first bank in Argentina was founded in 1822, the Banco de Buenos Aires, a chartered deposit and discount private bank, which was granted a monopoly of issue for twenty years.

In 1820, after ten years of war, the national authority had collapsed and each province had set up its own government. Exempt from the burden of sustaining an army, Buenos Aires, the large and wealthy province, was granted the right to collect customs duties, and profited from the period of prosperity which was to last until the Brazilian war (which broke out in 1826 and which, incidentally, coincided with a trade depression related to the English financial crisis of 1825). In 1827 the national government headed by Rivadavia fell; and the long period of internal fighting which followed helped seal the end of the economic expansion. The rising commercial activity of the early 1820s required an increasing amount of money, not only for external trade, but also for domestic transactions, which in colonial times had used silver coins. The scarcity of silver was doubtless an obstacle for increasing internal trade. In addition, the government was in need of financial institutions to enable it to overcome short-term gaps between revenue and expenditure or to obtain long-term finance for the Treasury.

For these reasons the idea of creating a discount bank with note-issuing rights arose. The bank was to be a private institution, although it had close links with the government as its financial agent, and thanks to the fiscal and other privileges it was granted. The capital authorized was one million pesos and the bank was empowered to discount commercial bills for ninety-day periods.

Some of the features of the first bank subsequently had an enormous influence on the business or banking in the country and are therefore listed here as follows:

1. Its strong link with the government. As a financial agent it had no autonomy. In return, it was exempted from complying with sound banking practices; but this created a lack of confidence that affected the banking business for many years.
2. Its lack of capital. The shareholders subscribed the shares with loans given by the same bank.
3. The lack of liquidity of the assets. Although the rule was that the bills of exchange were discounted for ninety-day periods, it was the custom to renew them automatically for longer periods.
4. A market with a barrier of entry. Owing to its privileged and domineering position, the bank was able to establish a rate of interest below market values and rationed the credit it extended. Only those who were friends or partners of the bank's board or the provincial government had access to it.

The suspension of convertibility: the Banco Nacional

During the war with Brazil (1826–8) the need for the government to pay for military expenditure abroad led the government to request the bank for a loan in gold. In order to comply, the bank used its gold reserves, which left it in a very difficult situation. When in January 1826 the government reiterated its demands, the bank asked for the implementation of a rule that exempted it from converting its notes into gold. A provincial law declared the inconvertibility of the bank-notes which the government guaranteed. As a consequence of that, the government took over all the metallic reserves.

At the same time, the establishment of a national bank was discussed (the Rivadavia national government was in office then) which was to

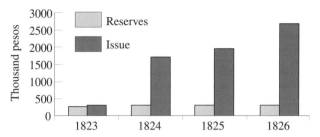

Figure 10.1 Banco de Buenos Aires, 1823–6. For the values used in this and the following figures see the note on p. 248.

succeed the Buenos Aires bank, taking on its assets and liabilities. On 28 January, in an atmosphere influenced by war and the flight of domestic paper money, the National Bank (Banco Nacional) was founded (the shareholders of the older bank received shares of the new institution to replace the previous ones). In May 1826 a decree was enacted stating that the bank-notes would be circulated and that they should be accepted at their face value. When the national government ended in June 1827 the Buenos Aires provincial government took over the bank, guaranteeing the issues for a total amount of 10 million pesos. The provincial bank had begun its operation in 1822 with a capital of 200,000 pesos. Four years later notes issued reached 3 million, with the consequent depreciation. Under the Rosas regime (1829–52), money issues were made through the mint (Casa de la Moneda). The circulation of this money rose from 15 million in constant dollars at the closing of the National Bank in 1829 to about $126 million at the end of the Rosas period. Figures 10.1, 10.2 and 10.3 give a rough indication of these developments. Figure 10.4 depicts in addition the estimated overall growth of the Argentinian money supply and the related premium on gold.

Banking during the national organization

In the second half of the nineteenth century, even after the country had become organized under the 1853 Constitution, its financial institutions were still very primitive or non-existent. That is because of the situation of generalized anarchy in the monetary system which reflected, in turn, the fragmentation of political power characteristic of Argentina at this time. For it is difficult to understand the delay in the appearance of financial institutions if we do not take into account that the monetary disorders stemmed from the collapse of the Spanish political regime that was followed precariously by a succession of rulers in the new country, in the former viceroyalty of the Río de la Plata. The cities, in colonial times,

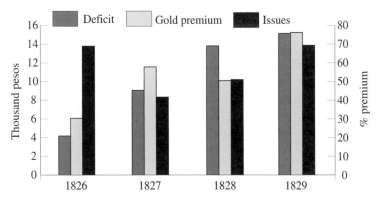

Figure 10.2 Banco Nacional issues and deficit, 1826–9

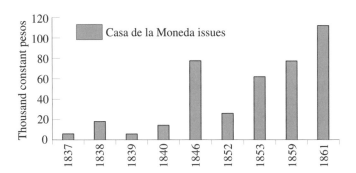

Figure 10.3 Casa de la Moneda issues, 1837–61

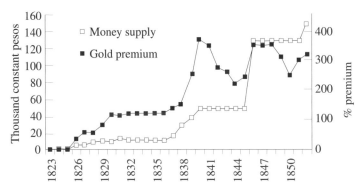

Figure 10.4 Money supply and gold premium, 1823–52

were mainly administrative centres, later on provinces, which claimed authority over vast spaces that formerly belonged to the colonial administrative units, although they were able to exercise that authority only in nominal terms. Such conflict produced political chaos, and that produced negative monetary effects.

The crisis of the Spanish Empire in America is in a sense reminiscent of the circumstances that affected Western Europe after the collapse of the Roman Empire, which led to a trend towards greater decentralization and fragmentation when the central political authority was replaced by local powers. Under the conditions of crisis and insecurity during most of the nineteenth century there was little basis for the development of financial institutions in Argentina. When it proved possible to return to a safer atmosphere, in which property rights were enforced, the need to create new institutions arose. In fact what remained from the former empire was the circulation of silver coins of *ocho reales* (*el peso*) as a means of payment. The attempts to create new financial institutions failed and the only monetary experiment that remained was the widespread use of paper money of the Buenos Aires provincial government (that had a fiduciary circulation). When the country entered a period of strong economic expansion, as in the 1850s for example, specialized financial institutions were still clearly absent.

But when new institutions made their appearance in the years which followed, they had a variety of characteristics. The banks of issues were both state-owned and a mixture of privately and publicly owned institutions. Then there were also the deposit banks that dealt with the savings of immigrants who sent money abroad to their families. These banks usually took the name of the country where the immigrants came from, but they were not foreign-owned. They also discounted commercial bills, especially those related to the financing of imports.

When we speak of foreign banks (those with capital and headquarters abroad) we refer mainly to two conspicuous cases: the Baring Brothers Bank and the Bank of London and the River Plate. These banks are discussed below.

Financial and monetary systems in Argentina

Money (silver and fiduciary issues)

In colonial times currency was mainly silver coins, among them the eight-reales peso, minted in Potosí (Bolivia). The coins, minted in Bolivia and called Bolivianos, were debased and because of this their market value fluctuated between 70% and 80% of the real value of the full coin (the Spanish or Mexican peso). In the interior provinces these coins had wide-

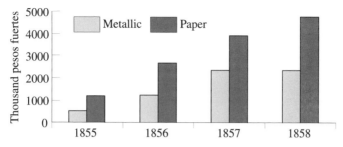

Figure 10.5 Banco de la Provincia de Buenos Aires, metallic and paper deposits, 1855–8

spread circulation owing to the positive balance of trade between the interior and neighbouring countries.

In Buenos Aires province in contrast, bank-notes were prominent: from 1822, the bank-notes of the Bank of Buenos Aires (Banco de Descuento) and from 1826 also the fiat money issued by the Banco Nacional and that of the provincial mint (Casa de la Moneda). But they did not circulate in the interior. The negative balance of trade between the interior and Buenos Aires was paid for with silver coins received from neighbouring countries. If we ignore the early and short-lived experience of the Confederacion (with its bank and Banco Maua) we may speak of a decisive step having been taken in 1854, when the Buenos Aires Provincial Bank (Banco de la Provincia de Buenos Aires) was founded. It was a deposit and discount bank that accepted the notes in circulation issued by the previous institutions. In 1866 it was given the exclusive right to issue convertible bank-notes backed by metal. From 1872 to 1881 this right was shared with the newly founded Banco Nacional. It is true that there were notes issued by some provincial banks, for instance in Mendoza and in Rosario through the Bank of London, but the number of notes issued was very small and these notes were not accepted in other Argentinian provinces. The Buenos Aires Provincial Bank continued the activities of the provincial mint (instead of minting coins they printed notes).

The banks

The Buenos Aires Provincial Bank

This bank, founded, as noted above, in 1854, deserves more attention. That is not so much because of its nominal business of deposit and discount, or its issue of metallic notes in 1866 (and the peso notes in the board of exchange in 1867). An idea of the development of its deposit business can be gained from Figure 10.5. Of great significance, however,

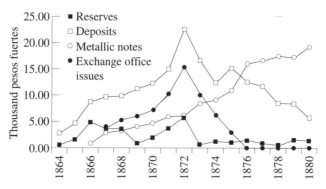

Figure 10.6 Banco de la Provincia de Buenos Aires, issues, deposits and reserves, 1864–80

is the fact that it was an official (or government-orientated) bank, a status which negatively affected its behaviour as a financial institution. For being a state monopolist bank, it developed certain habits of financial management which really belong to the political world. Banking policies were strongly affected by political interest. This affected: (a) its reserves policy; (b) its credit policy; (c) the appraisal of the solvency of its clients; and (d) the strong dependence on the need to finance the government.

It is true that the government was largely responsible for the continuous demand for funds, but the directors of the bank were also responsible for authorizing ample credits to their friends and associates. When there was a shortage of funds the board of directors tended to reduce the level of reserves to dangerously low levels. If questioned about the ratio of deposits to reserves levels the directors claimed that to establish this was their own responsibility. Being a state bank there were different degrees of confidence because it was felt that the government would never default on its liabilities to the public. Because of this belief and the presumed absolute need to expand credit, higher reserves–deposits ratios were felt unnecessary. Referring to vault reserves Quesada said that 'they were minimal in relation to the amount of deposits not reaching 1% of the currency, but the confidence in the bank was so great and the widespread opinion that it could not collapse and the lack of practice in reading bank balance sheets created a situation which was not perceived and which could not have happened in any other part of the world' (Quesada 1901: 154). In addition, one should note that the board of directors of the bank was not made up of people from business seeking profits, but of political figures, merchants, entrepreneurs or farmers appointed by the provincial government. Rather than bank profits they were concerned with helping their own businesses.

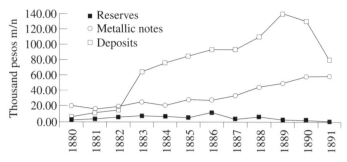

Figure 10.7 Banco de la Provincia de Buenos Aires, issues, deposits and reserves, 1880–91

It is true that the bank acted as a financial agent of the national government; and it is also true that the 1866 and 1876 loans to the government produced a huge monetary expansion (the loans to the provincial government during that period were smaller); but one can conclude from the bank balance sheet that it was larger than the expansion of private credit to subsidize rates of interest due to seignorage (Cortés Conde 1989). Until the 1880s the Buenos Aires Bank was way ahead of the Banco Nacional and other private banks in terms of deposits (see Figures 10.6 and 10.7). In 1880, when the city of Buenos Aires was declared a federal district, the rising power of the national government was reflected also in the growing importance of the reorganized National Bank. The Buenos Aires bank thus gained an important competitor. In 1887, with the passage of the so-called 'Free Banking Law', both banks were incorporated into the 'Guaranteed Banks' regime – an institution which emulated the US National Banking Act of 1864 by making note-issuing rights dependent on an equal purchase of national government bonds. We return to this law below. But first a brief description of the National Bank is necessary.

The National Bank (Banco Nacional)

In 1872 a new law of Congress led to the founding of the (second) National Bank. It was formally a private company, but with strong participation by the government. It was a bank of deposit and issue, agent of the national government, recipient of Treasury funds and endowed with fiscal privileges.

It began without completing the payment of the shares subscribed. To overcome this difficulty the government contributed to the capital with public bonds (Fondos Públicos Nacionales).

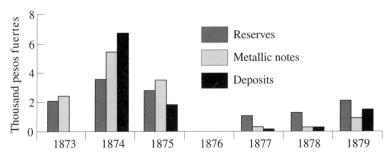

Figure 10.8 Banco Nacional, issues, deposits and reserves, 1873–9

The private shareholders only contributed 3 million $F from the 20 million agreed, leaving a deficit of 17 million. Consequently, what was intended to be the largest financial institution in the country started its operations with partners owing a large portion of the capital. The bank was authorized to issue convertible notes, maintaining 25% of the reserves in metal (gold or silver), but this was a requirement that later on was not enforced. At the beginning of its operations it received a large amount of gold from a public works loan deposited by the government in the bank's vault. This produced an enormous credit expansion. Subsequently, when the government withdrew the funds a severe credit contraction followed. But the bank did not just have problems in collecting shareholder contributions. It proved difficult to recover the money lent: 'The lack of payment on the loans overcame us' (Quesada 1901: 163). In widespread use were loans called 'habilitadores', that is to say, short-term loans which were permanently renewed. 'The memory of the second year', according to Quesada, showed 'that the difficulties of collecting capital contributions remained and that the banking situation had not improved' (1901: 163). When in May 1876 the Buenos Aires government suspended the convertibility of the Provincial Bank, the national government did the same at the National Bank. However the rules established at the time of contracting the loan with the Provincial Bank limited the circulation of National Bank notes and worsened its already difficult situation. After the 1876 crisis the National Bank started a reorganization process which led to its recuperation – at the end of the decade (see Figures 10.8 and 10.9).

The private banks

Given their limited importance, discussion of private banks can be brief. The Bank of London and South America and the Banco de Italia were already established, in 1862 and 1872 respectively, as deposit and dis-

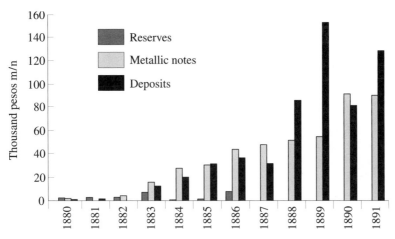

Figure 10.9 Banco Nacional, issues, deposits and reserves, 1880–91

count banks. New banks founded in this period were the Banco Carabassa and several banks in the interior provinces. The volume of deposits in these banks until the 1880s was significantly less than those of the official banks. In the interior, finally, the banks of issue printed notes in Bolivian pesos. This reflects the ongoing problem of incomplete monetary integration in Argentina referred to above.

The foreign banks

The main foreign banks were the Bank of London and the River Plate and the Baring bank. Both had an important influence on the Argentine economy and politics but they were quite different types of banks. The first was a deposit and discount bank. The second was a merchant bank; not only an early financial agent of the Buenos Aires provincial government and later underwriter of the national government, it also undertook direct intervention in some operations. The Bank of London had a branch in Buenos Aires, and others in Montevideo, Córdoba and Rosario. The Baring bank had a representative in Buenos Aires.

However, in a country like Argentina, where the financial institutions were primitive, these banks, especially the Bank of London, had a notable influence. There were other foreign banks, to be sure. In the early years of the confederation period (1853–62), for example, the Banco Maua operated a branch in Rosario. Later on the Banco Mercantil, owned by British capital, was active, at least until it went bankrupt following the 1876 crises. The Banque de Paris et des Pays Bas (now Paribas) was a merchant bank which played an active role in railways, promoting for example the construction of French railways in Santa Fé and Buenos Aires (Regalsky 1994). Finally, also worth mentioning are Stern Brothers, L. Cohen and other institutions which, like Baring Brothers, mainly specialized in the placement of the public debt (national, provincial or municipal).

The business of the public debt

At this point it is necessary to focus explicitly on the problem of government debt; for it is in this area that the foreign banks just described had their heaviest impact and most dramatic experience. While the government used the official banks to place its domestic debt, when hard currency was required it had to turn to foreign banks, to place its debt abroad. With Baring the relationship went back a long time, to 1824, starting with a loan that went into default in 1826 and remained so until 1857, when a new agreement was negotiated according to which the former debt and interest were paid. After the 1857 agreement Baring began to intervene directly in the market of the public debt, for example underwriting the national loan of 1865 for £2.5 million. Since the 1860s Baring had been the main financial agent of the government of Buenos Aires province and of the national government. As an underwriter it placed large amounts of the Argentine public debt (mainly national although some of it was provincial and municipal) in the London market. The capital raised this way contributed largely to activate the hitherto narrow capital market in Argentina. However, Baring did not limit its operations to financing the government. It took part in private business directly or indirectly. It lent money to colonization companies such as Eduardo Casey's Curamalan, which failed dramatically, being one of the serious difficulties of the firm in 1890; and it was Baring's direct intervention on behalf of the Buenos Aires Drainage and Water Supply Co. – whose shares could not be placed – that was the main reason for the liquidity problem that led to the suspension of payments in November 1890. There was also some intervention in the Banco de Italia y Río de la Plata.

The Bank of London and the River Plate

The Bank of London was a different case since it was chartered under Argentine law as a branch of the London headquarters. It mainly financed foreign operations. 'Credits were granted to European exporters against bills sent for collection. Acceptance credit was opened for importers in the River Plate . . . Mercantile business was the main staple of the bank's operation. It did not normally act as an issuing house . . . While quite willing to consider providing short term accommodations to the government, the director was adamant in refusing to jeopardize its stability as a commercial bank by excessive commitments of this type' (Joslin 1963: 30).

Contrary to the generalized interest in the business of issue, the Bank of London, at least in Buenos Aires (not in Rosario), limited its activities to the discount of short-term bills. The director Bruce rejected De la Riesta's suggestion to operate as a bank of issue (Joslin 1963: 32).

The 'style of management of the Bank of London was different in this and other respects from that of the other banks, whose operations were described in London as "gaucho banking"' (Ford 1962). The bank maintained a policy of large reserves which implied a large spread between the rates collected from the borrowers and that paid to the depositors (Joslin 1963: 35). The latter had the guarantee that they would collect their credits in the money in which they lent them. The management was very strict on the quality of loans and took special care on the seasonal variation of credit and in which *numéraire* it was demanded. The bank tried to minimize the exchange risk: 'paper became scarce when the trader sent it to the interior to make purchases and gold became scarce if it was shipped abroad or needed by traders up-river. Under these circumstances it was tempting for a banker to convert his resources into the medium most required by his customers at that time. By doing so, he ran a major risk of exchange loss', which, led to the strategy of conducting 'each business separately as far as possible' (Joslin 1963: 34).

The bank's policy consisted of lending on short-term commercial bills, paying out the currency it was to be repaid with, and without using the possibility allowed by the government of payment in depreciated paper pesos. Moreover, the Bank of London did not subscribe to and rejected government pressure to enter into the national system of guaranteed banks. This allowed it to maintain reserves outside of government hands (Cortés Conde 1989). These policies gave the bank a solid prestige and allowed it to avoid the suspension of payments that affected other banks during the crises of 1876 and 1890 (Joslin 1963). However the bank *was* involved in the disastrous operation of the Water Supply Co. in 1890 referred to above.

Financial intermediation or creation of money?

More than other financial intermediaries, the banks in the Río de la Plata then seemed to seek maximization of profits through the creation of money. In a country in the process of rapid expansion, the bankers probably assumed that there was an increasing demand for money and that the role of the banks was to provide liquidity. This was partially true, but not to the extent that the banks expanded the money supply greater than the demand for money, which is what happened in 1873–6 and 1885–90,

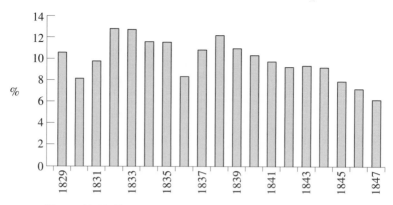

Figure 10.10 Interest rates, 1829–47

thus producing a run on reserves and the failure of the financial system in those years. (For interest rates see Figures 10.10 and 10.11.)

The Free Banks (Bancos Garantidos), 1887–90

The Bancos Garantidos, or 'Free Banks', certainly represented the most important financial experiment of the period. Since the basic organizational framework had been set up (in 1853) there had been a long debate concerning which regime was most suitable for Argentina. One position espoused the monopolist bank of issue, like the Bank of England (following Peel's Act), the other the system of the National Banks of the United States. In 1862 the Executive Branch sent Congress a bill of Free Banks, but it was turned down because of the strong opposition of Buenos Aires (and its bank). In 1887, another, stronger government succeeded in getting the Free Bank bill approved. It requested that all existing commercial banks join a system whereby the business of banking and the right to issue would be free, without requiring special charters.

The aim of the banks – it was said – was to have a uniform paper currency, which circulated in the whole country. As we have seen, the lack of a uniform currency was a chronic problem. It was not the aim to allow provinces to establish banks of issue, which some of them already had (Córdoba and Tucumán), and there was nothing to impede them from setting up new ones. The aim of the law was to establish a uniform currency, because the issues from these banks were accepted with different discounts outside the boundaries of each province. The winning political coalition formed by the governors of the interior provinces was seeking a mechanism by which the issues of the local official banks would obtain legal-tender status throughout the entire country. With this system the provincial issues gained that status. For the national government, whose

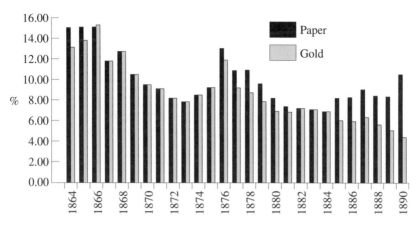

Figure 10.11 Interest rates, 1864–90

external debt had reached alarming proportions, the aim was to get its hands on the gold in the vaults of the private banks. After the 1885 suspension of convertibility, the government was desperately trying to obtain gold to intervene in the market, sustaining the peso parity (so as to avoid the erosion of its taxes due to the depreciation of the peso). They thought that all of the gold held in the country was hoarded by the private banks. The government's attempt to force them to enter into the Free Banks' regime was aimed at control over their gold. As a result the government obtained large amounts of gold (in relation to the inflow coming from other issues of external debt), but the provincial governments, each of them a founder of the new Banco Garantido, became beneficiaries of the system by obtaining the negotiation of their own external foreign debt for more than $100 million gold in international markets (mainly in London), using as collateral the national government's internal, gold-denominated debt which was supposed to serve as a guarantee for the issues of the Bancos Garantidos. Few private banks joined the regime, but all of the Argentine provinces founded their own official banks in order to have the chance, for years, to use the Buenos Aires institution to monetize their deficits. The provinces had issued external debt by which they obtained gold to buy the Bancos Garantidos bonds. They received the interest of their bonds and had to pay the interest on their external debt, a little above that of the bonds (around 1%). The difference was obtained by the interest paid by commercial loans or by subsequent borrowing.

Following the idea of the National Banks, entering the business of banking was made possible without the need of a charter. For any company could establish the right to issue bank-notes, if it complied with the following conditions:

1. It must have capital of a quarter million gold pesos.
2. Bank-notes must not exceed 90% of the capital.
3. It had to purchase, with gold, an amount of government bonds equal to the bank-notes issued.
4. These notes were provided by the Inspection of Bancos Garantidos, and would be uniform and guaranteed by the government. The notes would be legal tender in the whole country and should be received at face value for payment of all obligations, both public and private (art. 31). The previous issues were also inconvertible.
5. In the case that any bank should collapse, the Bancos Garantidos Inspection would sell the bonds, paying the holders of its notes with the receipts.

The authorities at the time argued that, with this regime, Argentina was following the National Banking Act of the United States of 1864. They said the new arrangements implied the abandoning of the monopolist chartered regime for a free banking one. But the legal and regulatory framework was different, as was its practice. In reality there was no competitive business, because although there were many banks, in each province there was only one, and an official (or government) one at that. Moreover, the bank-notes were not convertible into another currency used as legal tender as was the case in the US National Bank's system.

The requirement of guaranteeing bonds with gold was not completely fulfilled. The National Bank was exempt. The contribution of the Buenos Aires Provincial Bank was compensated with the debt that the national government had had with it since 1876. The Banco de Córdoba bought the bonds with promissory notes in gold. Finally the national government issued an enormous internal debt in gold, that was bought by the banks, a debt larger than the one that already existed. For this reason, it could never really be placed on the market, which made the guarantee illusory. Under the Free Banks regime the country's money supply (current and deposits) went from almost $200 million to $500 million.

This experiment, as well as many others which seemed very ingenious, ended in enormous failure, increasing the government debt by $158 million, coming from public bonds and producing a parallel increase in the amount of currency in circulation. The gold coming from these bonds was sold on the exchange market to support the parity of the depreciated peso, in an effort doomed to fail. The government sold gold-backed debt (the Bancos Garantidos bonds), and with these bonds the banks lent money with which the public bought back the gold that the government had sold. This was probably the main financial experiment in Argentina up to 1890. It was a big failure and delayed further development in financial institutions.

The gold of the Bancos Garantidos, capital flight and the 1890 crisis

The depreciation of the peso that took place after the suspension of convertibility in 1885 did not harm only the public. The government suffered the erosion of its revenues produced by the depreciation of the peso, for, because of the 1885 law, it was obligated to accept notes in paper pesos or other inconvertible moneys in payment of taxes. This was the problem that most seriously affected the deficit, because a large proportion of its expenditure had to be paid in gold (especially the external debt, and eventually the internal debt as well).

In order to overcome this problem the government had to attempt to defend the peso parity, trusting that the country was experiencing an extraordinary expansion. In the long run, it was felt, a continuous inflow of foreign capital would provide an ample supply of gold. In 1886 the government sold gold in the market, using the proceeds of the sale of the Andino Railway (see Figure 10.12). It was successful in maintaining the parity between 1885 and 1887 and, from the latter date on, the government had the chance to use the new funds of the Bancos Garantidos, which is what it did between 1887 and 1888 (see Figure 10.12). Until 1888, through selling gold it maintained pretty much the same parity. But noticing that the banks continued to expand credit, the public began buying gold with the notes. The banks' gold reserves ran out. The gold premium, which had been stable for about three years, jumped. Prices followed. But the attempts by the banks to attract deposits failed because the public remembered the experience in 1885 when metal-based deposits were converted into paper pesos at nominal and not at market rates. The public itself also withdrew deposits in paper, preferring to hold on to notes rather than deposit claims. As capital flight set in, the banks were denuded of their metallic reserves; and a run on deposits in paper followed. After the monetary crisis came a financial one. The Bancos Garantidos finally collapsed when the interest payments on the bonds ceased. The official banks as well as the majority of private ones suspended their payments and a general moratorium was declared. When gold was 300% above parity the government was no longer able to fulfil its obligation *vis-à-vis* its internal and external debts. The government could not afford the services on its foreign debt. This produced the 1890 crisis, which represented, just as it caused, a new institutional setback (Cortés Conde 1989).

Financial and monetary institutions up to 1890

The year 1890 appears to have been a watershed in Argentinian financial history. Therefore it makes sense to summarize developments up to that

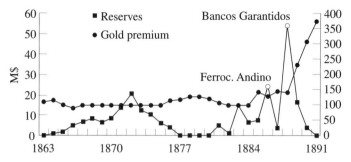

Figure 10.12 Reserves and gold premium, 1863–1891

point. I wish to emphasize two characteristics which negatively influenced the development of financial institutions in the pre-1890 period.

The first was that the principal business of the banks was, in effect, that of seignorage. Acting on the assumption of a secularly rising demand for money, the official and semi-official banks supplied generous credit through a large expansion of money supply. The other characteristic was government intervention in the banking business. Financial institutions were used mainly to dispense funds to the government, and to its friends and political clients in the private sector.

When the money supply significantly exceeded money demand this was reflected by rising prices and inflation. Consequently, savings left the financial circuits and were hoarded or left the country, an outcome which had negative consequences on the rate of interest, on investment and on the development of the financial sector. In spite of that, owing to enormous possibilities for the exploitation of untapped natural resources, the expansion of the real economy continued, but did not occur without serious cyclical fluctuations, retrogression and crises, which in the short term created repeated setbacks.

In this process the role of the banks was complex. We have already underlined the negative characteristic of the state banks, which instead of channelling savings confiscated them through the creation of money, giving them to the government. This was reflected not only in the recurrent inflation but also in the chronically high rate of interest.

The debate at that time confused demand for money with demand for credit. Increasing the supply of money when demand for domestic money was falling tended to push international money away. The price of credit for loans depended upon the magnitude of savings and the risk premium. Although the amounts of savings were not negligible, the risk premiums were usually high, because they anticipated and incorporated the risk of the eventual depreciations that would take place when convertibility was suspended owing to the mismanagement of the monetary and financial systems.

The 1890 crisis and the evaluation of financial institutions

The 1890 crisis led to the closure of two official banks, the National Bank and the Buenos Aires Provincial Bank. This was accompanied by a run on deposits at private banks, which were also forced to close down for different periods of time. A general moratorium was in force from April to November. The banks that entered into the system of Bancos Garantidos lost their right to issue currency and their uncovered liabilities were converted into a liability for the federal state. The Banco Nacional closed down for good and the Provincial Bank for fifteen years. At the height of the crisis, in 1891, the Banco de la Nación (a state bank) was created, but without the right to issue notes and with a reserve ratio of 75%. It started its operations very slowly owing to the generalized lack of confidence, but later on, thanks to the development of a large number of branches in different provinces (which gave it almost exclusive control of the transactions in the interior), its deposits increased (Table 10.1).

Lending to the government was limited to the federal government (which thus excluded provincial governments or municipalities) and this, in turn, was limited to not more than 20% of its capital.

Consequences of the crisis for the financial system

Among others, there were two important consequences:

1. The banks would no longer have, as their main activity, the issuing of notes. The creation of currency lay in the hands of the national government. The private banks specialized in commercial activities, discounting bills of exchange and lending money through deposits. The use of cheques increased and banks established a clearing house.

2. Deposits in private banks rose significantly and by the end of the century they exceeded those of the state (Table 10.2). Argentinian financial institutions had now finally reached a more mature stage.

The 1899 monetary reforms

Almost the whole of the 1890s was a time of monetary contraction. The gold premium represented an inverse index of currency depreciation, and it rose by 400% by 1893. In the second half of the decade, owing to the contraction, it fell by 200%. This led the government to take a

Table 10.1 *Deposits of the Banco de la Nación,*
1892–1909.

	Deposits*	
Year	Gold	Paper
1892	0.30	48.37
1893	1.50	66.50
1894	0.43	71.58
1895	0.68	72.27
1896	0.79	74.44
1897	1.04	75.25
1898	1.33	82.56
1899	1.32	87.88
1900	0.81	93.75
1901	8.41	92.33
1902	1.67	92.67
1903	1.76	123.77
1904	1.34	140.40
1905	2.90	170.19
1906	1.79	167.99
1907	4.94	192.57
1908	5.29	234.18
1909	5.09	335.03

Note:
* in millions of pesos
Source: Banco de la Nación Argentina, *El Banco de la*
Nación Argentina en su cincuentenario (Buenos Aires, 1941)

serious look at the need for monetary reform. In 1899 a new law was
enacted that put Argentina on the gold standard. A currency board
(Caja de Conversión) was already exercising the right to issue notes
(paper pesos) to anyone who required notes against gold at a fixed parity
of 1 *peso moneda nacional* which equalled 44 cents gold. The Caja was
obliged to return to gold at the same rate, to anyone who presented the
notes to that end. Starting in 1899, the new issues were backed with
reserves in gold, which did not cover the previous emission for an
amount of 300 million paper pesos or 163 million in gold. The system of
the currency board started slowly but in the following years, up until
World War I, it had a tremendous success, maintaining exchange parity
and price stability, which in turn encouraged an enormous inflow of
direct capital investments. As occurred throughout the world, in 1914
convertibility was suspended, with the commitment to return to the

Table 10.2 *Deposits in private banks, 1897–1909.*

Year	Banco de la Nación (Millions of paper pesos)	Other banks (Millions of paper pesos)
1897	78.27	61.21
1898	86.01	68.45
1899	90.87	82.06
1900	95.6	228.22
1901	11.4	225.30
1902	96.6	246.90
1903	127.8	310.27
1904	143.5	365.42
1905	176.8	454.87
1906	172.1	466.58
1907	203.8	464.12
1908	246.2	504.62
1909	346.6	642.52

Source: Dirección General de Estadística de la Nación, *Estrato Estadístico de la República Argentina 1915* (Buenos Aires, 1916).

same parity when the external conditions returned to normal. During the first decade there was an important increase in the proportion of currency backed by reserves. During the whole suspension the currency board maintained the same proportions of reserves to currency, which implied that it followed the rules of the gold standard, in spite of the suspensions.

In sum, monetary stability was an indispensable framework for the growth of the financial system, for the lowering of unusually high interest rates and for the mobilization of savings, all of which took place in the first half of the twentieth century. Throughout most of the period covered in this chapter, such monetary stability was rarely obtained, and was never sustained over a long time.

NOTE

The monetary units used in this chapter are defined as follows:
$F (unit of account) = Peso Fuerte and equals the old Spanish silver peso of 8 reales = 1 US dollar.
$m/cte (medium of exchange) = Peso Moneda Corriente; originally was at par with silver peso. It was devalued in 1867 so that 25$m/cte = 1$F.
$Gold = Peso Gold; 1.033 $Gold (unit of account) = 1$F.
$m/n = Peso Moneda Nacional; in 1883 was equal to $1Gold; after the suspension of convertibility in 1885 the $m/n depreciated, and in 1889 1$m/n = 0.44$Gold.

Appendix: Monetary statistics, 1863–1900.

Year	Money supply (in millions of $)	Money supply (in millions of $ gold)	Metallic reserves (in millions of $)	Metallic reserves variation	Reserves/ money supply (%)	Paper reserves (in millions of $)	Total deposits (in millions of $)	Currency in hands of public	Reserves/ deposits (%)	Currency/ deposits (%)
1863	25.38	22.64	0.50	–	1.97	–	–	–	–	73.91
1864	24.73	21.30	1.10	0.60	4.45	0.19	14.22	10.51	9.07	66.80
1865	29.09	28.61	1.80	0.70	6.19	1.80	17.44	11.65	20.64	71.28
1866	33.81	37.53	5.00	3.20	14.79	0.08	19.74	14.07	25.73	85.01
1867	39.13	39.13	6.71	1.71	17.15	0.27	21.15	17.98	33.00	86.53
1868	42.10	42.10	8.50	1.79	20.19	0.72	22.57	19.53	40.85	86.57
1869	46.27	46.27	6.48	–2.02	14.00	0.24	24.80	21.47	27.10	88.14
1870	49.80	49.80	8.80	2.32	17.67	0.41	26.47	23.33	34.79	93.01
1871	56.90	56.90	14.23	5.43	25.01	0.94	29.48	27.42	51.46	74.01
1872	72.98	72.98	20.91	6.68	28.65	2.02	41.94	31.04	54.67	82.27
1873	66.11	66.11	12.66	–8.25	19.15	0.75	36.27	29.84	36.97	69.16
1874	62.54	62.54	10.64	–2.02	17.01	1.51	36.97	25.57	32.86	65.01
1875	68.15	68.15	6.24	–4.40	9.16	1.83	41.30	26.85	19.54	99.05
1876	66.66	58.27	4.29	–1.95	6.44	1.38	33.49	33.17	16.93	101.99
1877	73.89	62.28	0.26	–4.03	0.35	1.12	36.58	37.31	3.77	132.06
1878	73.70	57.67	0.25	–0.01	0.34	1.00	31.76	41.94	3.94	129.44
1879	79.73	61.71	0.44	0.19	0.55	0.71	34.75	44.98	3.31	138.99
1880	74.23	61.51	0.44	0.00	0.59	0.69	31.06	43.17	3.64	69.56
1881	82.70	76.77	5.10	4.66	6.17	0.00	48.77	33.93	10.46	60.64
1882	86.46	86.32	0.94	–4.16	1.09	0.00	53.82	32.64	1.75	60.64

1883	125.97	125.97	14.20	13.26	11.27	1.20	75.71	50.26	20.34	66.38
1884	153.71	153.71	6.81	−7.39	4.43	1.20	95.51	58.20	8.39	60.94
1885	187.60	132.11	7.70	0.89	4.10	9.40	116.91	70.69	14.63	60.47
1886	210.30	163.02	23.90	16.20	11.36	4.10	130.00	80.30	21.54	61.77
1887	280.00	193.10	3.92	−19.98	1.40	3.04	144.90	135.10	4.80	93.24
1888	403.07	283.85	54.53	50.61	13.53	36.76	231.07	172.00	39.51	74.44
1889	576.55	247.45	16.54	−37.99	2.87	37.49	312.55	264.00	17.29	84.47
1890	570.09	184.50	3.86	−12.68	0.68	21.70	304.09	266.00	8.41	87.47
1891	519.66	138.58	0.07	−3.79	0.01	—	258.66	261.00	0.03	100.90
1892	409.88	176.67	2.20	2.13	0.54	—	127.88	282.00	1.72	220.52
1893	429.94	191.94	4.38	2.18	1.02	—	122.94	307.00	3.56	249.72
1894	421.18	163.88	2.47	−1.91	0.59	—	123.18	298.00	2.01	241.92
1895	452.47	185.44	5.83	3.36	1.29	—	156.47	296.00	3.73	189.17
1896	440.95	224.97	4.46	−1.37	1.01	—	145.95	295.00	3.06	202.12
1897	432.48	226.43	2.92	−1.54	0.68	—	139.48	293.00	2.09	210.07
1898	446.46	282.57	5.79	2.87	1.30	—	154.46	292.00	3.75	189.05
1899	463.93	371.14	9.49	3.70	2.05	—	172.93	291.00	5.49	168.28
1900	695.10	547.32	35.10	25.61	5.05	—	169.10	526.00	20.76	311.06

BIBLIOGRAPHY

Balbín, Francisco 1877. *La Crisis*. Buenos Aires.

Banco de la Nación Argentina 1941. *El Banco de la Nación Argentina en su cincuentenario*. Buenos Aires.

Cameron, Rondo 1967. *Banking in the Early Stages of Industrialization*. Oxford.

Cortés Conde, Roberto 1989. *Dinero, deuda y crisis: evolución monetaria y fiscal argentina 1862–90*. Buenos Aires.

   1995. 'Estadisticas monetarias y fiscales Argentinas 1810–1914' (mimeo).

   1997. *La economia Argentina en el largo plazo*. Buenos Aires.

Ford, A. G. 1962. *The Gold Standard, 1880–1914: Britain and Argentina*. Oxford.

Garrigós, O. 1873. *El Banco Provincia*. Buenos Aires.

Joslin, David 1963. *A Century of Banking in Latin America*. Oxford.

Maddison, Angus 1991. *Dynamic Forces in Capitalist Development*. Oxford.

Quesada, Sixto J. 1901. *Historia de los bancos modernos, bancos de descuento, la moneda y el credito*, vol. 1. Buenos Aires.

Regalsky, Andrés M. 1994. 'La evolución de la banca privada nacional en Argentina (1880–1914). Una introducción a su estudio', in Pedro Tedde and Carlos Marichal (eds.), *La formación de los bancos centrales en España y América Latina*, vol. 2: *Sudamérica ye el Caribe* (Banco de España (Servicios de Estudios), Estudios de Historia Económica 30).

Segreti, Carlos 1975. *Moneda y política en la primera mitad del siglo XIX: contribución al estudio de la historia de la moneda Argentina*. Tucumán.

Ziegler, Philip 1988. *The Sixth Great Power*. London.

11 Shaping the US financial system, 1690–1913: the dominant role of public finance

Richard Sylla

> If the individual Capital of this Country has become more adequate to its exigencies than formerly, 'tis because individuals have found new resources in public *Credit*, in the funds to which *that* has given value and activity. Let Public Credit be prostrated, and the deficiency will be greater than before. Public and private Credit are closely allied, if not inseparable. There is perhaps no example of one being in a flourishing, where the other was in a bad, state.
>
> Alexander Hamilton (1795 [1973])

When Hamilton penned these words in his last major report to Congress prior to stepping down after serving for five and a half years as the nation's first Secretary of the Treasury, he could look back with considerable satisfaction on the accomplishments of his tenure in President Washington's cabinet. For he and his supporters, including the president and the Federalist majorities in Congress, had just engineered a financial revolution in the United States. Although quicker and neater than what has been termed the financial revolution in England during the eighteenth century (Dickson 1967), the US financial revolution was every bit as important for the nation's subsequent political strength as well as its economic development.

In 1795, the United States was prosperous; a decade before it was mired in depression. Revenues flowed into the Treasury from customs duties and domestic excise taxes. They were used to finance the federal government and pay interest on a national debt of some $77 million (GDP then was about $200 million). New securities representing the debt had achieved a high credit rating at home. They were actively traded in securities markets that sprang up in Philadelphia, New York, Boston and other American cities. Abroad, where many of the securities had migrated after 1790, they were traded in the markets of London and Amsterdam. Foreign investors had begun to transfer liquid capital to the United States, a practice they would continue on a vast scale in the years ahead. A decade earlier the US government had been essentially bankrupt, making payments due on its Revolutionary War debts only by issuing new debt because it had no powers of taxation, only what it could requisition from its constituent state governments, which often proved reluctant to pay. There were no active securities markets then, although speculators could buy evidences of US debt for as little as 5 or 10 cents on the dollar.

By 1795 a US mint was in operation, offering to coin gold or silver in dollar-denominated coins. A decade before there were no US coins. Some twenty banks had been established and were being shaped into a US banking system by the Bank of the United States, a nation-wide branching institution established by Hamilton and the Federalists in 1791. These banks converted their note and deposit liabilities into specie on demand. A decade before, there were just three banks – one three years old, the other two just a year – working in isolation from one another in Philadelphia, New York and Boston. The three early banks provided credit to local merchants and furnished convertible currency to their immediate communities, but most paper currency used by Americans was still the inconvertible fiat paper issued on the colonial precedent by state governments. With the adoption of the Constitution in 1788, however, US states would forever lose the authority to issue inconvertible paper money.

The Hamiltonian Federalists' financial programme is customarily discussed in terms of taxation, public credit, the national bank, and the mint and the dollar, that is, in terms of public finance and the monetary system. But it was equally if not more important for launching a banking system and a securities market. The banking system and the securities market were to the new nation's economy what independence and the Constitution were to its political life – fundamental institutions that determined the course of all subsequent development. Hamilton and his party disappeared from the scene shortly after 1800. By then, however, their financial system was so embedded in American life that few Americans, apart perhaps from Thomas Jefferson and other erstwhile foes of the Hamiltonian Federalists, had any desire to return to the old, pre-1790 system.

Hamilton, in the headquote, was surely correct about the alliance of public and private credit in a country's financial system. But like a good public servant, he was perhaps more modest in his argument than he might have been. The financial requirements of the state (in the European sense, or the government in the American sense) do not only interact and ally with private finance. Very often, particularly when countries are newly establishing or reforming themselves, the state's financial requirements and policies *determine* the ways in which private financial institutions and markets emerge and develop.

That is a recurring lesson of US history. It provides the theme of this chapter. I hope to establish the lesson by exploring several episodes of American financial history during the eighteenth and nineteenth centuries. What emerges from the study is that virtually every major innovation in financial institutions and markets arose in response to government's financial needs and policies. There is a pattern: the state, or the government, needs to raise new money for ordinary purposes or extraordinary ones such as wars. These public financial needs place stresses upon existing financial arrangements. Such stresses lead to financial innovation. The more pressing the public financial need, the greater is the financial innovation it elicits, and the longer lasting is its impact on the development of the financial system. The Federalist financial revolution of two centuries ago is the leading example illustrating the pattern, but it is not the only one. Well before the new nation emerged, public finance already had determined key parameters of the colonial American financial system.

Colonial governments and financial innovation

The thirteen colonies of British North America that in 1776 became the United States constituted the most rapidly expanding economy in the world of the seventeenth and eighteenth centuries. Population growth of 3% per year on average combined with modest increases in product per person to foster a long-term overall rate of expansion of 3% to 3^{1}/$_{2}$% per year. This was a modern rate in a pre-modern world. Inevitably it led to problems in supplying an adequate amount of means of exchange to grease the wheels of local and long-distance trade. Whatever English or European money the colonists brought with them or gained in other ways was spent to finance trade deficits – a common characteristic of newly established economies (as well as old, mature ones) – almost as quickly as it came in. This led to considerable experimentation and innovation merely to supply local means of exchange (Sylla 1982a, b). Wampum, the token shell money of the native Americans, was adopted by the European colonists. Various commodities – corn, rice, tobacco and beaver pelts, for example – were also given monetary status. In the early 1790s, when the US dollar became the official currency unit, counties in Virginia still collected local taxes in tobacco money. Precious metals gained from trade, mostly that with Latin America, circulated in the colonies. There were even attempts to provide a local coinage from such specie inflows, although the British torpedoed them as violations of royal prerogatives. The colonists also made extensive use of book credits, with settlements of accounts spread out over many months and even years.

The crowning achievement of all this colonial American monetary innovation was something that everyone, everywhere, now uses: paper notes issued by the state and declared by governmental fiat to be money. When the Massachusetts colony launched the innovation in 1690, it was without precedent in the history of any Western country (although the Chinese, according to Marco Polo, may have used it for a brief time centuries ago). What circumstances led to the American innovation? Colonial governments were tiny operations by modern standards, even by European standards of the time. Late in the colonial era the New York colony, for example, spent five-sixths of its budget on the salaries of just six officials; one of them, the crown-appointed governor, received nearly half of the total budget. Such governments could finance their minimal peacetime functions with limited duties on imports and exports, and with small property and poll taxes.

In colonial America, however, peacetime was as much the exception as the rule. Numerous wars with hostile native Americans and non-English Europeans vying for control of North America strained the small peacetime budgets of the English colonies. In 1690, such strains led to the innovation of fiat paper money, called bills of credit. During King William's War (1689–97), Massachusetts sent an army to capture a French fort at Quebec. Anticipating success, it planned to pay the army with loot from the fort. But success did not come, and the soldiers returned, demanding to be paid. The colony treasury was empty, however, and so the Massachusetts legislature authorized that the troops be paid with bills of credit issued in standardized format and in round denominations.

Initially, the bills of credit – which embodied a totally new concept of money – were greeted with scepticism and sank to discounts from their denominated value. In 1691, Massachusetts solved the problem when it issued a new batch of bills sufficient to discharge all of its war debts and made the bills receivable in public payments (taxes, fines, fees) at a 5% premium over their denominated value. It promised to levy taxes to be collected a year or two later to redeem the bills. Recognized by then as non-interest-bearing public debt that also served the purposes of money, the bills rose to par in terms of specie and remained there for some two decades. So useful were bills of credit as money in the expanding economy that the government happily found that it could meet most of its limited ordinary expenses simply by issuing more bills along with pledges of future taxes to redeem them.

Like most promising innovations, bills of credit were soon adopted by other colonies (Brock 1975; Perkins 1994). During Queen Anne's War (1702–13), the French and Spanish along with their native American

allies seemed to threaten the English colonists from all sides. To finance
the conflicts, the South Carolina colony issued bills of credit in 1703. It
was followed by Connecticut, New Hampshire, New York and New
Jersey in 1709, by Rhode Island in 1710, and by North Carolina in 1712.
Some of these issues bore interest, and some were made legal tender for
all payments, not just payments to the colonial government. Most
promised redemption through future taxes to be levied for that purpose.
And in just about every case, the colonial governments discovered, as had
Massachusetts, that they could go on meeting normal governmental
expenses by issuing currency long after the war exigencies that had
prompted the initial issues had passed. They also discovered that it was
not necessary to pay interest on the bills or to receive them at a premium
in payments to the government for the paper money to be acceptable in
private transactions. In addition to solving a financing problem of government, bills met the need of an expanding economy for more means of
exchange.

Also, like many other innovations, colonial bills of credit were altered
and extended to meet needs not anticipated when they first appeared.
One such alteration was to finance the operations of colonial loan offices
or land banks. Here South Carolina was the innovating colony. In 1712,
nine years after its first emission of bills, South Carolina put out most of
new issues as loans to individual borrowers on landed security. The
private borrowers were to pay back $12\frac{1}{2}\%$ of their loans each year for
twelve years. In this way the colony not only would have the principal of
the loan returned but would also earn interest amounting to 50% (or
$8\frac{1}{3}\%$ annually) over the life of loan on the amount of principal lent. Loan
issues, like bills of credit, were standardized and in round denominations,
and they passed interchangeably with bills in the colonial money supply.
The chief difference was that they were secured by pledges of private
assets instead of by promises of redemption through taxation. Colonial
loan office or land-bank notes served three functions. Citizens received
loans at a time when other sources of credit were limited. The colonial
government received an interest revenue that allowed it to keep taxes low.
And the expanding economy received an infusion of new currency.

Like bills of credit, the loan office innovation quickly spread. In New
England, Massachusetts adopted the South Carolina innovation in 1714,
followed by Rhode Island (1715), New Hampshire (1717) and
Connecticut (1733). In the Middle Colonies, Pennsylvania and Delaware
issued bills on loan in 1723, New Jersey in 1724 and New York in 1737.
In the South, North Carolina emulated South Carolina in 1729, followed
by Maryland in 1733 and Georgia in 1755. Of the colonies that later
revolted to form the United States, only Virginia failed to implement loan

office bills, but it considered doing so when it issued its first bills of credit in 1755.

The experience of the American colonies with bills of credit and loan offices provides a near-perfect example of how the needs of public finance can shape the financial system of a country. In their case, what initially were short-term expedients of public finance turned out to have long-term financial results. For a century after the Massachusetts innovation of 1690, fiat paper money was an important component of the American money supply, a cheap and easily augmented component that sustained rapid economic expansion. When independence came in 1776, Congress financed much of the Revolutionary War effort by issuing, and over-issuing, bills of credit, the 'Continental' currency notes. States, the former colonies, did the same, and they continued to do so after the war ended.

There were inflationary abuses, which surely will come as no surprise to those who have lived with fiat paper money in the twentieth century. Too much of a good thing is often a part of the human condition. Inflationary abuses of fiat paper money led eighteenth-century Americans, after adoption of the Constitution and the Federalist financial revolution it authorized, to abandon fiat paper money until the twentieth century. There were two noteworthy exceptions prompted, as one might guess, by war exigencies – the war of 1812 and the Civil War; in each case, after the war the United States by consensus resumed specie convertibility of paper money. But fiat paper money eventually did return, to America and nearly everywhere else. And it prevailed. During the twentieth century the whole world became Massachusetts.

The Federalist financial revolution

New nations, especially those born during costly revolutions, do not soon become countries with pristine international credit and world-class financial systems. The United States furnishes an exception to this rule. Another rule is that great institutions such as financial systems – as distinct from particular organizations such as banks – seldom owe their origins to the efforts of one person, however gifted. Again, the US financial is an exception. Its architect was Alexander Hamilton (1757–1804), who along with Franklin, Washington, Adams, Jefferson and Madison ranks as one of the pre-eminent founding fathers of the United States. Hamilton was the youngest of these noted statesmen and the only one who was an immigrant. Nonetheless, he played a prominent role in most of the major events of US history from the time he arrived as a youth from the West Indies in 1772 until he was killed in a duel by Aaron Burr, the sitting Vice-President of the United States, in 1804.

Hamilton was many things, but most of all he was a statesman and public administrator equipped with architectonic financial insights and abilities that were unsurpassed in his time.

When Hamilton arrived in colonial America, there were no banks and no securities markets as we now know them. There was no central bank, unless one counted the mother country's Bank of England, on which Hamilton would make himself something of an expert. Indeed, there was no country, only a collection of colonies issuing fiat paper money and running government-sponsored loan offices that funded their lending with paper money printed up and issued for that purpose. After independence was declared in 1776, the national congress and the new state governments borrowed what they could from domestic and foreign supporters, but they financed their revolution mostly by printing money, by 'currency finance', as had been the American practice for decades. The revolution was protracted. Fiat paper money was greatly overissued, and it greatly depreciated. All the while, Hamilton was in the Continental Army, rising from captain of a New York artillery company in 1775 to lieutenant colonel and aide-de-camp to General Washington by 1777, and he then became a hero of the Yorktown victory of 1781 that effectively ended the war.

During military lulls, Hamilton mused on how financial weakness and chaos threatened the American cause. He studied economics and finance, and began to formulate his vision of a future American financial system. In 1779, 1780 and 1781, while still in his early twenties, he wrote lengthy letters to national leaders calling for a great national bank based on specie and convertible bank-notes to cure the obvious problems of fiat paper that he had observed. The last of these letters went to Robert Morris shortly after Morris had been appointed Congress's Superintendent of Finance. Morris was thinking along similar lines, was encouraged by Hamilton's plan, and soon led the drive for the chartering of an institution more modest than the one Hamilton had sketched, the Bank of North America, which opened in 1782 as America's first bank. Hamilton's 1781 letter to Morris also dealt with the war's legacy of debts: 'A national debt, if it is not excessive, will be to us a national blessing. It will be a powerfull cement to our nation. It will also create a necessity for keeping up taxation to a degree which, without being oppressive, will be a spur to industry' (Hamilton 1781 [1961]). Here we can see the germ of the sweeping financial reforms that Hamilton, as the first Secretary of the Treasury under the Constitution, would sprout not quite a decade later: a national bank issuing a bank-note currency convertible into specie, and a national debt serviced by revenues from taxes – customs duties – that would at the same time give mild protection to domestic American industries.

We can also see in the quote the germ of American nationalism. Most men of the time were loyal to their states, the former colonies. Their country was seen as a loose league or confederation of states designed first and foremost to coordinate interstate efforts in the war of independence. (Analogies with today's European Union would not be strained, although that confederation is more about preventing war than about prosecuting it.) Hamilton on the other hand was an immigrant, in the country for less than a decade. He was not particularly attached to any state. Or to any old-world nation, since he was the illegitimate and later orphaned offspring of a Scottish father and a mother of French descent. (John Adams later called Hamilton 'the bastard brat of a Scotch peddler', showing that American political rhetoric has not changed much in two hundred years.) Hamilton's only loyalties were to the new nation that was forming itself, and he perceived that state particularism and state loyalties were a barrier to forming the nation he envisioned.

After the letter to Morris, Hamilton distinguished himself militarily at Yorktown, studied and practised law, and was appointed receiver of national levies in New York State. In the latter post, he discerned the difficulties of getting states to pay Congress' requisitions under the weak Articles of Confederation that had left the national government without tax powers. He served in the Confederation Congress and was instrumental in the founding of America's second bank, the Bank of New York, in 1784. Hamilton was a New York delegate to the 1786 Annapolis Convention that met to deal with trade disputes between states, and he drafted that convention's report calling for the constitutional convention of 1787.

At the Philadelphia convention, Hamilton was again a New York delegate and a member of the small committee that drafted the Constitution. When the document was submitted to the people for ratification, he recruited James Madison and John Jay to join him in explaining and defending it in *The Federalist*, writing the majority of the eighty-five classic essays himself. Then he led the successful fight for ratification in the New York state convention. The Constitution's supporters celebrated the feat by parading a model-ship float labelled 'Hamilton' through the streets of New York City. Hamilton was only 32 years old then, and he had come a long way from his boyhood in the West Indies. But his greatest work, foreshadowed in the letters a decade earlier, was yet to come.

In 1789, after Hamilton had drafted the bill establishing the Treasury Department, President Washington appointed him the country's first Secretary of the Treasury. He set about organizing the department and its machinery for collecting customs duties and internal excise revenues implemented by Congress, usually at his request. He also drafted his classic reports of 1790 and 1791 on funding the revolutionary debts of Congress and the states into long-term federal securities, on establishing a national bank, on creating a mint (including defining the dollar and the monetary base), and on promoting American manufactures. The essential provisions of all but the last report were quickly adopted by Congress. By the time of the Report on Manufactures in the Fall of 1791, Hamilton's astonishing successes in organizing the finances of the new federal government had provoked an organized political opposition to Federalist policies. Led by Thomas Jefferson, the Secretary of State, and James Madison, then a Virginian congressman, this Republican party defended the rights of states against what they saw as too much power building up in the federal government. The eternal cleavages and two-party system of US political life thus were born in Hamilton's financial initiatives, and they became well established during President Washington's first term, 1789–93. Why the President, who like Jefferson and Madison was a Virginia slave-owning planter, backed Hamilton at virtually every step of the way is a question that still has not been answered by historians. But he did.

The ostensible purpose of Hamilton's financial programme was to strengthen the credit of the new federal government. In this it was remarkably successful. When the government first formed in April 1789, evidences of public debt left over from its essentially bankrupt predecessor, the Confederation, traded in informal markets at 15% to 23% of nominal par value, and that was up some from where they had stood in previous years (Davis 1917: 338). Hamilton used the new revenues Congress had enacted and his Treasury Department would collect to promise debt holders that, with Congress' authorization of his plan, the government would fund the old debt, including arrears of interest and state debts from the Revolution, into newly issued federal securities that would pay interest quarterly and ultimately be redeemed at par in specie. Some state leaders in Congress, particularly Virginians, opposed the assumption of state debts on grounds that their states had paid many of them and that under the plan they would become responsible for debts of states that had not done so. This opposition was overcome in mid-1790 when Hamilton struck a deal with Jefferson and Madison to move the national capital to a new city on the Potomac River adjacent to Virginia in return for vote switches to pass the funding bill. After Hamilton's plan was enacted in July, old debt advanced to as much as 55% to 60% of par. When the new 'Hamilton 6s', a 6% issue paying interest in specie quarterly, appeared in October, they were valued in the market at 70% of par; by December 1790 they rose to 93%.

December 1790 was also the month that Hamilton laid before

Congress his plan for a Bank of the United States. Despite fierce opposition from Madison and other congressmen, the bill was soon passed. Washington asked Jefferson and Randolph, the Attorney General, for their opinions on the measure. Both said it was unconstitutional because the Constitution said nothing about chartering banks. He then asked Hamilton for his response to the opponents' arguments. Hamilton dissected and dismissed them while advancing a new doctrine of powers implied by sovereignty even if not explicitly enumerated in the Constitution. The President was persuaded by Hamilton's argument and approved the Bank bill in February 1791.

The Bank of the United States, when organized in 1791–2, was the country's fourth bank and, capitalized at $10 million, was by far the largest. Hamilton modelled its charter on that of the Bank of England, and many of the charter provisions were subsequently adopted in the charters of American banks organized under state laws. There were differences from the English model. The Bank was partly owned (20% initially) by the federal government, for example, and it could and did establish branches throughout the United States. Neither was the case in England at the time. But like the Bank of England, the Bank of the United States was a large corporation with a special relationship to the government and government finances, and it soon developed some of the functions that later would become known as functions of a central bank.

A clever feature of Hamilton's Bank plan was to allow the newly issued public securities to be receivable, some at par, in private subscriptions for stock in the Bank. Since the Bank was the 'hot' initial public offering (IPO) of mid-1791, the effect was to raise the new 6s to par at that time, and a few months later to 120% of par. Thus the national debt supported the Bank, and the Bank supported the debt. The Bank also functioned as the fiscal agent of the government and it provided a new source of public revenue in the form of dividends paid on the government's shares.

Another device Hamilton urged, and Congress adopted, was a sinking fund that allowed the government to use surplus revenues, and loans if necessary, to purchase public debt in the market at or below par. Such open market purchases, as the Federal Reserve would independently discover more than a century later, could be used to support the government bond market, to ease the money market and to expand the economy, points understood and acted upon by Hamilton. Unlike the Fed, he could not sell government securities to achieve reverse results, but he could borrow from banks and build up the Treasury's cash to contract bank credit (Studenski and Krooss 1963: ch. 5). Few of the techiques available to modern finance ministers and central bankers were not known and used by Hamilton two centuries ago, although later

Congresses, ever suspicious of the discretionary powers they delegated, would rein in his successors.

Hamilton completed his architectural plan for the US financial system with his April 1791 report on establishing a mint. The dollar had been adopted under the Confederation as the new country's currency, but it had not been precisely defined and no provisions were made for a mint. Hamilton in his report did both, and Congress adopted the plan a year later. It turned out to be the weakest link in Hamilton's structure. Although partial to gold monometallism and aware of Gresham's Law, he nonetheless espoused bimetallism, defining the dollar in terms of both gold and silver and calling for coinage of both metals at the then market ratio of 15 to 1 (equal weights of gold and silver were valued in the market at that ratio). Hamilton hoped that bimetallism would give the country a larger monetary base, which it might have if the market ratio had remained at the mint ratio of 15 to 1. But that was not to be. Gold rose in the market relative to silver, and so no gold was offered for coinage at the US mint when it opened in 1794. The United States effectively was on a silver standard in its first decades until, in the 1830s, it reduced the dollar's gold content and switched to that base. Moreover, US silver dollars were slightly lighter than the Spanish pesos on which they were modelled, but they passed at par with pesos in Latin American markets. Therefore, most of the silver coined by the US mint in its early years left the country and was replaced by foreign coins. Fortunately, Americans were long used to paper money, which their rising banking system supplied in the form of bank-notes.

If establishing a high credit for the new government was the ostensible purpose of Hamilton's programme, its true purpose and lasting result was establishing a modern financial system of banks and capital markets for the United States. Given the political climate and the controversy sparked by the Bank of the United States at its inception, the banking system would for decades grow up under state rather than federal auspices (see below). That was fine with Hamilton, who had played a major role in the founding of the first state banks as well as the US Bank, and then, as Treasury Secretary, provided direction for meshing these institutions into a banking system. The capital market that emerged from Hamilton's programme was, however, more a private than a governmentally guided development.

The debt funding of 1790 in a short time provided nearly $65 million of new, high-grade public securities to Americans, with another $12 million owed to foreigners. The Bank of the United States brought an additional $10 million of prime equity shares. Almost overnight, securities markets were organized to trade these new instruments in the country's major cities, with those of New York, Philadelphia and Boston being the most active and deep. Only recently have historians come to appreciate these developments, which remained hidden in contemporary newspapers rather than in the public documents upon which so much of financial history is based (Sylla, Wilson and Wright 1997). Three series of US debt issues of 1790 and Bank stock were regularly quoted and traded in each of the cities and became the nucleus of a national capital market. Newspapers in each city published security price quotations from the local market and, with some days' delay, from the markets of other cities. There is ample evidence of inter-market arbitrage from this interest in information, from surviving letters of market participants, and, of course, from the behaviour of prices. Moreover, the new securities proved attractive to foreign investors, and large quantities of them began to migrate overseas to be quoted and traded in English and Continental markets. By 1795, London quotations of US securities were picked up by American newspapers, but they were published sporadically since they arrived in the United States with a two-month lag and were therefore of limited use to American market participants. By 1803, nearly half of the US debt was held by foreigners. In buying it, foreign investors transferred capital to the United States. This fulfilled Hamilton's 1790 prediction, and it marked the beginning of the great trans-Atlantic flow of capital that would peak a century later. He and his supporters thought that foreign purchases of US securities would be a good development, one they had hoped and planned for, but that did not stop their political enemies in the Jefferson camp from accusing them of selling out America's interests to foreigners.

Local as well as national securities soon joined the newspaper quotation lists. Each city market had its local bank, insurance and transportation shares, as well as state and local governmental debt issues to quote and trade. During the late eighteenth and early nineteenth centuries, the US states were far more lenient than the British and Continental governments in granting charters of incorporation to business enterprises, and so the US corporate stock market quickly became more integral to the US economy than was the case in other countries. Securities regularly quoted in newspapers were just the tip of the iceberg; many other issues were closely held or inactively traded, so they did not make it into the published lists. Yet through growing numbers of brokers who made it their business to match buyers with sellers, there was a market for such issues.

As noted at the start of this chapter, the banking system and the capital markets rapidly became fundamental institutions of American life from which later developments drew sustenance. When Napoleon in 1803 offered Jefferson, Hamilton's political archenemy, the opportunity to double the size of the United States by purchasing the Louisiana Territory, he found that the French would be pleased to accept in return $11.25 million of fresh federal securities that they in turn sold to Dutch bankers for distribution to, among others, Napoleon's enemies across the channel. When factory manufacturing came to America, banks and securities markets were there to finance it. When grand canals and railways came, governments and private corporations turned to these financial institutions and markets for funds. When the West was settled and its agricultural surpluses were moved to eastern and foreign markets, a modern financial system was in place to finance their movement. When the United States fought wars to preserve or expand the union, borrowing on the capital market supplied most of the resources. Banks and securities markets mobilized and efficiently allocated capital, giving it a liquidity that America lacked before 1790. The Federalist financial revolution thus released energies that gave rise to and propelled the modern economic growth that came to the United States before it came to most countries.

Hamilton used his position as head of the federal government's finances to build something far greater than the public credit he was charged with rescuing. He used it to construct a financial system that endured to shape US development. It happened so neatly, and became so engrained in the order of things, that many, forgetting how different was the previous financial order, failed to comprehend what he and the Federalists had wrought. Lord Bryce a century later in *The American Commonwealth* noted of Hamilton that 'his countrymen seem to have never, either in his lifetime or afterwards, duly recognized his splendid gifts' (Bryce 1914 [1995]: 687). But that is only partly true. Daniel Webster (1782–1852), US senator and orator, grew up with Hamilton's system and in the 1830s said of it: 'The fabled birth of Minerva from the brain of Jove was hardly more sudden or more perfect than the financial system of the United States as it burst forth from the conception of Alexander Hamilton' (quoted by Gordon 1997: 41). Later, long after the fledgling agrarian country of 1789 had become the industrial colossus of the twentieth century, the great historian Charles Beard summed up, in a dated but still insightful way, the larger meaning:

Hamilton's measures were primarily capitalistic in character as opposed to agrarian . . . and constituted a distinct bid to the financial, commercial, and manufacturing classes to give their confidence and support to the government in return for a policy well calculated to advance their interests. He knew that the government could not stand if its sole basis was the platonic support of genial well-wishers. He knew that it had been created in response to interested demands and not out of any fine-spun theories of political science. Therein he displayed that penetrating wisdom which placed him among the great statesmen of all time. (Beard 1915: 131)

Beard's financial, commercial and manufacturing classes of the 1790s probably comprised less than 5% of the US population. But they were the primary agents of economic change, and the Federalist financial system provided them with powerful tools to effect it.

Public finance and state-sponsored banking, 1790–1860

The Federalist financial revolution directly created but one bank, the Bank of the United States. From 1791 to 1836 (with a hiatus from 1811 to 1816), it and its successor, the Second Bank, nonetheless were the dominant banking institutions of the country by their size, their interstate branch system and their central-bank influences on the rest of the banking system. The Bank of the United States was also important for the precedent it set in committing the country to a modern banking system. The nation's first modern bank, the Bank of North America, was chartered by Congress on the last day of 1781, but subsequently also by several states because they doubted that Congress had the power to charter a bank. In 1785, Pennsylvania revoked its charter for the Bank of North America, only to reinstate it with further restrictions a year later. The nation's second bank, the Bank of New York, could not even obtain a charter from the state when it was founded by Hamilton and others in 1784. It had to wait until 1791. Banks were controversial institutions during the 1780s. Only three were formed in the decade, and two of them had trouble in obtaining or keeping state charters. Many, perhaps most, Americans preferred the old order of state fiat money. They viewed banks as elite, privileged institutions contrived by and for the benefit of merchants, and a threat to the old order. The 1790–1 debates in Congress over chartering the Bank of the United States featured many of the same concerns. Only after Hamilton persuaded Washington that his Bank was constitutional did the United States become committed to the development of a modern banking system. Even then, doubts remained and would surface periodically in some states until the middle of the nineteenth century (Hammond 1958).

Given such a climate of opinion, so curious to us now yet perhaps understandable in a premodern polity composed overwhelmingly of farmers, how are we to explain the rapid development of the US banking system? The states chartered thirty banking corporations by 1800, 100 by 1810, 300 by 1820, 700 by 1836 and 1600 by 1860. In Europe during these decades, incorporated banks were the exception, most banks being private proprietorships or partnerships. America also had such institutions, but they were the exceptions to the rule of banks sanctioned and chartered by state governments. Banks were useful, of course, to their owners and their customers. Nonetheless, to understand the rapid spread of chartered banking in the United States, the utility of banks to the governments that chartered them is equally important. Considerations of public finance once again shaped the American financial system.

Although the Constitution made the Federalist financial revolution possible, it was a mixed blessing for the powers and the finances of state governments. Prior to the Constitution, states had full sovereign powers of taxation, including the power to levy duties on imports from other states as well as from foreign countries. The Constitution took away their power to tax imports, ceding it to the new federal government. The Constitution also gave the federal Congress control over money, negating the states' power, dating from the colonial Massachusetts innovation of 1690, to issue bills of credit and other fiat moneys. But the Constitution also eased burdens on state finances. The federal government assumed state Revolutionary War debts. It also took over most previous state responsibilities for defending the country. Moreover, when the accounts of the Revolution were settled, creditor states – those that had contributed more than their fair share of the costs of independence – were rewarded with interest-bearing federal securities for balances due, while debtor states, in an implicit extension of debt assumption by the federal government, effectively had their negative balances forgiven (Perkins 1994: ch. 10). Their burdens lightened, several states found that they could reduce or even eliminate their always unpopular property taxes. But that would not last long, and so states became interested in finding new sources of revenue.

Banks conveniently furnished such a source, although it took a little time for state legislatures to realize it. The first American banks were viewed more as public utilities than as the competitive business enterprises they soon became. Although sponsored by merchants, they were chartered by legislatures on grounds of the public good they would promote by making loans, by receiving and transferring deposits, and by furnishing the community with a bank-note currency convertible into specie. The essentially public purpose of banks was reinforced when the Constitution took away the rights of states to issue money. States could no longer circulate fiat currencies, but at least they could charter banks that issued a bank-note currency, thus ensuring a continuity in the provision of convenient paper means of payment. In keeping with the ancient concept of the corporation that still prevailed at the end of the eighteenth century – namely, a grant of monopoly privileges in return for promoting some aspect of the public good – state legislatures reinforced the public-utility notion of banks by granting only one bank charter per town (Sylla 1985).

Soon, however, state legislators discovered that their local banking monopolies were highly profitable to their private owners. Dividends of the nation's first bank, the Bank of North America at Philadelphia, for example, averaged 10% annually during its first forty years. Other Americans, dedicated to equal opportunity and resentful of special privileges, began to demand bank charters. Such demands on democratically elected politicians proved difficult to resist, but with them came political opportunity. Since bank charters possessed value to their owners, legislators could demand something of value in return.

The something of value could and did take many forms. One of the earliest was for the state to demand that it be granted rights to subscribe for bank shares, which it would pay for with a loan from the bank. Since dividends would probably exceed the interest on the loan, the state would profit and be enabled to keep taxes lower than they otherwise would have been. Alternatively, the state could demand a bonus payment in return for granting or renewing a charter; this had a similar effect on state finances. Still another method was to enact special taxes on banks; such taxes were a more politically palatable means of raising public revenue than direct taxes on the property of voting citizens. Or the state, in return for granting a banking charter, could exact on favourable terms a more or less permanent loan from the bank.

Many states derived a substantial portion of their public revenues from banks. Massachusetts, a leading example, between 1811 and 1860 derived more than half of all its ordinary revenues from a tax on the capital of banks. Since more banks meant more bank capital to tax and more state revenue, the state legislature routinely granted virtually all requests for charters (Sylla, Legler and Wallis 1987). Its banking system was the largest in the country in relation to its population, and, fuelled by abundant bank credit, the state became a leader of the US industrial revolution in the early nineteenth century. When states relied more on investments in banks or on bonus payments rather than on taxation of banks, their fiscal interest made them more restrictive in granting charters. Often the result was slower economic development than occurred in states such as Massachusetts (Wallis, Sylla and Legler 1994).

Still other methods states used to extract something of value from granting bank charters were less direct in their impact on state revenues but equally useful in meeting demands of citizens. Bank charters often directed banks to employ their own funds in ways the legislature deemed appropriate, such as by directing a portion of them to particular groups of citizens or particular private projects and institutions deemed worthy of public support. The latter included, in virtually every state, institutions such as state literary and school funds, schools themselves, colleges, and homes for orphans. This method of privately financing worthy public causes by directing banks to do so was an additional means of keeping taxes lower than they would have been had the legislators decided to give such support through the state budget. The two extremes of extracting something of value from bank charters came when the state entirely owned and operated a bank (which might or might not have been a monopoly bank) and, at the other extreme, when corrupt individual legislators and coalitions of legislators demanded personal payments or political contributions in return for their votes in support of charters on favourable terms to the banks.

Every one of these methods of extracting a *quid pro quo* for a bank charter was employed during the years 1781–1838, when every bank charter in the United States, some 700 of them, was granted by a specific legislative act. Since the number of state (and territorial) legislatures increased from twelve to twenty-nine in these six decades, the result was great variety in the terms of charters and the types of banks states created. Banks were ordered by their charters to supply cities with water, gas lights and hotels, and the countryside with roads, bridges and canals. Others were ordered to lend some percentage of their capitals to citizens engaged in agriculture and manufacturing. In the South, states helped found banks specifically to lend to planters on mortgage security. Banks were even chartered to relieve citizens victimized by depressions.

The US banking system developed rapidly compared to those of most countries in the early decades of the nineteenth century. It also developed differently, with the typical bank being a corporation with limited liability chartered by a state legislature rather than a proprietorship or partnership with unlimited liability. But it is evident from what has just been said that many banks were far from typical; their charters often specified that they serve particular public purposes. The rapidity of banking development and the variety and sheer numbers of banking institutions reflected the intimate relationships that developed from the 1790s, the decade of the Federalist financial revolution, between American banks and the finances of the governments that chartered them. The role of the financial revolution was critical. Its Bank of the United States supplied not only a model for state bank charters, but also a lesson in how a private financial institution could support public finance.

Even more important in the long run was the capital market that arose in the financial revolution. It provided the means by which all the banking and other corporations, financial and non-financial, chartered by states could raise capital by issuing shares that were then traded in US securities markets. A single issue of a New York newspaper, the *New-York Price Current* of 29 June 1811, indicated how extensive the securities markets had become by that early date. In addition to US debt securities, the New

York market listed and quoted the shares of six banks and ten insurance companies. Philadelphia's list included five banks, nine insurance companies, seven bridge and turnpike companies, and three municipal securities. The Baltimore list had twelve banks, six insurance companies, four turnpike companies, a manufacturing company and a municipal security. The Boston market listed, besides the US securities traded in every city, four banks, two insurance companies, and Massachusetts state securities. These, of course, were just the published quotations, presumably of relatively larger companies and more actively traded securities. Securities of many other banks and non-banking companies existed in each market but did not make it into the lists published in New York. Two decades after the Federalist financial revolution was launched, the essential contours of the US financial system were well established.

Civil War finance and the financial system

By many measures, absolute (total casualties) and relative to the economy and population of the time, the Civil War of 1861–5 surpassed all wars in US history in its human and financial costs. It supplies another illustration of this chapter's thesis that public financial stresses lead to lasting financial change.

The most significant and lasting developments came in the areas of banking and currency. From the Federalist revolution of the 1790s to the 1860s, most American banks, as discussed above, were state-chartered institutions that individually issued bank-notes. On the eve of the war there were some 1600 such banks, most issuing several denominations of notes, so that there were an estimated 8,000 to 10,000 differently designed and denominated varieties of bank-notes in circulation. This had costs. It encouraged counterfeiting and loose banking practices such as circulating large batches of notes far from the office of the issuing bank in order to delay their return. Countering this were resources devoted to note brokerage, the gathering of notes at a discount and returning them to the issuing bank for the spread, and to printing up and circulating bank-note reporters and counterfeit detectors so that merchants and others could know if notes were good, and how good.

A more uniform national currency was clearly desirable. The war provided the opportunity to achieve it. First came the greenbacks, the fiat United States notes issued by the federal government after it and the nation's banks suspended specie payments at the start of 1862. The suspension lasted until 1879, but when specie payments were then resumed a large portion of the greenbacks remained in circulation, convertible into specie at the Treasury.

Next came the National Banking System and national bank-notes, in 1863. With them the federal government attempted to solve two problems (Sylla 1975). The most pressing problem was its need to borrow for war purposes. The new banking law, modelled on New York State's free banking law of 1838, made it easier to borrow by granting federal charters to 'national' banks, and requiring them in return to invest a good portion of their capital in federal debt securities. The secondary objective of the new law was a more uniform national currency. The national banks could deposit their federal securities as collateral with a newly created Treasury official, the Comptroller of the Currency, and receive uniform national bank-notes to be lent out in ordinary bank operations. Then, if a bank failed, noteholders would be compensated by liquidation of the bond collateral. Congress expected that all state banks still in the union, for reasons of patriotism and self-interest, would switch to national charters and the country would have close to a uniform currency. Apart from being patriotic, banks would earn a double return from participation in the new system, in the form of interest on their federal bond holdings and interest from lending the national bank-notes they received from the Comptroller's office against their bond collateral.

Unfortunately, there were less appealing features of the law, and many established state banks chose not to join the new system. This frustrated Congress' twin objectives, and Congress responded in 1865, as frustrated legislative bodies sometimes do, by passing a prohibitive tax on state bank-note issues. Even that was only partly successful. State bank-notes disappeared, but some state banks had discovered that note issue was not necessary to carry on a banking business and they chose to keep their state charters rather than join the national system.

In the end the federal government achieved most of its objectives. Aided greatly by bond-issue borrowing, it won the war, ended slavery and preserved the union. And the country came out of the war with a more or less uniform national currency composed of US-minted coins, United States notes convertible (after 1878) into gold at the Treasury, and national bank-notes convertible into gold at the issuing banks and backed by US debt securities held by the Comptroller. State-chartered banks remained. By the twentieth century they would increase in numbers and resources to rival in size the national banking system (James 1978). But the federally chartered national banks also remained in the American 'dual banking system' of federal- and state-chartered institutions.

That the national banks of the Civil War era persisted provides a suggestive contrast with the first national banks, the First and Second Banks of the United States. These quasi-central banks left the scene in 1811 and 1836, when politics prevented their rechartering. Eventually, however, they were reinstituted in 1913 as Congress' 'Third Bank of the United States', the Federal Reserve System. The Fed might seem an exception to this chapter's thesis, for it was not an innovation prompted by stresses of the public finances. But casting it as the 'Third Bank' should alleviate such concerns. For the Fed was less an innovation than a return to the financial system established by Hamilton and the Federalists in the 1790s.

Conclusion

The United States at the end of the twentieth century is a very different country from what it was at the end of the eighteenth. Now some 260 million Americans, a twentieth of the world's people, produce upwards of a fourth of the world's total output of goods and services, with endless varieties in both categories. Two centuries ago, the country of 4 million produced mostly agricultural goods. Other changes – political and military power, the ethnic composition of the population, for example – are equally striking.

But the essential contours of two great underpinnings of American society are very much the same as they were two centuries ago. One is the federal political system of sovereignty divided between the national and state governments. Put in place in 1789, it proceeded in an unbroken line of Congresses and presidents, of state legislatures and governors, of federal and state courts. The other is the financial system, the descent lines of which are less unbroken but nonetheless discernible. Then, as now, there were national and international markets for the debt of the federal government. Then, as now, there were active markets for corporate, state and local government securities. Then, as now, there were banks chartered under federal and state laws. Then, as now, there was a great central bank chartered by Congress. Then, as now, capital flowed regionally and internationally from relatively developed and wealthy areas and countries to newer, developing ones that could promise capital a higher return. The accomplishments of the Federalist era in politics are widely understood and celebrated. It is probably time to recognize that the Federalist financial revolution deserves the same understanding and praise. It was no less central to the American experience.

The world at the end of the twentieth century also has countries with weaker financial arrangements than America's, both then and now. They include many of the less developed countries and those in Eastern Europe that are attempting to restructure their economies after decades of socialist planning. Private and official organizations, for example the International Monetary Fund and the World Bank, are engaged in advising these countries and recommending new policies and institutions. They all could learn a basic lesson from historical US financial development. If the public finances are put in order, orderly private financial institutions and markets will probably follow. True in Hamilton's time when governments were small, it is likely to be all the more true today when governments have considerably larger relative roles in their economies. US history certainly provides ample lessons that public finance can shape a country's financial system.

BIBLIOGRAPHY

Beard, Charles A. 1915. *Economic Origins of Jeffersonian Democracy*. New York.

Brock, Leslie V. 1975. *The Currency of the American Colonies, 1700–1764*. New York.

Bryce, James 1914 [1995]. *The American Commonwealth*, 3rd edn updated. Indianapolis.

Davis, Joseph Stancliffe 1917. *Essays in the Earlier History of American Corporations*, vol. I. Cambridge, Mass.

Dickson, P. G. M. 1967. *The Financial Revolution in England: A Study of the Development of Public Credit, 1688–1756*. New York.

Gordon, John Steele 1997. *Hamilton's Blessing: The Extraordinary Life and Times of Our National Debt*. New York.

Hamilton, Alexander. 1781 [1961]. 'To Robert Morris'. *The Papers of Alexander Hamilton*, ed. Harold C. Syrett, vol. II. New York.

1795 [1973]. 'Report on a Plan for the Further Support of Public Credit'. *The Papers of Alexander Hamilton*, ed. Harold C. Syrett, vol. XVIII. New York.

Hammond, Bray 1958. *Banks and Politics in America, from the Revolution to the Civil War*. Princeton, NJ.

James, John A. 1978. *Money and Capital Markets in Post-Bellum America*. Princeton, NJ.

Perkins, Edwin J. 1994. *American Public Finance and Financial Services, 1700–1815*. Columbus, Ohio.

Studenski, Paul and Krooss, Herman 1963. *Financial History of the United States*, 2nd edn. New York.

Sylla, Richard 1975. *The American Capital Market, 1846–1914*. New York.

1982a. 'Monetary Innovation in America', *Journal of Economic History* 42: 21–30.

1982b. 'Monetary Innovation and Crises in American Economic History', in *Crises in the Economic and Financial Structure*, ed. Paul Wachtel, pp. 23–40. Lexington, MA.

1985. 'Early American Banking: The Significance of the Corporate Form', *Business and Economic History*, Second Series, 14: 105–23.

Sylla, Richard, Legler, John B. and Wallis, John J. 1987. 'Banks and State Public Finance in the New Republic: The United States, 1790–1860', *Journal of Economic History* 37: 391–403.

Sylla, Richard, Wilson, Jack W. and Wright, Robert E. 1997. 'America's First Securities Markets, 1790–1830: Emergence, Development, Integration',

Working Paper presented at Cliometrics Conference, Toronto (May); a shortened version of the paper appears in *Financial History* 61 (Winter 1998), 14–31.

Wallis, John J., Sylla, Richard and Legler, John B. 1994. 'The Interaction of Taxation and Regulation in Nineteenth-Century U.S. Banking', in *The Regulated Economy: A Historical Approach to Political Economy*, ed. Claudia Goldin and Gary Libecap, pp. 121–44. Chicago.

12 Cosmopolitan finance in the 1920s: New York's emergence as an international financial centre

Mira Wilkins

New York City became in the 1920s a hub of international finance.[1] This was a new role. The city had long been America's largest.[2] It had long been an important port. It had long been an entry point for immigrants from Europe. Throughout its history it had been international, but in the 1920s it assumed a new prominence within the world economy.

Before 1914, the United States had been a debtor nation in world accounts, attracting more monies from abroad than it sent abroad.[3] Yet, as a debtor nation it had certain distinguishing features that made it unlike contemporary debtors. First, it was by far the greatest debtor nation, drawing in more foreign capital than any other single country (Wilkins 1989: 145). Second, by 1900, it already had the world's largest industrial output – and by 1913, almost 36% of global manufacturing was done in the United States (1989: 142). Third, the great bulk of America's vast *industrial* production had been financed domestically; a large part of the inward foreign capital had gone into infrastructure, namely railways. Fourth, many of America's largest, most innovative industrial companies were already multinational enterprises (Wilkins, 1970). Other debtor nations had multinational enterprises, but none had as extensive a collection as that from the United States. Fifth, there had emerged in the United States a coterie of investment bankers, who over the decades had acquired (had learned) skills in intermediating domestic *and* foreign capital, *into* American public and private uses.[4] In this respect, the United States was hardly unique among debtor countries; for example, Russia and Sweden had similar financial intermediaries, but none appears to have had the stature or the scale of business of Morgan or Kuhn, Loeb.[5] Sixth, the United States had another set of banking institutions, including National City Bank, First National Bank and Chase National Bank, that while neither national nor international in terms of branches, none the less had become large, sophisticated money market institutions; they were, however, fettered by US law and not until 1913, when the Federal Reserve Act was passed, could American federally chartered banks branch abroad.[6] These big American banks had counterparts in Russia, Canada and Australia, where banks had broader geographical operations; Japan and Sweden also developed strong domestic banking institutions. What seems to have distinguished the American banks from those in other debtor nations was that, with one obvious exception, they had greater resources at their command.[7] Seventh, and of significance, no debtor nation had a stock market anything like that in New York City. Not in St Petersburg, nor in Toronto or Montreal, nor in Tokyo or Osaka, nor in Stockholm, nor in Buenos Aires was there any institution that approximated the New York Stock Exchange. The New York Stock Exchange was, however, fundamentally a domestic market (some foreign securities were traded, but few). Foreigners traded on it – in *American* securities. Unlike the London market, it was not a hub for international issues (Michie 1987; 1988a, b).

In 1914, while the United States had a positive trade balance (exports exceeded imports), its foreign trade was in the main financed from abroad; prior to the 1913 passage of the Federal Reserve Act, American federal law, as interpreted by the courts, barred national banks from handling international acceptances. American cargoes were in large part carried on foreign ships. And US international trade was, to a great extent, insured by foreign insurers (Wilkins 1989; see also Wilkins 1991: 247–8). In these regards, it was like some but unlike other contemporary debtor nations.[8]

The First World War had a dramatic impact on the foremost creditor nation – the United Kingdom – and consequently radiating global impacts. When Britain needed to liquidate its world-wide investments to finance the war, each debtor nation reacted differently.[9] In the United States, because the inflow of foreign capital had been complementary to domestic savings and because the external dependency had stimulated the growth of domestic institutions, the country was able not only to respond to the British withdrawal but also to be 'proactive' in filling the gap and building on the new opportunities.

During 1914–18, Americans paid attention to providing dollar acceptances, i.e. financing US commerce (the 1913 passage of the Federal Reserve Act opened up new possibilities); to building a shipping industry (subsidized by the US government); to providing insurance; to replacing foreign with domestic capital at home; *and* to lending and investing abroad on an unprecedented scale (Wilkins forthcoming).

By the end of World War I, by 1918–20, the dollar was being used to finance US trade; over 50% of American cargoes were transported on US flag carriers; American marine insurance had greatly expanded. The nation's exports soared. New York City bankers recognized they were in a position to play a significant international leadership role; the newly authorized branches abroad of national banks multiplied. The New York Stock Exchange was prepared to handle foreign securities. The US Congress passed legislation to encourage further *American* directed international transactions: the Webb-Pomerene Act (1918) allowed US exporters to combine, exempt from antitrust prosecution; the Edge Act (1919) authorized American banks to form federally incorporated corporations for international banking. American businesses were poised to continue their international expansion. Most crucial, the United States had become a creditor nation.

After the transition

Some of the remarkable changes that took place during and in the immediate aftermath of the First World War proved ephemeral. The surge in US exports, for one, did not persist. They peaked in 1920 and that level was not again achieved in the 1920s, and, indeed, not surpassed until 1943! (US Department of Commerce 1960: 537). The commitment to American shipping sagged after the 1920–1 recession, and by the end of the 1920s the United States was again dependent on foreign carriers.[10] Most of the newly established Edge Act banks were shortlived, while the number of foreign branches of American banks, which had soared to a high of 181 in 1920, was by 1925 reduced to 107.[11] By the autumn of 1920, certain British bankers in New York had become wary of dollar acceptances and returned to the use of sterling credits for their Latin American and Far Eastern trade.[12]

Yet, what did *not* change was the firmly established creditor position of the United States, which became ever more evident as the 1920s progressed. American businesses continued their international expansion, which was not new. What was novel was that the New York Stock Exchange listed numerous foreign securities. New York became a truly international financial hub, as never before in its history. Dollar acceptances survived and flourished. America was, relative to the rest of the world, the wealthiest nation. US capital and capital markets were available to finance governments and industry – at home and abroad.

The leading pre-war creditor nations, the United Kingdom, France and Germany, had all been deeply scarred by the war. Germany, burdened by reparations, became the foremost debtor nation (replacing the United States in that role). The United Kingdom had to struggle to resume its pre-war standing; it became obsessed with returning to gold at a pre-war parity, which was not achieved until 1925. France was unable to take the initiative in world finance (Lévy-Leboyer 1977; Schuker 1976;

Leffler 1979). The United States filled the gap left by the disabled former great creditors. From 1924 through 1929, according to one estimate, American 'foreign lending' was almost double that of Britain, still the largest European lender.[13]

We almost take for granted the rise of the United States in the global economy. No other debtor nation was in the running to step in when the former great European creditor states stumbled. As for other pre-war debtor nations, Russia had had its revolution; it renounced its debts. World War I changed the name of St Petersburg and the face of the country; Russia became less international – a pariah in the world community. By contrast, Japan had the fastest growth rates of any country (1913–19); it emerged from the war as a creditor nation, but its attention was to domestic savings; Japanese stock markets remained underdeveloped; no Japanese city could even dream of playing the role New York assumed in the world economy.[14] Sweden, too, became a creditor, with healthy financial institutions and aggressive international businesses, yet the country was not rich enough to be a global lender.[15]

Canada, deprived of the inflow of monies from the United Kingdom, turned to the United States for funding. Toronto and Montreal were active financial centres, but not global ones. Australia showed no hint of world leadership, while Argentina sank into economic decline after being cut off from massive British capital inflows (Taylor 1992: 907–36).

European creditors – Holland and Switzerland – seem to have increased their relative position in the interwar period, but none could assume the role of the United States.[16] The United States, in contrast to all other pre-World War I debtors, had emerged from World War I with new wealth and prestige, fully able to challenge the former supremacy of Western Europe. New York could build on and transform its pre-war financial infrastructure to serve the needs of America's domestic economy and the world economy as well.

There now exist a large number of valuable studies on America's creditor position in the 1920s. I do not want to discuss the Dawes or Young loans or the excitement of international financial diplomacy in this decade.[17] Nor do I want to dwell on the vast expansion of American multinational enterprises.[18] Rather, I want to focus on one of the most fascinating novelties of the 1920s – the creation of New York as an international financial entrepôt – and consider how this was linked with international *industrial finance*.[19] There has been substantial confusion over the relationships between short- and long-term international finance, which became intermixed in America's new capital market; my interest is in the latter, in the functioning of capital markets. I like the definition of capital markets by George David Smith and Richard Sylla: 'They are . . .

the organized processes by which funds for long-term investment (or capital formation) are raised, securitized, distributed, traded, and – perhaps most important of all – valued' (1993: 5). These are the international processes that we need to study in the 1920s.

My current research has been on America as a *recipient* of long-term foreign investment (Wilkins forthcoming). After the United States became a creditor nation, it still continued to attract inward foreign investments. In investigating the inflow of foreign monies, I have been dealing with continuities and discontinuities. Clearly, the major disjuncture was the dramatic shift from debtor to creditor during the years 1914–18. Yet every historian knows that the past creates paths,[20] that, discontinuities notwithstanding, underlying continuities always lie beneath the surface. America's achievement of prominence and New York's emergence as an international financial centre grew out of, built on, those foundations.

Throughout its history as a creditor nation, from the end of the First World War to the mid-1980s, America continued to be a recipient of investment from abroad and these investments were *both* direct and portfolio ones, with a greater quantity of the latter than the former. In the 1920s, what became remarkable were the institutional structures that evolved to combine the *inward* investments with the far more substantial outward ones.

The blending of inward and outward finance

Capital moves internationally through channels. In the 1920s, long-term foreign 'finance' typically took the form of new issues and traded securities. In addition, multinational enterprises moved capital over borders internally within the firm. Such a description – dividing portfolio and direct investments – greatly oversimplifies.[21]

In the intermediation of capital external to the enterprise, bankers and securities dealers were central to the process. By 1929 one estimate indicates that there were 6,445 securities dealers in the United States of which 3,000 could be classified as investment bankers. The truly elite group of investment bankers *qua* securities dealers was far smaller (Carosso 1970: 267).[22] The 1920s saw the democratization of American securities markets. As America became a consumer society, so too middle-class Americans began to participate as never before in securities transactions.

New securities issues multiplied during the 1920s. The largest number were domestic issues, generally for American corporations (domestic and multinational ones) – representing both debt and equities.[23] Many of the investment bankers and securities dealers had, and the new ones developed, contacts in Europe, and their affiliates, associates and correspondents were given a tranche in the domestic issues. Particularly easy to sell abroad were the securities of American multinational enterprises, since their names were well known in Europe. There was a market abroad for American securities. Initially, at the beginning of the decade, the securities sales had been principally of bonds, but as the market priced common stock at ever higher valuations, especially at decade's end, there were new European purchases of and trading in American shares – new issues and existing securities. The Morgan House, with its British and French affiliates, typically offered a tranche to its European associates in all its American securities offerings. The dealing in American securities by foreign investors was not unlike that in the pre-war era where railway bonds had been particularly popular abroad; the channels were the same, albeit there were by the late 1920s many more participants in selling these securities at home and abroad. And there were more purchases and sales of the securities of American industrials and, particularly, public utilities. Many of these corporations were multinational enterprises, and they in turn as multinational enterprises exported capital world-wide. Thus, there was the *outward* direct investment (by Morgan, for example, in its affiliates abroad), that encouraged *inward* portfolio investment (monies coming into the United States to buy American securities), and, in turn, there was once more the *outward* direct investment (the allocation within the US-head quartered multinational enterprise to its business operations world-wide).

If this is not complex enough, what was truly novel with the *inward* portfolio investments was what was happening with the so-called 'foreign securities', dollar-denominated securities issued and traded in the United States to finance governments and corporations outside the United States (*outward* investment).[24] The largest percentage of these foreign securities represented lending to foreign governments (Fishlow 1985: 419). Both governmental and corporate borrowers *from abroad* sought funds in America where abundant capital seemed available. All the experienced (and as the decade progressed, the less experienced) New York based international bankers underwrote foreign issues.[25] Commercial banks set up securities affiliates that handled domestic *and* foreign issues. The amount of business done was unprecedented (Carosso 1970: 240).

Just as in the underwriting of domestic securities, so, too, the underwriting of foreign issues involved the pricing of the securities and the distribution of them at home and abroad. Foreign issues could be bonds, but like domestic ones, as the decade progressed, they were often in the case of corporate issues shares. Bankers and securities dealers handled the transactions and sought out additional business. Both new issues and existing securities were traded.

Foreign issues were sold to the American public, but were also distributed abroad. Why did investment bankers and securities dealers – through their international contacts (and through their branches' outward direct investments abroad) – market the foreign issues outside the United States, and why did foreign investors buy foreign dollar-denominated issues? The answer to the first question is that American underwriters and securities dealers sought as large a market as possible for the securities. It was said that because Americans were unfamiliar with foreign securities, the bankers needed to rely on European investors (Burk 1992: 364).[26] A superior reason was that American investment bankers in particular *had* the international networks (long established from the days of selling US railway securities abroad) and these very same clusters of foreign banks and securities dealers could be used and expanded to market in the 1920s American domestic as well as the foreign issues. The model was there and newcomers followed the pattern.

The more interesting question is the second one: why did foreigners buy foreign securities in the United States? In the 1920s, in the period when the United States was a creditor nation, foreign investors bought both domestic American securities and foreign issues in the United States, and more of the former than the latter.[27] The foreign issues purchased by individuals and institutions outside the United States were of two sorts – issues for a third country (a British investor bought dollar bonds issued for Chile) or issues for the same country (a German investor bought a dollar-issued loan to Germany or to a German firm). When each occurred, we are talking about an *inward* investment in American-issued foreign securities that was serving to disperse capital world-wide (*outward* investment).

Foreigners bought foreign securities in the United States for a number of reasons. (1) Often, foreign issues to the *same* foreign borrower carried a higher coupon rate when the issue was in New York rather than in London, *because* American bankers had argued that to sell the bond to Americans, who were unfamiliar with foreign issues, the interest rate had to be higher; foreign investors buying the foreign issue in the United States could take advantage of the higher returns (Davies 1927: 44–5). (2) German investors were more confident about German securities bought through New York; they could also evade turnover taxes and income taxes in the international transactions.[28] (3) When Britain returned to the gold standard in 1925, there were restrictions imposed on foreign issues but none on the purchase of outstanding foreign issues traded in New York (Moggridge 1972: 215). Britishers, much to the annoyance of contemporaries, bought on Wall Street (and the commissions and fees went to Americans). And (4) sometimes the reason was arbitrage – buying an internationally traded security on one exchange (say New York) and selling it on another market, London or Amsterdam; at times, securities could be bought in New York and sold for a higher price on a foreign bourse. Yet, in the 1920s, because of the speed of information (cable connections were rapid), markets quickly adjusted and the possibilities of arbitrage narrowed. None the less, inter-exchange arbitrage did exist and was by 1929 widely discussed.[29]

Loans issued in New York to a German steel company, Vereinigte Stahlwerke, for instance, would be sold to the American public and also to British, Swiss, Dutch, German and other European investors. Dillon, Read, a major participant in American underwriting for German loans in the 1920s, carried out a survey in 1929 on where bond coupons were presented for payments and found that about two thirds of some of its earlier high-interest German loans had moved to German ownership by that time (Schuker 1988: 117).

To add to the complications of cosmopolitan finance, a British banking house with an affiliate in New York (inward direct investment) might join in the underwriting of a German issue. An example of this was the British merchant banker, J. Henry Schröder & Co., which established in New York in 1923 the J. Henry Schroder Banking Corporation. The British Schröder house had long experience in Anglo-German financial relationships. Its New York subsidiary participated in banking and selling syndicates led by the American investment bank Dillon, Read, which underwrote many German loans including the ones mentioned to Vereinigte Stahlwerke. Since J. Henry Schroder had no special US distribution system for such securities, it would forward its tranche abroad (Roberts 1992: 231).

J. Henry Schroder Banking Corporation also served a second even more valuable function. Its London parent not only provided a network to market some portion of the issues, but directed its clients in Central Europe and Latin America to its New York affiliate. Indeed, many of the fifty-seven foreign bond issues in which J. Henry Schroder Banking Corporation participated in these years were for its parent's clients (Roberts 1992: 231). The J. Henry Schroder Banking Corporation had been set up to handle dollar acceptances, but it had moved rapidly into underwriting foreign issues as well.

Similarly, the International Acceptance Bank (IAB), formed in 1921 to finance trade, became deeply involved in long-term foreign finance. IAB was founded by Paul Warburg, who before World War I had been a partner in Kuhn, Loeb; Paul Warburg's brother's firm, M. M. Warburg &

Co., Hamburg, participated in the organization of IAB, as did a number of other European banks (*inward* foreign direct investment).[30] Yet the inward foreign direct investment aspect was small compared with the outward flow of capital arranged by IAB, assisted by its stockholding banks. IAB set up a group of affiliated companies, which served to intermediate monies to Germany and other Central European countries.[31]

A key feature of the cosmopolitan finance of the 1920s was the growth of affiliates, clusters of companies. Not only IAB, but numerous financial intermediaries, spawned affiliated companies with different purposes, but many of which engaged in providing the channels for the export of capital. Such companies included wholesalers and retailers of securities, holding and finance companies, investment trusts, asset realization units, and so forth.[32] And, here too we get into the intricacies of cosmopolitan finance, for foreign investors often participated as shareholders in these affiliates (inward foreign investment) *and* at the same time used them as mechanisms for raising money for their own foreign requirements.

A related way for foreigners to generate capital in the United States was to form their own companies (inward direct investments by industrial corporations) that would then issue securities and the funds obtained would go to finance their business outside the United States. The monies were amassed by issues sold principally to Americans. The capital allocation process was then done within the corporation. Thus, Framerican Industrial Corporation raised money in the United States for Schneider-Creusot, while Patiño Mines and Enterprises Consolidated (run by the Bolivian tin entrepreneur, Simon I. Patiño) attracted American capital to finance Bolivian mining.[33] International Match Company, Ivar Kreuger's intermediary, collected large amounts of money in the United States (and abroad), ostensibly for Kreuger's match business (Wilkins forthcoming).

Such foreign-controlled US companies typically had investment bankers underwrite their US issues. Thus, Kreuger used Lee, Higginson as the lead banker in his issues. Again, to add complexity, some part of the securities of such companies might well be sold abroad. The International Match Company was internationally traded. Later, when the Kreuger empire collapsed, bringing down Lee, Higginson, a partner of the latter noted that all the European bankers participating had trusted Kreuger.[34] Cosmopolitan finance in the 1920s involved international networks of information that were not always reliable, since often, in the enthusiasm for new business, there was self-deception (and sometimes actual deception). Questions were not asked that should have been. As George Smith and Richard Sylla point out (1993: 29), new bank affiliates, utility holding companies, and investment trusts, created to promote and float securities – domestic and foreign – often did so without attention to the underlying values.

Some of the complications of cosmopolitan finance are evident in the behaviour of the Belgian Alfred Loewenstein, 'an operator' involved in rayon and public utilities. Loewenstein set up a Canadian-registered company in 1926, Hydro-Electric Securities Corporation, to acquire public utilities securities. Hydro-Electric was internationally traded. By 1929 (after Loewenstein's death), it had obtained financial interests in utilities in Spain, Italy, Belgium, Brazil and Mexico, but roughly 90% of its investments were in US public utilities, some of which in turn had foreign investments. The rise in American stock values in the summer of 1929 made Hydro-Electric the object of substantial international attention. Most of the buying of its securities was by Americans or Canadians, yet British 'speculators' purchased, seeking quick profits. The holding company, Hydro-Electric, had been established in Canada for tax reasons and because Canadian entrepreneurs had become specialists in this type of public utilities endeavour.[35] Cosmopolitan finance involved outward US long-term lending to Europe, Latin America, Canada and Asia, and inward US investments, often made to facilitate the outward flows. Sometimes it involved outward investments (as in those by Americans in Hydro-Electric) to facilitate the inward flow.[36]

Cosmopolitan finance was short term as well as long term. A speculator in securities engaged in short-term buy/sell propositions, but frequently traded long-term securities, equities or debt. It is, however, impossible to separate out statistics on the 'speculator' versus the 'investor'. Sometimes 'speculators' held securities longer than they intended; sometimes 'investors' decided that they did not want to hold for long periods.[37]

Call loans and brokers' loans, in which foreigners participated in the United States, were short term, yet they provided the basis for a dynamic securities market, creating the possibilities of more investments, particularly in shares.[38] Companies – domestic and foreign – could raise more monies than ever in history. So could foreign governments.

The role of the US government

Viewing the extremely complicated financial architecture erected in the process of cosmopolitan finance, this author is struck by the relative absence of American government participation. The Federal Reserve System, set up to provide stability to the banking system, had come into being in 1914. At the outbreak of war in Europe, the New York Stock Market had closed (to avoid massive withdrawals by foreign investors). The decisions on when to open it were made by stock market officials, monitored to be sure by the New York Federal Reserve Bank (the New York Fed).

During World War I, the US government had become deeply involved in the world economy, including its activities as lender to the Allied Powers. US government officials after the war participated in international conferences that affected the world economy. Benjamin Strong, governor of the New York Federal Reserve Bank from its origins to his death on 16 October 1928, was *au courant* in international finance. His biographer, Lester V. Chandler, writes that Strong, together with Montagu Norman of the Bank of England, was 'a principal architect of world monetary reconstruction after World War I and a leader in . . . international central bank cooperation'. Yet, as Chandler also indicates, while Strong was head of the New York Fed there was no willingness on the part of the US government 'to lead or even to cooperate officially in international financial matters' (Chandler 1958: 3). While Strong himself was savvy in financial matters, the story of cosmopolitan finance in the 1920s was one of virtually no regulation.[39]

Bankers were expected to clear their foreign lending plans – particularly loans to foreign governments – with the US State Department, but fundamentally it was up to the partners in the House of Morgan, in Dillon, Read, and in Lee, Higginson and the like to make the decisions in the sphere of international finance. They knew men in Washington. Yet they and the many other participants who joined them in international finance in the 1920s acted, in the main, on the basis of their own judgement.[40] This was especially true in industrial finance. The New York Stock Exchange was 'self-regulating'. It imposed certain listing requirements for securities; the amount of information given to investors was very limited.

The financial pyramids relating to outward and inward international investments were by the late 1920s affected by the US government only in that some were mechanisms for tax evasion or tax avoidance. Since World War I had imposed the first truly heavy corporate taxation and since after the war the wartime tax structures had not been fully dismantled, part of the elaborate financial architecture was linked with reducing tax burdens; this was true of Americans and foreigners alike and added to the complexities.[41]

Scholars have used US government records and seen government monitoring of the Dawes and Young loans, government attempts at monetary policies and government scrutiny of international economic activities (there are records in Washington on International Match Company and its raising of money), and government compilations of statistics on international transactions. From such archives, there has come to be a belief that there was (or could have been) a major US government role – one that is frequently exaggerated by virtue of the narrowness of the sources.

By contrast, the business historian who studies business records sees the locus of decision-making about the international financial transactions in the 1920s in enterprises (banks and other businesses).[42] Indeed, the regulatory structures that evolved in the subsequent decade, the 1930s, were a consequence of the abuses that were perceived as caused by the *absence* of an effective government role in the 1920s.

What emerged in the 1920s was New York as a world financial emporium, financing governments and industry. This came about not because of any action or lack of actions of the US government, but because the United States was where the capital and the capital markets were. It occurred because the United States had in its economic growth generated surpluses and at the same time had the presence of financial intermediaries able to mobilize and disperse these surpluses domestically and internationally. Cosmopolitan finance in New York in the 1920s was basically *not* US government regulated – not by the State, Commerce or Treasury Departments. The New York Stock Exchange set its own rules. Banks made their own decisions. The New York Federal Reserve was aware, informed, monitored, but gave no directions. In Washington, there was similar attention (and occasional interventions), but the locus of activity came from the private sector. And, equally important, as American multinational enterprises expanded abroad (allocating capital within the business enterprise on an international scale), they were providing industrial finance completely unregulated by the US government.[43]

The culmination

American international lending slowed in the summer of 1928. Why? It was due in part to rising interest rates in America and in part to the growing involvement of Americans with domestic securities and the upward move in stock prices on the New York Stock Exchange that attracted domestic and foreign money to American equities. In 1928, the value of stock issues in the United States surpassed debt ones for the first time. Americans were buying securities at home – and foreigners joined in. There was no slack in the quantities of securities issued, but domestic securities soared at the expense of foreign ones. New holding companies, investment trusts and other financial intermediaries – all seeking to offer their shares – multiplied. In 1929 the New York Stock Exchange had its first billion dollar year. The effects of the reallocation of monies to Wall Street and the slowdown in international lending on the world community were devastating.[44] Perhaps we have not thought through how new to world finance New York was, and how dramatically its long-established financial structures had altered in their domestic and global involvements. The frenzy of American finance was both domestic and international.

American financial institutions, along with the American public and foreign investors (inward investors), looked to Wall Street and by the summer of 1929 stock prices were heading towards new peaks. Historians debate whether Strong's illness in the summer of 1928 and his death in October 1928 made a difference in what followed, whether his successor at the New York Fed, George Harrison, was less able to cope with the situation, less able to engage in effective international cooperation (Eichengreen 1992: 208–9). I think the emphasis on the 'untimely death' of Strong elevates the role and the impact of the Federal Reserve to undeserved heights.

Cosmopolitan, international New York in the 1920s was a singular post-World War I creation – the consequence of new domestic and international conditions. The financial architecture of the 1920s – the holding companies, the investment trusts, the securities dealers, the investment bankers, the brokers' loans and the call loans, the scale of transactions – all of which directed capital to uses at home and abroad, was elaborate and not fully tested. Architectural design of financial institutions became flamboyant. There was 'an orgy of financial speculation' (Eichengreen 1992: 14).[45] It was unregulated. When there was a tightening of monetary policy to try to control the situation, the results were not as anticipated.

It seems likely (in retrospect), with the financial pyramids and the lending, the stock market boom had to collapse. Whether the Hatry Affair in Britain and/or the raising of the British bank rate triggered the downturn as contemporaries thought, or whether it was bad US monetary policy, or whether the market simply lost artificial values that had been created by overspeculation, are important factors (and the reasons given are not irreconcilable) in considering how the depth of America's international economic involvements influenced the market, and subsequently the US and the world economy. The financial pyramids would crumble after the stock market crash of October 1929 and in its wake. By the early 1930s, the ornate financial architecture constructed in the 1920s lay in ruins and disrepute.

An evaluation

Were there any redeeming features? Did cosmopolitan finance serve industry? Did the fancy financial market structures provide the basis for *industrial* finance, for technological innovation and for real economic progress? Or was it all a monetary illusion, a world of paper values, with little substantive worth? Before I attempt to answer these questions, it is important to indicate that even though we are talking about a time when the US government role was limited, we are not talking about 'free markets'. There were all kinds of market imperfections. There was a lack of full information, essential for markets to function properly. Certain actors in the economy had more information than others. There was not in the 1920s perfect competition – by any stretch of the imagination – not in financial markets or in goods markets. Market imperfections were, to repeat, the norm. There were many 'visible hands', in international financial as well as in corporate managerial allocations.[46]

Second, as we analyse the data it becomes clear that the line is not easily drawn between investment (traditionally thought of as 'a good') and speculation (traditionally thought of as 'a bad'). If the function of capital markets is to allocate 'real' resources, to price securities, to provide 'values', the speculator plays an important role as a communicator of information.

And, third, the sizeable role of foreign government borrowing in the 'foreign issues' has to be taken into account. Albert Fishlow (1985: 420) points out that the purposes for which governments borrowed included currency stabilization, reconstruction, deficit financing, repaying old loans and so forth; much of the government borrowings of the 1920s was not reinvested in productive activities and in no way contributed to industrial finance.

The answers to the questions that I posed in the first paragraph of this section are complex and debatable. On the one hand, there was in the 1920s (and certainly in the collapse) seemingly an immense amount of waste. As Smith and Sylla have written on this decade: 'The new, popular investment vehicles were subject to enormous abuses, through intra-holding company underwritings, through the flotation of excessively large securities issues, and through outright self-dealing, manipulation and fraud' (1993: 29). This was true in both domestic and international securities issues.

The pain of the aftermath of 1929 cast a dark shadow on the existing institutional structures.[47] In the wake of the New York Stock Market crash, the international financial architecture was tempered – by defaults, bankruptcies, reorganizations, and then extensive US government regulations in the 1930s. Never again, it was thought, would private sector decision-makers be allowed such a free rein. When World War II began in Europe, government officials in the United States started to plan for the peace, reviewing the events after World War I and in the 1920s. There would be a major role for the US government in the international economy of the post-World War II years.

In the 1990s, however, we have become less confident about the wisdom of government decision-making and are returning to reliance on private-sector markets. We pay more attention to 'financial capitalism'. And, as we do so, we need to look again at the 1920s private-sector international financial structures – with caution, knowing as we do of the aftermath, but also with a new sense of the functions of financial markets. Waste notwithstanding, beneath the flashy cosmopolitan financial structures of the 1920s perhaps there were certain redeeming features. What were they? Before we discuss the possible redeeming features, it is important to stress, as we have earlier, that the international financial structures built in the 1920s were in response to new conditions after World War I. America was for the first time in its history a creditor nation. There is no question that there were immense abuses, fraud and waste and the fact of the subsequent collapse cannot help but make us aware of faults in the structure. Yet at the extreme, should one see these structures as merely financial 'churning' with no effective reallocation of 'real' resources? It does seem clear that, however imperfect these financial institutions were, they did move capital internationally; the vibrant new electrical and chemical industries were not starved of capital; the spread of electrical public utilities was dramatic (financing *was* provided); the financial structures did provide for the continued economic growth in much of the world in the 1920s.

Beneath the elaborate and pyramided cosmopolitan structures, networks of information developed and resource allocation occurred. Financial institutions emerged that did dispense long-term capital – to the private sector as well as to governments. Capital was raised, 'securitized, distributed, traded . . . and valued' (Smith and Sylla 1993: 5). Aspects of the financial infrastructure of the 1920s, combined with the totally new US governmental regime of the 1930s, did offer the basis for future US world leadership after the Second World War. Survivors used their knowledge of the past. Stock markets ultimately do serve an important and real function in the allocation of international financial information and in the allocation of resources.

It is interesting to consider the juxtaposition of resource allocation within the firm (as the multinational corporation spreads over borders and allocates resources) and external to the firm as financial markets price the securities of these very corporations and of governments (that may use funds towards productive or non-productive uses). In the 1920s, as America became a new creditor nation, the experimentation with financial edifices resulted in many flimsy structures. International finance created new vulnerability. In retrospect, this seems almost inevitable. Yet, the waste was in part (maybe in large part) offset by the learning experience.[48] Americans (and the rest of world) came to understand the worth and the perils of international (and purely domestic) financial intermediation. Multinational enterprises survived to provide a platform for financing industry. Perhaps the allocation of funding for industry within the framework of the multinational enterprise was (and remains) more important to the financing of industry than the financial markets. But would the former have been possible without the developed financial institutions?

NOTES

1 This chapter owes much to discussions with the late Vincent Carosso, with Dick Sylla, Rondo Cameron, V. I. Bovykin, Boris Anan´ich, Geoffrey Jones, Youssef Cassis, Jean-François Hennart and many others.

2 Throughout I am using the word 'America' as synonymous with the United States.

3 On America's first debtor nation era, see Wilkins 1989.

4 By 1914, sovereign debt constituted only a very small part of America's foreign obligations; this had not, however, always been the case (Wilkins 1989: *passim*).

5 For the achievement of Morgan in putting together in 1901 US Steel, the world's first billion dollar corporation, see Smith and Sylla 1993: 2–4 and Carosso 1987: 466–74.

6 For American banks in international finance, see Carosso and Sylla 1991. See also Cleveland and Huertas 1985: esp. 73–4.

7 The one exception was the Imperial Bank of Russia, which had far larger deposits than any American bank. For the size of its deposits in 1913, see Wilkins 1989: 454.

8 Japan, for example, had a negative trade balance, yet seems to have financed a greater portion of its own trade than Americans did; its cargoes were carried to a large extent on its own ships; and its insurers appear to have covered more of its trade than was the case with the United States. See Lockwood 1954: 257; Wilkins 1986: 199–231; 1990: 586–8; Mason 1992: 435–44.

9 I am currently working on a sequel to my history of foreign investment in the United States, which will deal with the US responses in great detail. In the notes this will be cited as Wilkins forthcoming. If there is no citation, it can be assumed that I have drawn on research collected for that forthcoming book.

10 In 1913, 14% of the shipping employed in American foreign trade was under an American flag; in 1920, the percentage was 50.8% and in 1929, 37.6% (Sturmey 1962: 130).

11 The decline was already evident to Phelps (1927: 211). Theodore J. Grayson (1928: 136) wrote that 'the Edge Act has been a decided failure'. An excellent work on 'American independence in international finance', is Abrahams (1976).

12 Based on data in file 792, Federal Reserve Bank of New York, New York.

13 Particularly useful on the general picture are Einzig 1935; Aldcroft 1977; Eichengreen 1992. See also Kindleberger 1973: 56 (US 'foreign lending' equalled $6.4 billion, while UK 'foreign lending' came to $3.3 billion; these figures are totals of annual lending based on League of Nations balance of payments data; they do not correspond with other figures that measure US foreign lending by capital issues. The latter also show the United States far in the lead).

14 See Maddison 1991: 212–14, on comparative growth rates and Hirschmeier and Yui 1975: 186, on the Japanese stock markets.

15 I found of great interest the work of the sociologist, Gordon Laxer (1989: ch. 3, entitled 'Sweden: Out of the Staple Trap'). Sweden, however, had not prospered during World War I (Maddison 1991: 212–14).

16 Broder (1991: 7–38) emphasizes the important role of Holland in interwar German finance.

17 The bibliography of Eichengreen's splendid *Golden Fetters* (1992) offers a good introduction to the enormous literature.

18 I did that in Wilkins 1974.

19 On the entrepôt concept, Geisst (1992) was helpful in clarifying some of my 'simmering' ideas. Particularly useful is Carosso 1970: chs. 12–14.

20 The path dependency notions of Paul David have been very influential in my thinking.

21 Jean-François Hennart (1993) has been very stimulating to me – albeit I do not use his vocabulary.

22 The Investment Bankers Association had 650 members.

23 Domestic issues far exceeded foreign ones. See Federal Reserve Board, *Annual Report 1931*, 199.

24 For the amounts and regional distribution of American foreign securities issues, see Eichengreen 1989: 114.

25 I am emphasizing New York as a centre. The important Boston firms – Kidder, Peabody and Lee, Higginson – had New York offices. It is clear that the quality of foreign lending fell during the 1920s as more participants competed and less experienced lenders saw opportunities for profits.

26 This may have been true in the early period, but it is doubtful that it was true as the 1920s progressed. See Stallings 1987: 73–4.

27 For two sets of figures on international movements of outstanding American and foreign securities, see National Industrial Conference Board 1929: 64; Lary 1943: 107. While the figures from these two sources are different, both show that the trade in American-issued domestic securities exceeded that in American-issued foreign securities.

28 On German individuals who purchased 'units in the Dutch or Swiss *tranches* of American loans (to Germany), or who invested funds directly in such issues on Wall Street', see Schuker 1988: 116–17.

29 British journals such as *The Economist* regularly reported on American market transactions, as they had for years; there was an international spread of information. The same was true of Dutch publications – and of the press in much of Continental Europe.

30 Wilkins forthcoming (on IAB). Paul M. Warburg is best known as one of the original members of the Federal Reserve Board and for his role in the found-

ing of the Federal Reserve System (see Chernow 1993). Warburg resigned as a partner in Kuhn, Loeb on joining the Federal Reserve Board; he never rejoined Kuhn, Loeb.

31 See, for example, Ránki 1983: 390, for IAB's participation in financing the Hungarian General Credit Bank.

32 Carosso 1970: 276, for a list and the rationale behind each.

33 Wilkins forthcoming. I am indebted to Jean-François Hennart for discussions on the similarity of Patiño's behaviour to that of many European seekers after capital.

34 Donald Durant, US Senate, Committee on Banking and Currency, *Stock Exchange Practices, Hearings*, 72d Cong., 1st sess. (1933), pt. 4, 1233.

35 *The Economist*, 10 Aug. 1929: 282; Wilkins forthcoming; Armstrong and Nelles 1988: 256–71 (for background on Loewenstein).

36 An American investor who invests in the United States through a foreign holding company is using the latter often to save taxes and in doing so facilitates the US investment (more is invested if less goes to taxes!).

37 Most scholars solve the statistical problems by looking at the security; if the security has a life of longer than a year (with a bond) or an indeterminate life (with a stock), then the investment is considered to be long term, no matter what the investor intends or how long in fact the investor holds the security.

38 On brokers' loans and the participation of foreign investors in them, see Beckhart 1932.

39 Strong was a banker by background. In 1898 he was a neighbour of Henry P. Davison and Thomas Lamont, both of whom would become Morgan partners. In 1903 he became secretary of Bankers Trust Co., rising to chief executive. See Schwartz 1990: 402–3.

40 As Barry Eichengreen points out (1989: 123–4), the State Department asked banks originating foreign loans to consult with them prior to offering the issue to American investors; the State Department then checked with the Treasury and Commerce Department. The programme was entirely voluntary and informal. An embargo was placed on lending to the Soviet Union. The State Department disapproved of a Romanian loan in 1922 (since there had not been a war debt funding agreement). There were some other interventions (the best-known cases are the German Potash loan and the São Paulo Coffee Institute loan). See Fishlow 1985: 421–2. There were, unquestionably, certain 'politically linked loans'. Overall, however, with the frenzy of finance, it is the absence of US government interventions that is most striking. Barbara Stallings, considering Latin American lending in the 1920s, writes that the best description of the US government position was 'passivity'. Stallings 1987: 74–5.

41 Tax avoidance was universal in the 1920s – for Americans and foreigners alike.

42 I share with Eichengreen (1992: 14) the view that 'there is no evidence that monetary policy played a significant role in the great bull market of the 1920s'. He argues, and I would agree, that the Wall Street boom was what influenced monetary policy rather than the other way round. One could go further and say there is no evidence that any government policy (beyond mon-

etary policy) played a significant role in the bull market. Certain state governments within the United States passed 'blue sky' laws, regulating securities, but these had little impact on the international financial pyramids. On blue sky laws, see Smith and Sylla 1993: 32.

43 While the US Department of Commerce looked on with alarm as American companies set up European plants, fearing the export of jobs and competition with American goods (see Wilkins 1974: 52–3), there was no effort to stop such expansion abroad. Unlike bankers that were expected to clear foreign government loans with the State Department, there was nothing similar *vis-à-vis* direct investments. Also, since so many of the foreign issues were to governments, there was a foreign policy facet of international finance that was not as much in evidence with the growth of multinational enterprise investments.

44 Eichengreen (1992: 12–14) puts the emphasis on rising interest rates in the United States; see Smith and Sylla 1993: 28 on the general Wall Street boom.

45 Professor Maurice Lévy-Leboyer objected to the designation 'orgy of financial speculation', seeing the connotation as negative, which is the case. I am, however, happy with Eichengreen's (and many other authors') description, as reflective of this era.

46 The phrase 'visible hand' comes from Alfred Chandler.

47 Even before the collapse, there were warnings that the financial frenzies had perils. The articulated warnings were not, however, loud and clear at the time; only in retrospect do we emphasize their prescience.

48 The 1980s saw substantial flamboyant finance, with leveraged buy-outs and debt financing – and what many defined as great waste (misallocation of resources). Yet, when the stock market crash of 1987 took place, there was no terrible aftermath affecting the US and the global economy such as had occurred in the years 1929–33. The institutional structures of the 1980s were different from those of the 1920s.

BIBLIOGRAPHY

Abrahams, Paul Philip 1976. *The Foreign Expansion of American Finance and Its Relationship to the Foreign Economic Policies of the United States, 1907–1921.* New York.

Aldcroft, Derek H. 1977. *From Versailles to Wall Street 1919–1929.* Berkeley, Calif.

Armstrong, Christopher and Nelles, H.V. 1988. *Southern Exposure.* Toronto.

Beckhart, Benjamin Haggott 1932. *The New York Money Market,* vol. III, *Uses of Funds.* New York.

Broder, Albert 1991. 'Les mouvements de capitaux dans l'entre-deux-guerres: l'Allemagne, la France, les Etats-Unis, les Pays-Bas', *Economies et Sociétés,* 2: 7–38.

Burk, Kathleen 1992. 'Money and Power', in Y. Cassis (ed.), *Finance and Financiers in European History, 1880–1960.* Cambridge.

Carosso, Vincent 1970. *Investment Banking in America: A History.* Cambridge, Mass.

1987. *The Morgans.* Cambridge, Mass.

Carosso, Vincent P. and Sylla, Richard 1991. 'U.S. Banks in International Finance', in Rondo Cameron and V. I. Bovykin (eds.), *International Banking*, pp. 48–71. New York.

Chandler, Lester V. 1958. *Benjamin Strong*. Washington DC.

Chernow, Ron 1993. *The Warburgs*. New York.

Cleveland, Harold van B. and Huertas, Thomas F. 1985. *Citibank 1812–1970*. Cambridge, Mass.

Davies, A. Emil 1927. *Investments Abroad*. Chicago.

Eichengreen, Barry 1989. 'The U.S. Capital Market and Foreign Lending, 1920–1955', in Jeffrey D. Sachs (ed.), *Developing Country Debt and Economic Performance*, pp. 107–55. Chicago.

    1992. *Golden Fetters*. New York.

Einzig, Paul 1935. *World Finance 1914–1935*. New York.

Fishlow, Albert 1985. 'Lessons from the Past: Capital Markets during the 19th Century and the Interwar Period', *International Organization* 39.

Geisst, Charles R. 1992. *Entrepôt Capitalism*. New York.

Grayson, Theodore J. 1928. *Investment Trusts*. New York.

Hennart, Jean-François 1993. 'International Financial Capital Transfers: A Transaction Cost Framework', Working Paper 93–004, Center for International Business Education and Research, University of Illinois, Urbana.

Hirschmeier, Johannes and Yui, Tsunehiko 1975. *The Development of Japanese Business*. Cambridge, Mass.

Kindleberger, Charles P. 1973. *The World in Depression 1929–1939*. Berkeley, Calif.

Lary, Hal 1943. *The United States in the World Economy*. Washington DC.

Laxer, Gordon 1989. *Open for Business*. Toronto.

Leffler, Melvyn P. 1979. *The Elusive Quest: America's Pursuit of European Stability and French Security, 1919–1933*. Chapel Hill, NC.

Lévy-Leboyer, Maurice (ed.) 1977. *La position international de la France*. Paris.

Lockwood, William W. 1954. *The Economic Development of Japan*. Princeton, NJ.

Maddison, Angus 1991. *Dynamic Forces in Capitalist Development: A Long Run Comparative View*. Oxford.

Mason, Mark 1992. 'The Origins and Evolution of Japanese Direct Investment in Europe', *Business History Review*, 66: 435–44.

Michie, Ranald C. 1987. *The London and New York Stock Exchange 1850–1914*. London.

    1988a. 'The Canadian Securities Market 1850–1914', *Business History Review*, 62: 35–73.

    1988b. 'Different in Name Only? The London Exchange and Foreign Bourses, c. 1850–1914', *Business History* 30: 46–8.

Moggridge, Donald E. 1972. *British Monetary Policy, 1924–1931*. Cambridge.

National Industrial Conference Board 1929. *The International Financial Position of the United States*. New York.

Phelps, Clyde William 1927. *The Foreign Expansion of American Banks: American Branch Banking Abroad*. New York.

Ránki, G. 1983. 'The Hungarian General Credit Bank', in Alice Teichova and

P. L. Cottrell (eds.), *International Business and Central Europe, 1918–1939*. New York.

Roberts, Richard 1992. *Schroders*. Basingstoke.

Schuker, Stephen A. 1976. *The End of French Predominance in Europe: The Financial Crisis of 1924 and the Adoption of the Dawes Plan*. Chapel Hill, NC.

  1988. *American 'Reparations' to Germany, 1919–33: Implications for the Third World Debt Crisis*. Princeton, NJ.

Schwartz, Anna 1990. 'Benjamin Strong', in Larry Schweikart (ed.), *Banking and Finance 1913–1989*. New York.

Smith, George David and Sylla, Richard 1993. 'The Transformation of Financial Capitalism: An Essay on the History of American Capital Markets', *Financial Markets, Institutions and Instruments*, 2, 2 (May 1993).

Stallings, Barbara 1987. *Banker to the Third World: U.S. Portfolio Investment in Latin America, 1900–1986*. Berkeley, Calif.

Sturmey, S. G. 1962. *British Shipping and World Competition*. London.

Taylor, Alan 1992. 'External Dependence, Demographic Burdens, and Argentine Economic Decline after the *Belle Epoque*', *Journal of Economic History*, 52: 907–36.

US Department of Commerce, Bureau of the Census, 1960. *Historical Statistics of the United States*. Washington DC.

Wilkins, Mira 1970. *The Emergence of Multinational Enterprise: American Business Abroad from the Colonial Era to 1914*. Cambridge, Mass.

  1974. *The Maturing of Multinational Enterprise: American Business Abroad from 1914 to 1970*. Cambridge, Mass.

  1986. 'Japanese Multinational Enterprise before 1914', *Business History Review*, 60: 199–231.

  1989. *The History of Foreign Investment in the United States to 1914*. Cambridge, Mass.

  1990. 'Japanese Multinationals in the United States: Continuity and Change, 1879–1990', *Business History Review*, 64: 585–629.

  1991. 'Foreign Banks and Foreign Investment in the United States', in Rondo Cameron and V. I. Bovykin (eds.), *International Banking*, pp. 233–52. New York.

  forthcoming. *The History of Foreign Investment in the United States after 1914*.

Index

Andino Railway, 241
Argentina, 14
  bank notes, 228, 230, 241–2
  banking and seignorage, 233, 237, 242
  bills of exchange, 225, 226
  currency board, 245
  depreciation of peso, 227, 241–2
  free banking, 14, 233, 238–9
  interest rates, 238–9
  monetary reforms of 1899, 244–5
  money supply in, 237–8, 240, 242–5,
    246–7
  national debt, 236
  war with Brazil, 226, 227
assignats, 6, 22–35, 46
  Russian, 210
Austrian National Bank, 128

Baden, Grand Duchy of, 7
Bagehot, Walter, 121–3, 189
Banca Commerciale Italiana, 189–90, 197,
  199, 203
Banca Generale, 185, 189, 194
Banca Nationale nel Regno d'Italia, 183
Banca Romana, 183
Banco de Buenos Aires, 226
Banco Central, 174–5
Banco de Descuento (Bank of Buenos
  Aires), 224, 231
Banco Garantidos, 238–42, *see also* free
  banking
Banco Hipotecario, 163
Banco Hispano Americano, 167
Banco de la Nación, 243
Banco Nacional, 227–8, 231
  (second) Banco Nacional, 233–4, 240,
    243
Banco di Napoli, 197
Banco de la Provincia de Buenos Aires,
  231–3, 240, 243
Banco de San Carlos, 12
Bank of England, 9, 29, 78–80, 82, 83, 87,
  105–8, 125–6

Bank of France, 6, 37, 38–45, 47, 50n,
  128–9
Bank of Italy, 13, 183–9, 192–3, 194–206
  and *Consorzio per sovvenzioni*, 204
  Superior Council, 184
Bank of Japan, 130
Bank of London and the River Plate, 235,
  236–7
Bank of Manchester, 85, 87, 93, 102, 108
Bank of North America, 255, 262
Bank of Portugal, 131
Bank of Prussia, 16–17n, 137
Bank of Spain, 131, 158–78, 160–1
Bank of the United States (First), 262
bank failures
  in Great Britain, 81–2, 83–5, 89, 102
  in Germany, 138
Banking Act of 1826, 76–7, 83–6, 102–3
Banque de Belgique, 61–2, 65–6
Banque Terrotoriale, 36
Baring Brothers Bank, 235–6
Baring Crisis of 1890, 14, 126, 236,
  240–2
Bark, P. L. (Russian Finance Minister),
  210, 218–19, 220–2
Bavaria, Kingdom of, 7
Belgium
  an industrialization, 53, 63, 65
  and revolution of 1830, 11
  and crisis of 1848, 65–6
billet de confiance, 31, 32
bills of credit (Massachusetts), 256–7, *see
  also* fiat money
bills of exchange
  in Argentina, 225, 226
  discount business in: in Belgium, 57–8,
    66–7; in France, 27, 37, 40; in Great
    Britain, 105–8, 124–5
  rediscounting of: in Great Britain, 105; in
    Italy, 187, 197
Bleichröder & Co., 189
Bolivianos, 226, 230
Bourse of Berlin, 140–1, 142–8, 153–4

and issue of securities, 140–5, 149–51
and Law of 1896, 140–1
and pricing of securities, 146–51
Bubble Act of 1720, 16n
Buenos Aires Drainage and Water Supply
 Company, 236

Caisse de Comptes Courants, 36, 40–2
Caisse d'Epargne, 65
Caisse d'Escompte, 27–30, 37
Caisse d'Escompte du Commerce, 41–2
caisse patriotique, 31
Cajá Federal de Fondes de SudAmérica,
 226
Cajá del Potosi, 225
capital markets
 in Belgium, 63
 in France, 201
 in Germany, 134–55
 in Great Britain, 142–8, 150–1, 235
 in Italy, 191
 in United States, 163–5, 169–70,
  175–90
 see also Bourse of Berlin; New York,
  securities markets
Casa de la Moneda, 228
central banking, 118–32
 in Germany, 11, 137, 152
 in Italy, 182–205
 in Spain, 163, 171–7
 in United States, 258, 267–8
Chase National Bank, 271
City of Glasgow Bank, 126
Commission of Debt Redemption
 (Russian), 211, 212
Consorzio per sovvenzi, 204
Credit Office (Russia), 13, 212–22
Credito Italiano, 189
Credito Mobiliare, 185
Creditanstalt (Vienna), 189–90
Cuba, 160, 165

Danish Nationalbank, 130–1
Deutsche Bank, 190
discount business, *see* bills of exchange
Du Pont de Nemours, 29

Edge Act, 273
England, *see* Great Britain

Federal Reserve Act of 1913, 272
Federal Reserve System (US), 268, 280,
 281
fiat money
 in American colonies, 9–10, 252–5, *see*
  also bills of credit

in France, 28
in Argentina, 231
financial innovation, 17n
 in Belgium, 59–63
 in France, 26, 35
 in Spain, 171–3
 in United States, 251–69
financial revolution, 4–8, 135, 249, 254–62
France
 Directory, 24–6
 fiat money, 23, 28
 free banking in, 29, 31
 gold reserves, 47–8, 50n
 government finances, 6, 20, 46
 maximum, 22, 23, 25
 money supply in, 23–4, 25, 48
 National Convention, 21, 32
free banking
 in Argentina, 14, 234, 238–42
 in France, 29, 31
 in United States, 267
Frère-Orban, Walthère (Belgian politician),
 65–7, 69

Germany
 company law and securities markets,
  134–55
 concentration in banking, 141, 152–3
 crisis of the 1870s, 11, 137–8, 152–3
 Franco-Prussian War of 1870, 137–8
 government finances, 7–8
 money supply in, 138, 152, 155n
 Napoleonic Wars, 7
 regulation of motgage banks, 221
 Revolution of 1848–9, 7
 Zollverin and monetary integration, 8
gold standard, 14, 15, 163, 176
 in Great Britain, 77–8
 in Italy, 186
Great Britain
 banking and legislation, 76–117
 gold standard, 77–8, 79
 government finances, 4–6, 78–9
 national debt in, 5
 securities market in, 103–4, 141–51, 235
greenbacks (US), 266

Hamilton, Alexander, 10, 249, 250, 254–62
haute banque protestante, 27
holding companies, 61

incorporation (of business enterprises)
 Germany, 139–40, 152–3
 Great Britain, 142–6
 Prussia, 138–9
 Spain, 161–2

International Acceptance Bank (US), 278–9
International Match Company, 279
Italy, 12–13
    and central banking, 183–9, 191–205
    and gold standard, 186
    and government finances, 186
    and uindustrial finance, 191, 203
Japan, 278
Jefferson, Thomas, 257, 260
Joel, Otto, 190, 193–5, 199–202
Joplin, Thomas, 80–1, 88, 94–5

Kokovtskv, V. M. (Russian Finance
    Minister), 216, 217

land banks, 257, *see also* United States,
    colonial loan offices
Law, John, 6, 26
Lee, Higgison, 279
Loewenstein, Alfred, 280
London
    as capital market, 142–8, 150–1, 154
    Clearing House, 87
    money market in, 9, 17n, 105–6, 107–8,
    124
London & Westminster Bank, 87
Lussatti, Luigi, 201

Madison, James, 256, 257
mandats territoriaux, 23, 35
Mangili, Cesare, 193, 194–5, 196, 203–4
Meeûs, Ferdinand, 59–61
mixed banking
    in Belgium, 53, 54–8, 61, 71–2
    in Italy, 190–1
    in Spain, 169–76
    see also universal banking
money supply
    in Argentina, 242–5, 246–7
    in France, 23–4, 25, 48
    in Germany, 138, 152, 155n
    in Spain, 165–6, 167
Montagnards, 20, 21, 33
Morris, Robert, 255

Napoleon Bonaparte, 40, 41, 42, 44, 45–6
Napoleonic Wars, 7, 135, 158
National Bank of Belgium, 67, 71, 129–30
National Bank Act of US, 267
National City Bank, 271
National Debt
    Argentina, 236
    Great Britain, 5
    Italy, 201–2
    Prussia, 7
    Russia, 211

Spain, 160, 164–5, 167, 170–1
United States, 249–50
Necker, Jacques, 28–9, 38
Nederlandsche Handel-maatschappij,
    57
Netherlands
    public finances, 4, 10–11
New York
    Federal Reserve Bank of, 281, 283
    securities market, 10, 265–6, 271–2,
    282–3, 284; new issues in, 275–77;
    foreign participation in, 276–8; foreign
    loans in, 284
New York Stock Exchange, 272, 282
Northern & Central Bank, 83, 94, 96, 97,
    99, 102, 108

Paribas (Banque de Paris et des Pays Bas),
    167, 190, 193, 235
Peel, Robert, 82
Peel's Act of 1844, 8, 98, 108, 125
Plan Villaverde, 166–7
portfolio diversification, by Spanish banks,
    173
Potosi, 225, 230
Prussia
    government finances, 6–7, 135, 154n
    incorporation law of 1870, 138–9,
    154–5n

railways
    in Belgium, 59–60, 67–8
    in Spain, 12, 162
rediscounting, *see* bills of exchange
Reichsbank (German), 128, 137
Riksbank (Sweden), 130
Rothschilds, 7, 59, 161, 201
Russia
    banking regulation in, 219–22
    foreign loans, 14, 213, 214, 218, 274
    gold standard, 13–14, 215
    Institute of Court Financiers, 211, 213
    joint-stock banks in, 218–19
    private bankers, 216
    State Bank, 213, 215, 218
    State Loan, 210–11
    State Mortgage Bank, 215
    Stieglitz & Co. (court banker), 212
    World War I, 218–22

sans-culottes, 20, 21, 31
J. Henry Schröder & Co. (Great Britain),
    278
J. Henry Schroder Banking Corporation
    (US), 278
seignorage, by Argentinian banks, 233, 237,
    242

silver standard, Spain, 12
Società Bancaria Italiana, 197
Société Belge des Chemins de Fer, 67–8
Société Générale de Belgique, 11, 53–72
Société Générale de Commerce, 36–7
Société Metallurgique Russo-Belge, 68
Spain
    bank portfolios in, 171–4
    central banking in, 163, 171–7
    credit companies law, 161–2
    Cuban War of Independence, *see*
        Spanish-American War
    industrialization in, 159–60, 174, 176
    money supply in 165–6
    Spanish-American War (1898), 158–9,
        160, 166
    Supreme Banking Council (Consejo
        Superior Bancario), 171
stock market in New York, *see* capital
    markets
Stringher, Bonaldo, 13, 182, 188–9

Talleyrand, 29, 32
Thornton, Henry, 120–2

United Kingdom, *see* Great Britain
United States
    banking and state finances, 264–5
    civil war and banking, 266–8, *see also* US
        National Banking Act of 1864
    colonial government finance, 251, 252;
        colonial loan offices, 253; fiat money,
        252–3; *see also* bills of credit

Constitution of 1787, 9, 263
Federalists, 250, 256
financial revolution in, 249, 254–62
foreign investment, 274
foreign investment in, 260–1, 271
investment banking in, 275–81
open market operations, 258
securities markets in, 249–50, 259–60,
    264–6
World War I, 272–3
United States National Banking Act of
    1864, 233, 240
United States Report on Manufactures
    (1791), 257
universal banking, 134, 153–4, 173, *see also*
    mixed banking

Vereinigte Stahlwerk, 278
Villaverde, Raimundo (Spanish Finance
    Minister), 166

wampum, 255
Washington, George, 256–7
William I, King of Netherlands, 11, 54–7,
    59
William of Orange, 4
Wilts & Dorset Bank, 100–1, 103
Württemberg, Kingdom of, 7

Zentralverband des deutschen Bank- und
    Bankiergewerbes, 221
Zollverein, German, 8